CONCENTRATION OF BANKING

CONCENTRATION OF BANKING

The Changing Structure and Control of Banking in the United States

BY

JOHN M. CHAPMAN

ASSISTANT PROFESSOR OF BANKING
COLUMBIA UNIVERSITY

NEW YORK : MORNINGSIDE HEIGHTS
COLUMBIA UNIVERSITY PRESS

M·CM·XXXIV

PUBLISHED 1934

PRINTED IN THE UNITED STATES OF AMERICA
GEORGE BANTA PUBLISHING COMPANY, MENASHA, WISCONSIN

TO

M. G. C.

FOREWORD

The passage of the Banking Act of 1933, which became effective on June 16, has for the first time given national banks an opportunity to provide banking service by branches in rural communities under direct authority of Federal law, without working through consolidation with, or conversion of, state banks already operating branches. Even though the authorization was grudgingly granted and is limited by state laws—so that progress must necessarily be slow (only thirty-seven branches of national banks had been established under its provisions three months after its enactment) the publication of Professor Chapman's book is most timely. If the history of banking development in other commercial countries which have escaped our serious recent epidemics of bank failures is a criterion, branch banking is certain to continue to make progress, and to overcome the prejudices and the legislative obstacles which have so long prevented a natural development of banking in the United States.

Professor Chapman has in this volume presented by far the most complete and thorough study of branch banking that has been published in the United States or elsewhere. He presents the history of branch banking under state banking laws during the early years of American banking, when branch banking was regarded as the natural means of providing banking service in the smaller places, particularly in the West and South. He explains the almost complete disappearance of branch banking following the Civil War and the inauguration of the national banking system, the revival of branch banking principally within the limits of a few large cities following the Panic of 1893, the branch banking development in California following the passage of the Bank Act of 1909 in that state, and the more recent movement growing out of the effort to find a remedy for the numerous bank failures of the decade 1920-30, and finally the agitation that culminated in the curtailed authorization for branch banking by national banks in the Banking Act of 1933.

Arguments for, and against, branch banking are fully, fairly and impartially presented and examined as to validity and reasonableness, with the conclusion that a considerably wider authorization for branch banking than that contained in the Glass-Steagall Act would be to the advantage of American banking and of American business. The discussion and presentation should be of particular interest to business men, and to depositors in banks generally. They are really as vitally concerned in the development of a sound banking system able to stand up under adverse circumstances as are bankers.

NEW YORK CITY
January 15, 1934

EDMUND PLATT
Former Vice Governor
Federal Reserve Board

PREFACE

Much controversy has raged around the subject of branch banking in the United States during the past two decades. This controversy has been carried on very largely by unit bankers on one side, while on the other may be found economists, business men and certain other bankers who have believed that a branch banking system would, in the long run, give us a safer and sounder banking system. The unit bankers and others who have opposed the development of branch banking have maintained that our unit system has worked far better than the branch system across the border in Canada. Branch bankers have contended that under a branch system we should have had fewer bank failures and that there would be proportionately less concentration of banking capital in our large cities.

A phase of banking which is very closely related to branch banking and which, until very recently, was much neglected, is afforded by bank mergers and consolidations. The developments in this particular field of banking have assumed great importance in the movements and changes that have been taking place in the general field of banking in this country since the close of the World War. The large increase in the average size of the unit bank, the growth of chain banking and the more recent appearance of group banking are other phases of the current banking situation each of which has a close relationship to the subject of branch banking. This five-fold development constitutes the major element in the concentration movement that has been going on in the field of commercial banking in this country.

An interesting and important phase of this study is found in connection with the availability of bank credit for the business community. How will these changes finally affect the Federal reserve system? These and many other questions should be considered in appraising finally the concentration movement in its entirety. Public sentiment has been undergoing certain fundamental changes in regard to branch banking and the reasons for its expansion during the past decade. Interest in it has broadened and a better understanding prevails now than at any time heretofore.

This book is intended to deal with the various changes in the field of banking which we have just indicated and to attempt to evaluate them. Special attention has been given to branch banking and bank mergers. Statistics are presented to show the growth of these two movements in relation to our banking system as a whole. The arguments for and against branch banking are considered with a view to ascertaining the effects of various changes upon the scope and character of the services rendered by banking institutions. Effort has been made to outline the reasons for the appearance and spread of chain and group banks, and to show how this will be affected by a growth of branch banking and a further extension of the merger and consolidation movement.

The growth of branch banking in California and the large increase in bank failures in the United States as a whole following the depression of 1920-21 was instrumental in inducing a group of bankers in California to sponsor a careful study and investigation of bank failures and branch banking. This study was conducted in 1925-26 long before the most destructive period of bank failures had set in. The actual investigation was placed in charge of Professor H. Parker Willis who was given absolute freedom in selecting his personnel and in the directing of the research project.

The writer had the privilege, with others, of being associated with Professor Willis in carrying out this research project which was nation-wide in scope. He was assigned to, and directed, the major part of the work involved in preparation of the statistics relating to branch banking, chain banking and bank mergers, and in addition wrote very largely the sections of the report which dealt with these subjects. When it became clear that the results of this study would not be immediately published, although filed with the Senate Banking Committee as a public document, the author asked, and received permission from Professor Willis, and approval and assistance of the bankers, to use the statistics thus assembled, together with any additional data which might be secured. The material submitted to the Banking Committee of the United States Senate included data for the years 1919 to 1924, inclusive. Statistics used in this book covering branch banking and bank mergers for the years 1925 to 1929 are the result of the author's own work as above described. For the last two years, 1930-31, the data was compiled by him but financed by funds provided from appropriations designed to maintain a study on the *Present Banking Situation* made in favor of Professor Willis by the Social Science Research Council, in which these statistics were needed.

I take this occasion to express my sincere appreciation to Professor Willis for his suggestions and constructive criticisms in the preparation of the manuscript. I am deeply indebted to the bankers who sponsored the investigation for permission to use the original data on branch banking and for constructive suggestions on branch banking policies and management received from Mr. Edward Elliott of Los Angeles. A special obligation is acknowledged to Hon. Edmund Platt for reading, criticizing and supplying me with material and suggestions otherwise unavailable. To Dr. Mildred Hartsough, Professors W. H. Steiner and Earnest L. Bogart, I am indebted for most valuable criticisms and suggestions. Mr. V. D. Kazakevich assisted me in compiling much of the data and has read and criticized constructively the entire manuscript and in other ways rendered valuable assistance. Mr. David Dangler rendered valuable assistance in compiling and tabulating the statistics.

I am deeply indebted for the invaluable aid received from my wife, Mary G. Chapman, who read and criticized the manuscript and assisted in the collection and tabulation of the statistical data.

COLUMBIA UNIVERSITY JOHN M. CHAPMAN
January 15, 1934

CONTENTS

CHARTS

CONCENTRATION OF BANKING

CHAPTER I

INTRODUCTION

EVOLUTION OF BANKING AND BUSINESS

All modern, progressive business enterprise must be dynamic. To expect the present methods of doing business to remain in practice indefinitely is to ignore the records of all past improvements in commerce, industry, and finance. When domestic economy was no longer suitable to meet the needs of the growing community or state, the factory system developed, an outgrowth of the industrial revolution. While many had to suffer severe hardships and losses, the final outcome is now generally accepted as an improvement or a benefit to the world at large. More goods are now being produced and consumed than could ever have been had domestic economy not been supplanted.

Fundamental changes in methods of production, distribution, and consumption are continuously being made as a result of inventions and discoveries. It is an almost everyday occurrence to see, as a result of these improvements, manufacturers, transportation companies, and merchants losing not only the profits of earlier and more fortunate days but their capital as well. Many cases could be cited to illustrate this point. The severe competition between bus lines and railroad companies at the present time is causing not a few railroads to modify, if not to abandon entirely, their passenger traffic. This is true in the case of short-line roads. Interurban railway systems have been affected to a far greater degree than have the steam railroads. The manufacturers of ice are struggling against severe and increasing competition from the makers of electric and gas refrigerators. In the field of mining the same type of competition exists. This is especially applicable to the coal producers in their struggle with the producers of gas, oil, and electricity. Entrepreneurs or stockholders who have a prosperous and successful business today have no assurance as to what may befall them on the morrow. Changes and improvements may be normally expected so long as there is freedom of invention and operation.

Just as there have been marked changes in mining, agriculture, and commerce, there have, likewise, been striking modifications in the field of banking. Banking institutions perform a middleman's function. Their primary purpose is to serve business and commerce. To do this satisfactorily, the banking system must change to meet the needs of an ever-changing business and commercial organization. Larger business units require larger financial institutions to finance them properly and efficiently. Such changes and modifications will come, despite the fact that there appears to be a strong group in our community that, for some unexplained reason, thinks and believes that the small commercial bank, which met the requirements of our society a few decades ago in a fairly satisfactory manner, should do equally well or even better for the present and for a long time to come.

In the past two or three decades important changes have taken place in the institutional framework of the banking system, in the prevailing practices, and in the position of the banking system as a whole relative to other parts of the national economy. The institutional framework of the banking system was altered fundamentally through the establishment of the Federal Reserve system and Federal Farm Loan system, the War Finance Corporation, the Reconstruction Finance Corporation, the Home Loan Banks and the (Glass-Steagall) Banking Act, 1933. From the viewpoint of prevailing banking practice the most outstanding changes were the extension to national banks of certain privileges such as lower reserve requirements and the right to do a trust business and to make loans on real estate. In regard to the changing position of the banking system relative to commerce and industry one may point out the growth in the size of the banking unit, the increase in the number of banks operating branches, extensive bank mergers and consolidations, introduction of new methods of financing foreign trade, the expansion of the American capital market and the entry of banks into the security field, and, finally the epidemic of bank failures during the last decade.

One of the most fundamental changes which has been taking

place has been the concentration movement. The reduction in the number of commercial banking institutions and the corresponding increase in the size of the individual bank are almost world-wide in their scope and effects. The movement has reached maturity in Great Britain where the number of banks has already been reduced to a very few. Likewise in Germany and Canada, as well as in certain other countries, the total number of commercial banks remaining is very small. The movement started earlier in these countries than in the United States; consequently it is more fully developed with them than in this country. Nevertheless, the movement has been under way here for a great many years. The large reduction in the number of existing banks before 1920 was largely offset by the number of new banks chartered in the several states. Since 1921 the number of banks has been gradually declining despite the large number of banks newly organized each year. The principal immediate causes for this decline are found in: (1) a large number of bank failures, (2) a small number of voluntary bank liquidations, and (3) a large number of bank mergers and consolidations. Other phases of the consolidation movement in the United States are illustrated in the growth of group banking and branch banking, and the existence of chain banking and the security affiliates.

THE CONCENTRATION MOVEMENT

A study of the concentration movement involves a discussion of the changing unit bank, the growth and extent of bank mergers and consolidations, the development and status of branch banking, the history and problems involved in chain banking, and a consideration of the more recent appearance of group banking. Of these various phases of the movement, the subjects of bank mergers and consolidations and branch banking will be treated more fully than group and chain banking. The concentration movement has attained an importance today that makes it a live and interesting current banking problem. The scope and meaning of this development is more completely and more widely realized today than ever before. Before discussing further, at this time, the concentration movement, it is desirable to outline briefly some of the more salient features of the unit system, which are being greatly changed by the development of banking concentration.

THE UNIT BANKING SYSTEM

A strong and determined sentiment in the banking community in support of the unit banking system has existed in this country from the very beginning of its history. This feeling was highly developed during the periods covering the existence of the First and Second Banks of the United States. Despite an extensive development of branch banking in this country during the period before the Civil War, this struggle and the passage of the National Bank Act, together with the amendment taxing bank notes out of circulation, gave branch banking a severe setback. From the close of the Civil War until after the passage of the Federal Reserve Act in 1913, the sentiment was strongly in favor of unit banks. The acceptance of the principle of unit banking implied the chartering of a large number of small independent banks designed to meet the needs of the communities in which they were located. Following the Civil War there was a gradual increase in the total number of banks and trust companies until 1921, when the total number of separate banking institutions reached its peak.

The very nature of the unit system gave it certain elements of strength as well as points of weakness. It had a personal touch that has not been attained by the branch system in other countries. The individual bank was a local affair devoted largely to the interests of its immediate community. On the other hand, such a system implied the operation of many banks by management not particularly capable or experienced. There was a lack of coöperation among the unit banks in times of stress. There was no pooling of reserves and no agency to which the many small banks could turn for assistance in times of trouble. Another fundamental weakness was unavoidable in many cases in connection with the portfolio; many banks found it difficult properly to diversify loans, discounts, and investments. If a depression hit the major industry of a given community, the banks found it difficult to maintain liquidity, sometimes even to prevent a bank failure.

The unit banks were in many instances not able to meet long periods of depression. Each panic or depression of major consequence was accompanied by a large number of suspensions and bank failures. Many bankers and economists thought the proper coördination had been attained through the enactment of the Federal Reserve Act and that in the future there would be very few, if any, bank failures. The situation growing out of and following the World War has utterly demolished that belief. The worst period of bank failures in this or any other country has occurred in the United States since 1920. A very large proportion of these failures has been among the much-praised local unit banks. The results of the past ten or twelve years of banking in this country have proved beyond doubt that there has been and is something fundamentally unsound in our system of banking. The unit banks have suffered an irreparable setback. Today there is general recognition of this condition. It is hard for many to give up their belief that a system of from 20,000 to 30,000 small, medium, and large banks will not work. Yet there is unmistakable evidence that not only bankers themselves but members of the business community in general recognize this fact. There is scarcely a community in the United States that has not been "hit" either directly or indirectly in some way by the long list of bank failures since 1920.

The unit banking system as constituted in this country has failed to meet the acid test. This does not mean that all unit banks have failed or gone into the hands of receivers; this is far from being the case. But many sections of the country have as a result of bank failures been left without adequate banking facilities. There seems to be little hope now that there will be a new development of unit banks such as will provide these various sections with banking offices. If these communities are to be properly and adequately served in the near future, it must be by some other type of banking. There is good reason for believing that the number of unit banks in the United States will continue to decline even though the present epidemic of bank failures be definitely stopped. Many banks now in existence are not making a profit and are not likely to do so for many years to come, if at all. Banks will be liquidated and many others will be merged or consolidated with other banks. With the decreasing number of banking institutions the need for some kind of banking office for the small cities and towns will gradually become more and more evident.

This need may be satisfied by either branch or unit banking.

There will be, of course, many unit banks in this country for a number of years to come. This would be true even though a system of branch banking should be adopted on a nation-wide basis. It now seems clear, however, that there will be a further gradual reduction in the number of unit banks and a general increase in the number of banks operating branches, together with the establishment of a large number of small branches designed to serve the small local centers. With intelligent, capable management this change will bring about a marked improvement not only in the banking situation but in the general field of business and commerce.

THE CONSOLIDATION MOVEMENT

Much has been said and written upon the subject of bank mergers, mergers of public utility companies, consolidation of railroads for the purpose of creating certain trunk-line systems, and consolidation of industrial concerns. All these mergers or consolidations are a part of a great and fundamental change which has been going on for years in our economic system as a whole. None of these changes in a particular industry or line of business is separated completely from similar changes taking place in every other line of business or industry. The large increase in the number of chain stores during recent years would not have been possible without a corresponding growth in the concentration of financial resources within a few hands, or at least under the control of a limited group, comparatively speaking. On the other hand it would not be worth while to effect this concentration unless there were opportunities for using these funds on a large scale. Before the chain store could be profitably operated there had to be more or less concentration of population in certain communities, and this concentration could not have taken place without the increase in total population which occurred in the latter nineteenth century.

In banking the concentration movement has made far-reaching progress through the gradual increase in the size of the American bank, while at the same time the number of banks has decreased. The larger operating unit in banking, as in other lines of business, is without doubt one phase of the concentration movement. In some states and cities the increase in a few large banks, which make up a large proportion of total banking assets of such states or cities, is most emphatic and denotes basic modifications in our banking structure. While comparatively little attention has been given to this phase of the movement, it is an important one and deserving of far more consideration than it has received.

The merger and consolidation movement has been in progress for many decades. It is far older in England than in the United States. The most important phase of the American development has occurred very largely since the close of the World War in 1918. There were a great many mergers before that date, but the movement was less marked and did not attract any considerable amount of attention. The most interesting period, and certainly the most important from the standpoint of the banking system as a whole, is that dating from 1924. It was during this latter period that a large percentage of all mergers in the United States occurred.

The growth of bank mergers and consolidations has been closely related to other changes going on in our banking system. It has been especially closely tied up with the efforts to prevent bank failures in certain parts of the country, to secure trust business and hence the expansion of trust departments, and also the extension of branch banking. The most important causes tending to bring about bank mergers have been (1) the desire to secure branches, and (2) the wish to prevent bank failures. Mergers and consolidations have been quite influential in reducing the number of banks in operation. The growth in recent years in the number of bank mergers involving the largest banks of the country has constituted one of the most important and far-reaching phases of the concentration movement in this country. It has been a powerful factor in concentrating the banking business in fewer and larger banking institutions. It is certain to affect in the future the problem of bank management.

The concentration movement represents notable and important changes in the field of banking as well as in the fields of commerce and industry. Many phases of banking which have been considered separately are severally and jointly a part of this great fundamental movement. So long as unit banking or small independent units were recognized and encouraged as the best means for providing the most suitable and desirable type of business organization, there was little chance for mergers and consolidations to bring about any basic change in the size of the business units. The larger business organizations, however, soon demonstrated their ability to surpass in productivity the smaller units in a great many lines of business. The use by certain organizations of machine methods and specialized labor soon outstripped the less specialized organizations.

In the field of banking, an extension of branches has made possible the bringing together of large resources under the control of centralized management while at the same time continuing the banking services formerly provided by the smaller unit banks. In this respect, then, branch banking may be regarded as one of the means of effecting consolidations. As long as certain states in this country prohibit branch banking, there is a distinct limit beyond which bank mergers and consolidations will not reduce the number of banking institutions. Of course there are many communities in which there are too many banking houses. Some of these will normally disappear in the course of time regardless of the development of branch banking, but the movement in this direction has its limitations. Branch banking may, then, be considered as one of the important phases of banking concentration. Other distinct phases have been noted, as for example, group and chain banking. Let us now review briefly the branch-banking question as it has existed in this country during the past several decades. It will then be desirable to consider group and chain banking, which have developed partly as a result of the legal restrictions on branch banking.

THE BRANCH BANKING PROBLEM

The uncertainty which exists has driven many bankers and business men in their search for a better type of banking to consider more seriously, perhaps, than ever before in this country, the subject of branch banking. No doubt many who are today advocating branch banking are doing so, not because they are absolutely certain in their own minds that branch banking will correct the present situation, but because they realize that our banking system is faulty and that branch banking may mean an improvement. They look upon it as promising and are willing to give it a trial in the face of the heavy reverses suffered by the independent banks. If they cannot legally have branches then they look with favor upon the development of group or chain banking in order to insure a new type or class of management.

The development of branch banking in some states and the discussion of the problem in other states has led many to give this subject a great deal of attention. The fact that branch banking has been carried on in most of the leading commercial countries, with the exception of the United States, has been a factor in the growth of interest in the subject. Undoubtedly branch banking is one of the most interesting and important factors at work in this country to bring about a concentration of banking resources within the hands of a comparatively limited number of bankers. The extent to which this movement has grown in the United States varies considerably from state to state. In a large number of states branch banking is not permitted by law in any form whatever at the present time. In about 50 percent of the states which permit branch banking, some restrictions are placed upon the extension of branches. In approximately fifteen states banks are allowed to establish branches on a state-wide basis. Interstate branch banking is unknown with the exception of a few isolated cases, developed under unusual conditions which prevailed during the past.

Regardless of all the restrictions placed upon both national and state banks in establishing branches, the extension of branches either locally or state-wide in those states permitting branch banking has been rather rapid. It will continue to be more and more important as the legal provisions permitting branch banking are extended or liberalized from time to time, as now appears evident from the great interest which has developed all over the country. The vital point in this growth of sentiment is the fact that it is generally in favor of an extension of the branch movement, which will mean a greater concentration of banking resources as well as of banking power and responsibility.

A complete survey of branch banking in the United States would involve a study of the history of banking in the United States from the time our independence as a separate nation was established.

The discussion of the advantages and disadvantages of branch banking began with Alexander Hamilton and has continued in one form or another to the present time. Even today the problem is a very difficult one to solve. Neither the policy of the Federal government nor that of the individual states has been uniform. At times it appeared that branch banking was recognized as the natural form of banking in this country, while at other times the attitude of the national government was directly the opposite. The same uncertain, indefinite, and varying course has been followed by a large number of states. The attitude of the state legislatures has fluctuated, first in favor of branches and then against them. The unsettled attitude toward this type of banking has served to make impossible the development of what might be termed a permanent or long-time policy in connection with the growth and development of banking facilities by means of branches.

NATIONAL BRANCH BANKING POLICY

The difficulty of adopting and maintaining a national policy with regard to banking in this country has been intensified by the fact that there is a dual form of banking supervision and regulation. The country would doubtless have been saved much of the sad, disgraceful, and disappointing experience of bank failures and losses, had the right to charter and regulate the banking business been reserved to the national government. There have been no uniform standards established for the operation of banks. The unsound policies followed by the early American bankers have, without doubt, played a very important rôle in bringing into existence the immense number of banking laws which have been enacted with a view, very largely, to protecting the noteholders and the depositors. These laws did not attain the ends desired and consequently with each breakdown in the system there was added a new body of laws. This practice has been followed down to the present.

The fear of and opposition to banks of all kinds which existed during the early development of the country increased the difficulty of establishing a national banking policy. These conditions made possible many changes which would not have arisen, had the national government been able and willing to take a firm stand in regard to the future development of a nation-wide system of banks. The efforts of the Federal government in connection with the two Banks of the United States were unsuccessful. The growth of state banking systems left little hope for the development of a sound and uniform banking system. Each state tended to develop its own peculiarities. The states in the South and the West generally favored the extension of banking by means of branches, while the eastern part of the country tended in the direction of unit banks. The failure of a few of these early state banks with branches had a depressing effect upon the sentiment in favor of an extension of banking facilities by means of branches.

Before 1860 the wide geographical limits of the country, the bad roads and the difficulty of communication between different sections made it almost impossible for a bank to keep in close touch with distant offices. Branches often found it difficult to secure a sufficient volume of business to make branches profitable. In many instances, therefore, bankers hesitated to extend their branches because of the unfavorable economic conditions. Moreover, one of the principal sources of income for the banks was that of note issue. The larger the number of branches the more difficult it was for the bank to keep its notes outstanding. On the other hand, of course, the larger number of offices increased the ease with which such notes were originally put into circulation.

EARLY BRANCHES DISCONTINUED

The coming of the Civil War had a tremendous influence upon the decline of branches during the early sixties. The conditions brought about by the efforts of the Confederacy to finance the war forced many of the southern branch banks to go out of existence during the war. Some of the banks in the West experienced a similar fate. The states which remained loyal to the Union and which permitted branches, faced an entirely new situation which was, in turn, brought about to a very considerable extent by the war. The national banking system was created by an act of Congress in 1863. The national act did not recognize branch banking in any effectual way. The early amendments to the act were distinctly unfavorable to a continuance of branches, even by the banks which had been engaged in that type of banking for many years. The most effective part of the legislation regarding branches was that of taxing the note issues of state banks out of existence. Note issue was at that time fundamental to the very existence of most banks. Deposit business had not yet been developed. After the enactment of certain Federal legislation in 1865, which provided for the conversion of state banks into the national system and placed a tax on the note issues of state banks, the logical course for state banks was to enter the national system. This they did in large numbers. Within a comparatively short time thereafter the state banks had been almost wiped out.

The type of management which had been established by the branch banks in Ohio, Indiana, Iowa, and Missouri was such that it was easier for the branch banks there to convert the branches into individual banks than to convert under the provisions which permitted them to enter the national system and retain their branches. The disappearance of the branches in the southern states during the war and the policy of the western banks resulted, within a short time after the close of the war, in practically bringing to a close the branch-banking business in this country. The rather extensive systems of branches which had been brought into operation before the Civil War were either closed or converted into national banks. The country therefore lost nearly all of its branch banks and developed, instead, a system of unit banks. The strong position of the national banking system was such that for the next several decades there was very little sentiment in any of the states in favor of the development of a state-wide system of branches, much less any concerted effort to bring about a change in our banking laws which would make possible the establishment of a national branch-banking system.

To summarize, the two principal factors which virtually ended branch banking in the United States in the sixties were the Civil War and the amendment passed in 1865 to the National Bank Act taxing state bank notes.

REVIVAL OF INTEREST IN THE NINETIES

The depression of the early nineties revived a great deal of the discussion regarding the desirability of having banks with branches. The office of the Comptroller of the Currency at that time sent out a questionnaire or two designed to secure data about banks. One of the questions dealt with the subject of branch banking. During the decade from 1890 to 1900 at least two Comptrollers of the Currency recommended some kind of branch banking—James H. Eckles and Charles G. Dawes. It is true that they favored an extension of branches for the reason that the capital requirements of national banks were so large that many communities were unable to secure banking facilities. Branches of large banks were intended to fulfill that need. President Cleveland in one of his presidential messages to Congress recommended branch banking of the type which had been approved by the Comptroller of the Currency. Needless to say, such legislation never passed Congress.

The Indianapolis Monetary Commission held its meeting in Indianapolis in 1897 and brought out a report in 1898. The report contained a recommendation for a branch-banking system. The provisions of the proposed bill, which was included in the report, were wide in scope and were intended to give banks very wide and extensive privileges in the establishment and operation of branches. The return of prosperity in the late nineties, and the modification of the laws relative to the organization of national banks and their capital requirements changed the situation to a very considerable extent, so that the demand for branches began to wane shortly after 1900. A large number of those advocating branches in the nineties desired to provide banking facilities for smaller communities. The change in the National Bank Act permitting the organization of national banks with a minimum capital of $25,000 made it possible to establish banks in many of these smaller communities, thus lessening the demand for branches for such localities.

The next important move in this country in connection with branches came after the panic of 1907. During the period following that fiasco, much attention was given to the subject of banking reform in this country. The state legislature of California in 1909 enacted a law which was destined to have far-reaching consequences with regard to the future of branch banking not only in that state but also in the United States as a whole. The law made possible important changes in the banking system in California providing for state-wide branch banking which, in turn, has influenced the development of branch banking in certain other states and has been very powerful in shaping public opinion upon this important question in many other states. The 1909 Branch Banking Law of California may rightly be regarded as one of the landmarks in branch-banking history in the United States.

BRANCH MOVEMENT IN CALIFORNIA

The development of branch banking in the state of California was slow, and had it not been for the efforts of one or two groups in that state it is doubtful if the issue would be as important in banking discussion as it is. The earliest domestic agencies or branches were organized there prior to 1890, but the number was small and without any important influence either for or against branch banking. The period of slow growth continued for many years. The number of branches increased gradually after the passage of the act in 1909, but the number did not show a marked increase until after 1922. Since then the growth has been very rapid. It was during this latter period that the subject received its greatest attention. It was during this period also that the growth has been the most marked in other states, many of which were greatly influenced by branch-banking developments in California. The growth of branches was marked by the rapid increase of "outside branches,"[1] showing that the growth was state-wide in scope. Other states provided a method for establishing branches on the same basis, but the growth was less marked than in California.

THE FEDERAL RESERVE SYSTEM AND BRANCH BANKING

The ruling of Comptroller of the Currency Crissinger, in 1922, was one of the most important steps taken towards branch banking prior to the passage of the McFadden Act. This action of the Comptroller in 1922 was epoch-making in the development of branch banking in this country. While it did not extend to national banks the full rights then enjoyed by certain state banks, it

[1] "Outside branches" are those operated by the branch bank outside the corporate limits of the city of the parent bank.

placed the national banks in a position to develop a certain type of branches (teller windows or additional offices, so-called) in several states.

The original Federal Reserve bill included a provision for the establishment and operation of branches by national banks. The Comptroller of the Currency, the Federal Reserve Board, and the Federal Advisory Council were, for several years after the Federal Reserve banks went into operation, strong advocates of an extension of branches by national banks. Shortly after the 1922 ruling of the Comptroller of the Currency, the Federal Reserve Board reversed its former policy. In 1923 the Board adopted a definite set of resolutions designed to curb a further extension of branches by members of the Federal Reserve system. The next major development in branch banking culminated with the passage of the McFadden Amendment, which was designed to equalize branch banking to a degree between state and national banks, but at the same time aimed to check a further extension of state-wide branch banking. The number of branches of national banks increased quite rapidly following the enactment of that legislation.

Public sentiment in favor of branch banking has developed quite rapidly during the past two or three years, especially since the depression which started in 1929. The large number of bank failures has tended to increase the desire on the part of many bankers to create branches. Not a few state banking officials, who were a short time ago opposed to any extension of branches, have now come out in favor of branches. The development of branch banking has been very slow in this country, but there now appears to be little doubt that a considerable extension of branches will take place in the near future. Unit banks will be with us for many years to come, but it is becoming more and more evident that a growth of branch banking will be accompanied by a decline in the number of unit banks.

THE BANKING ACT OF 1933

The year 1933 will doubtless prove to be a memorable one in the history of branch banking in the United States. As a result of the enactment of the Glass-Steagall bill into law, national banks were given essentially the same rights and privileges as those enjoyed by state banks and trust companies in the state in which the national bank or banks were located. This was the first time that legal provision has been made for national banks to establish and operate branches on a state-wide basis, and marked, therefore, an extremely important modification of branch banking in this country. In addition to the specific provisions of the Act regarding the operation of branches by national banks, there are also certain provisions of this Act which will probably have an important bearing upon the future development of branch banking. The provisions are those relating to the guaranty of bank deposits, the capital requirements of national banks, and the prohibition of the payment of interest on demand deposits. The carrying out of these provisions will tend to bring about gradually an extension of branches.

In addition to the changes in the National Bank Act relative to branch banking, there has been a pronounced growth in state bank legislation in favor of state-wide branch banking. No less than seven states (Connecticut, Idaho, Michigan, Nevada, Oregon, Utah, and Washington) have passed laws since January 1, 1933, providing for state-wide branch banking under certain conditions. This is unquestionably the greatest advance in this direction for any single year to date. It means that the opposition to branch banking is crumbling. The changes in Federal and state laws in this connection mean to some that the fight for branch banking is won.

CHAIN AND GROUP BANKING

Other phases of our subject which have received an unusual amount of attention and consideration during the last few months, or perhaps years, are the questions of chain banking and group banking, each of them a major factor in this movement. In some cases writers regard the two as quite similar, while other writers make a distinction and hence treat them independently. Whichever point of view we adopt, we must recognize that this line of development has been very influential in bringing a larger and larger number of banks under the management of one group of individuals or of a holding company. The rapid growth of these two types of organization brought them forcibly before the public in such a way as to create a vast amount of interest in the whole subject. The rapid progress made by some groups in buying up and controlling a large number of small banks marked the movement as one which would modify or limit the whole concentration movement in this country. The activity has subsided somewhat in the past year or two from the peak of the period before the depression began, but it is reasonable to suppose that unless branch banking is legalized in many states, we shall see in the near future another rapid increase in the formation of chains or groups.

Chain banking had its origin in this country during the last part of the nineteenth century. The exact place where it first appeared is uncertain, but it had its greatest development in the Northwest centering in St. Paul and Minneapolis, and in the Southeast concentrated largely in and around Atlanta, Georgia. The chains in the Northwest extended into the states of North and South Dakota, Montana, and in a few cases to other states of that general section. The area in the Southeast included the Carolinas and Florida and later broadened out to include a few banks as far north as New York and New Jersey. The movement made some headway elsewhere, but these two cities may be regarded as the centers of the movement. By 1925 the number of states had greatly increased and the number of banks involved in the movement had mounted to more than a thousand. Complete information is not available to show the exact number of banks involved in these chains.

There developed quite early certain very glaring weaknesses in the chain systems as they were operated. These evils appeared in the form of dishonest management—efforts on the part of the management to use the bulk of the funds for their own individual ends to the great detriment of the depositors. In not a few cases the chains were built upon a "shoe string" with the result that they were underfinanced and consequently very easily brought to ruin in the case of an emergency. There was a tendency also for chains to be built up whose real owners were unknown. Secrecy as to the owners tended to produce a very serious situation, since the owners could not be held responsible for the policy of the banks. In general the banks were very small and very loosely knit together so that they were frequently unable to stand any serious strain. This method of control early fell into disfavor among conservative bankers and able and thorough superintendents of banks who had to deal with the problem. It was difficult to examine the chains properly since they often extended through two or more states. This system is now generally considered unsound and unsuitable for the future in this country.

Group banking, as distinct from chain banking, refers to that type of banking control or ownership in which the stock of the bank is held by a holding company, whereas in the case of chain banking the stock of the member banks of the chain is held or owned by an individual or a group of individuals.[2] In many cases the member banks of a group system are centered or clustered around a large metropolitan bank. The holding-company form of banking control dates back many years. It developed, in fact, simultaneously with chain banking. The earlier holding company type was quite similar in purpose to the early chain organizations. The stock of these early holding companies was held by a small number of stockholders, whereas the bank-holding companies of the present time generally have a large number of stockholders, and in some cases have their stock listed on a security or stock exchange. Present types seek to raise sufficient amounts of capital to own and control large metropolitan banks. They exercise more definite supervision over the various group members than was done by the earlier holding companies.

The development of the present-day bank-holding company, or group banking, has taken place very largely since 1925 and more especially since 1927. It had its greatest growth during the years 1928 and 1929, just before the depression began. The reasons for the rapid expansion of this type of banking control were: (1) legal restrictions against branch banking; (2) the desire for profits on the part of some, at least, of the organizers through stock-

[2] For a fuller discussion of group and chain banking the reader is referred to Chap. XIX and XX, especially Chap. XIX, pp. 322-23.

jobbing, and the increase of earning power of the member banks through the introduction of better management; (3) the "bad" reputation of chain banking; and (4) the fear of losing correspondent bank business. More positive reasons are found in the advantages of this method of control, which include (1) economies of operation; (2) the possibility of granting larger lines of credit; (3) greater diversification of loans and discounts; and (4) more centralized control.

Group banking is regarded by many as a temporary development in our changing banking system. Not a few group bankers openly state that they will convert their group systems into branch systems as soon as the law will permit. Some of the same difficulties regarding supervision and control exist in group banking that are present in chain banking. Branch banking will accomplish all that group banking can do. Branch banking will secure these advantages with a less complicated financial set-up, thus leading to economies in legal and other expenses, and will in the end provide banking services for many small localities in which the group systems would find it unprofitable to establish small banks.

THE SECURITY AFFILIATES

There can be no doubt that security affiliates have had a most important influence on the merger movement, especially in connection with group banking and the holding company. In such cases the security company can buy and hold the stock of the banks, which the commercial banks themselves cannot always do. In many cases these security affiliates played an active part in the purchase of stock in unit banks for the purpose of effecting mergers between certain banks. Here again the affiliate could do something which the bank was not permitted to do legally. While we realize the important place occupied by the affiliate in the growth of banking concentration, we prefer in our discussion of concentration to consider the affiliate not as a separate factor but as one used by the affiliated bank to assist in bringing about an interbank relationship which the individual bank could not do itself legally.

THE PRESENT SITUATION

The experience of unit, chain, branch, and group bankers has shown in a most convincing manner that the present banking system in this country has failed to serve in a safe, adequate, and satisfactory way the financial needs of the various elements in the community which require the help and assistance of a well-organized and efficiently-operated banking system. This inability to measure up to the requirements has been most noticeable in connection with the enormous number of bank failures, with their attendant losses to all classes of the community. It must be evident that there is something fundamentally wrong with any banking system in which more than 11,125 banks fail during a period of twelve years. Despite the laws and public supervision of commercial banking in the United States, it is still patent to all thoughtful individuals that the methods of supervision and regulation so ardently supported and tenaciously followed have failed to protect the depositors and the public. There does not exist sufficient encouragement in the present situation to justify the blind adherence of many to the idea that the past ten years of experience have been an exceptional outgrowth of conditions over which the country had no control. The administrative relief measures may succeed in checking the failure of banks temporarily, but what hope have we for the future, when the Federal government shall no longer wish to hand over billions of dollars to a Reconstruction Finance Corporation to assist weak, inefficiently-managed banks and railroads? Moreover, it is not believed that the guarantee provisions of the Glass-Steagall Act will prove at most more than a temporary make-shift for handling weak and failed banks. Surely there is abundant evidence that our banking system is, as a whole, in a very bad condition and needs the most capable, thoughtful and constructive consideration that can be given it by the best bankers and economists of the United States.

The small unit banks have weaknesses which are basic in their effects upon the success or failure of the system. The inability of the bank properly to diversify its portfolio and to secure and retain able management, and the ease with which new banks are chartered and brought into existence, clearly indicate grave defects which make it an extremely difficult task to modify the laws and practice so as to make the unit system a safe and sound one. The small bank finds it practically impossible to diversify its portfolio of loans, discounts, and investments in such a way as to protect itself against the demands placed upon it. The smallness of the fund and the similarity of the types of business to be financed in a given locality make it almost impossible to prevent tying up too large a portion of the fund in one or a few closely allied lines of business. This has been and can be avoided in most cases if the management of the bank is well informed and is willing to risk the criticism of the local business community by buying commercial paper or by lending a certain percentage of the funds to borrowers outside the community. To do this requires courage and skill which have, in far too many instances, been lacking.

Small banks have had and will continue to have a most difficult task to secure and retain the kind of management necessary to operate a bank safely through all the various stages of the business cycle. It is hard to keep first-class management in small banks where the opportunities for promotion and salary advances are definitely limited. Such banks are not in a position to compete with the large institutions for the best banking talent. The final results are unfavorable to the small bank. Of course, there are many small banks so situated that they can, for some local reason hold good men, but the number of cases where this is impossible is far too large for us to pass over without serious question to the whole problem of management of small unit banks. This, it is believed, is one of the very weak spots in the unit system, and the chances of overcoming it appear extremely doubtful.

CHAPTER II

THE UNIT BANKING SYSTEM

The history of unit banking in this country began with the founding of the Bank of North America in Philadelphia during the Revolutionary War. That bank was brought into existence very largely through the efforts of Robert Morris, one of the leading financiers of that period. Within a comparatively short time thereafter, the Bank of New York and the Bank of Massachusetts were established. None of these banks established branches. The first two are outstanding examples of successful unit banks. From the founding of the Bank of North America to the present time, unit banking has prevailed in this country at all times, and during much of this time has had practically a free field so far as branch banking was concerned.

Branch banking made considerable progress in the United States before the Civil War. After that there was comparatively little branch banking in the United States until after the close of the World War in 1918. Since then branch banking has made important strides, but even today branch banking, if measured in terms of total resources, occupies a minor place in our system of banking. Certain questions may well be raised regarding the present and future status of unit banking. What are the underlying causes for so many bank failures in this country? Will unit banking meet the needs of the business community in the future? What are the reasons for the decline in the number of banks in operation in this country?

The total number of banks reached a peak in the United States on June 30, 1921, with 30,812 commercial banks, trust companies, savings banks and private banks in operation. At that time these banks had total deposits amounting to $35,849,000,000. On June 30, 1931, there were 22,071 banks with total deposits of $52,036,000,000.[1] The immediate reasons for this decline in the

[1] On June 30, 1932, there were 19,163 banks with total deposits amounting to $45,390,269. *Annual Report of the Comptroller of the Currency* (1932), p. 561.

number of banks in operation are found in the large number of bank failures, bank mergers, the decline in the number of new charters in certain states, and the voluntary liquidation of a small number of banks.

Fundamental and underlying causes for this remarkable change are found in certain basic economic modifications in our economic structure. The desire on the part of certain groups in the community to own and operate either banks with branches or larger unit banks has also played a rather important rôle in some states in the decline of independent banks. What type of bank has been most likely to fail, or to be merged, or to go out of existence during this concentration movement? Why has one particular type been more likely to be discontinued than other classes? What is the result of the closing of small banks? Is the present economic situation more favorable for large banks than for small ones?

BANK FAILURES

Among the immediate factors tending to reduce the total number of unit banks in this country, none has been more striking than bank failures. Bank failures since 1920 have been exceedingly heavy and the rate has increased in general during the period. The peak year in so far as actual number of suspensions is concerned was 1931, during which year nearly 2,300 banks were closed.

From 1921 to March 1, 1933, inclusive, the number of failures totaled 11,130, or 36.12 percent of all banks in operation on June 30, 1921. The losses to depositors, stockholders, and the public have been stupendous. The total loss cannot be ascertained. The total deposits of suspended banks for the period from 1921 to March, 1933, inclusive, were approximately $5,203,000,000. If from this we deduct the total amounts of deposits of banks reopened, it leaves a net total of $4,435,000,000 deposits for banks being liquidated. Further, if we should assume that approximately 25 percent[2] of this amount will never be realized, the approximate

[2] ". . . The average percentage of all dividends paid on the aggregate of secured and unsecured claims proved against the 1,086 receiverships that have been finally closed, but not including the 109 restored to solvency which paid 100 per cent, was 67.19 per cent. If payments to secured and preferred creditors, offsets, and other disbursements, as indicated above, were included with the dividends paid in this calcula-

direct loss to depositors would be something approaching $1,108,750,000. This last figure does not take into account the loss to depositors arising from their inability to make use of their funds during the liquidation period, nor the results of the tying up of working capital, resulting in the curtailing of the business operations of the community for a long period of time. Nor does it include the loss to stockholders. Table I indicates the extent of bank failures during the period from 1921 to March 1, 1933, inclusive.

TABLE I

DATA OF BANKS SUSPENDED AND REOPENED*

(In millions of dollars)

YEAR	TOTAL NUMBER OF BANKS IN OPERATION IN THE UNITED STATES	NUMBER OF FAILED BANKS	FAILED BANKS AS PERCENT OF ALL BANKS IN OPERATION	DEPOSITS OF ALL BANKS IN OPERATION IN THE UNITED STATES	DEPOSITS OF FAILED BANKS		BANKS REOPENED		
					Amount	*Percent of All Banks in the United States*	*Number*	TOTAL DEPOSITS *Amount*	TOTAL DEPOSITS *Percent of All Failed Banks*
1921	30,812	501	1.63	35,849	196	0.55	60	17	8.67
1922	30,389	354	1.16	37,876	111	0.29	65	36	32.43
1923	30,178	648	2.15	40,631	189	0.47	37	12	6.35
1924	29,348	776	2.64	43,771	213	0.49	94	22	10.33
1925	28,241	612	2.17	47,612	173	0.36	62	17	9.83
1926	28,146	956	3.40	49,726	272	0.55	149	61	22.43
1927	27,061	662	2.45	52,446	194	0.37	95	36	18.56
1928	26,213	491	1.87	54,332	139	0.26	39	16	11.51
1929	25,330	642	2.53	54,281	235	0.43	58	26	11.06
1930	24,079	1,345	5.59	55,510	865	1.56	147	62	7.17
1931	22,071	2,298	10.41	52,036	1,692	3.25	276	158	9.34
1932	19,163	1,456	7.60	42,178	716	1.70	290	276	38.54
1933†		389			208		41	29	
TOTAL		11,130			5,203		1,413	768	

* Source: *Annual Reports of the Federal Reserve Board*, and *Federal Reserve Bulletin* (Washington, D.C.: Government Printing Office).

† Includes only the preliminary data for the first two months of the year, Jan. and Feb. See *Federal Reserve Bulletin*, Mar., 1933, p. 144.

An analysis of bank-failure statistics shows clearly that the smaller the bank in this country the more likely it is to fail. This statement does not imply that all small banks will fail, or that no

tion, the total disbursements to creditors would amount to $414,701,237 or 77.06 per cent of claims proved," *ibid.*, p. 14.

large banks are likely to encounter serious difficulties. If all suspended banks be classified according to size, it will be found that a large percentage of all failed banks had a capital of $25,000 or less at the time of failure. This situation is most emphatically shown in Table 2, which gives the number of bank failures of each particular class, based upon the capital of the banks at the time of failure.

TABLE 2

BANK SUSPENSIONS CLASSIFIED ACCORDING TO CAPITAL STOCK*

BANKS HAVING STOCK OF	NUMBER OF SUSPENSIONS										
	1921	*1922*	*1923*	*1924*	*1925*	*1926*	*1927*	*1928*	*1929*	*1930*	*1931*
Less than $25,000	194	117	295	319	234	384	247	191	223	466	548
$25,000	104	85	151	191	135	230	165	106	143	296	513
$25,001– $49,000	31	39	49	55	46	100	60	38	67	140	220
$50,000– $99,000	78	53	91	130	133	164	122	94	120	221	457
$100,000–$199,000	47	24	32	61	43	46	47	46	58	131	285
$200,000–$999,000	12	15	16	15	18	16	13	11	19	70	227
$1,000,000 and over	4†								5‡	11§	32
Not available	31	21	14	5	3	16	8	5	7	10	16
TOTAL	501	354	648	776	612	956	662	491	642	1345	2298

* *Annual Report of the Federal Reserve Board* (1931), p. 127.

† Includes one bank with a capital of $1,309,000.

‡ Includes one bank with a capital of $1,225,000.

§ Includes one bank each with capital of $1,218,000, $1,750,000, $2,500,000, $4,000,000, $4,877,000, and $25,250,000.

More than 5,300 banks with a capital of $25,000 or less failed out of a total of 9,285 bank failures during the period 1921-31, inclusive.

The comparative position of the smaller banks is clearly shown by the recent study of the Federal Reserve Committee on Branch, Group and Chain Banking. That study classified banks according to the volume of loans and investments. The Report showed that approximately 80 percent of all failed banks had total loans and investments of less than $500,000. Table 3 is reproduced here in order to show more fully the relative position of the failed banks grouped according to size.

If the number of bank failures be classified according to the size of the town or location in which the failed banks were situated, the result shows that more than 55 percent of all bank failures took

TABLE 3

BANK SUSPENSIONS DURING 1921–31, BY SIZE OF LOANS AND INVESTMENTS*

SIZE OF GROUP LOANS AND INVESTMENTS (000 OMITTED)	NATIONAL BANKS		STATE BANKS		NATIONAL AND STATE BANKS	
	Number	*Percent of Total*	*Number*	*Percent of Total*	*Number*	*Percent of Total*
Under $150	154	11.5	3,350	44.2	3,504	39.3
150– 250	253	18.9	1,501	19.8	1,754	19.7
250– 500	413	30.9	1,478	19.5	1,891	21.2
500– 750	170	12.7	481	6.3	651	7.3
750– 1,000	89	6.7	248	3.3	337	3.8
1,000– 2,000	157	11.8	285	3.8	442	5.0
2,000– 5,000	74	5.5	158	2.1	232	2.6
5,000–10,000	20	1.5	47	0.6	67	0.7
10,000–50,000	5	0.4	31	0.4	36	0.4
50,000 and over	1	0.1	1	0.01	2	0.02
TOTAL	1,336	100.0	7,580	100.0	8,916	100.0

* Report of the Federal Reserve Committee on Branch, Group and Chain Banking (1932), on *Bank Suspensions in the United States, 1892–1931*, p. 51.

place among the banks located in towns or villages with a population of less than 1,000. Approximately 36 per cent of all bank failures occurred in towns with a population of less than 500. Table 4 gives the number of bank failures by years for the period 1921-31

TABLE 4

BANK SUSPENSIONS, BY SIZE OF TOWN OR CITY*

PLACES WITH POPULATION OF:	NUMBER OF SUSPENSIONS										
	1921	*1922*	*1923*	*1924*	*1925*	*1926*	*1927*	*1928*	*1929*	*1930*	*1931*
Less than 500	181	120	331	335	226	372	266	207	240	442	666
500– 1,000	99	75	104	158	130	204	142	93	128	278	402
1,000– 1,500	47	23	58	71	67	115	61	48	77	128	202
1,500– 2,500	39	44	55	75	56	88	65	52	63	137	225
2,500– 5,000	33	30	35	55	60	79	53	33	35	119	214
5,000–10,000	32	18	24	28	32	30	22	18	35	60	140
10,000–25,000	21	12	14	22	18	22	30	17	24	57	134
25,000 and over	49	32	27	32	23	46	23	23	40	124	315
TOTAL	501	354	648	776	612	956	662	491	642	1,345	2,298

* *Annual Report of the Federal Reserve Board* (1931), p. 127.

inclusive, classified according to the size of the town in which the failed banks were located at the time of failure.

The Report of the Federal Reserve Committee on Branch, Group and Chain Banking shows results similar to the reports of the Federal Reserve Board, though the Board's figures are less favorable for the smaller banks. The Federal Reserve Committee's findings are presented in Table 5.[3] This table gives not only the total number of banks for each class of towns, but it gives the percentage distribution, indicating that approximately 75 percent of failures took place in towns with a population of less than 2,500.

TABLE 5

BANK SUSPENSIONS DURING 1921–31, BY SIZE OF TOWN

POPULATION OF TOWN	NATIONAL BANKS		STATE BANKS		NATIONAL AND STATE BANKS	
	Number of Suspensions	*Percent of Total Suspensions*	*Number of Suspensions*	*Percent of Total Suspensions*	*Number of Suspensions*	*Percent of Total Suspensions*
Under 500	171	12.8	2,982	39.3	3,153	35.4
500– 1,000	255	19.1	1,476	19.5	1,731	19.4
1,000– 2,500	408	30.6	1,348	17.8	1,756	19.7
2,500– 5,000	202	15.1	568	7.5	770	8.6
5,000– 10,000	118	8.8	309	4.1	427	4.8
10,000– 25,000	92	6.9	297	3.9	389	4.4
25,000– 50,000	36	2.7	112	1.5	148	1.6
50,000–100,000	19	1.4	130	1.7	149	1.7
100,000 and over	35	2.6	358	4.7	393	4.4
TOTAL	1,336	100.0	7,580	100.0	8,916	100.0

A careful study of the bank-failure data reveals one of the most alarming weaknesses of the unit banking system. This system has demonstrated its inability to provide safe and adequate banking facilities for small communities. The economic and business conditions surrounding the small towns and cities are such as to make it difficult to adjust the capital investment of banks to meet the needs of the locality, and at the same time have a sufficiently large capital to enable a board of directors to carry on a sound and well

[3] Report of the Federal Reserve Committee on Branch, Group and Chain Banking (1932), on *Bank Suspensions in the United States, 1892-1931*, pp. 72-73.

diversified banking business. The banks located in towns of 1,000 or less must of necessity be small. If a bank with a large capital be established, it will be unprofitable to its stockholders unless the bank engages in business which should be avoided by commercial banks. If this policy be followed the risk will be very greatly increased for the depositors who, in the end, will be likely to undergo heavy losses as a result of unsound banking practices. The capitalization of banks must, therefore, be kept in harmony with the needs of the communities in which the banks are located. Under such conditions it is evident that many small towns in this country are not able to maintain an independent banking institution with the amount of capital required by the national banking laws for national banks. The same applies to many communities also so far as operating banks under state banking laws is concerned.

It is more and more fully recognized that the unit banking system as operated in this country has not provided the small communities with the kind of banking services they need. Anti-branch bankers have contended that one of the principal advantages of the unit system is to be found in the services rendered small communities, which would not be provided by the large city branch banks. These small localities are entitled to adequate banking facilities, and no banking system is satisfactory to the country that does not provide just such advantages to all classes. Thus far, the unit system has not made good in this respect.

SHIFTING POPULATION

One of the factors increasing the difficulties of operating a successful unit bank in a small community is encountered in the tendency of the population to shift from place to place. This is true to a marked extent in certain mining and industrial communities. Moreover, there has been a notable improvement in good roads in many parts of the country. Good roads have been a great boon to many localities and have, in turn, made it easy for those living in the country or in small towns and cities to go to the larger places for shopping, business, and entertainment. With this shift of business and other activities to the larger centers, there will be a natural tendency for the banking business to follow to a marked extent. In addition many business men who are still active in the smaller communities, will transfer a part, if not all, of their banking business to larger banks. Such transfer of business and banking to larger banks affects the banker in the small town in the same way as though the business men had actually deserted the small locality.

These changes are robbing the small banker of a large part of the business which he enjoyed for many years, and which he had come to regard as his own. While the loss of any considerable part of this business is detrimental to these communities, the transferred business frequently represents some of the most desirable banking business of the community. It indicates, moreover, that the banker is losing one of the most desirable means for diversifying the portfolio and thus his position is materially weakened. The banker working under such conditions finds it more and more difficult to earn a fair return upon his invested capital and to keep the bank in a liquid, solvent condition. The task becomes increasingly difficult as time goes on. The disappointing feature is that he is unable to improve matters materially through his own efforts.

CREDIT INVESTIGATION

The increasing size of the business unit in this country during the past few decades has increased the necessity for more careful and extensive credit work by the banker and has, at the same time, made the task more difficult for the reason that business organizations often establish branch offices and extend their operations over a wider area. The reports and statements of borrowers become more and more involved and hence require greater effort and knowledge by the analysts. A large unit bank is usually qualified to do this credit work and the volume of business transacted is large enough to make the cost of providing the necessary personnel and equipment a reasonable one. This is not true of the small bank in a great many places. Under such circumstances the small bank must go ahead making its loans and advances to small local borrowers, in far too many cases on insufficient information, with a corresponding increase of risk. There is no way by which the small unit bank, acting alone, can reduce credit investigation costs to a basis commensurate with its ability to pay.

In the future more, and not less, credit work will be needed. This makes the future for the small bank still more doubtful unless a number of small banks coöperate in some way to have this credit work carried out jointly in order to spread the costs over a larger number of banks in proportion to the services received. This coöperation has not been found feasible in the past and it is doubtful if it will be in the immediate future. Under a unit banking system there is, therefore, inevitably a large number of banks which are unable to afford the proper credit work. Many of the large banks have such facilities but the unit banking system, in which there is a large number of banks operating on an unsound basis, will sooner or later find itself in dire distress. Under such a banking system the lack of credit work by many members will continue to be one of its weak spots and, in the long run, is apt to prove rather costly.

BANK EARNINGS

An important phase of the banking problem is the question of the earning power of banks. A bank to be successful must, over a period of time, yield a fair return upon the invested capital and make adequate provision for a surplus. A bank or banking system which fails in this important respect will be unable to endure the vicissitudes that will overtake it. This should not be interpreted to mean that each and every member must make a good profit. There will be some institutions that will not be properly operated and there will be others which, by their very location, will not find it possible to secure and retain a sufficient volume of business to make the undertaking successful. Such cases must be exceptions, or must be regarded as marginal, or, perhaps, even as banks operating below the margin. Even though the number of banks in this class may not be large in the aggregate, they must inevitably go out of business for the reason that only successful banks can live.

If the system is so constituted that any considerable number of banks are unable to make a fair return, granted honest and efficient management, judgment must be rendered against the system as being one which is not meeting the needs of the community. It may not be amiss to state again that the system must be so organized that banking facilities will be provided for all classes. Where this is not done, the system as such cannot be said to be satisfactory. Since profits are regarded as a basic test, it is in order to study the earning records of various types of banks to ascertain which, if any, are not meeting this test.

The Federal Reserve Board and various Federal Reserve banks have made cost studies to ascertain the profit of various classes of banking institutions. Several state banking departments and certain state bankers' associations have given considerable time and study to this question. Reports of the Federal Reserve banks show in many cases that the banks with a small volume of earning assets realize relatively larger gross earnings than banks with a larger volume of earning assets. The average cost of operating the smaller banks is considerably greater in proportion to their size, however, so that the net earnings are less for the small banks. Losses and depreciation charged off are greater proportionately for the banks with small earning assets. This gives the large bank a much better showing when net profits are considered.

Gross earnings for member banks in the Chicago Federal Reserve district for 1928,[4] for banks with earning assets of less than $250,000, were 7.15 percent, as compared with 6.03 percent for member banks with earning assets of over $15,000,000. Total expenses for these classes of banking institutions were 5.65 percent and 4.68 percent respectively. Net earnings were favorable for the small banks but the losses were heavy, leaving the banks with earning assets of less than $250,000, a "net addition to profits" of 0.08 percent as compared with 1.05 percent for the banks with a larger volume of earning assets. No group of banks with earning assets of less than $2,000,000 showed net additions to profits of as much as one percent. Similar data for the Chicago district for the year ending December 31, 1926, showed practically the same results, though the actual percentages of net additions to profits were

[4] *Analysis of Member Bank Earnings and Expenses in 1926 and 1928*, Chicago Federal Reserve District Federal Reserve Bank of Chicago, Oct., 1929, and May, 1928.)

larger in most cases for the same class of banks. In regard to losses the report stated that:

As was the case in the preceding study, the 1928 compilation shows that groups comprising the smaller banks in general wrote off heavier losses than the larger institutions.

The study[5] of non-branch banks for the year 1927 in the San Francisco Federal Reserve district showed in general much the same results as those given for the Chicago district. Average total earnings of 620 banks in the twelfth district were $6.77 per $100 of earning assets, as compared with $7.67 for banks with earning assets of $1,000,000 or less. Banks with earning assets of $5,000,000, and over, earned $6.38 per $100 of earning assets. Net addition to profits was $0.95 for all banks, $0.74 for banks with earning assets of $1,000,000 and under, and $0.98 for banks with earning assets of $5,000,000 and over. Here again, net losses for the small banks were much greater proportionately than either those for the large banks or the average for all banks. If the results be stated in terms of the profits to invested capital, the average was $6.88 for all banks. The least favorable showing was made by the banks with the smaller volume of earning assets, while the most favorable results were registered by banks having total earning assets ranging from $4,000,000 to $4,999,999. This group earned $8.11. The banks with earning assets of $5,000,000 or over made $7.95. All groups with earning assets of less than $3,000,000 showed returns below the average for all banks. In comparing the gross and net earnings of banks of different sizes it would be interesting to know the rate of dividend paid by each class of banks. Unfortunately such information is not available at this time.

Recent reports of the Federal Reserve Bank of Boston do not show net profits to capital funds, but the report covering the year 1926 showed that the banks with gross loans and investments of under $500,001 had less net profits to capital funds than any other class. It should be noted, however, that the statistics showed the most profitable class of banks on this basis to be that with total loans and investments ranging from $1,000,001 to $2,000,000, and

[5] For a detailed study of the banking costs of the banks in the twelfth district, see *Monthly Review of Business Conditions*, Federal Reserve District of San Francisco (Federal Reserve Bank of San Francisco, Dec. 20, 1928, p. 96).

not the class with the largest volume of loans and investments—that with over $10,000,000.[6]

In general the results are the same for national banks, state banks and trust company members in the Philadelphia Federal Reserve district for the years 1927 and 1929.[7] In each of these groups for each of the three years, the banks with loans and investments of under $250,000 for national banks and under $1,000,000 for state bank and trust company members showed a lower yield than the groups holding larger amounts of loans and investments when measured in terms of net profits to capital funds (capital, surplus and undivided profits).

The studies made by the Federal Reserve Bank of New York[8] took as the lower class all banks with loans and investments of under $500,000. Based upon this minimum, the banks in this class made the least favorable showing of any class reported. Net earnings to capital funds for the "under $500,000" class were 10.6 percent and 11.8 percent for 1928 and 1929 respectively. For the class with earning assets ranging from $5,000,000 to $9,999,999, the percentage ratio was 14.0 for 1928 and 15.5 for 1929. The percentages for the various classes ranging between the two just referred to vary somewhat, with a decided tendency to increase as the total loans and investments increase.

Difficulties of the small bank are well illustrated by the conditions existing among the state banks of Iowa. Data including net earnings and net profits were prepared by the Iowa State Bankers' Association for the period 1924-29, inclusive. Banks with loans and investments of less than $150,000 as a group showed a loss after having written off losses. In 1924 all banks with total loans and investments averaging less than $1,000,000 registered a net loss when considered as a group. Conditions improved for the small bank, especially during 1928 and 1929, but in the meantime a large number of small banks failed. A summary of the data prepared by the Bankers' Association is presented in Table 6.

[6] *Operating Costs and Profits in 1926*, Federal Reserve Bank of Boston, p. 4.

[7] *Analysis of Operating Costs and Profits of Member Banks in the Philadelphia Federal Reserve District* (Federal Reserve Bank of Philadelphia, 1928, 1930).

[8] *A Comparison of the Operating Ratios of the Representative Member Banks in the Second Federal Reserve District, for the Year 1929* (Federal Reserve Bank of New York, April 29, 1930).

TABLE 6

ALL BANKS IN THE STATE OF IOWA*

LOANS AND INVESTMENTS OF:	PERCENT OF NET EARNINGS TO CAPITAL SURPLUS AND UNDIVIDED PROFITS†						PERCENT OF NET ADDITIONS, IF ANY TO PROFIT AND LOSS ACCOUNT TO CAPITAL, SURPLUS AND UNDIVIDED PROFIT‡					
	1924	1925	1926	1927	1928	1929	1924	1925	1926	1927	1928	1929
Under $75,000	0.9	0.3	0.2	0.9	2.7	3.5	−6.6	−9.6	−7.6	−9.5	−6.6	−0.6
$75,000–$100,000	3.0	2.5	3.4	4.8	4.4	4.7	−5.6	−8.8	−0.1	−5.2	−1.0	−0.0
$100,000–$150,000	2.5	3.4	4.0	4.5	5.4	6.2	−7.3	−6.3	−5.4	−5.9	−1.8	−1.2
$150,000–$250,000	5.0	4.5	6.0	6.0	7.0	8.1	−2.2	−4.7	−2.2	−4.1	0.1	1.9
$250,000–$500,000	6.8	6.8	7.7	7.4	9.2	11.2	−0.9	−1.0	−0.9	−1.6	1.0	3.7
$500,000–$750,000	7.2	7.8	8.7	9.6	10.2	13.5	−1.2	−0.4	−2.3	1.6	3.4	6.0
$750,000–$1,000,000	7.6	8.5	10.1	10.4	10.2	12.8	−1.5	0.8	2.7	1.0	3.9	5.0
$1,000,000–$1,750,000	8.9	8.6	9.1	9.1	11.0	12.7	4.1	0.5	4.3	1.4	3.2	4.4
Over $1,750,000	9.2	10.7	10.9	9.7	11.2	13.4	3.3	6.3	6.2	4.4	3.5	4.7
TOTAL	7.5	8.0	8.7	8.5	9.7	11.9	0.5	1.0	1.6	0.8	2.3	4.2

* *Proceedings of the Forty-fourth Annual Convention of Iowa Bankers' Association* (1930), facing p. 320.

† "Net earnings" include gross earnings less (1) salaries; (2) interest and discount paid on borrowed money; (3) interest paid on deposits; (4) all other expenses.

‡ After "charge-offs" have been deducted, but dividends still undeducted.

These data form a sad commentary upon the state banking system of Iowa, indicating the plight into which the banks of that state have fallen. Especially is this record most striking among the smaller banks.

National banks, when measured either in terms of percentage of banks reporting net deficits or no net profits, indicate conclusively that the national banks with a small volume of loans and investments, as a class are at a great disadvantage as compared with banks doing a larger amount of business. The net average income for banks with total loans and investments below $1,000,000 is too low to be satisfactory. The situation is more clearly shown in Tables 7 and 8.

TABLE 7

PERCENTAGE DISTRIBUTION OF NATIONAL BANKS GROUPED BY SIZE OF LOANS AND INVESTMENTS AND BY RATE OF NET PROFITS ON INVESTED CAPITAL: AVERAGE 1926–30*

SIZE OF GROUP LOANS AND INVESTMENTS	TOTAL 100 PER-CENT	REPORTING NET DEFICITS OR NO NET PROFITS		REPORTING NET PROFITS				
		6 Per-cent or more	*0.0 to 5.9 Per-cent*	*Less than 3 Per-cent*	*3 to 5.9 Per-cent*	*6 to 8.9 Per-cent*	*9 to 11.9 Per-cent*	*12 Per-cent and Over*
Under $150,000	100	14.6	20.4	18.8	20.2	13.8	7.0	5.3
150,000– 250,000	100	11.3	16.7	15.3	18.8	17.5	9.9	10.6
250,000– 500,000	100	8.7	11.9	12.8	19.4	20.8	13.5	13.1
500,000– 750,000	100	5.9	8.7	11.4	18.8	23.8	15.1	16.4
750,000– 1,000,000	100	5.7	7.5	11.2	19.5	24.2	16.2	15.7
1,000,000– 2,000,000	100	4.0	6.6	10.0	19.5	25.6	17.8	16.5
2,000,000– 5,000,000	100	3.2	5.2	7.6	17.7	26.9	20.6	18.8
5,000,000–10,000,000	100	2.3	4.5	7.2	17.2	28.7	21.6	18.6
10,000,000–50,000,000	100	1.9	3.4	6.5	15.8	29.9	25.1	17.5
50,000,000 and over	100	1.0	1.5	4.6	12.7	31.5	28.9	19.8
AVERAGE ALL GROUPS	100	6.4	9.4	11.3	18.9	23.2	15.8	15.0

* Report of the Federal Reserve Committee on Branch, Group and Chain Banking (1932), on *Banking Profits, 1890–1931*, p. 15.

National banks located in towns with a population of less than 10,000 show as a class, heavy losses. The proportion of national banks earning less than 3 percent in towns with a population of less than 50,000 varies with the size of the town but as a group the percentage ranges from 20.2 to 35.9, the latter being for banks located in towns with a population of less than 500. National banks located in the smaller towns and cities are at a great disadvantage. Often the volume of business is too small. In other cases, the business is of a one-type nature, the banks being unable to diversify

TABLE 8

ANNUAL GROSS EARNINGS AND NET PROFITS PER $100 OF LOANS AND INVESTMENTS OF NATIONAL BANKS GROUPED BY SIZE OF LOANS AND INVESTMENTS: AVERAGE 1926–30*

SIZE OF GROUP LOANS AND INVESTMENTS	GROSS EARNINGS	NET PROFITS
Under $150,000	$9.18	$0.02
150,000– 250,000	8.06	0.50
250,000– 500,000	7.35	0.70
500,000– 750,000	6.99	0.98
750,000– 1,000,000	6.74	0.99
1,000,000– 2,000,000	6.58	1.05
2,000,000– 5,000,000	6.55	1.13
5,000,000–10,000,000	6.37	1.14
10,000,000–50,000,000	6.39	1.21
50,000,000 and over	6.09	1.37

* *Ibid.*, p. 38.

their portfolios easily so as to attain safety. In not a few cases, the volume of business is not large or profitable enough to make possible the employment of the proper type of management. All these factors are present in many cases, making the road of the small bank a rough and thorny one indeed. The percentage distribution of net profits on invested capital of national banks in towns of various sizes for the period 1926-30 is shown in Table 9.

The data presented in the preceding pages regarding the earnings of banks are by no means complete. They are sufficiently extensive, however, to show the average position of the banks grouped according to size. Certainly there is nothing in these data to indicate that all unit banks are a failure from the income point of view. What the data do show conclusively, it is believed, is the fact that banks with a small volume of business cannot offer much hope of a satisfactory financial return to their stockholders or adequate protection to their depositors. These statistics indicate that the small bank is doomed. Either there must be larger unit banks or there must be substituted some type of multiple banking. If neither of these changes occurs, then it must be patent that many communities in the future will be obliged to forego the services of local banks, a thing which they have come to expect in this country.

TABLE 9

PERCENTAGE DISTRIBUTION OF NATIONAL BANKS IN THE UNITED STATES, GROUPED BY SIZE OF TOWN, AND BY RATE OF NET PROFITS ON INVESTED CAPITAL, 1926–30*

POPULATION OF TOWN	TOTAL, 100 PER-CENT	REPORTING NET DEFICITS OR NO NET PROFITS		REPORTING NET PROFITS				
		6 Percent or more	*0.0 to 5.9 Percent*	*Less than 3 Percent*	*3 to 5.9 Percent*	*6 to 8.9 Percent*	*9 to 11.9 Percent*	*12 Percent and Over*
Less than 500	100.0	8.6	14.3	13.0	19.2	19.4	13.7	11.8
500– 1,000	100.0	9.1	11.8	12.0	17.7	20.7	13.7	14.9
1,000– 2,500	100.0	7.7	10.8	11.6	18.5	21.5	14.6	15.3
2,500– 5,000	100.0	5.8	8.0	11.4	17.4	24.6	15.8	17.0
5,000– 10,000	100.0	5.5	7.7	10.2	20.9	24.2	16.0	15.5
10,000– 50,000	100.0	3.7	6.4	10.1	19.9	26.1	19.4	14.4
50,000–100,000	100.0	2.6	6.7	8.9	19.4	29.0	18.9	14.4
100,000 and over	100.0	3.3	6.7	11.5	20.2	26.6	18.1	13.6
ALL GROUPS	100.0	6.4	9.4	11.3	18.9	23.2	15.8	15.0

* Report of the Federal Reserve Committee on Branch, Group and Chain Banking (1932), on *Banking Profits, 1890–1931*, p. 210.

It would be foolish to think of raising the capital requirements of banks in these small towns, since the banks already there cannot earn a fair return upon the capital employed. It is certainly desirable to have stronger banks, but these cannot be maintained long unless the banks can secure a sufficient volume of business to make the undertaking a success. Capital requirements should be raised, but only after modifications have been made in our banking statutes so that the banks may extend their services in the form of branches to the many small towns and cities which are not able to support a unit bank on their own account. The present situation does not hold out much encouragement for these small towns in the way of financial relief through the organization and operation of sound and prosperous unit banks. Economic conditions have changed and with these changes in business there must come in the course of time corresponding changes in our banking methods.

BIG BUSINESS AND THE INDEPENDENT BANKS

Economic conditions have changed rapidly in this country during the past three or four decades. The development of large corporations and trusts has brought about marked changes in the methods of financing business as compared with the way in which small business was and may be financed even today. The appearance of mail-order houses and large chain stores has done much to alter the position of the country or small-town banker. As a result of these changes, the banker has seen a sizeable portion of his most desirable business pass out of his hands and go to larger banks. The small bankers still have considerable business, but that which they have lost has, no doubt, reduced many bankers below the margin at which the banking business may be conducted profitably.

The large business, industrial or commercial concern, requires a large financial institution to handle its finances. This cannot be done by a small bank. It is true that there are, and will continue to be, many small business units, but the number and the variety of financial services they require are not of sufficient quantity to make the small bank a profitable venture in many cases. There is nothing that the small banker can do to help himself. He is the victim of a changing business world and must to a certain extent, at least, give way to larger banks with better management and more capital.

SUMMARY

Business of all kinds has passed through extensive and far-reaching changes during the past few decades. In many respects banking has lagged. The banks did not grow or expand as a class in keeping with the modifications made by the various lines of business enterprise which the banks proposed to finance. A few large banks have been developed, but on the whole the banks have not kept pace with many other types of business. The large banks have for the most part made a favorable showing from the standpoint of profits to the stockholders, but the smaller classes of banks have not been so fortunate in many parts of the country. The small banks have shown their fundamental weaknesses:

1. In the large number of bank failures throughout the country;
2. In the failure to provide adequate banking services to their localities;
3. In the small financial returns, this being strikingly evident in the large number of banks (1) showing net losses, or (2) earning less than 3 percent on invested capital;
4. In the unfavorable showing of banks located in towns with a small population.

The data studied do not show that all unit banks are insolvent or about to fail. Many of them are quite profitable and will continue to be so. These data do show that the system as now constituted cannot provide unit banks for a large number of towns and small communities. Since this is true, it must be admitted that the unit-banking system has failed in this important particular. A satisfactory system should and will, in the long run, provide financial services for all types of towns and cities. The past experience of the unit system in this country would certainly indicate that it is losing ground and that we cannot look forward to the future banking situation in the smaller localities with anything but grave concern. The unit system has not made good in this respect and we should realize the fact and make such changes or modifications as will provide adequate services for all classes in our economic community.

CHAPTER III

LEGISLATIVE PROVISION FOR BANK MERGERS AND CONSOLIDATIONS

The terms "merger," "consolidation," and "amalgamation" are used extensively in current financial discussions and writings. In most cases, however, no attempt is made to draw a precise difference in the meanings of these three terms in so far as they are applied to changes going on in the field of banking. It is customary to make a distinction when using these terms in connection with certain forms of concentration among railroads, public utilities, or industrial concerns. In relation to the latter types of institutions, "consolidation" generally refers to the bringing of two or more existing corporations under the control and management of a single corporation or group of individuals.

With regard to railroads and corporations other than banks, this unified control and management does not necessarily mean that any of the corporations involved surrenders its charter. It does mean, however, that all the corporations come under this central management. A merger is said to occur when two corporations are united in such a way that one is taken over by the other, the absorbing institution assuming the assets and liabilities of the absorbed concern. The absorbed institution surrenders its charter and becomes an integral part of the absorbing corporation which, in turn, retains its original charter. "Amalgamation" is used, on the other hand, to designate the process when two or more corporations unite to form an entirely new concern which assumes the assets and liabilities of the old corporations involved.

With reference to banking, amalgamation is a term more commonly used in England than in the United States. It is important to note, also, that these terms—merger, consolidation, amalgamation—are not generally employed in connection with banking concentration with the same meaning as in the case of other types of corporations. They are used generally in the field of banking to refer to the formation of one financial institution by combining two or more banks in order to form a larger bank, to carry out the liquidation of an old bank, or to prevent a bank failure. Many state banking laws and banking departments make no effort to classify them separately. In practically all instances of a merger or consolidation, there is only one remaining bank. There is a limited number of exceptions, as, for example, the merger between the National City Bank of New York and the Farmers Loan and Trust Company of New York City. In that case the business was so segregated that two separate legal entities were retained: the National City Bank and the City Bank Farmers Trust Company. The trust business was given to the latter while the former assumed the functions in connection with the commercial banking business. A brief survey of the laws governing mergers and consolidations will be outlined in the following paragraphs, but in general we may say that, from a practical banking point of view, the difference in the meaning placed upon each of these terms is insignificant except in a very few states.

The National Bank Act does not make any provision for the "merger" of banks, but it does provide for the "consolidation" of national banks or for a consolidation of national and state banks which is not in contravention of the laws of the state under which such state bank is incorporated. Before the passage of the Consolidation Act of November, 1918, there were no national laws providing specifically for the consolidation of national banks. Prior to that time it was necessary for at least one of the banks to go into liquidation and sell its assets to another bank or banks. In that event it was usually said that one bank was "absorbed" by the other. In some cases both banks went into voluntary liquidation and a new bank was formed which assumed the assets and liabilities of both liquidated institutions. Despite these legal difficulties many national banks carried through mergers or consolidations with both state and national banks.

Since the passage of the Consolidation Act of November 7, 1918, and the McFadden-Pepper Act of February 25, 1927, national and state banks may consolidate directly without either bank liquidating. In the act of 1918 there was provided a way for the consolidation of two national banks, while the act of 1927 provided, for the first time, for the direct consolidation of a state bank and a national bank. In both these acts provision was made for "consolidation." Even though the legislation governing national banks provides for consolidations only, this way of designating the process does not simplify our problem in defining the terms, for the reason that while the process is referred to as a "consolidation" in the national system, the same results are obtained in a number of states where the process is designated as a bank merger.

The state banking laws are not uniform as to terminology in the various statutes relating to banking concentration. The North Dakota laws[1] define mergers and consolidations as follows:

> The term consolidation as used herein shall mean the consolidation of the liabilities, assets and corporate existence of the two or more associations into a single association, which shall issue its stock to stockholders in the consolidating associations in return for the assets of the consolidating associations.
>
> The term merger as used herein shall mean the taking over, or the absorption of the assets of one association by another, and the assumption of the liabilities of the association, or associations, whose assets and liabilities are taken over.

New York and New Jersey use the term merger exclusively. In New York one writer points out that there is a distinction between mergers and consolidations. To quote:[2]

> The terms merger and consolidation are not synonomous. Consolidation implies the bringing together, the uniting, the combination of two or more companies in order to make a third. In merger one company is swallowed up in the other. In consolidation the identity of both companies disappears and an entirely new company takes the place of the companies consolidating. In merger only the identity of the weaker company is extinguished, the stronger company continuing its own corporate name and identity.

A sale of the assets is not considered a merger: (1) "One trust company may purchase the assets of another under Sec. 16 of the Stock Corporation Law, instead of merging under this section"

[1] *Laws Relating to State Banks, Savings Banks and Trust Companies, in the State of North Dakota,* compiled by Gilbert Semingson, State Examiner (Bismarck, N.D.; July 1, 1929), p. 52.

[2] Baldwin, W. E., *New York Banking Law, Annotated* (New York: The Bank Law Publishing Co., 1926), pp. 339-40.

(Report of Attorney General, 1913). The banking laws of Michigan on the other hand provide that such corporation "which is in good faith winding up its business for the purpose of consolidating with some other state bank may transfer its assets and liabilities to the bank with which it is in the process of consolidation."[8]

By far the larger number of states have adopted terminology similar to that used in the national banking system, using exclusively the term "consolidation." Among the states falling in this class are Arkansas, Connecticut, Florida, Idaho, Illinois, Maryland, Michigan, Ohio, North Carolina, South Dakota, and Wisconsin. Both terms are used in the texts of the banking laws in a limited list of states. When so used the wording is "merge or consolidate" or "consolidate and merge." The following states may properly be grouped in this general class: Alabama, Georgia, Massachusetts, Missouri, North Dakota, and Tennessee. North Dakota is perhaps more specific in the use of terms than the other states in this group. The law in North Dakota reads as follows: "Any two or more banking associations organized under the laws of this state may consolidate their capital, assets, and liabilities, or one or more of such associations may be merged into another." The states of the fourth group do not use either term specifically with reference to banking concentration. Among this group may be mentioned Colorado, Indiana, Kansas, Texas, and Utah. It is clearly evident that in no case does any class or group as outlined appear to be based on any geographical division of the country. Neither are we warranted in assuming that the state laws have been based on or modeled after the National Bank Act as amended, for the reason that much of the state legislation in this regard antedates the national law.

PROCEDURE FOR CONSOLIDATING OR MERGING

The state laws governing the general procedure for bank mergers and consolidations may be roughly divided into two groups. First there are those which make definite provision for either bank mergers or consolidations or both, while the second class contains no specific provisions covering such changes, the process being

[8] *Laws Relating to Banking, Revision of 1929*, compiled by John S. Haggerty and Sydney A. Schulte (Lansing, Mich.: Franklin Dekleine Co., 1929), p. 40.

covered in general terms. In the latter case the details must be worked out by the state banking department of the state concerned. The results are essentially the same regardless of which plan or method is followed. The banking laws in the state of Missouri illustrate the former, outlining the procedure in considerable detail. Other states like Georgia or Florida cover the subject in a few words, leaving the details to be covered by the regulations of the state superintendent of banks.

Regardless of the variation in the laws, the actual methods followed are practically the same in the different states. After the preliminaries have been "ironed out" among certain directors or officers, the directors of the banks involved must agree to the conditions under which a merger or consolidation may be effected. Such an agreement should specify the rights and privileges of the stockholders of all institutions participating. In cases involving mutual savings banks, the trustees occupy the same position as directors in state banks and trust companies. Stockholders must approve the merger or consolidation by a two-thirds vote of all stock. A mutual savings bank has no stockholders. In the state of New York two or more mutual savings banks may be merged with the approval of a three-fourths' affirmative vote of the trustees of the banks. In all states such a merger or consolidation must have the approval or recommendation of the state banking department. Savings banks in New Hampshire must secure the approval of the court, which grants permission only after the banking commissioner has certified that public convenience and advantage and the interest of said institutions, their members, stockholders, and depositors, will be promoted by the union.

The same principle applies with equal force to national banks participating in banking consolidations. If one bank is buying the assets of another bank, it is not usually necessary for the board of directors of the buying bank to submit the deal to its stockholders, since it is an outright purchase and does not alter the relative rights of the existing body of stockholders. Stockholders of the liquidating or selling bank are generally required to approve the sale by a two-thirds' vote of all stock.

There are many details involved in the actual completion of a merger or consolidation. First, there is the question of agreeing on the terms by which stockholders are given the right to convert their old stock into the stock of the new institution. There are no general bases for exchanging the stock, but it is frequently worked out on the basis of the liquidating value of the stock of the banks involved. In other cases the market price is used as a guide. In either case, it is customary to offer the stockholders the right to exchange, share for share, or two for one, or on whatever basis has been agreed. Frequently the value of the shares of one bank varies so widely from that of the other that it is necessary to exchange a share or shares of one bank for one or more shares, or even a fraction of a share of the continuing institution plus a cash payment, in order to arrive at a satisfactory and equitable settlement for all stockholders involved. In some cases options are offered to the stockholders of the absorbed bank so that they may exchange their stock for stock in the continuing bank on a certain pro-rata basis which has been definitely stated, or they may sell their stock for cash to the consolidated banking group at a certain price, also agreed upon.

Second, there is a method whereby two banks unite to form a new bank, both of the old institutions disappearing. The method of dealing with the two sets of stockholders is similar for the most part to the plan or plans outlined in the preceding paragraph. A third method is offered when one group buys out the assets of another bank. Here there is only one problem or question to be met, and that is the price at which the total assets will be disposed of. This is a fairly simple process. A more involved case arises when one bank is in difficulty. The "absorbed" bank under such circumstances often faces an embarrassing situation. The bank may be, often is, in danger of failing. If this be true, the liquidating, or the selling, bank frequently has to turn over the assets without any definite agreement regarding the amount, if any, to go to the old stockholders. The buying bank agrees to take over the assets with the idea of working out the situation. A definite period of two, three, or five years may be agreed upon during which time the buying bank undertakes to collect all claims possible and retire the debts or liabilities. During this time the retiring group of stockholders is frequently forced to agree to a continuation of the double-liability feature of the stock in order to protect the buying bank. If in the end the assets of the selling bank are insufficient to meet the liabilities, the stockholders must make up the difference to the extent of double liability of the stock. On the other hand, if there should be a balance after the liabilities have been met, the retiring stockholders will benefit accordingly in that each shareholder will receive his proportionate share of this remaining fund.

MERGER AGREEMENT BINDING

A merger agreement in the state of New York must be submitted by the board of directors, or trustees in the case of a mutual savings bank to the superintendent of banks for his approval. If, in the case of mergers involving commercial banks and trust companies, two-thirds of the stockholders owning at least two-thirds of the stock approve the terms of the agreement, it becomes binding upon such corporations. In the case of mutual savings banks the agreement, after being approved by the superintendent of banks, must be resubmitted to the trustees. If three-fourths of the trustees vote in the affirmative, the agreement thereupon becomes binding upon such savings banks. The two following sections of the New York law outline the final steps in the merger process and show when the merger becomes effective:

Sec. 492. After such merger agreement shall have become binding upon the respective corporations who are parties thereto, as provided in the two immediately preceding sections, one of the duplicates thereof with a copy of the superintendent's written approval and a sworn copy of the proceedings of the meeting at which such agreement was finally approved, made by the secretaries thereof respectively, shall be filed in the office of the superintendent, and the other duplicate of such agreement with the written approval of the superintendent and another sworn copy of such proceedings, shall be filed in the office of the clerk of the county in which is located the principal place of business of the corporation into which the other corporation or corporations are to be merged.

Sec. 493. Upon filing the duplicates of such merger agreement, together with copies of its approval by the superintendent as prescribed in the last preceding section, the merger agreement shall take effect according to its terms and the merger shall thereupon take place as provided in the agreement.

The methods of approving and recording the terms of the agreement vary from state to state, but in general the New York law as quoted above sets forth the procedure for completing the final legal details for mergers and consolidations. The latter steps of a merger or consolidation between banks are very similar to those of other corporations effecting mergers and consolidations. In fact the banking laws in this respect correspond quite closely to other corporation laws covering similar points. In some cases the two are identical.

THE MERGER BECOMES EFFECTIVE

Upon the completion of the agreement and the filing of the same, the corporate existence of each of the consolidating or merging banks, all the rights, franchises, and interests of said (absorbed) bank and its right, title, and interest in and to all property, shall be deemed to be transferred to and vested in such bank into which it is consolidated or merged, without further act or deed, and such corporation shall have and hold the same in its own right as fully as the same was possessed and held by the merged corporation from which it was, by operation of the provisions of this article, transferred.

The rights, obligations, and relations to any person, creditor, depositor, trustee, or beneficiary of any trust of the bank to be absorbed, remains unimpaired and the corporation into which it is being merged or consolidated succeeds to all such rights, trusts, and liabilities. All obligations and liabilities continue as fully as before such merger was consummated. This and the previous paragraph are based upon the New York and Wisconsin state laws. Other state laws are similar. Owing to the similarity of the state laws in this respect, we may assume that this sets forth very briefly the final steps of the banks participating in the merger or consolidation.

An important problem which banks must meet under these conditions is the question of what to do with the personnel of both institutions. The statement is frequently made by the banks that the entire force will be retained. Such an announcement cannot be taken literally. One of the principal reasons assigned for most mergers is that of economy. To retain indefinitely the full staff of both banks would prevent a proper reduction in labor costs. There can be no doubt that such statements are often honestly made, but the truth of the matter is that even though the full force is temporarily retained it will be cut down in the near future by one method or another. Employees often find that there is no definite field in the new organization for them and they take the first opportunity to find a new connection—which is what the management desires. Vacancies under such circumstances are left unfilled. This is considered a more humane way of cutting the force than simply telling the men they must find new jobs. In other cases, the new organization notifies certain officers and employees that they will be carried on the pay rolls for a certain length of time, after which their services will no longer be needed. Whatever the method adopted, it usually results within a reasonably short time in a reduction of the personnel of the two banks.

The desire to retain all or as much of the business of the absorbed bank as possible affects the problem of dealing with the officers and directors of the absorbed bank or banks. The name of the new bank or consolidating bank, at times, takes part of the name of the other bank, in order to keep as much of the good will of the old customers as possible. In the same way part of the directorate is elected to the new board to retain the confidence and good will of each group of depositors—or they may be designated as advisory council for the branch in question. This same plan usually applies to a part of the officers and employees of the absorbed bank. The principal point involved here is retention of as much business as possible, rather than preservation of the established personnel.

CHAPTER IV

THE SCOPE AND EXTENT OF BANK MERGERS IN THE UNITED STATES

Bank mergers and consolidations have taken place at a moderate rate in this country for many years. Public interest has been directed seriously to this phase of banking, however, for only a short time. It is primarily a postwar development so far as the public is concerned. No figures of any general nature were compiled prior to 1925. Since then the movement has been tied up closely with the bank-failure epidemic in many states. In certain states mergers and consolidations have been one of the principal means by which branches have been obtained by branch banks. Especially has this tendency been marked in the state of California. This chapter is intended to furnish a statistical picture of the movement, beginning with 1900.

The amalgamation movement has been going on in England for many years. In fact it has almost spent its force there, leaving but a very limited number of banks behind. A large number of English bankers, business men, and economists feel that a further development along these lines would result in greatly reducing or limiting competition among the banks. This, it is thought, would be a detriment to public policy[1] and would bring about a situation which the government would be fully justified in preventing. The consolidation movement made no significant progress in the United States until after it had reached maturity in England.

Although our discussion will deal primarily with the period in the United States since the close of the World War in 1918, it is interesting to trace the changes prior to that time in so far as available data will permit. To attempt to give a chronological list, such as that proposed by an able English writer[2] covering bank

[1] *Report of the* [*British*] *Treasury Committee on Bank Amalgamations*, (London: His Majesty's Stationery Office, March, 1918).

[2] Sykes, Joseph, *The Amalgamation Movement in English Banking, 1825-1924*, (London: P. S. King and Son, Ltd., 1926).

amalgamations in Great Britain, would be an almost hopeless task, since there are so many unit banks in this country. The total number of bank mergers and consolidations has run literally into the thousands when both state and national banks are considered.

TABLE 10

THE NUMBER OF BANK MERGERS AND CONSOLIDATIONS REPORTED FOR BANKS IN THE UNITED STATES, 1900–09 (INCLUSIVE)*

STATE	1900	1901	1902	1903	1904	1905	1906	1907	1908	1909	TOTAL
Arizona										1	1
Connecticut						1		1			2
Florida						1			1		2
Georgia									13	10	23
Idaho							1	1	4		6
Illinois		6		4	1	6	7	4	4	2	34
Indiana			1		1		1	1	1	1	6
Kansas	1	1	1								3
Louisiana			1	1	2	5	4	2			15
Michigan					6		2	4	7	4	23
Minnesota		1	1		1		3	2	5	9	22
Missouri		3	3	3	5	7	6	7	5	11	50
Nebraska	1	5	5	2	1	4	2		4	2	26
North Carolina			2	1			2	3	5	2	15
Ohio					1	3					4
Oklahoma									2	8	10
Oregon									4		4
Pennsylvania		1	2	4	3	4	1	1	1	1	18
Rhode Island	1	2	1		2	1	1			1	9
South Carolina									4	2	6
South Dakota			6		1	1					8
Texas							1			1	2
Utah						1					1
Washington									7		7
West Virginia	1		2				2	1			6
Wisconsin				2	5	2	1				10
Wyoming					2						2
TOTAL All State Banks	4	19	25	17	31	36	34	27	67	55	316
All National Banks	16	22	25	20	32	33	22	27	30	25	252
GRAND TOTAL	20	41	50	37	63	69	56	54	97	80	568

* Source: Annual reports and files of various state banking departments. The totals of this table are presented graphically in Chart I, p. 60. The reader should consult p. 53 for a statement concerning the nature of these data.

DEVELOPMENTS FROM 1900 TO 1910

Prior to 1910 the data were few and there were, moreover, no definite trends of importance. Yet the total number of mergers reported by several of the states was surprisingly large. Efforts to secure complete data for this period were not as satisfactory as was desired. In fact the incompleteness of the state banking reports and records made it practically impossible to do more than secure an estimate. The reports actually received show that more than 300 state bank mergers took place between 1900 and 1910, while during the same period more than 250 consolidations were reported for national banks. Thus, there was a total in excess of 550 for both classes of banks taken together. There were included in these statistics regarding state bank mergers reports from only twenty-seven states. It is fairly certain, therefore, that our data are incomplete and that the figure of 550 is too small. It seems, on the basis of our data, reasonable to estimate that there were, on an average, from 60 to 75 mergers and consolidations for each year for that ten-year period. That would have been an exceedingly large number for any other country, but in view of the large number of small unit banks here, it is certainly not out of line with other banking changes.

Table 10 is presented to show in statistical form the data obtained for the decade 1900-9.[8]

The distribution of these mergers by states is very interesting. Two hundred and twenty-six, or approximately 50 percent, of all the consolidations for that period were in the following states:

Georgia	23	Missouri	50
Illinois	34	Nebraska	26
Louisiana	15	North Carolina	15
Michigan	23	Pennsylvania	18
Minnesota	22		

A large percentage of the total number occurred in states in which there were no large cities. Even in the states which had

[8] The omission of certain states from Table 10 should not be taken as proof that there were no mergers in those states. It means that no data were received from the missing states. Moreover, the table is not presented as being complete for the states included. The table does indicate, it is believed, the trend of bank mergers and consolidations for that decade.

large cities, concentration was common in the smaller cities and towns, and only to a limited extent in the large cities. Of the total mergers which had taken place in these nine states a large proportion was limited to the states located in the South and Middle West.

During this period (1900-10) unit banks were increasing rapidly in number. Many people became for the first time directly interested in the banking business. The easiest way to enter the business, in many cases, was by establishing a new bank, even though the capital funds were small. Public sentiment, so far as it had developed at that time, was largely opposed to branch banking. Unit banking had no opposition. The growth in large-scale business had not, as yet, reached a stage in its development where it had a marked effect upon the size of the unit bank. Certainly there was no noticeable tendency to increase the size of the unit banks by absorbing other banks. That form of concentration was not to appear in its present form until a decade later.

The opposition that existed to branch banking at that time had a decided influence upon the type of concentration. Bankers had not become accustomed to operating banks with a widely distributed list of depositors and borrowers. Methods of controlling banking resources apart from branch banking had not yet developed. The growth of chain banking had not reached serious proportions outside of perhaps two sections of the country, namely the Northwest and the South. Minneapolis had been for a number of years a hotbed for the growth of chain banks. The banks were all small and had been brought together in many instances by an individual or individuals who sponsored the chain. Business men were accustomed to doing business with a community bank. The merger movement, as a means of creating larger banks, was not so important as it is at the present time. Another obstacle to consolidations has been found in the provisions of the various banking laws relating to bank mergers and consolidations. Especially was this true in connection with proposed mergers between state and national banks.

This earlier period of banking development may well be regarded as a period of extensive rather than a period of intensive banking, a general situation which also applied to other lines of business. The country was not so closely knit together and banks were organized to meet local conditions by men actually engaged in carrying on the principal business enterprises of the locality. Capital was scarce and the opportunities in other lines were far greater than in the limited field of banking. The United States was still a debtor country and entrepreneurs and capitalists found difficulty in obtaining sufficient capital to meet all their needs. Banks often sprang up, therefore, in response to a local need, and the result was in most cases a small bank. The bank, small at first, grew with the growth of the community. In most sections a long period of time was needed for the community to grow large enough to support a large bank. Moreover, the additional needs for banking accommodation were frequently met by the organization of another small bank rather than by the expansion of the older bank. Over a period of years, the country naturally tended to outgrow this system. Many business men and bankers realized that there was considerable waste in the operation of so many small banks. This feeling did not become very effective until many bank failures had occurred. Gradually, however, the country came to demand larger and larger banking units until today we have many large banking institutions throughout the country as a whole. The bank-merger movement has played an important rôle in this larger concentration movement. Although not all bank mergers were effected for the primary purpose of creating larger banks, in most cases one of the results was just that, even when the motive was to be found in the effort to secure branches or to prevent a bank failure. It would appear that the latter cause (bank failures) was especially marked in the last two years of the decade.

STATISTICS OF BANK MERGERS AND CONSOLIDATIONS

The discussion of the merger and consolidation movement is based on the statistics and data which show the total number of mergers and consolidations, including the various classes of banks and the total resources of all banks involved in the mergers. The period included in our study covers the years 1900-31 inclusive.

The data for the ten-year period 1900-9, as has been pointed out, are not complete. The results of the investigation for the earlier years have been presented in tabular form on page 52. The data for that decade are interesting, but form only an introduction to our study of later years. A varying number of consolidations was reported for each of the years 1910-31 inclusive, but there was no marked tendency upward prior to the close of the World War in 1918. The turning point, however, came during the year 1919

TABLE II

SUMMARY OF ALL BANK MERGERS AND CONSOLIDATIONS IN THE UNITED STATES FROM 1910 TO 1931 INCLUSIVE, INCLUDING NATIONAL BANKS, STATE BANKS, TRUST COMPANIES AND SAVINGS BANKS*

[*Dollar amounts to thousands of dollars*]

YEAR	NUMBER OF MERGERS	NUMBER OF BANKS	NUMBER OF BANKS ABSORBED				
			Total Number of Banks Absorbed	*National Banks by National Banks*	*State Banks by National Banks*	*State Banks by State Banks*	*National Banks by State Banks*
1910	127	250	128	32	13	70	13
1911	119	235	119	25	18	66	10
1912	128	253	128	39	13	67	9
1913	118	229	118	16	10	78	14
1914	142	276	143	29	24	76	14
1915	154	305	154	33	24	75	22
1916	134	263	134	36	15	62	21
1917	123	232	123	26	15	62	20
1918	119	231	125	16	20	73	16
1919	178	345	178	32	19	101	26
1920	181	349	183	29	30	88	36
1921	281	559	292	38	50	159	45
1922	337	616	340	49	53	182	56
1923	325	584	325	47	41	172	65
1924	350	668	352	56	60	174	62
1925	352	657	356	41	46	214	55
1926	429	814	429	70	57	243	59
1927	543	955	544	69	95	286	94
1928	501	916	507	71	88	277	71
1929	571	1,060	575	96	108	261	110
1930	699	1,346	698	130	135	322	111
1931	706	1,363	719	164	107	320	128

* Source: *Annual Reports of the Comptroller of the Currency; Annual Reports of the Federal Reserve Board; Annual Reports*, state banking departments; also special reports and direct assistance from officers and employees of various state banking departments and from the office of the Comptroller of the Currency.

TABLE II (*Continued*)

YEAR	DATA OF BANKS BEFORE THE MERGER OR CONSOLIDATION[a]						
	Member, Federal Reserve System	Branches			*Capital*	*Surplus and Undivided Profits*	*Resources*
		In	*Out*	*Total*			
1910		2		2	$ 67,391	$ 71,166	$ 888,172
1911		1		1	44,371	61,007	687,312
1912					107,606	145,826	1,638,878
1913					44,099	38,476	479,040
1914		5		5	74,310	63,581	832,001
1915	113	4		4	51,476	47,114	583,353
1916	107		5	5	36,797	31,162	398,353
1917	90	3	3	6	60,278	69,768	1,058,265
1918	74	7	3	10	55,444	68,028	1,137,802
1919	134	11		11	161,982	99,077	1,862,270
1920	164	21	25	46	132,349	163,148	3,059,974
1921	222	40	11	51	183,811	225,138	3,797,644
1922	259	76	45	121	188,673	210,554	3,266,248
1923	261	6	25	31	258,745	265,235	4,354,158
1924	277	26	23	49	187,018	152,975	3,318,037
1925	227	220	187	407	179,787	196,497	3,605,720
1926	310	275	238	513	331,152	407,614	6,973,957
1927	362	276	188	464	378,178	422,766	7,402,678
1928	338	394	361	755	379,722	494,610	7,454,705
1929	474	366	197	563	1,015,675	1,404,665	20,053,151
1930	564	756	492	1,248	743,079	952,133	11,597,567
1931	612	843	501	1,344	674,311	790,583	10,729,241

[a] For "Data of banks after the merger or consolidation completed" *see* p. 58.

with 178 mergers, which was a larger number than for any preceding year.

The number of mergers, shown in Table 11, declined during the years 1916-18. There were 154 mergers for 1915 as compared with 119 in 1918. The lowest numbers recorded for any other years were 119 and 118 for the years 1911 and 1913 respectively. Following 1918, there was a very striking upward tendency both in the number of mergers and the number of banks involved. This movement continued in general to gain momentum throughout the remaining period of our study, or to the close of the year 1931. There were slight declines in some years, but the movement became more and more pronounced as time went on.

The number of mergers during the period 1910-18, inclusive, was much larger than during the preceding decade, the average

TABLE II (Continued)

YEAR	DATA OF BANKS AFTER THE MERGER OR CONSOLIDATION COMPLETED						
	Member, Federal Reserve System	Branches			*Capital*	*Surplus and Undivided Profits*	*Resources*
		In	*Out*	*Total*			
1910		1	4	5	$ 74,312	$ 72,467	$ 899,781
1911		1		1	42,692	54,727	712,183
1912		1	1	2	98,197	127,165	1,587,878
1913					36,581	30,805	452,373
1914		7		7	53,881	50,610	810,428
1915	56	3	3	6	46,148	41,767	622,136
1916	46		5	5	27,803	23,662	423,897
1917	42	3	3	6	57,206	58,311	1,132,231
1918	40	12	3	15	57,587	60,118	1,257,023
1919	70	17	1	18	106,472	122,047	2,070,543
1920	92	33	33	66	141,819	157,824	3,801,756
1921	130	68	16	84	203,612	211,175	3,702,476
1922	144	88	56	144	190,202	204,121	3,588,873
1923	129	11	27	38	255,272	216,646	4,582,236
1924	151	22	35	57	174,037	138,685	3,626,370
1925	118	244	231	475	165,422	184,478	3,686,222
1926	163	296	295	591	329,004	379,431	6,668,888
1927	190	309	467	776	378,885	419,905	7,378,064
1928	179	398	462	860	392,373	541,717	7,712,070
1929	229	408	599	1,007	1,113,625	1,482,311	19,952,196
1930	308	771	509	1,280	591,410	921,199	11,069,153
1931	302	671	540	1,211	537,656	607,795	9,270,088

being slightly less than 130 for each of the nine years. The years 1914 and 1915 had the largest number, 142 and 154 respectively. From that time until the close of the World War the number declined continuously, reaching 119 for the year 1918. During the latter part of this period, the country was undergoing fundamental economic changes as a result of the war. There was an almost unlimited demand for goods of practically all kinds and people were generally more interested in organizing new banks and other corporations than in trying to effect mergers and consolidations among those already in existence. There seemed to be business enough for all. It was much easier to open new banks than to buy out established enterprises. Prices were rising higher and higher and paper profits were being made by most business concerns. Competition was not seriously felt so that there were not present the active forces to bring about a large number of bank mergers. During this whole war period the number of bank failures, one of the underlying causes of bank mergers today, was small. Branch banking had not, at that time, taken on its present importance so that force was not working strongly in the direction of greater concentration.

The aggregate changes in the number of mergers, the number of banks involved in these mergers, together with the number of member banks participating in these mergers, are shown in Chart I.

A very brief study of Chart I and the data upon which it is based will show clearly the close correlation between the growth of and changes in the number of banks, the number of consolidations, and the membership in the Federal Reserve system. The year 1919 is distinctly indicated as the year in which the trend turned sharply upward.

RELATIVE IMPORTANCE OF STATE AND NATIONAL BANKS

The total number of banks participating in the various mergers and consolidations from year to year has been large (see Table 11). If all the banks involved are classified according to their membership either in the national banking system or the state systems, the total number of state banks is much larger than that of national banks. This is not surprising for the reason that the total number of state banks in the United States is greater than that of national banks. Comparisons show, moreover, that a larger number of banks were absorbed by state banks than by national banks.[4] The total number of state banks absorbed by national banks is not greatly different from the number of national

[4] The classification is not as exact as we should desire. The reason for the variation is to be found partly in the difficulty of getting accurate statistics for the earlier years, but more in the unfavorable laws governing the actual process of bringing the physical assets of the institutions together. Under the earlier laws, if a state and national bank were merged into one institution, the continuing management had to decide under which laws the bank would be operated. If it was determined to have a state bank, the national bank was quite frequently converted into a state bank before the actual merger was effected. Under such circumstances it was customary to report the merger as that between two state banks, whereas it was really between a state and a national bank. If the management wished to carry on as a national bank, the opposite procedure was followed.

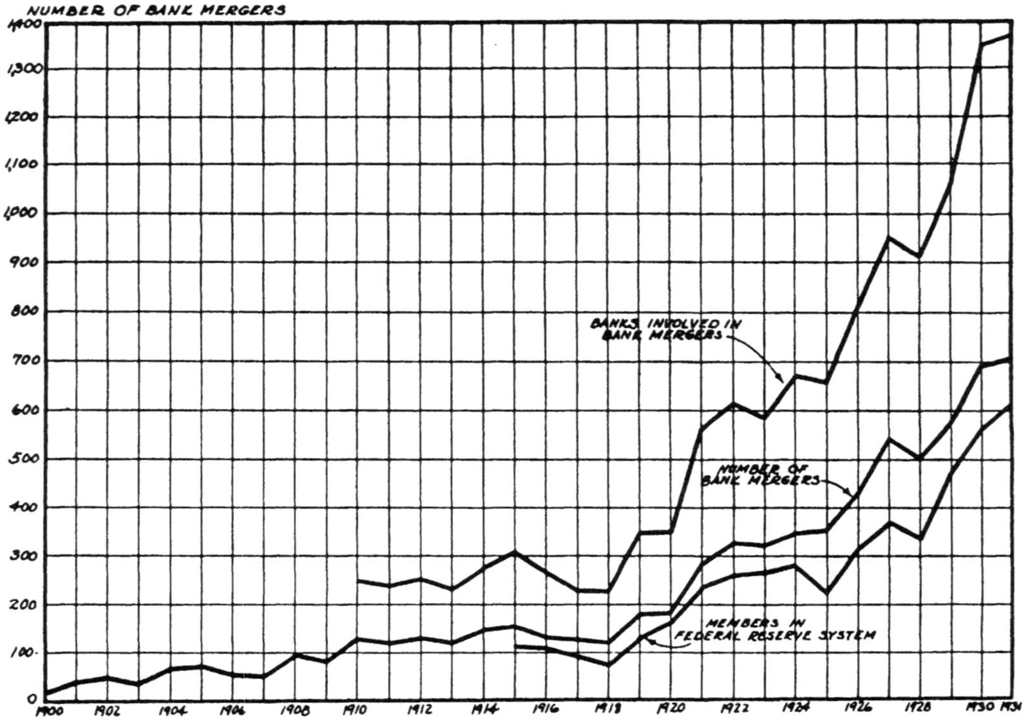

CHART I. NUMBER OF BANK MERGERS AND CONSOLIDATIONS

banks taken over by state banks. The shift, therefore, from one system to the other is approximately equal. The laws of the different states and the National Bank Act have proved to be a hindrance to the merging or consolidation of the banks in one system with those in the other. This was modified by the McFadden Amendment to the National Bank Act in 1927.

For purposes of comparison the data have been divided into four groups as follows:

1. State banks absorbed by state banks
2. National banks absorbed by state banks
3. National banks absorbed by national banks
4. State banks absorbed by national banks

The total number of banks in these four groups were: 3,428, 1,057, 1,144 and 1,041 respectively, or a grand total of 6,670 from 1910 to 1931, inclusive.

The movement of banks from one system to another has not been uniform. Different factors or causes have been at work to bring about alterations in the tendency for state banks to go into the national system and vice versa. As a matter of fact the forces at work have varied considerably in different parts of the country during the same period of time. The prestige of being in the national system and the opposition to the passage of a law providing for the guaranty of bank deposits have induced many banks to enter the national system at the expense of the state systems, both by consolidations and by the direct process of conversion. On the other hand the state law and state supervision are preferred in some sections of the country; hence we find a tendency to leave the national system for the state systems. These changes have been caused in part by a court decision regarding the continuity of the fiduciary powers of national banks. Another factor, doubtless, has been the ability of national banks as a class to withstand the failure movement more successfully than have the state banks and trust companies.

The outcome of the movement of banks from one system to the other as a result of the mergers and consolidations is presented in Table 11, which gives the number of banks in each class year by year. The results, expressed as percentages, are given in

Table 12. The same data are given in Chart II, which indicates clearly that the state system has received a larger number than the national system when the country is considered as a whole. This tendency is quite marked in later years. It should be observed, however, that there has been a very marked increase in the aggregate number of state banks passing into the national system, especially since 1926.

RELATIONSHIP TO THE FEDERAL RESERVE SYSTEM

The number of banks participating in consolidations which are, or were, members of the Federal Reserve system has varied great-

TABLE 12

PERCENTAGE DISTRIBUTION OF BANK MERGERS AND CONSOLIDATIONS INDICATING THE NUMBER OF BANKS ABSORBED*

(Each class expressed as a percentage of the total)

YEAR	TOTAL NUMBER OF BANKS ABSORBED	NATIONAL BANKS ABSORBED BY NATIONAL BANKS	STATE BANKS ABSORBED BY NATIONAL BANKS	STATE BANKS ABSORBED BY STATE BANKS	NATIONAL BANKS ABSORBED BY STATE BANKS
1910	128	25.0	10.2	54.6	10.2
1911	119	21.0	15.1	55.5	8.4
1912	128	30.5	10.2	52.3	7.0
1913	118	13.6	8.5	66.1	11.8
1914	143	20.3	16.8	53.1	9.8
1915	154	21.4	15.6	48.7	14.3
1916	134	26.8	11.2	46.3	15.7
1917	123	21.1	12.2	50.5	16.3
1918	125	12.8	16.0	58.4	12.8
1919	178	17.9	10.6	56.9	14.6
1920	183	15.8	16.4	48.1	19.7
1921	292	13.0	17.2	54.4	15.4
1922	340	14.4	15.6	53.5	16.5
1923	325	14.5	12.6	52.9	20.0
1924	352	14.2	17.1	49.4	17.3
1925	356	11.5	12.9	60.1	15.5
1926	429	16.3	13.3	56.6	13.8
1927	544	12.7	17.4	52.6	17.3
1928	507	14.0	17.4	54.6	14.0
1929	575	16.7	18.8	45.4	19.1
1930	698	18.6	19.4	46.1	15.9
1931	719	22.8	14.9	44.5	17.8

* These percentages have been computed from the data presented in Table 11.

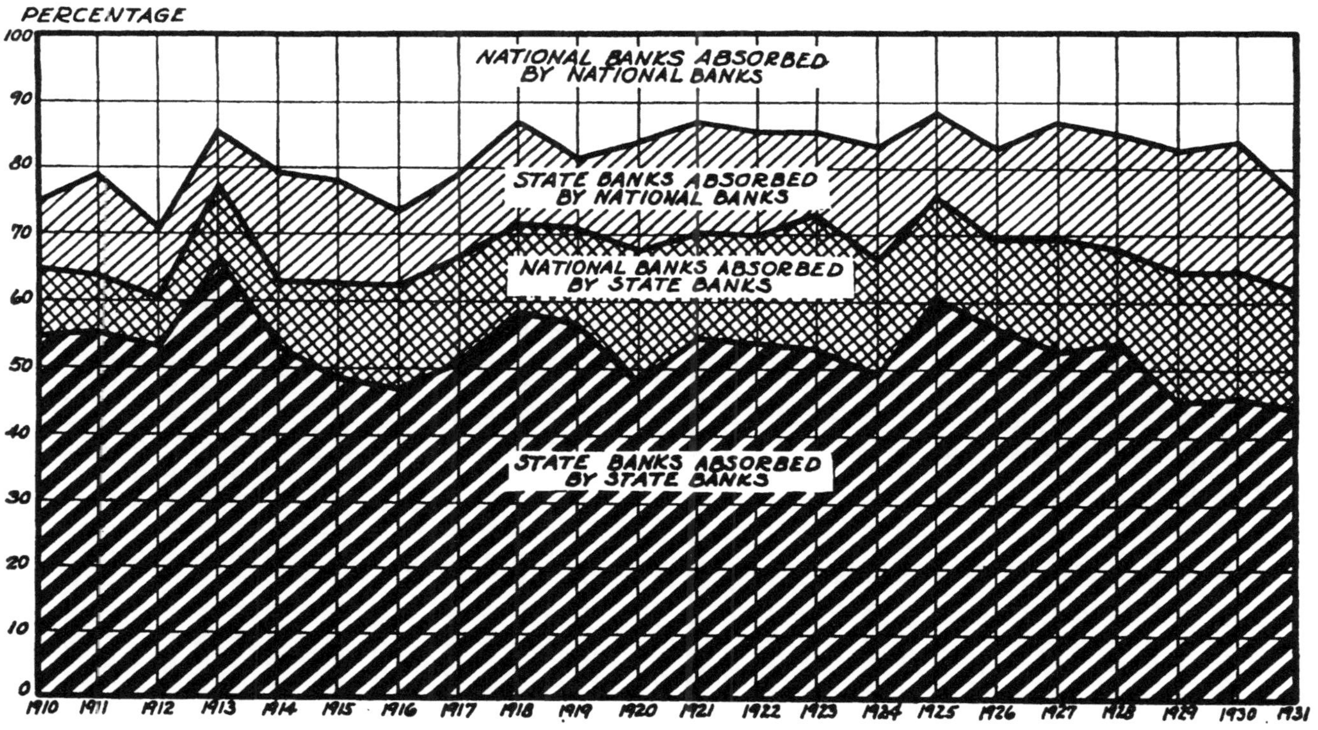

CHART II. PERCENTAGE DISTRIBUTION OF BANKS ABSORBED THROUGH MERGERS AND CONSOLIDATIONS

ly from year to year, but it is quite evident that the tendency has been distinctly upward when we consider either the absolute annual figures or the chart showing the movements from 1915 to 1929. The smallest number of member banks came in the year 1918, a year in which the total number of mergers was very low. The number of member banks ranged from 74 in 1918 to 474 in the year 1929. The upward trend is easily seen by a study of Chart I. This increase is quite significant when it is recalled that the total membership of the Federal Reserve system has been on the decline during the period 1923-29 inclusive. This decline has occurred both in state-bank membership and in the number of national banks. The aggregate number of member banks participating or involved may be studied in Table 11. Figures are not available to show to what extent the decrease in membership is due to the taking over of member banks by other banks which are not members and which do not become members after the merger has been completed. It is fair to assume, however, that the loss in membership in this way has been substantial. This assumption is justified for the reason that every absorption of a national bank by other national banks or member state banks results in a direct loss of membership in the Federal Reserve system. In addition to this, a considerable number, *in toto,* of member banks has been absorbed by banks that were not, or did not become, members of the Federal Reserve system.

The total number[5] of commercial banks in this country has declined from 30,812 on June 30, 1921, to 19,163 as of June 30, 1932. During the same period the average size of banks throughout the country has gradually increased, despite the fact that many banks have suffered heavy losses on account of declining business and for other reasons. In this connection the following statement is interesting and to the point:

> During the year 1930 more outside banks were absorbed by member banks than were lost to the Federal Reserve system by merger with non-member institutions, although in the five-year period the net movement in this connection was in the opposite direction.[6]

It is interesting to compare the actual number of participating

[5] *Annual Reports of the Comptroller of Currency* (1932), p. 561.
[6] *Annual Report of the Federal Reserve Board* (1930), p. 21.

member banks each year before the mergers or consolidations with the number remaining after the mergers have been completed. In practically each year since 1915, less than half of the number of banks participating in mergers remained in existence after the mergers had been completed.[7]

The importance of the movement should not, in fact cannot, be measured entirely by taking the number of consolidations. The total number is significant, but it does not tell the whole story by any means. We are interested in knowing whether the volume of assets or resources has increased or declined. In view of this we should, in considering the effects upon the Federal Reserve system, give considerable weight to changes in deposits and resources of the member banks of the system in comparison with the changes in the volume of total deposits and resources of the banking system as a whole. Is there a distinct tendency for the movement to take in a larger and larger volume of banking assets from year to year? Are the banks involved made up of the larger banks or smaller banks? The data in this connection are most interesting and decisive. The volume of resources has increased at a rapid pace, indicating that larger banks have been involved to a greater extent in recent years than in the early stages of the development. The total amount of resources involved for all banks prior to the mergers in 1929 was more than $20,000,000,000, or approximately one-third of all the banking resources in this country.[8]

In 1912 the total resources of all banks directly interested in consolidations amounted to more than $1,600,000,000. Beginning with the year 1917 the total resources of such banks never dropped below $1,000,000,000. In most years it was decidedly above the one-billion-dollar mark. The banks remaining in operation after the completion of the mergers followed the same

[7] These figures do not represent the actual number of members for any definite time. These two totals include many duplications. They are used here only for comparative purposes.

[8] Attention is called to the fact that all the duplications have been eliminated. That is to say that if bank X has participated in a number of mergers during this year, the total figures for that bank have been taken as they were reported for that period just prior to the first merger in which it was involved. This has been necessary in order to make the figures indicative of the change. Furthermore, the total amount would have otherwise been greater than that for all banks in the country.

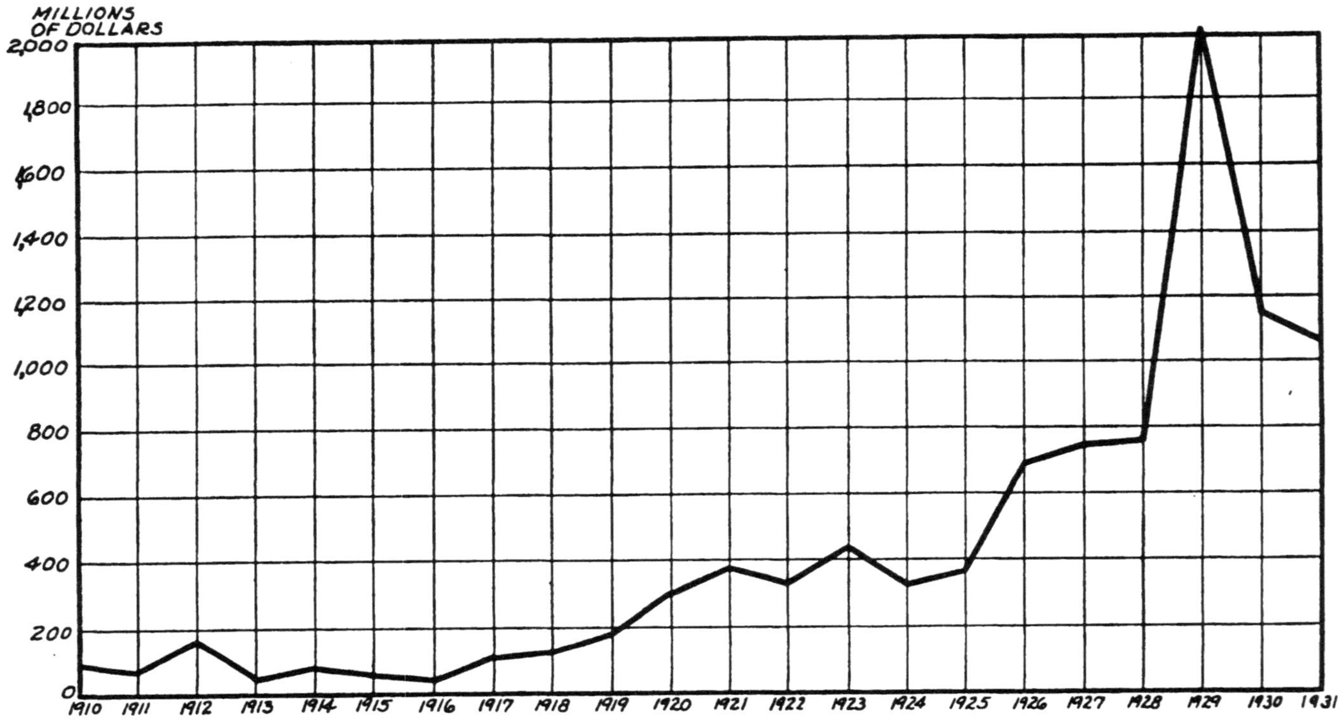

CHART III. RESOURCES OF ALL BANKS INVOLVED IN MERGERS JUST PRIOR TO THE COMPLETION OF THE MERGERS OR CONSOLIDATIONS

tendency. In fact, a study of Table 11 will reveal that there was only a slight variation in the volume of the resources after the mergers as compared with that before the mergers.

The trend in the volume of resources involved in the movement is very interestingly shown by Chart III for all banks prior to the merger, for the years 1910-29 inclusive. Although there was a gradual increase for the greater part of the period, the change became more marked from 1918 to 1925, while it was sharply upward for the five-year period from 1925 to 1929 inclusive, followed by a sharp decline during 1930-31.

INFLUENCE ON BANKING ASSETS

There has not been a marked change in the total assets of banks as a result of the consolidations of banking institutions. A comparison of the total resources of all banks which have participated in mergers and consolidations, as shown by official statistics of these banks before the mergers had been effected, with the total resources of all continuing banks after the mergers had been fully completed, reveals a slight increase for thirteen years and a small decline for seven years. In no case has the change been very significant when compared with the total volume of resources involved. Moreover, there has been no long-term trend in either case. There appears to be little reason to anticipate a great change either way unless there are special conditions surrounding the merger. We would normally expect the volume of deposits to increase in the near future in those cases where one of the banking institutions was in a weakened condition, especially if the consolidation resulted in a genuine "clean-up." Restoration of confidence would take place and tend to result in the attraction of a larger volume of business than the banks had previously enjoyed.

In many cases the merger should result in a shift of the assets. This should be striking in those cases where the large banks were carrying accounts of large firms and corporations which had conducted business with the different institutions directly interested in the consolidation. Where certain corporations had felt the need of two bank accounts, their business would naturally be transferred to other banks not directly involved in the merger. Where this took place, we should normally look for a decline in deposits within a short time after the business had been fully consolidated, in so far as the continuing bank was concerned.

An important phase of this problem is the writing off of worthless assets, not covered by our data. In not a few cases the management realizes fully that a considerable volume of the assets must ultimately be written off as a loss. This is frequently postponed in order to prevent a "bad impression" upon the community. The situation bringing about the consolidation may be so tense that it is important to restore confidence in the community. Under certain conditions it may seem wise to delay the marking down of assets. To answer this question statistically would involve so vast an amount of work as to make it impossible for an individual to undertake it unless he had large financial resources at his command. Another interesting point may well be raised as regards the decrease which takes place in many cases where the combined bank fails after the merger has been effected. A comparison of the list of failures with the list of continuing banks shows definitely that many banks fail within a year or eighteen months after they have absorbed another bank. In many such cases it is a result of a weak or semi-weak bank trying to save an insolvent bank from the odium of failure and indirectly trying to save the pride and reputation of the officers and directors.

The significant results of bank mergers are not to be found in the alteration in the size or volume of banking business carried on. Some business is shifted, as we have already observed, but that does not tend to increase the total volume of business. The two important questions are: (1) did the merger make for stronger and more ably managed banks, (2) did the merger tend to prevent losses and to provide banks better adapted to serve their respective communities? The answer to the second question is probably in the affirmative in a large percentage of cases, but unfortunately that has not always been the case. Reports and statements of banking superintendents indicate that the weight of evidence with respect to this point is on the whole favorable to the concentration movement. These questions are considered more fully in Chapter V (Principal Causes of Bank Mergers).

CAPITAL INVESTMENT DECLINING

The total capital reported as shown in Table 11 for all participating banks in bank consolidations prior to the mergers, compared with that of the continuing banks after the mergers had been effected, shows that, of the twenty years studied, the capital increased in only six years, whereas the total resources increased in thirteen of these twenty years. The actual capital declined during fourteen years. The total surplus and undivided profits increased during the years 1910 and 1919, and showed substantial declines during the other eighteen years of this period. Perhaps a sufficient explanation of the decrease in surplus and undivided profits is found in the fact that certain losses had to be written off in most cases, which of course directly reduced the sum of these two items. In many instances where two or more banks merged the process was carried through by one bank purchasing the assets of the other without any change in the amount of capital stock of the continuing bank. This reduced effectively the amount of outstanding capital.

The reduction of capital unaccompanied by a similar change of resources and total liabilities is in harmony with the general trend in banking toward a decline of capital in comparison with the volume of business being carried on by the banks. On the surface it appears that the shareholders are putting up less capital and consequently giving less protection. In actual practice this may not be exactly true because the reduction in capital may be a result of the writing down of the total amount of capital and surplus to its real value. To the extent that this is not true, we are justified in concluding that the protection decreased.

The relative reduction of capital funds may be offset by a better type of management or by a more economical use of bank funds, but so far results do not lead one to believe that this has taken place, at least not generally. The decline in capital funds proportionate to the resources of banks resulting from mergers, as compared with banks before the mergers, is in harmony with the general trend in this country as a whole to increase deposits, loans and discounts, and investments at a rate considerably greater than that of the increase in the stockholders' funds.

METROPOLITAN BANK MERGERS

The largest and, in some respects, the most interesting and influential bank mergers and consolidations have occurred among the large banks within the large metropolitan centers, or have been promoted or consummated by such large banks through the absorption of smaller banks in the smaller cities and towns. It is true, of course, that a great many small banks have been absorbed by other small banks outside the large financial centers, but such mergers and consolidations have received very little attention from the public in general.

The Bank of America of California (formerly the Bank of Italy), located in San Francisco, and its affiliated institutions have been instrumental in bringing about more bank mergers than has any other organization in this country, though many of the banks absorbed by this group have been quite small. The efforts of the Bank of Italy reached a peak in the early part of 1927 just before the passage of the McFadden-Pepper Act. The underlying reason for the large number of absorptions was the desire to secure branches. By these mergers the Bank of Italy was enabled to expand much more rapidly than by any other means. In Los Angeles the Security-First National Bank (formerly the Security Trust and Savings Bank) has attained a large volume of capital and business. The rapid increase has been due, in no small degree, to the absorption of a few large banks located in Los Angeles. The number of branches has been increased considerably by this method. The branches have been situated, for the most part, either within Los Angeles or in contiguous territory. Other interesting individual cases have developed in the cities of Detroit, New York, and Boston. The Peoples County Bank of Detroit,[9] the Chase National Bank, the National City Bank, and the Irving Trust Company of New York City, and the First Na-

[9] Later this became the First National Bank of Detroit.

tional Bank of Boston have participated in large mergers with important results as regards the concentration of banking resources in the hands of fewer managers (or managements). The Chase National Bank attained its position as the largest bank in the world through the absorption of the National Park Bank of New York City and the Equitable Trust Company, which latter in turn had absorbed the Seaboard National Bank and the Interstate Trust Company. Both the National City Bank and the Irving Trust Company secured huge increases through mergers in which they were the leading participants. The same results were attained by the Guaranty Trust Company of New York and the First National Bank of Boston. The same general situation developed among the large banks in Chicago and Cleveland.

The immediate result of these large metropolitan mergers and consolidations has been an increase in the size of several very large banks. The building up of these huge financial institutions is not confined to any particular section of the country or to any specific city. These financial giants are to be found from the Atlantic to the Pacific, and from the Great Lakes and Canada to the Gulf of Mexico. They are to be found more specifically in the following cities: Boston, New York, Buffalo, Philadelphia, Cleveland, Chicago, Detroit, Minneapolis, St. Louis, New Orleans, Los Angeles, and San Francisco. The largest of them are of course in New York, Chicago, San Francisco, Los Angeles, Cleveland, and Detroit. In all these cities, with the exception of Chicago, Minneapolis, and St. Louis, branch banking is carried on quite extensively, which is one of the factors involved in bringing about many of these consolidations. Not only do we find that a number of individual banks have grown in aggregate size, but they have accomplished something else which is more significant: they are doing a larger and larger percentage of the total banking business in these cities.

CHAPTER V

PRINCIPAL CAUSES OF BANK MERGERS

In the preceding chapter there was presented a detailed statistical picture of the growth of bank mergers and consolidations in the United States since 1900. The great increase in the number of mergers occurred after the close of the World War in 1918. The earlier period is interesting in itself but it does not indicate that there were any major changes or developments in process toward a concentration in our banking system. During that period larger and larger corporations were being developed in other lines of business, which were destined, in the course of time, to make it more difficult for the small bank to secure and maintain sufficient business to show substantial or adequate profits.

The rapid expansion in the number of small, weak banks contributed to the development of a situation in which credit was granted, in many cases, on unsound bases. As a result of this unwise extension of credit, a considerable number of banks were in danger of failure. The existence of that condition made it desirable for the stronger banks to get together and take over many of these smaller institutions to prevent their being closed. Thus there was created a situation very favorable to the development of a consolidation movement of world-wide significance. It is desirable to consider more fully the underlying reasons for this movement, as well as the effects it has had and will have upon our banking system. Are the reasons the same as or similar to those which have brought about the growth and development of large commercial and industrial corporations, public utility companies, chain stores, and other large business units?

This question is twofold: (1) what are the principal causes of these consolidations and, (2) what effect will these changes have upon the economic life of the community and upon the operating methods of banks themselves? The relation to economic conditions in general is more important from a broad point of view. Mergers and consolidations appeal to the banker since he, in most cases, looks upon his bank as a profit-making institution rather than as a service-giving institution through the extension of credit and the safe-keeping of the funds of the community. The banker may not appreciate the desirability of keeping his bank liquid and of being in a position to render an unusual service in the time of panics or depressions.

With this general statement regarding the background of the merger movement, it is desirable to consider the principal causes in a more specific way. It is useless to attempt to classify them in the order of their importance, although it is fairly easy to select two or three major causes which are outstanding for the country as a whole. This difficulty in classification is due to the fact that business and economic conditions vary considerably in different parts of the country. For example, the danger of bank failures may be the predominant cause in the Middle West and branch banking on the Pacific coast.

A public utility, chain store, or industrial concern of any kind is faced with certain definite overhead expenses. Such businesses must be prepared to pay adequate salaries in order to secure capable officers to direct the business once the enterprise is in operation. In order to justify the assumption of such expenses and charges, there must be available a potential volume of business which will, if secured on a reasonable basis, provide income large enough to pay all the expenses incurred in conducting the business. Even though the volume of business may be admittedly small in the beginning, yet it must be great enough to meet the normal expenses, or must at least give promise of expanding to that point within a short time. Otherwise the business venture is doomed to failure from the beginning. As population increases and business expands, it becomes necessary for each business unit to take on more and more business. If this is not done, new institutions will come into existence to take care of this normal growth. As a matter of fact both means will probably be employed to handle the increasing volume of business. All these conditions apply with equal force to banking. The small bank must from time to time increase its capital in order to meet the needs of new business which is coming into or being developed in the community. New banks have also been organized in many places, whereas it would have been far better in many instances had fewer banks been chartered, and larger banking units made out of the existing institutions.

A bank must grow, and, as it grows, its field of operation expands. This gradual expansion makes necessary a larger and better trained force of employees. The bank goes after more business. The development of new business and the increase in the personnel of the bank go hand in hand. The development of trust, investment, and other types of business by the banks frequently make it necessary for banks to reorganize themselves in order to insure the most economical operation. The requests of larger commercial concerns for financing make it incumbent upon the banker to grant larger loans. The loan unit cannot be increased safely without a more careful credit analysis on the part of the banker, hence the need for more scientific credit analysis.

Referring again to the earlier period when the commercial and industrial possibilities were as yet largely unexploited, there was organized a tremendously large number of small independent banks. The presence of this large number made it impossible for all of them to grow and to expand, as commercial business units increased in size and scope. Many small banks for one reason or another have not, therefore, kept pace with other lines of business. The larger business organization had to go to the larger banks simply because the smaller banks could not supply them with the needed funds. In some cases, to be sure, a few corporations used a number of small banks. The entrepreneurs who did this, however, found it necessary to carry a number of bank accounts, which tied up large amounts of funds in bank balances and at the same time increased the trouble and cost of conducting their banking business. This practice was adopted by relatively few enterprises and even in those cases it tended to be gradually discarded for the more desirable connection with a large bank which could give better service at a lower cost. The increasing number of small banks and the shifting of the business, in many cases, to the larger banks have cut down the volume of commercial banking business for the smaller banks and thereby reduced their income and profits. The loss of business in this way, as well as the "freezing up" of the assets of many banks, has brought many of these unprofitable institutions to seek a merger with a larger bank in order to avoid further loss or even failure. At the same time the larger institutions have been able to reduce their per-unit cost in many cases, owing to the larger volume of business handled.

Nowhere in the field of banking are the advantages of large-scale business more evident, perhaps, than in connection with the trust business. In order to handle trust funds efficiently the bank or trust company must have a considerable force of well-trained men. Once the organization is completed, it may do a large volume of business without a corresponding increase in expenses. Men with large financial interests do not wish to turn over large estates to small banks. Hence the small banker finds it difficult, if not impossible, to secure this type of business. The larger institutions are indispensable, especially in connection with corporate trust business. Hence, we frequently find the managements of two or three small banks agreeing on a merger in order to handle more economically a type of business that would be unprofitable for them if handled by the banks individually. In the large cities like New York, Chicago, or San Francisco the large banks have increased in size to the point where it is questionable whether they can make further economies in operation merely by increasing their size and obtaining a larger and larger volume of business.

Among the reasons assigned, oftentimes, by bankers for merging certain banks, is the claim that a greater and better service to the community may be rendered by the consolidated or continuing institution. It is undoubtedly true that the large banks perform many services for their customers which cannot be provided by the small banks. In this connection reference has been made to the trust business as being unsuitable for a bank with a limited capital fund. The liabilities incurred in the handling of large trust estates and corporate business are such that the small institution should not undertake it. The same reasoning applies to the business of financing foreign trade and the carrying on of all international banking business. In the same way the bigger institutions can afford to develop and maintain well-organized credit departments with highly trained credit men who are in a position to get more and better credit information than is possible for the small unit bank. Such men are better qualified to analyze and pass upon the risk. Information given by such a group of men would be very valuable to the bank customer. In fact the small bank itself oftentimes relies upon the larger institution for credit information. In no particular phase of credit work is greater dependence placed by the small bank upon the larger institution than in the purchase of commercial paper from the so-called commercial-paper houses.

Several large banks maintain a service department whose function is mainly that of preparing and disseminating information of an economic and business character to its customers. The reports and publications along these lines, issued by some banks, contain a great amount of useful information. The Irving Trust Company of New York published booklets on the Far East and other parts of the world which have been received with favor by exporters and importers. The Chase National Bank of New York has made a collection of various kinds of money which it keeps on display. This has proved of great interest to bankers, business men, and students of the subject. These are services that a small bank could not perform without incurring expenses out of proportion to its income.

In the matter of granting credit, there can be no question that the large corporations must go to the large banks where they can secure funds in amounts proportionate to their individual needs. The small bank has only limited amounts of funds to lend and these must be distributed among several borrowers.[1] It would not be sound banking to lend all the funds to one borrower, as the bank would have to do were it to cater to large business as the principal source of lending. Even if the small bank did undertake such a policy, it would not have a sufficient volume of funds to meet the needs of large corporations. Again in the matter of

[1] It should be observed that national banks are prohibited from lending to one borrower on his unsecured note an amount in excess of 10 percent of the capital and surplus of the lending bank.

services to tourists, only the large bank is in a position to render the best services to its customers who are going abroad.

Enough has been said to show conclusively that the large financial institutions can perform many services which are outside the scope of the smaller banks. In many cases these factors have been quite adequate to bring about a consolidation of certain financial institutions for the purpose of creating banks with capital and resources in keeping with the size of the business units to be financed, and to provide the kind of services needed by that element of the community. Even if we take for granted that the small institutions have a very important function to perform in our present economic organization, it is true that the larger institutions have a more important place in our financial and economic system, and that the most desirable way of bringing them into existence is, in many cases, through the consolidation of banks already in operation.

The volume of business carried on by the smaller banks is necessarily limited in scope. The capital funds are so small and the volume of deposits so limited that the bank cannot afford the necessary expenses for going outside its community to secure new business. Often the only way to obtain the needed funds is to bring all the banking interests of a community together and have them pool their resources into one institution so that they can attract the business desired. Often, too, there are advantages apart from a mere increase in size to be gained by the consolidation of two or more existing institutions. No one who has observed financial developments in New York in the past few years can have failed to observe the growing importance of the trust business there, and the rôle it has played in the consolidation movement. Commercial banking business has become more competitive as the years have gone by, making it desirable for many banks to develop a trust business. Many trust companies have been organized in the past and have over a period of years developed a very attractive and profitable trust business, even where the trust company itself was much smaller than many of the commercial banks. When the commercial banks began to solicit trust business in an aggressive manner, it was soon realized that there were certain advantages in absorbing a trust company rather than in developing this type of business, even though they might be forced to pay a high price for the controlling interest. In such mergers the commercial banks not only obtained directly a considerable volume of profitable business, but secured also a well-trained and organized staff of trust experts to carry on and develop still further the trust departments of these larger banks. Obtaining the trust business in this way not only shortened the time otherwise required to develop that type of business, but it also lessened mistakes which were likely to be made in this extension of the activities of the commercial banks.

In other cases the commercial banks have found it profitable in the development of their investment and security business to make connections with other banks or investment companies which have been engaged in the security business for a number of years. Some very interesting developments of this sort have occurred during the past few years among New York banks. The so-called security affiliates have played a particularly important rôle in this connection.

In still other sections of the country some large banks have used concentration of control as an entering wedge to secure mortgage-lending business. One method has been to have a holding company buy up a mortgage company without an actual merger or consolidation being affected. The holding company or security company, as the case may be, continues to operate the mortgage company or land bank for the benefit of the banking group as a whole. This possibility has been exploited particularly by certain western bankers.

In the branch banking states, where some of the large banks have gone into branch banking on a rather extensive scale, the method of securing new offices is very important. In most states permission must be secured from the banking commissioner before a new branch is opened. New branches are in many cases created very easily, while in others permission is much harder to obtain, on the ground that the banking facilities are already adequate to provide all the banking services needed in the community. In many instances the branch bank will resort to the consolidation plan in order to obtain the controlling interest in a local bank which has been in operation for some time. In this way a merger is effected between the large branch bank and the small local bank whereby the smaller institution becomes a branch of the larger bank. This has been a very important factor in several mergers in such states as New York and California. It is a method used widely by the Bank of Italy in California[2] both before and after it joined the national banking system, as a means of taking over a large number of both state and national banks. Some of the New York banks have secured a considerable number of branches in the same way. In Detroit and Cleveland, as well as in Philadelphia, banks have followed the same plan, with the result that the number of banks has decreased while the number of branches has been very greatly augmented.

The desire to secure branches has been only one reason for bank mergers in New York, Detroit, Cleveland, and other cities. In fact many mergers have been consummated within these cities within the last few years which had no direct relationship to the branch movement. Among motives causing a branch bank to take over another bank is the desire to avoid developing more banks in the locality than can be efficiently operated there and to lessen the competition which may exist if new branches are established. The larger bank may oftentimes secure new business in this way at a much lower cost than to develop it anew. This method, moreover, is usually the least expensive, since it is likely that the local bank has a banking office which will afford space sufficient for the branch. Where this condition exists, it is often unnecessary to invest additional bank funds in bank buildings and fixtures. All these things are important to the individual banks as well as to the banking system.

During the past few years some sections of this country have become "overbanked" with the result that the banks in such localities are, for the most part, unprofitable, and too often even unsafe. The Northwest is a notable example of a section where too many banks have been chartered. When a community becomes overbanked, the banks are unable to obtain the volume of busi-

[2] Now the Bank of America National Trust and Savings Association, San Francisco, California.

ness necessary to make them successful. The competition becomes so keen that too high interest rates are offered to secure both time and checking accounts. The high cost of obtaining these deposits makes it incumbent upon the banks to realize a large income from the use of the funds. The cost of obtaining business in this way is so high that the bank very frequently takes speculative risks in order to secure business or to obtain borrowers who are willing to pay a very high rate of interest. The result is likely to be the same in either case. The banks soon find a portion of their loans frozen and in the course of time some of them become doubtful or even worthless. The bank must then write off these bad loans as a total loss or carry them in the statement in order to avoid showing this loss to depositors and stockholders. Where the latter plan is followed the bank is only postponing the evil day. If such a practice is carried too far it will, in the end, mean failure and heavy losses to the depositors.

What is true of the Northwest, or rather what was true before the epidemic of bank failures had reduced the number of banking institutions in that region, has been almost equally true of other parts of the country. In some cities and towns there are more banking offices in operation than there is business to support them. In many cases spite work and pure "cussedness" have been the principal motives for the organization of too many banks. Such methods usually produce a weak, dangerous bank as well as frequently injuring the bank or banks already in operation. In order to overcome the situation thus created in certain sections of the country, banks have been forced to get together to work out plans for merging the institutions. In this way a better and more efficient management may be secured and wasteful and dangerous competition eliminated. There are still in this country today many cities and towns where undesirable competition exists. Bankers and business men are to be most highly complimented when they can effect a union of these small banks, creating larger and better-managed institutions. It is in such cases that the merger and consolidation movement may be said to bring about one of its most desirable results. Whenever a merger between two or more banks results in a better and stronger bank, it is to be encouraged. In so doing not only are the interests of the depositors and stockholders served, but the economic and business condition of the community is greatly improved.

One of the most fundamental causes of bank mergers in this country is found in connection with efforts to prevent bank failures. Especially is this true in the South and the West. Many banks, through bad management, theft, competition, poor business conditions, or one-man control, have found themselves in an unsound condition. Depreciation of assets through bad loans, speculation, and theft, as well as investment in local and unmarketable securities, have left many of these institutions in deplorable situations. In not a few cases they are absolutely hopeless. Such banks cannot restore themselves to solvency without the addition of new capital, which is sometimes supplied but far too often is not forthcoming. Bank officers and directors are willing to take their losses in some instances if only they can free themselves from further liability. Many stockholders prefer to take their losses once for all and have it over.

When bank officers find their banks in a dangerous condition they naturally seek a way to avoid, if possible, the odium of failure. Bankers often give up their shares partially, if not wholly, without reservation, to escape double liability. Under such circumstances it is frequently possible to interest the management of another bank in the assets and deposits of the weak institution. The time is then ripe for considering a merger between the two institutions, the strong bank assuming the liabilities of the weak bank and receiving whatever business there may be. Under such conditions it is customary for the banks to work out their plans secretly with the advice, consent, and assistance of public banking officials, in order to avoid a run upon the weak bank. When the plans are agreed upon by the directors of the two institutions, the stockholders are informed of the serious situation and asked to confirm the plans proposed by their board for a merger. It is a sad day for the stockholders who invested their funds in the bank stock in the hope of future profits. Yet the damage is done and they have lost. To prevent further depreciation of assets they consent, and the merger is rushed through, often without the business community knowing the real reasons for the merger. If the community has been tipped off, confidence is frequently restored because of the injection of a new personnel in the bank. In the process of the merger, the bad loans are written off, leaving the depositors in a much stronger position even though the stockholders of the merged bank may have lost all they originally invested in the enterprise.

The reason assigned for the merger is often wholly misleading. In several mid-western and southern states we know that the motive generally present is that of preventing bank failures. This is likely to be more uniformly true in the smaller cities and country districts, though it is not entirely confined to rural sections. One superintendent of banks, in discussing bank mergers in his own state, remarked that he did not know of a single merger which had not been consummated to prevent a bank failure. In Arizona the superintendent has definitely stated that he has used that method to prevent failures. If we could isolate the mergers that have taken place as a result of strained conditions within some bank, we should probably find the number of other causes much smaller than we are at present led to believe. This statement might be interpreted to mean that the consolidation movement is less important than is generally supposed. In fact, however, the chief factor leading to consolidation in the case of the large banks is not usually the danger of a bank failure. And, from the point of view of assets, the most important mergers are those involving large banks. We must recognize the failure factor, however, as a strong element in the consolidation movement.

The personal element is also a very strong factor in banking consolidation. Many officers and directors go in for size. They regard it as a distinction to be associated with the management of a large, growing bank. Not infrequently in such cases the officers or directors, or both, strive to have the largest bank in the city or county and to keep ahead of their competitors. In some cases this practice works out very well, but frequently it leads to bad banking. There is likely to be a tendency to take less desirable business in order to expand. Large losses may, and often do, follow this method of securing new business. The character of the credit work under such conditions frequently deteriorates greatly. On the other hand the community at large regards a growing bank with favor unless there are present certain unfavorable aspects. In order to attain this growth in size, the banker relies principally upon two methods.

The first method is to increase the volume of deposits and from time to time sell more stock to the old stockholders or to the public, in order that the amount of capital funds may keep pace with the deposit liabilities. Where competition is not too keen and where the community is prosperous, it is often comparatively easy for an aggressive management to bring about rather rapid growth. This method on the other hand often proves to be very slow and tedious. For some bankers it is too slow to meet their demands. Hence the officers and directors are likely to find another method which frequently brings about more rapid development. Yet the old method just discussed will continue to be a very important part of the program of any sound bank desiring to increase its volume of business.

The other method which a bank may use is to take over an institution already in existence. In many instances large bankers have been primarily concerned in increasing the size of their bank in order to keep pace with a competitor. Some men desire to be the head of the largest bank in the community. Bringing about a merger with another bank often proves to be the quickest way of obtaining the desired end. Some banks have, in the course of time, grown far more rapidly by the addition of the business of another bank through a merger than by hard, day-to-day, consistent work on the part of the officers and directors of the bank. There are no objections to such a procedure, provided the buying bank does not pay too high a price for the control of the second bank. The process, if carried too far, however, may result in undesirable competition between two banks in their bidding for the control of a given bank. Where such a situation materializes, the merger should be condemned, and if possible it should be prevented by the Comptroller of the Currency in the case of national banks, and by state banking commissioners where state banks are involved. Where a prudent policy is followed, the community enjoys the beneficial results of mergers without the corresponding evils growing out of unsound mergers.

Still another factor to be considered in connection with this phase of the concentration movement is that of stockjobbing. The rapid increase in market prices for leading bank stocks has led promoters, as well as bankers themselves, to plan and effect a bank merger, with the sole idea of making a profit on the rise in the market price of the bank shares when information is given out regarding the proposed merger. The practice of splitting up the shares of banks has at times accompanied the announcement of an important bank merger. This method of splitting up bank shares so as to give the par value of the stock a much lower figure has been followed in some instances by an almost perpendicular advance in the market price of the stock.

It should be stated that the splitting up of the shares of a bank has not by any manner of means always been part of a consolidation. In fact there are many instances on record where a split up has been made for the purpose of driving up the market value of the stock so as to make it more expensive for a group to get control of the bank in order to effect a merger. A well-known case of the rapid advance of bank shares, where a merger was not effected, is illustrated by a comparison of the market price of the stock of the Bankers Trust Company and the Irving Trust Company in New York City after announcements of "stock split up" by the boards of directors of these two financial institutions, with the prevailing prices prior to the split up of the stock. Many other cases could be cited.

A split up in the stock at the time of a merger is less likely to occur in the mergers of small banks because the opportunities are much less, owing to the narrow market for such securities or stocks. Sometimes this method will be used, not to increase the price, but to effect a wider distribution of the stock.

CHAPTER VI

EFFECTS OF BANK MERGERS AND CONSOLIDATIONS

Statistics and other data regarding the growth and extension of bank mergers and consolidations have been supplied in the preceding chapters. The legal difficulties involved as well as the underlying causes which have been fundamental in the growth and development of bank mergers have been briefly presented. Conclusions have been drawn in some cases, but it now seems desirable to summarize what appear to be the outstanding facts regarding mergers and consolidations in the field of banking during the past three decades, with special reference to the period since the close of the World War.

1. *Large number of the total bank mergers and consolidations.* —During the period 1900-31 inclusive, there were more than 7,175 bank consolidations in the United States, of which 3,801 took place during the seven years from 1925 to 1931, inclusive. A total of more than 7,230 banks disappeared, at least in name, of which 6,670 were lost during the period following 1909. Of the number of banks which were lost through these consolidations after 1909, 2,201 were national banks and 4,469 were state banks. The total resources of all banks involved before the mergers amounted to more than $20,053,000,000 in 1929, as compared with total resources for the continuing banks after the mergers of over $19,952,000,000 for the same year. The lowest number of mergers reported for any one year covered by this study after 1909 was 118 in 1913; the highest number was 706 in 1931.

2. *Decline in the number of banking institutions.*—One of the outstanding results of the large number of bank consolidations has been the decrease in the total number of banks in operation. Three factors have been at work to reduce the actual number of banks: (1) the voluntary liquidation of banks, (2) the large number of bank failures, and (3) the merger movement. The

first is of less significance than either of the other two. Since 1918 there has been a total of 5,453 bank mergers involving 10,232 banks. During the same period 5,498 banks have disappeared as a direct result of these mergers. It is a fact, no doubt, that a number of these banks would have failed had they not been absorbed by a neighboring bank. It is also true that several of the absorbing banks have later failed, thus increasing the number of failed banks. It is difficult, if not impossible, to separate the influence of bank failures and bank mergers in reducing the number of institutions. We can say, however, that both have been extremely important factors. There is no doubt that we would have in operation today a considerable number of banks which have disappeared, had there been no way for banks to consolidate.

3. *An increase in the size of the banking unit.*—With a decline in the number of banks, there has been a tendency for the average size of banks to increase when measured by their total resources or total deposits. It is, of course, evident that the assets of many banks have declined rather sharply during the past two or three years, whether or not they participated in mergers. The decline would have been even greater for the continuing banks, had they not fortified themselves by taking over a weak or competing bank or banks. There has been a distinct tendency in this country for the large banks to become larger and to get a relatively greater share of the banking business in their respective communities. The most noticeable expansion has occurred in the large cities. Mergers and consolidations have been used directly by bankers to secure control of this business as well as to rid the field of competitors. This increase in the proportionate share of the banking business has in some cases been accompanied by an extension of branches, but in other cases branches have been entirely lacking. The decline in the number of banking offices has been especially marked in those states which do not permit the development of branch banking in any form.

4. *Prevention of bank failures.*—One of the most important reasons for bank mergers and consolidations in this country during the past decade, or perhaps, the past twelve years, has been the desire to prevent bank failures. The terms or conditions under

which two or more banks are merged are so frequently announced or reported in the local papers that one cannot mistake the consolidation for any other than a salvaging process. In some cases the conditions are such that the public is fully aware of what is taking place. In other instances, the reports of banking officials are quite clear in the matter. However, many mergers are carried out in such a way that the public is unaware of what is taking place. Superintendents of banking in some states let it be known that it is their policy to prevent bank failures whenever possible by bringing banks together so that the weak ones may be absorbed by larger or stronger institutions. The prevention of bank failures has been in the last analysis one of the most important factors in causing bank mergers and consolidations.

5. *Decline in capital relative to total resources.*—One of the interesting results of the consolidation of banks has been a general decline of capital funds relative to total resources. This may be accounted for in part by the fact that the bad paper has been written off, at least to a degree, so that the capital is more accurately and fully presented in published statements than it has been in the past. It is doubtful if the total decline in capital funds can be wholly accounted for in that way. It seems quite logical to conclude that there has been a real decline and that the depositors and general creditors of the banks now have less protection in the form of stockholders' funds than they have had in the past. This may not mean in all cases that the depositors have less actual protection or safety, though it undoubtedly does mean just that in many individual banks. The decline in protection in this way may be more than counterbalanced by a more capable and alert management with more up-to-date banking and credit-investigating methods. Where this is true, there has been a genuine improvement in the banking situation. The difficulty is of course to know when this condition has been realized.

6. *Increase in the number of branches.*—There has been a very close relationship between the development of branch banking in several states and the increasing number of bank mergers and consolidations. In several cases, the desire to obtain branches has been the underlying factor which has brought about the mergers.

In some mergers the continuation of the smaller banks as branches has made it easier for the officers and directors of the banks to get the consent of the banking authorities. Development along this line has been most marked in the state of California, where state-wide branch banking has attained its greatest growth. The same general effects have been accomplished in other states such as New York, Ohio, and South Carolina, though the results have been more limited. On the other hand, the number of mergers would have been much greater in some states had the laws been more favorable toward the creation and operation of branches. If there should be a liberalization of the branch-banking laws in the future, as now seems most likely, we may look for bank mergers to increase in those states proportionately to the changes in banking laws and the growth of branch banking.

7. *Membership in the Federal Reserve system.*—In a general merger and consolidation movement, one would expect the total number of member banks to decline, especially as any merger including two or more national banks must result in a loss of one or more individual members. On the other hand, there is a marked tendency for the large banks to become members of the system as compared with the small banks. One of the principal results of the merger movement is larger banks and in the course of time this should tend to bring a considerable number of such institutions into the system. Regardless of this tendency, there should be a large increase in the total resources brought into the system for the reason that, under the present methods of merging, more assets are brought into the system than are lost. In any event the merger movement does not reduce the actual resources of the system, but tends to increase them. Continuance of the consolidation movement should strengthen the position of the Federal Reserve system as a whole, rather than weaken it as is frequently contended.

8. *Tendency for large banks to become larger.*—There is a tendency for a larger and larger percentage of the total banking business of the country to pass gradually into the hands of fewer and fewer bankers. This development has been most rapid in the large cities. It has not been in any way limited to the large cities,

however, as may well be demonstrated by taking smaller cities or by taking a state as a basis for comparison. In either case the facts bear mute testimony that the large banks are gradually absorbing a larger proportion of the total banking business. If we take, for example, ten of the largest banks of a particular state at a given time and trace the history of these banks over a period of ten years, we shall find definite proof of this statement. If a smaller territorial unit be preferred one may take a large city, such as New York, Chicago, Cleveland, San Francisco, or any other of a number of the largest cities in this country and the results will be similar. The business in the larger cities will be found to be concentrating in fewer banks in almost all cases. Generally the same results will be obtained if five, or fewer of the larger banks be taken for purposes of study in the large cities. The objection to this method is that the individual banks change their relative standing and, in some instances, do not continue the largest bank, even though they may be, or might have been so, at a given time. The largest banks as measured by total resources are included each year, and not necessarily the identical banks of the preceding year or years.

9. *Investment policy of banking institutions.*—One of the arguments advanced for consolidating two banks is to create a larger institution which can build up and maintain a better investment department. If one were to judge the importance of this argument from the need of a sounder investment policy on the part of many banks, it would receive a very high rating. Certainly the banks need a much sounder policy regarding investments, for, if the truth be known, the losses during the past few years have been stupendous. "Write-offs" have been heavy in many cases but the losses have been faced in this way in far too few instances. Undoubtedly, therefore, the banks need to improve this phase of their work. Unfortunately this problem is not seriously affected in a large number of mergers. The banks are frequently so small both before and after the consolidation that they cannot afford to retain an expert or experts to guide them in their investment policy. We must conclude, therefore, that unless the continuing bank is a large one the benefits to be

derived in this way are too small to be of any general significance or importance.

10. *Increases in the lending power of banks.*—A bona-fide merger should increase the lending power of the merged institution as compared with the total of the individual banks working alone. This potential ability to increase loans, discounts, and investments is due to the greater concentration of bank reserves. It will not reduce the legal reserve requirements of banks in relation to their total deposits, but it should enable the bank to reduce its till money, which is a very essential part of the bank reserve. The bank should be in a position to secure greater diversification of its portfolio. If this diversification is properly and scientifically worked out, the bank should be able to increase its loans and discounts without reducing its ability to take care of its obligations. Of course there is a limit to this kind of expansion, but the increase should be large enough to add to the total income of the institution.

11. *Increase in the safety of banks.*—Although a considerable number of banks have failed following the merger, it is nevertheless true that mergers usually improve the financial standing of the banks. In most cases there is a certain reduction in the overhead assets, accompanied by a writing off of bad or worthless assets, thus putting the bank on a sounder basis. By this house-cleaning process the bank should be placed in a situation in which it can better respond to the demands placed upon it.

12. *Research advantages.*—One of the outstanding advantages that a large bank has over a small institution is its capacity for doing a larger amount of research and credit-analysis work. The total income is larger and the per-unit cost in doing this kind of work may be spread over a larger volume of business than in the case of a small bank. More and better credit work can be done because the large bank can keep a larger and more specialized staff of credit investigators and analysts. In this way a large bank can afford to undertake certain kinds of work which should be of great benefit to the institution as a whole and which would not be possible for the smaller bank by reason of the large costs involved. A large bank may, if it wishes, have the services of an

economist and a statistical staff which would be a luxury for the small institution. It is of course true that the small bank does not have the need for some services that are required for the large bank, but in general the advantage is with the larger institutions.

Some institutions have made considerable progress in this type of work regardless of the concentration movement, at least so far as mergers and consolidations are concerned. But there are still many communities which would benefit definitely by a consolidation of their banking resources so that it would be possible to employ people who could render most valuable assistance in the ways just outlined. The smaller institutions cannot hope to have such assistance until the number of banks has been reduced and greater specialization attained in the remaining banks. The most economical and advantageous way to bring about a situation in which this may be realized is by merging or consolidating a number of banks. This would result in a distinct improvement in our banking system if it were wisely adopted and efficiently and ably carried out.

13. *Relation to the personnel of the banks.*—Regardless of the statement so frequently made by the officials conducting a merger or consolidation that no employees will be dismissed, there has usually been a reduction in the total personnel of the merged banks as compared with the total employed by the individual banks prior to the merger. The reduction has frequently been delayed for some time so that it could be accomplished in the least painful way. The delay is sometimes due to the desire on the part of the new management to retain the good will of the depositors of all institutions involved. Another factor is that a delay will often be followed by the resignation of a considerable number of employees for one reason or another. Where this occurs, it relieves the bank of the unpleasant task of actually dismissing a number of men. The reduction usually affects both the employees and the officials of the bank.

CHAPTER VII

EARLY BRANCH BANKING IN THE UNITED STATES

Branch-banking history in the United States began with the discussions regarding the founding of a national bank in the early years of the American Republic.[1] From that time to the present the subject of branch banking has received more or less attention from those who have been interested in a sound and efficient banking system. The extent and scope of these discussions have varied greatly in different parts of the country as well as at different times. Alexander Hamilton, the first Secretary of the Treasury, included this subject in his well-known and brilliant *Report on a National Bank* in December, 1790. He considered both sides of the question but "for various considerations" did not deem it expedient to recommend branch banking at that time. However, he recognized that it might be desirable, or even necessary in the future, and for that reason, it was unwise to prohibit it. He thought it advisable to insert a provision which might "lead to it hereafter, if experience shall more clearly demonstrate its utility."

Hamilton recognized that there were certain advantages inherent in a system which permitted a "plurality of branches." On the other hand he feared that it might result in mismanagement "which might hazard serious disorder." He summarized his position as follows:

> The situation in the United States naturally inspires a wish that the form of the institution could admit of a plurality of branches. But various considerations discourage from pursuing this idea. The complexity of such a plan would be apt to inspire doubts, which might deter from adventuring in it. And the practicability of a safe and orderly adminis-

[1] The author wishes to acknowledge his deep obligation to the Hon. Edmund Platt, formerly Vice Governor, Federal Reserve Board, now Vice President, Marine Midland Corporation, New York. Much assistance was obtained from Mr. Platt through personal conversations and from the articles and addresses which have been published by him from time to time. Mr. Platt is one of the pioneers in the study of branch banking in the United States.

tration, though not to be abandoned as desperate, cannot be made so manifest in perspective, as to promise the removal of those doubts, or to justify the government in adopting the idea as an original experiment. The most that would seem advisable, on this point, is to insert a provision which may lead to it hereafter, if experience shall more clearly demonstrate its utility, and satisfy those who may have the direction that it may be adopted with safety. It is certain that it would have some advantages, both peculiar and important. Besides more general accommodation, it would lessen the danger of a run upon the bank.

The argument against it is, that each branch must be under a distinct, though subordinate direction, to which a considerable latitude of discretion must of necessity be intrusted. And as the property of the whole institution would be liable for the engagements of each part and its credit would be at stake, upon the prudence of the directors of each part, the mismanagement of either branch might hazard serious disorder in the whole.[2]

THE FIRST AND SECOND BANKS OF THE UNITED STATES

The First Bank of the United States, established in 1791, was located in Philadelphia. The act creating the bank did not specifically require it to establish branches. However, a general scarcity of banks and the disturbed economic conditions made such a course desirable. As the amount of capital in the country was limited, there was little hope that individual banks would be established by means of private funds at that time or within the near future. Means of communication and transportation were inadequate so that much time was required to go from one section of the country to another. The deplorable economic conditions of the country left little, if any, choice in the course to be pursued in regard to branches. Steps were taken, therefore, within a few months to establish branches in New York, Boston, Baltimore, and Charleston, the leading cities in the United States outside of Philadelphia.

The bank and its branches proved to be of unusual service to the Federal government in the receiving and transferring of government funds from one place to another. In addition to the various fiscal duties performed by the bank for the government, it rendered remarkable assistance to private individuals, firms, and

[2] Hamilton, Alexander, *Report on a National Bank* (Dec., 1790). See *Report of the Secretary of the Treasury* (1837), I, 69-70.

corporations in the financing of their business operations. Aside from the scarcity of banking knowledge in the states, the widespread feeling which existed at that time against banks in general was such that it was difficult to establish them. The situation offered opportunities for the Bank of the United States to perform a unique service to the country at large, through an extension of its branches. Regardless of the opposition to banking in general and to the ownership by foreign stockholders of the Bank of the United States in particular, this institution gave us the first successful experiment in branch banking. By the end of its career branches had been located in the following cities: New York, Boston, Baltimore, Charleston, Norfolk, Savannah, Washington and New Orleans.

The Second Bank of the United States, chartered in 1816 for a period of twenty years, was authorized to open and operate branches. Under certain conditions it became compulsory for it to establish branches. It established a total of twenty-five branches[8] which were well distributed geographically throughout the various sections of the Union. The act creating the Second Bank outlined, in part, the methods by which the branches were to be controlled and operated. Directors were required to be residents of the state, territory, or political division in which the branch was located. The central board of the bank designated or appointed the local boards of the several branches. Local boards were, in turn, each required to elect one from their number who would become the president of the branch.

Grave difficulties were encountered by the bank in supervising the various branches. Poor roads and transportation systems made it almost impossible for auditors or officers from the head office to check the work in the several branches. Branch managers were, therefore, to a considerable extent placed upon their own resources in the management of the branches. This was one of the difficulties of a branch system feared by Hamilton when he said that "each branch must be under a distinct, though subordinate

[8] Two other offices existed at one time. These two branches were located at Augusta, Georgia, and Chillicothe, Ohio. They were discontinued. See D. R. Dewey's *Second Bank of the United States* (Washington: National Monetary Commission Report, 1910), 195-96.

direction." Such direction had of necessity to be given "considerable latitude of discretion." The bank was able to overcome many but not all of its difficulties. In the main it can be said that branches were operated successfully and performed a real service to the country at large and especially to the various communities in which they were located.[4]

The principal functions performed by the First and Second Banks and their branches were those of providing a satisfactory bank-note currency, keeping such notes in circulation and, at the same time, preventing their depreciation. Branches rendered a particularly valuable service in issuing and distributing the notes of the parent bank through various sections of the country. They also kept and transferred public funds and in that way performed many fiscal services which the government could not have enjoyed in any other way at that time without great difficulty and considerable expense. They further reduced substantially the costs or charges for transferring funds. The condition of most state banks at that time was such that their notes circulated at a discount, if acceptable at all. In other respects, the state banks did not possess the facilities for properly safeguarding public funds or for transferring them to other localities when and where they were needed.

The First and Second Banks encountered serious opposition from the state banks, which regarded the branch system as monopolistic. Moreover the local banks did not wish to compete with branches which enjoyed a greater prestige and public confidence. In Ohio,[5] for example, the state undertook to tax, in the amount of $50,000, each of the two branches of the Second Bank located in that state. The bank "filed a bill in chancery in the United States Circuit Court asking for an injunction." On the pretense that the state had not been legally notified of the injunction, the sheriff seized $90,000 and turned it over to the state treasurer. The state officers involved were arrested and imprisoned, and the

[4] For a fuller discussion of the work of the bank and its branches, the reader is referred to R. C. H. Catterall's *Second Bank of the United States* (Chicago: University of Chicago Press, 1903).

[5] *Annual Report of the Comptroller of the Currency* (1876), p. 26. The First and Second Banks encountered bitter opposition in other states, notably Virginia.

funds were later returned to the branches. Even though the branches were eventually recognized from a legal point of view, the state banks never ceased to oppose the bank and its branches. Opposition of this kind from state banks, together with political forces, finally overcame the Second Bank of the United States as effectually as they had the First Bank of the United States. After the charter of the Second Bank had expired, the field was left free for a greater growth of state banks and their branches. Let us now consider the operation of the branches by state banks in the several states.

EARLY STATE BRANCH BANKS

State banks with branches appeared quite early. The Bank of Richmond, chartered in 1792, was authorized to establish branch offices in different parts of the state of Virginia.[6] The Bank of Pennsylvania, chartered in 1793, opened several branches which proved unsuccessful. Most of these offices were closed in 1810 or earlier. In 1810 the state legislature enacted a law making the head office responsible for all notes issued by its branches. In 1806 the State Bank of Vermont was chartered.[7] It established two branches in 1806 and two more in 1807. The four branches were located at Woodstock, Middlebury, Burlington, and Westminster. The last two branches were organized as a result of the "seeming" progress made by the first two. In the end, the experiment proved unsuccessful and the branches were finally closed in 1812, after the state had levied a land tax of one cent per acre to provide funds "with which to redeem the bills of the bank."

An experiment in branch banking was undertaken in Kentucky in the same year that the state of Vermont granted a charter for the Vermont State Bank. The Bank of Kentucky was incorporated on December 27, 1806. The capital was fixed at $1,000,000 and the number of branches at thirteen. The charter was repealed in 1822. This bank was unsuccessful chiefly because the state leg-

[6] Dewey, Davis R., *State Banking before the Civil War* (Washington: National Monetary Commission Report, 1910), p. 138. Students interested in the history of branch banking should consult George T. Starnes' *Sixty Years of Branch Banking in Virginia*. (New York: The Macmillan Company, 1931).

[7] For a discussion of the Vermont State Bank, see L. Carroll Root's *Sound Currency*, Vol. II, No. 10 (April 15, 1895), pp. 223-25.

islature took too active a part in the selection of the board of directors and in the management of the bank. The laws governing the bank were changed or modified at almost every session of the state legislature. Legislative influence was, perhaps, the most important factor leading to the closing of the bank.[8]

During the life of the First Bank of the United States and the earlier years of the Second Bank of the United States, several state legislatures either established banks with branches or made provision for such institutions. The Bank of Manhattan, New York, had branches at Utica and Poughkeepsie which were discontinued about 1819.[9] A partial list of state branch banks authorized during that period, together with the number of branches for each bank is presented on page 98.

This list is doubtless incomplete, but it is sufficiently inclusive to indicate the extent to which the movement had spread among the early state banks. It is clear that the presence of the First and Second Banks of the United States did not prevent the development of branches among state banks, although it is no doubt true that they did restrict the number very considerably. The lack of banking resources and the inexperience of the bankers themselves were, to a marked degree, responsible for the failure of these banks to function properly and successfully. It is interesting to observe that the greater number of these banks and branches were located in the South and the West. The banks located in Vermont, Pennsylvania, and Delaware were notable exceptions.

During the period which extends roughly from about 1833 to the opening of the Civil War, or perhaps to the passage of the amendment of the National Bank Act in 1865, which taxed the circulating notes of state banks out of existence, there was a gradual increase in the number of branches. The branches thus established extended geographically over a large part of the country. In certain states where banks were not authorized to establish branches, there existed a tendency toward the creation of a system that had many of the features of branch banking. In this last category are included especially the states of Rhode Island

[8] For a discussion of the Bank of Kentucky, see *ibid.*

[9] Platt, Edmund, "Branch Banking Before the Civil War," *Proceedings*, New York State Bankers' Association (1925).

and Connecticut. In these two states, the business was obtained through the creation of agencies, which had for their purpose the getting of new business, including both deposits and discounts. These agents or agencies were continued until they were virtually forced by the commissioners of banking to go out of business. Much the same situation existed in the state of Massachusetts during the fifties, when banks in the vicinity of Boston es-

Name of Bank	*State*	*Date Established*	*Number of Branches*
Bank of Richmond	Virginia	1792	
Bank of Pennsylvania	Pennsylvania	1793	
State Bank of Vermont	Vermont	1806	4
Bank of Kentucky	Kentucky	1806	13
Nashville Bank	Tennessee	1807	5*
Farmers Bank	Delaware	1807	3
Bank of Philadelphia	Pennsylvania	1809	8†
Bank of the State of South Carolina	South Carolina	1812	2‡
Bank of the State of Georgia	Georgia	1815	2§
Bank of Vincennes	Indiana	1816	4
State Bank	Tennessee	1820	1
Bank of the Commonwealth of Kentucky	Kentucky	1820	
State Bank	Illinois	1821	4¶
State Bank	Alabama	1823	4**
Bank of the State of Louisiana	Louisiana	1824	5

* Branch provided for in 1817. The bank had five branches in 1819.

† Eight branches were authorized. Four branches were established. See D. R. Dewey's *State Banking Before the Civil War*, pp. 137, 138.

‡ Dewey refers to the Farmers Bank of Virginia, 1812, which was to have six branches.

§ The State Bank of Georgia was required to open at least two branches; the Bank of the State of Louisiana was required to open five branches.

¶ Dowrie, G. W., *The Development of Banking in Illinois, 1817-63*, "University of Illinois Studies in Social Science," Vol. II, No. 4 (Urbana, 1913), pp. 27, 61, 67.

** These branches were established during the years 1834 and 1835, two for each of these two years. The charters for all these branches were repealed in the session of the legislature, 1842-43.

tablished or opened offices in State Street, Boston. The commissioners of banking finally eliminated this type of banking, but not until they had threatened to use the injunction in connection with certain banks.[10]

In 1833 the State Bank of North Carolina and the Planters Bank of Tennessee were authorized to establish branches. The Union Bank of Tennessee had been granted the same rights in 1832. In 1834 the State Bank of Indiana was granted certain branch-banking privileges, while other banks entered the field during the thirties. The number of branches tended to increase gradually until the state banks were forced out of existence both by the devasting effects of the Civil War and the results of the tax on note issues in 1865. The State Bank of Ohio, created by an act of the legislature, February 24, 1845, was modeled after the State Bank of Indiana. In all, the bank was authorized to establish sixty-three branches,[11] and in 1856 had thirty-six in operation. These branches were well distributed over the state, performed useful services, and gave the state a sound and efficient system during their existence. Since the central idea was security of note issue, each branch was liable for the notes of every other branch, but not for the general debts of other branches. Ohio was divided into twelve districts and a certain portion of the capital was apportioned to each district. Note issues were limited to a certain percentage of or ratio to the capital.

The State Bank of Iowa[12] formed an interesting and important link in the long list of state banks operating branches. It was reported to have fourteen branches at the time the National Bank Act went into effect. The Federal tax on state bank notes in the end of course drove the bank and its branches out of operation. However, during the life of the bank it formed a very strong element in the financial structure of that state.

The State Bank of Indiana, established in 1834, has received more attention, not only as a state bank but also as an early

[10] For a discussion of the conditions in these three states, the reader is referred to D. R. Dewey's *State Banking before the Civil War*, pp. 141-43.

[11] *Annual Report of the Comptroller of the Currency* (1876), p. 26.

[12] For an interesting and valuable discussion of the Iowa State Bank and its branches, see H. H. Preston's *History of Banking in Iowa* (Iowa City; State Historical Society of Iowa, 1922).

branch system, than any other state institution in the country. This emphasis was justified for two reasons: (1) it was very successful and profitable from the point of view of the stockholders, and (2) it gave the state a sound and effective banking system over a long period of years. In 1816 the constitution of the state forbade the creation of a bank unless it were a state bank with branches. The original bill creating the bank fixed the number of branches at ten, later increased to thirteen. The bank had a capital originally of $1,600,000 or $160,000 for each branch. Provision as regards the amount of capital for each branch was later modified so that the capital could be increased to $250,000. Although the chapter expired in 1857, the legislature in 1855 approved a charter for a new bank. This new bank was capitalized at $6,000,000 and was authorized to establish from fifteen to twenty branches. It was required to purchase the stock owned by the state in the old bank. This institution survived the Civil War. After the passage of the act of 1865 taxing the note issue of state banks, most of the branches then in operation were converted into individual national banks.[13]

THE EXTENT OF BRANCH BANKING, 1834-61

No available data give a complete picture of branch banking in this country prior to the Civil War. The *Reports* of the Secretary of the Treasury and the *Bankers Magazine* periodically printed lists of banks operating branches. This information was usually given in piece-meal fashion and was not prepared regularly; hence it does not present chronologically the changes that took place in the number and location of branches. Table 13,[14] has been prepared from the *Bankers Magazine* and shows the number of banks operating branches and the branches owned by these banks, grouped according to states for the three dates indicated.

[13] For a general discussion of the banking situation in Indiana, see Logan Esarey's "State Banking in Indiana, 1814-73," *Indiana University Bulletin*, Vol. X, No. 2 (Bloomington, Ind., 1912).

[14] This table should be compared with the tables on pp. 102 and 103. None of these tables are complete. It is believed, however, that they present a fairly representative picture of the branch-banking situation during these years.

TABLE 13

NUMBER OF BANKS OPERATING BRANCHES AND THE NUMBER OF BRANCHES, CLASSIFIED ACCORDING TO STATES, FOR THE YEARS 1848, 1856, AND 1860

STATE	1848		1856		1860	
	Number of Banks Operating Branches	*Number of Branches*	*Number of Banks Operating Branches*	*Number of Branches*	*Number of Banks Operating Branches*	*Number of Branches*
Alabama*	1	5				
Delaware	1	3	1	3	1	3
Georgia	3	7	6	30	2	5
Indiana	1	13	1	20	1	20
Iowa					1	13
Louisiana†			1	1	2	3
Kentucky	3	13	6	26	7	31
Maryland	1	2	1	1	1	1
Missouri	1	5	1	5	9	33‡
New York§	2	2				
North Carolina	2	14	3	17	3	19
Ohio¶	1	29	1	36	1	36
Pennsylvania	1	1				
South Carolina	1	2	1	2	1	2
Tennessee	3	17	3	15	3	17
Virginia	6	30	7	39	7	39
TOTAL	27	143	32	195	39	222

* *Bankers Magazine*, II (Feb. 1848), 464, 469.

† The Canal Bank, New Orleans, evidently had branches in 1848. This bank is not, however, included in the total in this table.

‡ For a valuable study of the Bank of Missouri, readers are referred to J. Ray Cable's *Bank of the State of Missouri* (New York: Columbia University Press, 1923).

§ *Bankers Magazine*, II (March, 1848), 518; (June, 1848), 774-76.

¶ There were reported thirty-seven branches for the State Banks of Ohio in 1848. See Wm. G. Sumner's "History of Banking in All Leading Nations," *Journal of Commerce and Commercial Bulletin*, I (New York, 1896), 441.

The total number of banks and branches in operation during this period, as reported by the Secretary of the Treasury, is shown in Table 14 which has been compiled from the *Reports of the Finances*.

Table 14 covers the period 1834-61, with the exception of two or three years in which no data were available. According to this table the number of branches increased considerably. This growth

TABLE 14

TOTAL NUMBER OF BANKS AND BRANCHES IN OPERATION IN THE UNITED STATES, 1834–61 INCLUSIVE*

YEAR	TOTAL NUMBER OF BANKS IN OPERATION	TOTAL NUMBER OF BRANCHES	YEAR	TOTAL NUMBER OF BANKS IN OPERATION	TOTAL NUMBER OF BRANCHES
1834	406	100	1849	654	128
1835	558	146	1850	685	139
1836	567	146	1851	731	148
1837	634	154	1852		
1838	663	166	1853		
1839	662	178	1854	1,059	149
1840	722	179	1855	1,163	144
1841	619	165	1856	1,255	143
1842	563	129	1857	1,283	133
1843	577	114	1858	1,284	138
1844	578	118	1859†	1,329	147
1845	580	127	1860†	1,392	170
1846	587	120	1861†	1,427	174
1847	591	124			
1848	622	129			

* The source of all these data except for the last three years is *Report of the Finances* (1857–58), pp. 358–60. Compare totals in this table with the totals for the corresponding years in the tables given on pp. 101 and 103. See also note, p. 100.

† *Report of the Finances* (1861), pp. 282, 285.

was, however, slow and not in proportion to the total increase in the number of banks in operation.

Branches operated by the various banks were distributed widely through the South and West. Only a limited number was owned by banks located in the eastern states. Table 15 gives the total number of banks in operation in the states in which one or more branches were reported, and the total number of branches in each of those states for the period 1856-61, inclusive.

These data are interesting even though they are admittedly incomplete for the years covered, as they indicate the extent of branch banking at that time.

A study of the available banking literature covering the last decade or two prior to the Civil War shows conclusively that there was a growing interest in the subject of branch banking. The number of branches was slowly increasing. Especially was that true

TABLE 15

BANKS REPORTED AS OPERATING BRANCHES IN CERTAIN STATES DURING THE PERIOD, 1857–61*

STATE	1856†		1857‡		1858§		1859¶		1860**		1861††	
	Number of Banks	*Number of Branches*	*Number of Banks*	*Number of Branches*	*Number of Banks*	*Number of Branches*	*Number of Banks*	*Number of Branches*	*Number of Banks*	*Number of Branches*	*Number of Banks*	*Number of Branches*
Connecticut	67	1	70	1	73	1	75	1	73	1	73	1
Delaware	8	3	8	3	8	3	9	3	9	3	5	3
Georgia	18	6	19	4	26	4	24	4	25	4	14	4
Indiana	33	13	33	13	20	20	17	20	17	20	20	20
Kentucky	7	26	8	27	10	27	10	27	11	34	10	33
Louisiana	9	10	9	10	12	3			12	1	12	1
Missouri	1	5			6	4	7	15	9	29	9	33
New York			310	1								
North Carolina	12	16	12	16	12	16	12	16	13	17	14	17
South Carolina	18	2	18	2	18	2	18	2	18	2	18	2
Tennessee	22	23	22	18	27	18	21	18	16	18	16	19
Virginia	19	38	19	38	22	40	22	41	24	41	25	41
TOTAL	143		133		138		147		170		174	

* Compare the totals in this table with the totals for corresponding years in the tables on pp. 100 and 102. See also note, p. 100.
† *Report of the Finances* (1855–56), p. 138.
‡ *Ibid.* (1856–57), p. 324.
§ *Ibid.* (1857–58), p. 356.
¶ *Ibid.* (1858–59), p. 368.
** *Ibid.* (1860), p. 446.
†† *Ibid.* (1861), p. 282.

during the fifties. During and following the close of the war the trend shifted. This change was due to two or three factors. First, many banks failed to survive the perils of the Civil War. This is clearly shown by a study of the number of banks and their resources before the war in comparison with what existed after the war.[15] The war wrecked and put an end to a considerable number of branches. Heavy losses sustained by the state banks tended to induce a few to shift to the national system, where they secured a new lease of life under the supervision and regulation of the Federal government. Especially in the southern states the Civil War affected both unit and branch banks disastrously.

Another reason for the decline in branches was the passage of the National Bank Act of 1863. There does not appear to be any convincing reasons given in the *Congressional Record* to indicate that there was any substantial opposition to branch banking in Congress when the bill was being considered. It was hoped, no doubt, that the state banks would enter the national system. Provision[16] was made in 1865 whereby state banks with branches could convert into national banks and retain any branches in operation at the time of the conversion. Few, if any, availed themselves of that privilege until many years later. It appears more probable that the Act of 1865, placing a 10 percent tax on the note issues of state banks, was the real driving force in the abandonment of branches then in operation. This, in conjunction with the fact that the national law made no provision for branches, is probably the primary reason for the rapid decline in the number of branches after 1865. A survey of the bankers' publications of 1865 and 1866 shows that many banks surrendered their state charters during those years and entered the national system. Note issue was, undoubtedly, the deciding factor in a large number of cases involving the closing of branches.

Deposit business had not yet reached the status where banks

[15] Knox, J. J., *A History of Banking in the United States* (New York: Bradford Rhodes and Co., 1900), *passim*.

[16] The Amendment to the Revenue Act of 1865 providing that any state bank with branches might convert into a national bank and retain all branches it had at the time of conversion was sponsored by Senator Van Winkle of West Virginia to protect the state banks in his state which were operating branches at that time. See *Congressional Globe*, 38 Congress, 2 Session, p. 1281.

could rely upon that phase of the banking business to the extent that they can and do today. When the right of note issue was taken away, the banks had, for the most part, to choose between closing their doors permanently or applying for admission to the national system. The rapid decline in the number of state banks and the equally rapid increase in the total number of national banks showed unmistakably that note issue was the fundamental question at stake. Banks had to rely upon the issue of notes in order to make loans and advances sufficient to secure a profitable banking business. It is only natural, therefore, that the decline in the number of branches should be definitely connected with the note-issue problem. In fact there is little doubt that the original motive for establishing branches in many cases was to have an outlet for notes. If the branches could be used to put notes into circulation at a considerable distance from the head office where they were redeemable, the notes could be kept in circulation for a much longer period, which was a distinct advantage to the note-issuing bank.

One of the most important as well as most interesting phases of the rise of branch banking in the United States before the Civil War, and its rapid decline during and immediately following the close of the war, was the question of branch management. What was the relation of the branches to the parent institution? To what extent was each branch governed and controlled from the head office and, on the other hand, to what extent was it independent? In the case of the State Bank of Indiana, the stock of the several branches was sold separately, and the earnings of each branch belonged to the stockholders of the branch. Branches were jointly liable for all the debts of the various branches[17]—independent as regards assets, but united as regards liabilities. The board of control at Indianapolis consisted of a president and four directors chosen by the state legislature, and, in addition, one director elected for each branch. The branches were managed by their own stockholders, but the board of control had the right

sponsible, hence the public lost nothing. This represents one of the best features of
irregularities. The management was not satisfactory. The other branches were responsible, hence the public lost nothing. This represents one of the best features of the system. *Bankers Magazine*, XV (June, 1861), 940.

to examine each branch every six months, to require reports from each of the branches, to equalize the public deposits, and to call upon the branches to make good any losses in any branch or branches. The State Bank of Ohio was modeled after the State Bank of Indiana. The head office was a mere board of control and was so recognized by law.[18] Each branch was liable for the circulating notes of all branches.

In some other cases the branches were merely agencies for the purpose of signing and issuing notes. This was the case with the Bank of South Carolina, while some of the offices in the state of Georgia were designated as agencies and others, as branches. In short, there was no general rule governing the operation of branches in different parts of the country. In most of the states the laws governing the creation of branches occupied a middle ground as compared with the two types explained briefly above.

It appears certain that there would have been a greater amount of branch banking in this country had it not been for the Civil War. Whether the country would have developed a nation-wide system of branches is a debatable question. The sentiment in the eastern states was strongly against branch banking. In the southern states the movement varied widely from state to state, although in the main it was favorable to expansion. A number of the western states strongly favored branches. The development in the states of Ohio, Indiana, Iowa, and Missouri has received much consideration by students of banking in this country. There was considerable interest manifested in Illinois and, to a lesser extent, in Kansas.[19] It is mere conjecture as to what the outcome would have been had the Civil War not occurred, and had the authorities not felt obliged to tax the state-note issue out of existence. Certain it is that these two developments brought to an end practically all the branch banking that existed in this country at that

[18] White, Horace, *Sound Currency*, Vol. II, No. 1 (New York: Dec. 1, 1894), p. 209.

[19] "The Kansas Valley Bank is the title of a bank bill that has passed both houses of the Kansas Legislature and approved by the governor. The principal bank is located at Leavenworth City, with a capital of $800,000. Five branches are to be located at the following places: Atchinson, Doniphan, Lecompton, Fort Scott, and Shawnee. Each of the branches are to be independent banks." *Bankers Magazine*, II (May, 1857), 904.

time. Since branches had virtually disappeared in the United States by the middle or late sixties, the next chapter will deal largely with the trend of thought regarding the advantages and disadvantages of this type of banking and finally with the reappearance of branch banking in such a form as to make it possible to study the subject statistically.

CHAPTER VIII

THE DEVELOPMENT OF A NATIONAL BRANCH BANKING POLICY

The period since the enactment of the National Bank Act in 1863 is of considerable historical importance to the banker and the student of branch banking in this country. This period may conveniently be broken up into different sections for the purpose of detailed study and analysis. First, there were about three decades in which branch banking received but slight attention from either the business community or bankers. Second, the decade beginning about 1892 or 1893 witnessed the development of much discussion and interest in the adoption of a plan of branch banking, within the national system, designed to provide banking facilities for small communities which were either not able to support an independent banking institution, or which did not have any banking facilities directly available in the community, or both. Third, interest in branch banking again declined greatly during the period from about 1903 to 1910 or 1912. Fourth, within a few years after the passage of the branch-banking law in California in 1909, there appeared a growing interest in branch banking in certain states. Excepting the war period, this interest has developed gradually, and with it has come a very marked growth in the number of branches as well as a change of public sentiment in favor of some type of branch banking. The growth has become especially important since 1922. There was a decline in the number of branches during the years 1930 and 1931. This decrease was due largely to the failure of a number of banks with branches. Despite this falling off in numbers, public sentiment seems more favorably disposed today than ever before.

The office of the Comptroller of the Currency has from time to time shifted its position regarding branch banking. For a number of years little attention was devoted to the subject. During the eighties, some opposition was registered to this type of banking. In the nineties, the sentiment shifted in favor of the development of a local or restricted form of branch banking. Comptrollers of the Currency James H. Eckles and Charles G. Dawes advocated branch banking. Other incumbents either ignored the subject or opposed it. John Skelton Williams and his immediate successor, D. R. Crissinger, favored the extension of branch privileges to national banks.

The attitude of the Federal Reserve Board was for a number of years clearly in favor of local national branch banking. The Board's attitude was expressed time and again in recommendations issued during the first ten years of the Federal Reserve system. Then the attitude shifted materially, owing (in large measure) to the changes made in 1923 in the personnel of the Board itself. The action of the Board during the years 1923 and 1924 is very indicative of the modified point of view held by that body.

The Federal Advisory Council of the Federal Reserve system went on record as early as 1915 in favor of the operation of branches by national banks on a local basis. This point of view was consistently maintained and advocated at regular intervals until the passage of the McFadden Act in 1927, which permitted the operation of branches on a restricted basis by national banks in those states which permit state banks and trust companies to own and establish branches. With these introductory paragraphs indicating in a general way the development of branch banking, attention will now be directed to the changes which took place during this period.

THE OFFICE OF COMPTROLLER OF THE CURRENCY

The attitude taken by the office of the Comptroller of the Currency in regard to branch banking has, as was pointed out, fluctuated greatly during the period since the office was created by the National Bank Act in 1863. These shifts have been especially marked during the past two or three decades. The variations have depended upon the personal feelings and convictions of the Comptrollers that have held the office from time to time. One of the strongest advocates of the development of branch banking was the recent incumbent of the office, John W. Pole. On the other hand, H. M. Dawes, who served during the year 1923-24, was one of the most severe critics of the movement, despite the fact that he sanctioned an extension of offices or teller windows by national banks. Practically all points of view between these two extremes have been represented at one time or another by the various men who have served in this capacity throughout the nearly seventy years that the national banking system has been in existence.

Very little is said on the subject of branch banking in any of the *Annual Reports* of the Comptroller of the Currency prior to 1920. Especially is this true as regards the period before H. M. Dawes became Comptroller of the Currency in 1923, with the possible exception of the reports for 1895 and 1896. During the early history of the national banking system, the subject was not viewed as an important phase of the banking and financial problem. Very few branches of any kind were in operation. It was a period in which branch banking was distinctly in the background in banking discussions and in the meetings of bankers. The enthusiasm for branches which had existed at one time or another before the Civil War was gone, at least for the time being. Other phases of the subject of banking were foremost. The ease with which new banks could be started lessened the need for any form of multiple banking. Much attention was devoted to proposals for increasing our currency supply. It was a period of "extensive rather than intensive banking."

When the National Bank Act was revised in 1864, the words "places" and "offices" were changed to "place" and "office" respectively, and the banking reports contain very little information regarding the subject of branch banking prior to the early nineties. The amendment to the Revenue Act of 1865, it will be recalled, provided that state banks with branches might convert into national banks and retain any or all branches in operation at the time conversion took place. It was assumed by most of the Comptrollers of the Currency for many years after the inauguration of the national banking system that the law did not authorize the establishment of branches by national banks. It should be noted, however, that the question did arise occasionally and that many doubted the accuracy of the position taken so generally by the Comptrollers during these many years.[1] The feeling was never strong or powerful enough to bring about any serious action on the part of those interested in branch banking.

LAW AGAINST BRANCH BANKING RECOMMENDED IN 1887

In 1887 the Comptroller of the Currency, William L. Trenholm, stated that he felt that the law enacted in 1865 permitting state banks with branches to convert into the national system, retaining any or all branches then being operated, had outlived its usefulness and should, therefore, be repealed. This was desirable, according to his opinion, for the reason that it was necessary to forestall any efforts to build up a system of branch banks within the national banking system. His statement was, in part, as follows:

> When the system was first established . . . there were some state banks with branches and as it was desired that these should be induced to become national banks, provision was made for their retaining their branches after conversion. This reason no longer exists and it would appear to be in line of public policy to take precaution in advance against any future development of the national system in the direction of combination and agglomeration similar to the development among railroad and other corporations controlling interests upon which the business and convenience of whole communities depend. In section 127 of the proposed code provision is made for national banks having more than one office under certain conditions.[2]

It is quite apparent from Trenholm's statement that he shared the feeling that an extension of branch banking would mean monopoly. He was most anxious to make such a development impossible in this country.

Much interest was displayed in the subject of branch banking during the nineties,[3] and for a short time thereafter. Many recom-

[1] The Waynesville National Bank, Waynesville, Ohio, opened a branch at Lebanon, Ohio. "This is, we believe, the first instance on record of the establishment of a branch by any national bank." *Bankers Magazine*, XXXII (Aug., 1877), 154.

[2] *Annual Report of the Comptroller of the Currency* (1887), I, 4.

[3] A considerable number of national bankers desired to establish branches. "It is reported that numerous applications from national banks have been made to the Comptroller for authority to organize branches, and he submitted the question to the Attorney General, who declared that it was not the intent of the law for national banks to do business in that manner." *Bankers Magazine*, XLVI (Jan., 1892), 528.

mendations, official and otherwise, were made to Congress suggesting that the National Bank Act be modified to permit national banks to establish and operate branches.[4] The growth of sentiment in favor of branch banking at that time was due to the general realization that the unit system, as then organized and constituted, had failed to provide banking facilities for many smaller communities, and, moreover, had not met the financial requirements of the country in many other respects.

The sentiment in favor of branch banking represented only a limited portion of the public. The opposition to the development of a branch-banking system at that time was still too strong to permit an extensive or very important modification of banking laws, either state or national, tending toward the development of a sound system of branches. The attitude of government officials and certain leading bankers toward a system of multiple banking was such as to make that period important and interesting in the history of branch banking in the United States.

During the term of office of James H. Eckles as Comptroller of the Currency, April 26, 1893, to December 31, 1897, a study was made of the various state laws regarding the legal status of branch banking. The study was broadened to include data on the status of branch banking in several foreign countries. The Comptroller had the assistance of two well-known economists, Professors David Kinley and N. A. Weston of the University of Illinois. The conclusions of that study were summarized in the *Annual Reports* of the Comptroller for the years 1895 and 1896. A questionnaire was mailed to each state in the Union as well as to several foreign countries. The report read in part at follows:

In furtherance of the attempt to collect information on banking systems now in vogue, a personal letter was addressed to the state officer having the banks in charge, or to the governor of each state and terri-

[4] Congress authorized the opening of branches at the Exposition Grounds of the World's Fair at Chicago in 1892 by an act of Congress, May 12, 1892 (27 Stat L., 33). By an act dated March 3, 1901, banks were authorized to establish branches on the Exposition Grounds of the World's Fair at St. Louis, Missouri (31 Stat L., 1444). Branches under both these acts were not to be operated for a period longer than two years. See also *Financial Laws of the United States Concerning Money, Banking, and Loans, 1778-1909*, Sen. Doc. 580, compiled by A. T. Huntington and Robert J. Mawhinney, National Monetary Commission Report (Washington, 1910), pp. 441, 451.

tory of the Union, requesting from such officer that this Bureau be furnished with as complete data as possible.[5]

The questionnaire included twelve questions dealing with various phases of banking. Question 7 related to branch banks. It read, "Are any of the banks permitted to conduct branch offices or banks?" The results of that questionnaire in so far as it related to branch banks was summarized by the Comptroller as follows:

Thirteen states do not allow branch banks. Ten states report no laws prohibiting them nor providing for their establishment. In twenty states branches are permitted, and to some extent encouraged by favorable legislation.[6]

During the period following the depression of 1890-93, there was much agitation for an increase in the volume of money in circulation.[7] Emphasis was placed by many bankers and other business men and by members of Congress on an increase in the amount of money in circulation, rather than on the advantages to be derived from a sound banking system. The Comptroller of the Currency held the opinion, however, that the difficulty was due, not so much to a lack of money as to a faulty distribution of credit. There was available sufficient credit and the important question was, "How could an equitable and satisfacory means be secured for distributing this credit throughout the various sections of the country where it was most needed?" The Comptroller felt that there was ever present a tendency for the funds of the country to flow to the great financial centers and to be used there. What was needed, therefore, was a means for transferring these funds to the more remote or less well-known communities where greater opportunities existed for the use of such funds.

The reason for the maldistribution of credit was to be found in the fact that there were not present banking facilities "to enable them to show to those in control of loanable capital why credit should be extended and to whom." The smallest agricultural communities and small industrial centers needed a portion of these funds if it could be shown that they had the "means of

[5] *Annual Report of the Comptroller of the Currency* (1895), I, 38.

[6] *Ibid.*, p. 40.

[7] This and the two following paragraphs are intended to be a summary of the Comptroller of the Currency's discussion. See his *Annual Report* (1896), I, 103-5.

availing themselves of that which elsewhere entitles and obtains credit which is equivalent to and does answer the purpose of money." That situation could be improved and the smaller localities be "given the advantage of available capital" by establishing a well-organized branch-banking system. Such a system of branches would not only provide with funds many sections which were too small to have independent banks, but it would make such funds available to those communities at "lower interest and a lessened cost of exchange." The Comptroller of the Currency added, "It is not an extravagant assertion to state that with these enlarged opportunities of gaining credit, all entitled thereto could readily obtain it."

With regard to the objections which were usually raised against branch banking, reference was made only to the arguments that such a system would result in monopoly and tend to weaken the head office of the bank engaged in that type of banking. Moreover, it was realized that the granting of permission to establish a new branch in a given community would be opposed by all local banks. These criticisms were considered untenable for the reason that it was proposed to prohibit the establishment of branches in places where banking facilities already existed. Banks would be required to supply additional capital for each branch in order to prevent the creation of a situation in which a bank would be weakened by reason of its extension of branches on too small amount of capital funds.

The attitude of the Comptroller of the Currency at that time was distinctly favorable to the development of a limited system of branch banking in the United States. He was especially desirous of providing with branches certain localities where no national banks existed. More specifically the following recommendation was made to Congress:

> That national banks be permitted under such regulations and restrictions as shall be made by the Comptroller of the Currency and approved by the Secretary of the Treasury to establish branch banks in towns and villages where no national bank is established and where the population does not exceed 1,000 inhabitants; such branch banks to have the right to receive deposits, make loans and discounts, and buy and sell exchange, but in no case to be permitted to issue circulating notes other

than of the parent bank. It shall in all respects be considered as a part of the parent bank, and in each case where such branches are maintained the Comptroller shall receive in the reports of the central bank a statement properly sworn to and attested of the condition of its branches. He shall also have the right of separate and independent examinations, and he may, whenever he deems it necessary, require, before granting the right to any bank to maintain branches, that the paid-up capital stock of such bank be increased to an amount to be fixed by him with the approval of the Secretary of the Treasury.[8]

CARLISLE RECOMMENDS BRANCH BANKING

Secretary of the Treasury J. G. Carlisle recommended in 1895 that a law be enacted permitting national banks to establish and operate branches, on the theory that the national banking system had failed to meet the local requirements of a large number of small communities throughout the country. Inasmuch as the National Banking Act required a minimum capital of $50,000 for a national bank, it was not profitable to operate national banks in many places. In fact many communities were too small, even though they needed banking facilities, to raise that amount of capital funds with which to start the institution. Even if the citizens of a given locality exerted themselves and succeeded in actually raising that amount of funds, the results were anything but promising, since the volume of business was in most cases inadequate to support profitably such an institution. It was therefore, according to Carlisle, impossible, as long as the then existing system was continued, to provide banking facilities for a large number of small communities.

Carlisle pointed out further that the capital requirement for national banks operating in cities with a population of between 6,000 and 50,000 was a minimum of $100,000, and that it was difficult for many such cities to raise that amount. Hence they had to rely on state banks or go without banking institutions. The Secretary stated:

The result of these provisions is that the people in the smaller classes of towns and cities, being unable to raise the amount of capital required by the law, are being deprived of the advantages enjoyed by the citizens of the larger places, and are consequently obliged to rely for accommo-

[8] *Annual Report of the Comptroller of the Currency* (1896), I, 100.

dation upon banks at a distance, or borrow from the commission houses, brokers, and others nearer home, at high and frequently at exorbitant rates of interest.[9]

Secretary Carlisle repeated his recommendations to Congress in 1896 in the following terms:

. . . that authority be given to establish branch banks for the transaction of all kinds of business now allowed, except the issue of circulating notes.[10]

He felt that branch banking was the most feasible plan and could be put into effect easily and quickly without "in the least impairing the strength or efficiency" of the system. At the same time it would be the "means of furnishing accommodations to people in times of need and in localities where adequate banking facilities do not now exist."

RECOMMENDATION OF BRANCH BANKING BY PRESIDENT CLEVELAND

The interest manifested in branch banking during the nineties was very great. There was fairly general recognition that the banking system had failed to function properly. Branch banking then, as now, was regarded by many as a sort of panacea. President Cleveland in his annual message[11] to Congress, December 7, 1896, followed the recommendations of the Comptroller of the Currency in his report regarding branch banking, and advocated the enactment of legislation designed to permit national banks to establish and operate branches in "small communities."[12]

The essential difference between the recommendations of the President and those of the Comptroller was in stating or designating where branches could be established. The Comptroller suggested places of "less than 1,000 inhabitants," whereas the President merely referred to "small communities."

[9] *Annual Report of the Secretary of the Treasury* (1895), p. lxxxiv.

[10] *Ibid.* (1896), pp. lxxix-lxxxi.

[11] Richardson, James D., *A Compilation of Messages and Papers of the Presidents, 1798-1908* (New York: Bureau of National Literature and Art, 1909), Vol. IX, 1898, p. 744.

[12] The *Bankers Magazine*, LIV (Jan., 1897), 15, contained the following comment: "The President in his message to Congress repeats the recommendations of the Comptroller of the Currency, that the banking law be amended to permit national banks to establish branches."

Again in 1898[13] the Comptroller of the Currency, Charles G. Dawes, made a recommendation favoring a limited extension of branch banking. The chief purpose of his plan was the same as that of the earlier suggestions of his predecessor—to provide banking facilities for communities too small to support an independent bank. His suggestion was as follows:[14]

> The Comptroller of the Currency recommends, in accordance with former recommendations of his predecessor, that domestic branch banking should be legalized in communities of less than 2,000 inhabitants, many of which are now unable to support independent banks. This would afford some smaller communities banking privileges which are now without them, but would not materially interfere with the scope of the work now so well performed by the existing banks of the smaller communities.

Comptroller Dawes was not willing to go beyond this in the development of a branch-banking system. He did not accept the arguments for a national system of branch banking.

Interest continued for a short time after 1900 to be widespread. Comptroller of the Currency William Barret Ridgely carried on the ideas that had been advanced by his predecessors, Eckles and Dawes. That the interest was general was indicated by the Comptroller in the following statement:[15]

> The inquiry is frequently submitted as to the right of a national bank to maintain a branch or agency, principally for the reception of deposits, elsewhere than at its banking house in the same or adjacent locality.

The Comptroller contended, and was supported in this conten-

[13] This was the year in which the well-known Indianapolis Monetary Commission Report appeared. This report represented the views of an entirely different group. A chapter of that report was devoted to a discussion of the branch-banking problem. The treatment was a very able and timely one, setting forth the advantages which may accrue from a branch-banking system. In framing a tentative bill designed to provide an improved banking system, a clause or section was included providing for branch banking. The provision was very broad and, if it had been adopted, would have made possible a wide and extensive development of branches throughout the country. The section providing for branches was as follows:
"Sec. 38. That it shall be lawful for any national banking association to establish branches under such rules and regulations as may be prescribed by the Comptroller of the Currency, with the approval of the Secretary of the Treasury." *Report of the Indianapolis Monetary Commission* (Chicago: University of Chicago Press, 1898), p. 71.

[14] *Annual Report of the Comptroller of the Currency* (1898), I, xl-xli.

[15] *Annual Report of the Comptroller of the Currency* (1902), I, 45-47.

tion by the solicitor and the courts, that national banks had been denied the right to establish and operate branches. In this connection he said:[16]

> The word place and at an office or banking house have always been construed by the Comptroller to mean the legal domicile of the corporation, of which it can have but one, and this construction is sustained by the Solicitor of the Treasury in an opinion rendered August 10, 1899, on the question of the right of a national bank to establish and maintain an auxiliary cash room at some point distant from its banking house, for the purpose of receiving deposits, paying checks.

Despite the fact that the Comptroller of the Currency at that time believed that national banks did not have the right to establish branches, he was very much concerned about what changes, if any, were taking place in the various state banking systems. "With a view to ascertaining the extent to which branches are legally operative in the various states," a questionnaire was sent out from the office of the Comptroller of the Currency in 1902. The following questions[17] were asked of the proper state officials in each state:

1. Whether or not branches or agencies are authorized by the banking laws of the state or the charter of the banks;
2. If authorized, the regulations and provisions of the law relative thereto;
3. The names and location of banks operating branches and the number and location of the branches.

The results of the inquiry[18] were not fundamentally different from those obtained by the Comptroller of the Currency in 1895.[19]

[16] *Ibid.*, p. 45.

[17] *Annual Report of the Comptroller of the Currency* (1902), I, 47.

[18] Attention is called to the fact that the Fowler bill was presented to Congress in 1902, providing for the operation of branches by national banks. The section referred to in the Fowler bill was as follows:

"Sec. That subdivision second of section fifty-one hundred and thirty-four of the Revised Statutes is hereby amended so as to read as follows:

"Second-location: The places where its banking operations are to be carried on, designating the particular villages, towns, cities, counties, states, territories, districts, possessions, and foreign countries.

"Any national banking association may amend its articles of association with reference to the places where its banking operations are to be carried on upon the unanimous vote of its board of directors by and with the approval of the Board of Control of Banking and Currency." (*Bankers Magazine*, LXIV, April, 1902), 540.

[19] See pp. 112-13 above.

A few states had changed their laws to permit banks to open and operate branches. Without attempting to give a complete list of the changes, attention is directed to those made in the states of Alabama, Arizona, and Louisiana. The importance of any differences found by a comparison of the results of these two investigations must not be over emphasized, for the reason that the reports from the various states were probably not very complete in either case.[20] The difference in some instances is due, no doubt, to the fact that either a different official reported or that a different method was used in stating the situation. In any event, the changes were not very fundamental. We are justified, therefore, in assuming that the branch-banking situation had not materially changed between the two inquiries. During the latter years of Ridgely's term as Comptroller of the Currency, there was a lull in the interest in branch banking. Very little attention was directed to the subject in comparison to the discussions of the preceding decade. His two immediate successors devoted their attention primarily to other phases of banking. Comptroller Murray took a position against the development of branches. He considered the national banking act as "ambiguous" in this respect and therefore recommended that the law should be amended providing that

> . . . each national bank shall have one office or banking house located within the space specified in its organization certificate, and no national bank shall maintain any office or branch, either in the same place or any other place, but banks converted with branches be permitted to retain and keep in operation such branches.

The position of the Comptroller of the Currency against branch banking was supported in 1911 by the widely known and influential opinion of Attorney-General Wickersham, in which he held that national banks were not authorized to do a branch-banking business. His opinion was, in general, in harmony with the interpretation of the law by the office of the Comptroller of the Currency in the past and also with that of the courts in so far as they had dealt with the subject. His opinion served to check for another

[20] The *Bankers Magazine*, LXV (Aug., 1902), 144, made the following comment in connection with banking opinion regarding the Fowler bill:

"The reports of bankers' conventions throughout the country bear out the belief that the branch banking features of the Fowler Bill, which failed even to pass the House at the recent session of Congress, is not at all popular with the majority of bankers."

decade any serious attempts to develop a system of branches by national banks.

John Skelton Williams became Comptroller of the Currency in 1915. He remained in office until 1920 and during this period took a very definite position in favor of a limited form of branch banking. In his annual report for 1915 he recommended to Congress that the National Bank Act be modified to permit national banks to engage in branch banking. It has been pointed out in another section[21] of this chapter that the original Glass Bill of the Federal Reserve system provided for branches of member banks of the system. The changes advocated by Comptroller Williams were similar in many respects to those contained in the original Glass Bill. More specifically the Comptroller proposed the following amendment to the National Bank Act:[22]

> National banks, with the approval of the Comptroller of the Currency, shall be allowed to establish and maintain branches within certain limits, for example, within city or county lines, but not without the boundaries of the state in which the parent bank may be located, and if such state be partly within one Federal Reserve district and partly in another Federal Reserve district such branches shall be established only in that portion of the state which is in the same Federal Reserve district as the parent bank. No national bank to be permitted, however, in this country, to have more than twelve branches. The capital of the parent bank to be increased with the establishment of each branch in the town in which the bank is located, in an amount equal to not less than 50 percent of the minimum capital which would be required for the organization of a national bank in the city wherein the parent bank is located, and the capital of the parent shall be increased with the establishment of each branch outside the city where the parent is located in an amount equal to the capital now required by the national bank act for the organization of a national bank in the place where the proposed branch is to be located.

D. R. Crissinger, who succeeded John Skelton Williams as Comptroller of the Currency in 1921, took a very decided position in favor of branches for national banks. He definitely recognized in his report of 1921 that only two types of national banks

[21] See p. 127 below.

[22] *Annual Report of the Comptroller of the Currency* (1915), I, 33-34. The same recommendation was repeated by Comptroller of the Currency Williams in each of his annual reports for the following five years, 1916-20 inclusive.

could own and operate branches: (1) the national banks which had been converted from state banks and which were operating branches at the time of conversion to the national system; and (2) the national banks which had obtained branches through consolidation with another national bank under the provisions of the Consolidation Act of November 7, 1918. He regarded the position of national banks in relation to their competitors, the state banks, as being quite unfavorable to national banks. Accordingly, in 1921 he recommended the following modification in the National Bank Act in order that national banks should have "like privileges" to state banks:[23]

> In order that national banks located in states the laws of which authorize the operation of branches by state institutions may be accorded a like privilege, a bill has been introduced providing for an amendment to section 5190 of the Revised Statutes, authorizing any national banking association located in such state to establish and maintain one or more branches in the same city, town, or county in which the association is located, provided that the capital of the national banking association shall exceed by 50 percent for each branch the capital required for the establishment of a national bank at the location of the branch or branches. The bill, however, limits the number of branches to not more than 12.

The changes proposed were very similar to those which had been recommended time and again by John Skelton Williams.

During the year 1922, the Comptroller modified his policy toward branch banking in such a way as to make a radical change in the establishment of branches by national banks in this country. In some respects his new policy was such as to make history in the field of branch banking. The Comptroller of the Currency let it be known that he would reverse the policies of his predecessors and would permit national banks to establish *agencies* or *additional* offices within the city of the parent bank. Such action had been held contrary to the provisions of the National Bank Act by those who had preceded him, on the ground that it would be branch banking and that branches could not legally be established by national banks. The Comptroller interpreted such offices as an extension of the activities of the head office and

[23] *Annual Report of the Comptroller of the Currency* (1921), p. 9.

not as branch banking, since he would not authorize such agencies to make loans except through the head office.[24] They were allowed to receive deposits and to cash checks. This change of policy he justified on the ground that it was necessary in order to protect and preserve the national banking system.

The change of policy is fully and clearly set forth in the Comptroller's letter to Senator McCormick of Illinois, in which he explained his position. The new policy was justified on the ground that it was necessary if the national banking system was to be preserved. The Comptroller's attitude is, perhaps, best set forth in the following statement of the Comptroller himself:

> The time has now come in this process of developing relations between national and state institutions, when it is necessary to give attention to the matter of branch banks, or additional banking offices or agencies. . . .
>
> To put the whole matter in a nutshell, we are in grave danger of losing our larger national banks in states where more liberal charters are granted to state banks. . . .
>
> In view of this situation, the present administration of the Comptroller's office has declined to hold that a national bank may not open additional offices in the city in which it is established. Nevertheless, it is deemed highly important that the whole matter be removed from the realm of possible uncertainty or controversy, and therefore it most earnestly recommended that Congress pass an amendment to the national banking law granting to national banks within the discretion of the Comptroller the privileges enjoyed in each state by its state banks. The bill H.R. 12415, now pending represents the general view of this bureau.[25]

The fact that Comptroller Crissinger had altered a policy of many decades' standing and had granted permission to many national banks to establish agencies or additional offices did not prove to be a final solution of this perplexing problem. The rapid opening of branches by state banks in certain states emphasized

[24] The theory underlying this change of policy is found in the fact that the Comptroller did not regard these "additional offices" or "teller windows" as branches, since they were not authorized to make loans. To be classed as branches according to this decision, they must have the right to make loans. The question of the right to "make loans" was the element which made such offices branches or mere places for the receipt of deposits and the cashing of checks. See also note 28, p. 125.

[25] *Annual Report of the Comptroller of the Currency* (1922), p. 4.

again the need of a more definite and lasting national branch-bank policy. Shortly after Crissinger had been made governor of the Federal Reserve Board and had been followed as Comptroller by H. M. Dawes, the Attorney-General of the United States was asked to render an opinion regarding the recent policy of granting to national banks permission to establish agencies or offices. The request included specifically the following questions:

1. Assuming that a national banking association is without power to establish and maintain a branch for carrying on a general banking business, has it the corporate power to open and operate an office or offices at a place or places other than its banking house for the performance of such routine services as the collection of deposits and cashing of checks for its customers?

2. If a national banking association has the corporate power to open and operate such an office or offices, must they be located within the city limits of the place designated in the organization certificate of the association as the place where its operations of discount and deposit would be carried on?

The Attorney-General reviewed the law, the decisions, and rulings bearing upon the question of branches and additional offices. He followed the Comptroller's earlier ruling, in that there was a technical distinction between branches as they were commonly regarded and the so-called offices or agencies sanctioned by the office of the Comptroller. He held that the law did not permit national banks to operate branches, but that the operation of additional offices or agencies might be conducted, provided they were within the corporate limits of the city of the parent bank.

Within a comparatively short time after the Attorney-General had rendered his opinion on October 3, 1923, the Comptroller of the Currency, H. M. Dawes, issued a set of regulations setting forth the conditions under which the Comptroller would authorize national banks to open and operate additional offices or agencies. These regulations are referred to in this chapter to indicate how far the Comptroller went in trying to regulate and control the establishment and operation of branches by national banks.

The attitude and efforts of the Comptroller of the Currency in the summer of 1923 involved another problem which was quite important. Under the Comptroller's direction, Charles W. Collins, Deputy Comptroller of the Currency, drafted a bill[26] which was introduced in the House of Representatives on February 11, 1924, by Mr. McFadden. In that bill as originally presented, there were two main provisions regarding branch banking. First, the bill provided that national banks would be given the right to establish and operate branches within the city of the parent institution. In the second place, provision was made whereby member state banks and trust companies were prohibited from further extending branches outside the corporate limits of the city of the parent bank. No less than four sections in the bill dealt with the branch-banking problem. In Section I, it was provided that state banks and trust companies could merge directly with national banks, but such national banks could not retain "outside" branches in operation at the time of consolidation except those which were in existence at the time this bill became a law.

The same provision was made in Section 7 regarding those state banks which were being converted into national banks and which were operating branches at the time of conversion. Section 8 provided for the operation of city branches by national banks in states in which state banks and trust companies were permitted to operate branches. Section 9 was intended to check a further extension of "outside" branches by member state banks and trust companies by requiring such state banks and trust companies to relinquish all outside branches which had not been established prior to the time of the approval of this bill.

During the time the McFadden branch-banking bill was under consideration by the House committee, it was modified in one important particular. The original bill had provided that, in case state banks and trust companies with branches were absorbed or were converted into national banks, the continuing institutions could continue to operate all branches owned by the banks involved at the time the said merger or conversion was completed, provided that no "outside" branches could be continued except those in existence at the time of the passage of this bill. The bill was also changed so that state banks and trust companies enter-

[26] *Annual Report of the Comptroller of the Currency* (1924), p. 2.

ing the Federal Reserve system had to relinquish all outside branches, whereas the original draft had made it possible for such state banks and trust companies to retain all branches in existence at the time the bill became a law. The bill and its amendments were clearly intended not only to curb a further extension of all branches located outside the corporate limits of the city or municipality of the parent institution, but to suppress branches of all banks in the system where such branches were located outside the corporate limits of the city or municipality of the parent institution. It was intended to strike directly at state-wide branch banking.

After the changes made in the personnel of the Federal Reserve Board in 1923 and the assuming of office by H. M. Dawes as Comptroller of the Currency, the policy of the Board and the Comptroller were quite similar. At least this was true so far as the majority of the Board was concerned. The Board undertook through its power of regulating member banks to prevent a further expansion of branches located outside the corporate limits of the city of the parent institution. For a justification of this plan, advice was sought and obtained from counsel.[27] The Comptroller on his part, as outlined in the preceding paragraph in connection with H. R. 6855, undertook to prevent national banks from obtaining, either through mergers or by conversions, branches located outside the city of the parent bank. At the same time he set forth as part of his policy the placing of national banks on a par with state banks by giving national banks the right to establish city branches.[28]

A brief summary of the points for and against branch banking, as developed by various Comptrollers of the Currency as outlined in preceding pages, seems desirable at this time. The advantages and disadvantages will be discussed more fully elsewhere.

[27] *Commercial and Financial Chronicle*, CXVII (Nov. 10, 1923), 2053.

[28] The Comptroller of the Currency regarded branches as being fundamentally different from the "additional offices" or "teller windows" which he advocated for national banks. The offices were considered a means for extending the services of the head office, whereas the branches represented absentee ownership and as such were undesirable. There was, according to his definition, no conflict in his position of opposing branches outside the city and the favoring of offices within the city of the parent. The latter he regarded as a modification of unit banking and under certain conditions very desirable. See note 24, p. 122 above.

Here we shall summarize only the leading arguments developed on each side of this important subject:

A. ARGUMENTS AGAINST BRANCH BANKING

1. It is clearly the intent of the National Bank Act to deny national banks the right to establish and operate branches.

2. Branch banking tends towards combinations and monopoly. This would be highly undesirable; therefore national banks as well as state banks should not be allowed to enter the field of branch banking.

3. Branch banking would mean absentee ownership. Banks would be operated for the benefit of the stockholders rather than for the purpose of serving the community.

4. Branch banking is not in harmony with the American idea of self-government.

5. Branches would be operated by managers who would not have the same interest in the community that a unit banker would have. It would be less personal and the branch would not be as apt to promote the general welfare of the community as would the unit bank.

B. ARGUMENTS IN FAVOR OF BRANCH BANKING

1. The existing banking system fails to meet the needs of small communities. Many such places are unable to raise sufficient capital to establish an independent bank and are therefore without local banking services.

2. The amount of capital would be less for a system of branches than for a large number of unit banks. Branch banking would result in a more economical use of banking capital funds.

3. The national banks will convert into the state system unless the National Bank Act is liberalized so that national banks may compete freely with state banks. This includes the right to establish and operate branches, at least in the states which permit state banks to operate branches.

4. Branches would aid or facilitate the flow of capital from the financial centers to the small localities where it is more urgently

needed. In the same way it would facilitate the flow of currency.

5. Branch banking would tend to reduce and make more uniform the interest rates charged borrowers throughout the country. Banks with branches would tend to charge the same rate for all loans made throughout their system of branches regardless of the location of the various offices.

FIRST COMPLETE DRAFT OF THE GLASS BILL

The basic principles of branch banking have been thoroughly understood by economists, bankers, and legislators for many years in this country. It has been the subject of discussion on numerous occasions. It received favorable consideration in the *Indianapolis Monetary Commission Report*, 1898. The framers of the Federal Reserve bill gave considerable attention to arguments for and against branch banking. The first complete draft of the Glass bill[29] contained a section designed to introduce branch banking into the national banking system on a definite basis in those states which permitted state banks to establish and operate branches. The following section was included in that draft:

Section 9. That it shall be lawful for any national banking association having a capital of not less than $1,000,000 to establish branches under such rules and regulations as may be prescribed by the Comptroller of the Currency, with the approval of the Secretary of the Treasury; Provided, that the number of such branches shall not exceed one for each $500,000 of capital stock issued by the parent institution; and provided further that no branch shall be located outside the Federal Reserve District in which the parent bank has its head office.

This section was dropped before the bill was introduced into the House of Representatives.

Public sentiment was not favorably disposed toward branch banking at that time. The proposal met with strong and powerful opposition in the early stages of the framing and drafting of the Glass bill. The opposition to branch banking was so marked that to have undertaken to push it through would have endangered the outcome of the whole legislative program for banking reform.

[29] Willis, H. P., *The Federal Reserve System* (New York: The Ronald Press, 1923), Sec. 9, p. 1537.

Political leaders understood the difficulties and were not, therefore, inclined to put the section forward as a part of the program.

THE FEDERAL RESERVE BOARD

After the Federal Reserve bill became law and the Federal Reserve system became operative, the sentiment in favor of banks operating branches remained comparatively weak and ineffective. In 1915, however, the Federal Reserve Board took an advanced position in favor of national banks operating branches when it recommended to Congress that the Federal Reserve Act be amended as follows:

> Permission should be granted to national banks to establish offices within the city, or within the county, in which they are located.[30]

It is interesting to observe that the Board advocated a limited branch-banking system by restricting branches to the city or county.

In 1916 the Board,[31] consistent with its action in 1915, recommended that Congress pass legislation which would permit national banks located in cities of more than 100,000 and having a capital and surplus of $1,000,000 or more to establish and operate branches within the corporate limits of the city of the parent institution. In 1917 the Board again recommended the granting of power to national banks to establish branches.[32] The provisions regarding the size of the city and the amount of capital were the same as had been recommended to Congress in 1916. The new features proposed were to limit the number of branches within the city to ten and to provide that no branches should be established in any state which did not permit state banks and trust companies to operate branches. The Board stated that the present policy of allowing state banks to operate branches in certain states where national banks could not was unfair to national banks. The one avowed purpose in such legislation was to put the national banks on a competitive basis with the state banks and trust companies.

The Federal Reserve Board renewed its recommendations again

30 *Annual Report of the Federal Reserve Board* (1915), p. 22.
31 *Annual Report of the Federal Reserve Board* (1916), pp. 29, 145.
32 *Annual Report of the Federal Reserve Board* (1917), p. 33.

in favor of branch banking in both 1918[33] and 1919,[34] on the ground that national banks were at a great disadvantage as compared with state banks and trust companies in certain localities. It was further argued that an extension of branch banking was necessary if there was to be a "proper development of the Federal Reserve system" in the coördination of the work among members of the system.

During the year 1919 the subject of branch banking was more favorably considered. The United States Senate passed a bill which proposed that national banks having a capital and surplus of $1,000,000 or more could establish branches in cities of 500,000 or more in population, provided the number of branches was not in excess of ten and that the branches were within the corporate limits of the city of the parent bank. The operation of these branches was further contingent upon the right of state banks to operate branches within that state. This bill was not favorably considered by the House of Representatives.[35]

The position of the Federal Reserve Board prior to 1920 was very clearly stated in the Board's report for 1919 as follows:

> The Board has on several occasions recommended to Congress that the Federal Reserve Act be amended so as to permit national banks under certain conditions to establish branches within the corporate limits of the city in which they are located. Under the present law the national banks can not afford the same facilities to the public as are given by state banks having branches, except in cases where state banks and trust companies operating branches have merged with national banks, when existing branches may be continued by the national banks. The Senate has passed a bill authorizing national banks located in cities of not less than 500,000 inhabitants and having a capital and surplus of $1,000,000 or more to establish branches not exceeding ten in number within the corporate limits of the cities in which they are located, provided the laws of the State extend a similar privilege to the banking institutions operating under State charters. While the Board would prefer to have this privilege extended to national banks in cities of not less than 100,000 inhabitants, or, failing that, have the population limit raised to 200,000, it wishes to point out that the limit fixed in the Senate bill does

[33] *Annual Report of the Federal Reserve Board* (1918), p. 83.

[34] *Ibid.*, pp. 64-65.

[35] The Hon. Edmund Platt, who was Chairman of the Committee on Banking and Currency of the House at that time, informed me that the bill failed to obtain a favorable report in the Committee by a tie vote.

not affect the principle involved, and it therefore respectfully recommends once more that national banks be permitted to establish branches in the cities in which they are located under such limitations as in the wisdom of Congress may be deemed desirable.[36]

The Board in 1922 reviewed briefly the development of branches by banks in certain states and drew the conclusion that the movement had gone so far in certain states, "notably California, and in a few large cities, including New York, Cleveland, and Detroit, as to greatly reduce the number of national banks." Further, the Board did not believe that the action of the Comptroller of the Currency in 1922, in granting permission to national banks located in cities in which the state laws permitted state banks to operate branches, had met "the situation in California and does not fully meet it in the cities mentioned." The Board added that "an amendment to the national banking act allowing national banks the same privilege given to state banks in states where branch banking is permitted is much to be desired."

It is clear that there was a keen desire to put the national banks on a par with the state banks and trust companies. The statements are not always precise and one is left in some quandary as to just how far the Board was willing to go in making the branch-banking laws provide an equal basis for the two classes of banks. It is very doubtful if the Board was willing to go so far in its recommendations as to urge state-wide branch banking in states where it was being carried on by state banks. To have provided the competitive basis they had been advocating would have implied that they were quite willing to provide state-wide branches for national banks in states like California, Georgia, Maryland, and North Carolina, where branches were being operated freely on a state-wide basis.

Another phase of the Board's policy or attitude in 1922 is interesting. The rural-credit situation at that time was highly disorganized and much dissatisfaction existed in many sections of the country, especially as regards the agricultural situation. The Joint Commission of Agricultural Inquiry in its report to Congress had suggested that "a system of limited branch banking might fur-

[36] *Annual Report of the Federal Reserve Board* (1919), pp. 64-65.

nish a possible solution of the problem."[37] In this suggestion the Board concurred and expressed their approval as follows:

Such systems are in fact already established in some sections of our country, notably California, and appear to have gone far toward solving the problem. Branch banking has lowered the rate of interest in some leading agricultural sections of California and at the same time has provided added security for the deposits of the farmers. There are interesting neighborhood branch banking groups in other states, which appear to be serving their communities well. State-wide branch banking is permitted in several southern states, but has not as yet been developed on an extensive scale. In the absence of laws permitting branch banking, there has been in certain sections a considerable development of so-called "chain banks"—banks owned and controlled in groups by individuals or holding companies. The largest of these includes some 175 small banks.[38]

Judging from the official record, there can be no doubt that the Federal Reserve Board had been definitely in favor of branch banking. At times they specifically advocated city or county branches, at other times they stressed city branches, while again they seemed to favor putting the national banks on a competitive basis with the state banks in those states where state banks and trust companies were permitted to operate branches on a state-wide basis. This would have involved the national banks in state-wide branch banking. At any rate the policy prior to 1923 was consistently one in which the extension of branches by national banks was strongly recommended each year.

It was officially stated by the Board in 1917 that state banks could enter the Federal Reserve system under the provisions of the 1917 amendments without any fear of interference on the part of the Board in their development of a state-wide system of branches. The act of 1917 had specifically provided that state banks could enter the system and retain all their charter rights:

Any bank becoming a member of the Federal Reserve system shall retain its full charter and statutory rights as a state bank or trust company, and may continue to exercise all corporate powers granted it by the state in which it was created, and shall be entitled to all privileges of member banks.

[37] *Report of the Joint Commission of Agricultural Inquiry (Report 408)*, House of Representatives, 67 Congress, 1 Session, Pt. II, p. 146.

[38] *Annual Report of the Federal Reserve Board* (1922), pp. 5-6.

The Board's regulations were in harmony with this provision. The Board stated its policy in part, as follows, on November 1, 1919:

Subject to the provisions of this act and to the regulations of the Board made pursuant thereto, any bank becoming a member of the Federal Reserve system shall retain its full charter and statutory rights as a State bank or trust company, and may continue to exercise all the powers granted to it by the State in which it was created and shall be entitled to all privileges of member banks.[39]

Additional proof was given of the Board's liberal policy in this connection in 1919 when the Security Trust and Savings Bank of Los Angeles was considering the advisability of entering the system. At that time the Security Trust and Savings Bank had declared definitely in favor of an extension of its branches and was therefore anxious to ascertain the probable course of the Board's policy toward branch banking in the future. That bank, in order that it might have a definite and satisfactory understanding of the matter before entering the system, addressed a letter to the chairman of the board of the Federal Reserve Bank of San Francisco for information regarding the future policy of the Board on this subject. The letter[40] read in part as follows:

We regret, however, that we are now unable to accept, unreservedly, all of the four conditions, without having first obtained additional approvals as provided in said conditions, and without some further information as to the probable attitude of the board in relation to the establishment of branch offices by California State member banks.

On November 3, 1919, John Perrin, chairman of the board of the Federal Reserve Bank of San Francisco, in a letter to J. F. Sartori, president of the Security Trust and Savings Bank, Los Angeles, assured Mr. Sartori that it was not the policy of the Board to interfere with the development of branch banking among the member state banks. The letter stated definitely that the Board was not opposed to the principle of branch banking as a general proposition. The following quotation from Mr. Perrin's letter,[41] shows more completely the Board's attitude:

[39] See *Board's Regulations of 1917, Regulation H*, p. 25.

[40] *Hearings before the Committee on Banking and Currency*, House of Representatives, 68 Congress, 1 Session, H.R. 6855 (April, 1924), p. 55.

[41] *Ibid.*, p. 59.

As to the Board's attitude regarding the establishment of branches, I can say that its sole concern will be to satisfy itself that any proposed extension will not impair the general strength and safety of your institution. In admitting state banks having branches the board has taken the view that State banks are not to be restricted in the exercise of their powers except where there is reason to believe that the exercise of such powers will impair the liquidity of the bank.

As you no doubt are aware, the Federal reserve board is not opposed to the principle of branch banking, so you need have no hesitation in bringing your bank into the Federal reserve system through fear that diffculties will be interposed to your maintaining branches or establishing new ones. The board simply reserves the right to approve the establishment of new branches in order that it may be assured that the bank's general strength and liquidity will not suffer.

For your information I wish to state that the same condition was imposed upon the Bank of Italy and all other State banks admitted to membership.

Prior to 1923 the Board had considered each application for a new branch upon its individual merits, "giving consideration to public convenience and to the parent bank's capacity for properly organizing the branch and assimilating the business taken over."[42] The Board had adopted a liberal policy and did not refuse permission to establish or acquire new branches if the extension was consistent with a sound banking policy, adequate supervision, and complete solvency. The basis upon which the Board's decision rested in the last analysis in each case is completely outlined by the following statement:[43]

As a matter of general policy, rather than specifically of branch banking policy, the Board in individual cases withheld its approval until satisfied that establishment of the additional branch or branches in question would not impair the solvency or liquidity of the parent bank. It gave consideration to the rate of expansion of the given branch system; coordination of branches already acquired; head-office control, supervision, and personnel; affiliation with outside corporations; relation of capital and surplus to deposit liabilities, especially in rapidly expanding branch systems; methods of acquiring branches; and generally to local conditions and needs in so far as these could be clearly defined.

In summary, the attitude of the Board prior to 1923 was that of letting the states determine the conditions under which state

[42] *Federal Reserve Bulletin,* Dec., 1924, p. 926.

[43] *Ibid.*

banks might operate branches in the Federal Reserve system, provided such practice did not violate the principles of sound and conservative banking. The Board on the other hand, as we have already pointed out, recommended legislation to Congress designed to broaden and liberalize the provisions of the National Bank Act in order to extend the privileges of operating branches on a restricted basis to national banks.

CHANGE IN THE FEDERAL RESERVE POLICY IN 1923

The Federal Reserve Board made a fundamental change in its branch-banking policy during the second half of 1923, especially as regards a further expansion of branches by member state banks and trust companies of the Federal Reserve system. This new policy was announced on November 7, 1923, and was to become effective February 1, 1924. The purpose underlying this modification was to check and control the growth of branches in the Federal Reserve system by denying member state banks and trust companies the right to establish additional branches or offices outside the corporate limits of the city of the parent institution. The resolution adopted by the Board on November 7, 1923, was not intended to interfere with the right of either state banks or national banks to establish offices or branches within the corporate limits of the city of the parent bank, or in town or city contiguous to the city of the parent institution. The alleged reasons for this action were to protect and preserve the Federal Reserve system and to equalize conditions between national banks and state banks in those states where state-wide branch banking was permitted.

What were the conditions at that time which gave rise to this sudden reversal of policy? Broadly speaking, the causes were twofold. In the first place, there had been a rapidly growing interest on both sides of the question of branch banking. In the state of California, branches had increased extensively and had gone far to stir up a wide discussion of the arguments both for and against branch banking. City branches in other states, notably in the cities of New York, Detroit, and Cleveland, had registered marked increases.

During the same period there was developing considerable opposition to branch banking, and not only in those sections where branches had their greatest growth. In states such as Illinois and Missouri much attention was given to methods which might be effective against a further extension of branch banking, especially of the state-wide variety. The growing interest in this subject, therefore, made it most important for the Board to formulate a definite policy concerning the further expansion of branch banking. There appears to be no doubt that each group was anxious to get a favorable hearing from the Board. This influence, probably, had considerable weight with certain members of the Board in formulating a new policy. Especially was this true in regard to the new members who had come from states which either prohibited branch banking or very definitely restricted the branch-banking area.

The second important factor to be considered in connection with the declaration of this new policy was to be found in the changes in the membership of the Federal Reserve Board itself during the year 1923. There were three new members added to the Board during the first half of that year. The Comptroller of the Currency was named as governor or the board, leaving a vacancy in the office of the Comptroller of the Currency. After the designation of Crissinger as governor, there were still two vacancies on the Board. H. M. Dawes was appointed Comptroller of the Currency, and George R. James and E. H. Cunningham were named to fill the vacancies on the Board. The other members of the Board at that time were Edmund Platt, vice governor, Charles S. Hamlin, A. C. Miller, and Andrew W. Mellon, Secretary of the Treasury. The adoption of the famous branch-banking resolution on November 7 was by a four-to-three vote of the Board, with Secretary Mellon[44] absent and not voting. The four members who voted for the resolution and decided the issue were H. M. Dawes, D. R. Crissinger, George R. James, and E. H. Cunningham, three of whom were newly appointed. The three votes against the resolution came from three old members who had long before declared their posi-

[44] It was reported that Mr. Mellon was "in general accord with the majority of the Board in the position taken in its new policy." *Commercial and Financial Chronicle,* CXVII (Nov. 10, 1923), 2051-55.

tion in regard to the development of branches among state banks in the Federal Reserve system as well as among the national banks.

A study of the reports of the Comptroller of the Currency for the years 1923 and 1924, and of the *Hearings before the Committee on Banking and Currency,* House of Representatives, 1924, leaves little, if any, doubt that the leading spirit in the opposition to a further development of branch banking was the Comptroller of the Currency himself. He came to Washington at a time when the bankers of his own community were strongly opposed to the idea of branch banking. Further support was given to that position by the resolutions and expressed views of the American Bankers' Association, which had gone on record at different times against branch banking.

The Federal Reserve Board in the summer of 1923, shortly after the new Comptroller of the Currency assumed the duties of his office, appointed a Committee on Examinations, consisting of Henry M. Dawes, chairman, Edmund Platt, and George R. James, to make a study of branch banking and to report its recommendations to the Board as regards what should or could be done by the Board to declare a more definite and effective branch-banking policy. There seems to be no doubt that the immediate aim to be attained was that of checking the growth of "outside" branches by state banks and trust companies within the Federal Reserve system until some legislation could be drafted and presented to Congress designed, if passed, to curb the extension of branches, if not to stop it altogether. The study by the committee for the Board ended in a disagreement, resulting in majority and minority reports. The minority report was signed by Mr. Platt, vice governor of the Board. That there was a sharp conflict between the members of the committee and the Board in connection with the final report and the resolutions of November, 1923, is attested by the testimony of Mr. Platt before the Banking and Currency Committee in 1924. In his testimony[45] Mr. Platt seems

[45] *Hearings before the Committee on Banking and Currency,* House of Representatives, 68 Congress, 1 Session, H.R. 6855 (April, 1924), pp. 206-7. See also C. W. Collins' *Branch Banking Question* (1926), p. 90.

to imply that the opposition was centered to a considerable extent in the office of the Comptroller of the Currency.

THE MAJORITY REPORT

The committee "had under study the development of branch banking, with a view to recommending to the Board the policy which the Board should pursue in admitting to membership in the Federal Reserve system state banks maintaining branches outside the corporate limits of the city or town or contiguous territory" in which the parent institution was located. It was stated that a "long and intensive study by all members of the Federal Reserve Board" was made. According to the report the Federal Reserve system was possible because of the power given to the Federal government to force national banks to become members. The majority report held, moreover, that an extension of branch banking would give to many state banks a decided advantage over national banks, and it was, therefore, the duty of the Board "to lay down a policy to the general end that all banks, national and state, may operate for the good of the system." It was stated, furthermore, that "in certain specific instances, the interests of the members require at the present time a clear and definite statement as to the limitations and privileges which will be recognized."

The report made by the committee was adopted by a majority vote of the Board. The resolutions as presented to and acted upon by the Board are summarized as follows:

Whereas,

1. National banks *must* and state banks *may* become members of the Federal Reserve system.

2. The Federal Reserve Act contemplates a unified banking system in which both national and state banks may participate.

3. State banks in certain states have been permitted to engage in state-wide branch banking, while national banks are limited to the city of the parent.

4. The Board believes this results in an inequitable situation as regards state and national banks in the Federal Reserve system.

5. In the interest of successful administration of the system,

it appears necessary to confine the operations of member banks within certain territorial limits.

Be it resolved:

1. That state banks entering the system must agree, as in the past, not to establish any branches without the consent of the Board.

2. That, as a general principle, state banks with branches outside the corporate limits of the city or town, or contiguous territory, ought not be admitted to the system unless they relinquish such branches.

3. That, as a general principle, state banks which are members of the system ought not be permitted to have branches outside the corporate limits of the city or territory contiguous thereto.

4. That the Board in acting upon individual applications after February 1, 1924, will be guided by the above principles.

5. That contiguous territory shall mean territory of city or town whose corporate limits at some point coincide with corporate limits of town or city of the parent bank.

6. That the resolution is not intended to affect the status of any branches or additional offices established prior to February 1, 1924, either of those banks now members or those subsequently applying for membership.

The resolution was made effective as of February 1, 1924, in order to give the banks time to adjust themselves to the new policy and also to give time for certain banks to establish additional branches before the doors were closed to state-wide branches in the system. There were, moreover, according to reports, a number of applications before the Board for consideration. A third factor in the postponement, no doubt, was to give Congress time to consider the desirability of enacting new legislation before the Board's new regulations became effective.

On January 7, 1924, two months after having adopted the new policy toward branch banking, the Board considered the applications of three banks which had requested permission to establish a number of branches over a period of time in accordance with their contemplated program of branch-banking development.

After due consideration the Board adopted the following resolution:[46]

> That no blanket authority to establish branches would be granted; that each application must be presented separately in regular form and manner, subject to approval of the state banking authorities and a recommendation of the Federal Reserve bank of the district; that applications to establish branches in noncontiguous territory, filed before February 1 (under the Board's resolution of November 7) might be considered by the Board after that date; and that the Board reserved the right to pass on each application on its merits.

The Board gave further consideration to the formation of its branch-banking policy at its meetings in March and April, 1924. The results of these meetings, in so far as they affected the status of branch banking in the Federal Reserve system, was made public in a definite form in the Board's regulations of April, 1924. The principal features of these regulations in regard to branch banking are summarized as follows:

1. That, as a general principle, branches would be restricted to the city of the location of the parent and the territorial area within the state contiguous thereto . . . excepting in cases where the state banking authorities have certified, and the Board finds that public necessity and advantage render a departure necessary or desirable.

2. That, as a general principle, applications for branches would not be considered unless state authorities "regularly made simultaneous examinations of head office and all branches," such examinations to furnish "information as to the condition of each bank and the character of its management" sufficient to enable the Board "to protect the interests of the public."

3. That, as a general principle, each bank operating branches would be required to maintain "an adequate ratio of capital to liabilities and an adequate percentage of its total investments in the form of paper or securities eligible for discount or purchase by the Federal Reserve banks."

4. That no application to establish a branch, agency, or additional office be issued until state banking authorities had approved

[46] *Federal Reserve Bulletin*, Dec., 1924, p. 929.

it, and the directors or executive committee and the Federal Reserve agent of the Federal Reserve bank of the district had made a report upon the financial condition of the bank, the character of the bank management, the effect such branch would have on other banks of the community, and whether such branches would be in the interest of the locality.

5. That a permit to establish branches by the Board would become void if not exercised within six months after it was granted.

6. That the Board reserved the right to cancel any permit granted in the future, wherever it should appear, after hearing, that such branch was being operated in a manner contrary to the interest of the public in the locality in which it was established.

SUMMARY OF THE MINORITY REPORT

The regulations of the Board regarding branch banking, as set forth in the preceding pages, remained in effect until the passage of the McFadden-Pepper Act of February 25, 1927. There was considerable opposition to the principles laid down, but the Board adhered fairly closely to that policy till the law was modified. It seems desirable to present a general summary of the minority report by Edmund Platt, vice governor of the Federal Reserve Board, in which he took issue with the majority report of the Committee on Examination which had filed its report with the Board on November 7, 1923. This is said to be the first minority report submitted by any member of the Federal Reserve Board. The report may be briefly summarized as follows:

1. The majority report was based upon the assumption that it is the duty of the Board to deny any state bank the right to exercise any powers granted in its state charter that appears to give the state a marked advantage over a competitive national bank.

2. If the Board adopted this policy, it would be tantamount to an attempt to force state banks to conform to national banking laws, and would be a complete reversal of the Board's past policy.

3. Such a policy would be contrary to the policy followed by the Board in regard to trust business.

4. Limited branch banking is permitted by the Comptroller of the Currency and it would appear to be a wise policy to find a way

for extending branch banking to certain communities rather than to try to check the movement.

5. National banks, through the provision of the act of 1865, have been permitted to own and operate branches obtained through conversion.

6. Branch banking is justified on economic grounds and is recognized by the foremost authorities on banking in this country, especially as regards the services which such a system could render to the smaller communities.

FEDERAL RESERVE AGENTS' CONFERENCE

At a meeting held by the Federal Reserve agents in October, 1921, the conference went on record[47] in favor of an extension of branch banking by national banks within the city of the parent institution, provided that the state banks were permitted to operate branches in that state. The position assumed by the agents is, of course, the same as that announced much earlier by both the Federal Reserve Board and by the Federal Advisory Council. The special importance to be attached to this resolution is that it was in harmony with the policy of the Federal Reserve Board. It is indicated that the various organizations within the system were favorably disposed toward a limited or local extension of branch banking by national banks with the idea of placing national banks on "a footing of equality" with state banks and trust companies.

The Council in 1916 renewed its recommendation[48] of 1915, but added that "such privilege should apply to all banks in the national system of adequate capital or to none." In its recommendation[49] made during the year 1917, the Council advocated limiting branches to "cities of more than 100,000" inhabitants, and again stated that the privilege should be extended to all national banks of adequate size regardless of the state laws. This last step is, perhaps, further than the Federal Reserve Board was willing to go in its recommendations to Congress at that time. In the year

[47] *Hearings on Branch, Chain and Group Banking before the Committee on Banking and Currency*, House of Representatives, 71 Congress, 2 Session, H.R. 141 (1930), p. 438.

[48] *Annual Report of the Federal Reserve Board* (1918), p. 816.

[49] *Ibid.*, p. 822.

1918 the Council stated[50] that it still adhered to and would repeat its recommendation of November 20, 1915. During the year 1919 it endorsed Senate Bill 170,[51] which was passed by the Senate, August 2, 1919, and provided that national banks could operate branches within the corporate limits of the city of the parent, provided the state laws permitted state banks to operate branches, and provided further that branches should not be operated in cities of less than 500,000 inhabitants. The Board was urged "to use every effort to secure the passage of Senate Bill 170 in the interest of sound banking and the granting of equal banking facilities to all people in the same business community."

Beginning with 1915, the Council made recommendations favoring the extension of branch banking by national banks on the following dates:

September 21, 1915	February 19, 1917
November 16, 1915	February 19, 1918
November 20, 1916	September 16, 1919

In addition to the recommendations made on these dates, the Council in 1923 approved the idea again but did not at that time accept the new ruling of the Federal Reserve Board, which was designed to restrict or prohibit a further extension of branches by member banks of the Reserve system. In this connection it was stated that:

> . . . the Council believes that the resolution, if carried into effect, will give a position of monopoly to those state banks that have already established state-wide systems of branches, while those state banks which have refrained from branch banking will be placed in a position of great disadvantage.[52]

During the next three years, 1924,[53] 1925,[54] and 1926,[55] the Council approved in principle, the provisions of the McFadden bill in Congress. In 1927 the McFadden bill was enacted into law. In

[50] *Ibid.*, p. 856.
[51] *Ibid.* (1919), pp. 528-29.
[52] *Annual Report of the Federal Reserve Board* (1923), p. 467.
[53] *Hearings on Branch, Chain and Group Banking before the Committee on Banking and Currency*, House of Representatives, 71 Congress, 2 Session, H.R. 141 (1930), pp. 437-43.
[54] *Ibid.*
[55] *Ibid.*

connection with the McFadden bill the Council took a position against certain features of the bill, even though it approved it in most respects. On November 19, 1926, the Council stated that it did not "believe it should let pass without explicit comment and which in its opinion may ultimately work a gross hardship on some national banks and perhaps seriously affect both State and national membership in the Federal Reserve system. It is the so-called Hull Amendment."[56]

The Council desired to place certain definite restrictions on the development of branches. The following were the principal restrictions desired:

1. No banks were to operate branches with a capital of less than $1,000,000. The reason for this was that a bank should have sufficient funds before embarking upon a policy of branch banking. It was believed that at that time the capital requirements for unit banks were entirely too low. The same applied to certain states regarding the provisions concerning the operation of branches. It was to remedy this weakness that a minimum requirement of $1,000,000 was proposed.

2. No branches should be established outside the corporate limits of the city of the parent institution. It was the object to retain in principle the unit bank, even though the privilege to establish city branches were granted. Such branches were not to be regarded as full-fledged branches in the same way that Canada or England carries on branch banking.

3. Branches were restricted to central Reserve or Reserve cities or, as later provided, to cities having a population of not less than 100,000 inhabitants. This meant, if put into effect, that a large part of the country would be without the advantages of branch banking.

4. All national banks located in a city of sufficient size and having a proper capital should be permitted to operate branches regardless of state laws covering the operation of branches by state banks. If this could not be done, then the privilege should be denied to all.

[56] *Annual Report of the Federal Reserve Board* (1926), p. 487.

THE MCFADDEN-PEPPER BANK ACT

The McFadden-Pepper Bank Act was approved February 25, 1927. This was the first act passed in the United States authorizing national banks to establish branches. The bill which was finally passed had gone through many stages in the two branches of Congress and emerged greatly modified from what it had been in the beginning. The bill was alleged to contain provisions designed to place the national banks on a competitive basis with state banks and trust companies. The greatest attention was directed to provisions dealing with the subject of branch banking. Branch banking was the center around which the controversy raged. The opposition to branch banking was well organized and carried on the fight with great skill and enthusiasm.

The amendments introduced or drafted by Representative Hull of Illinois proved to be the most disputed and fiercely debated of any provisions that became a part of the bill. These amendments provided that member banks, both state and national, should never be permitted to establish and operate branches in those states which did not at the time of the passage of this act allow state banks to own and operate branches. These amendments went so far as to prohibit the establishment of branches by state banks outside the Federal Reserve system. Regardless of the extreme form which these provisions took, they were approved by the American Bankers' Association and the bill, including the Hull amendments, was passed by the House of Representatives on February 4, 1926. The bill was approved by the Senate after having eliminated the Hull amendments. The Senate refused to accept the amendments and the session closed without any definite results so far as the McFadden bill was concerned.

The American Bankers' Association, which met in Los Angeles, California, in 1926, after a stormy session lasting many hours finally approved the McFadden bill with the Hull amendments eliminated. With this changed attitude on the part of the association, the supporters of the bill took up the task in the next Congress and pressed it through both houses. That meant that the House, which had sponsored the Hull amendments, had to yield. This it did only after a very desperate struggle. Some maintained that the bill was finally pushed through the Senate because of an alliance between the supporters of the McNary-Haugen Bill for agricultural relief and those who backed the McFadden bill.[57] Be that as it may, the bill was passed by both houses and approved by the President on February 25, 1927, marking the temporary end of a long and bitter struggle between the branch and anti-branch bankers throughout the country. The branch bankers had won a partial victory.

The provisions of the McFadden-Pepper Act relating to branch banking are summarized as follows:

1. National banks may retain and keep in operation any branch or branches which said national bank or banks had in lawful operation on February 25, 1927.

2. If a state bank with branches is converted into the national system, such national bank may continue to operate all such branches the state bank had in lawful operation on February 25, 1927.

3. Any national bank, which had operated one branch for a period of more than twenty-five years, could continue such branch regardless of the legality of the establishment of the branch at the time it was opened.

4. If two national banks are consolidated, the continuing bank may continue to operate any branches that either institution had in lawful operation on February 25, 1927, regardless of the location of the branch or branches.

5. If a state bank is merged with a national bank, the national bank may continue any branches which the state bank had in lawful operation on February 25, 1927.

6. National banks located in a state which permits state banks to establish and operate the branches may establish branches in the city of the parent bank, provided that no branches be established in a city or town with a population of less than 25,000 inhabitants; provided that no more than one branch may be established in a city of 50,000 or less; provided, further, that no more than two branches may be established in a city of 100,000 or less; provided that in any city or town which exceeds 100,000, the num-

[57] Tippetts, Charles S., *State Banks and the Federal Reserve System* (New York: D. Van Nostrand Company, Inc., 1929), p. 353.

ber of branches which may be established is left to the discretion of the Comptroller of the Currency.

7. The word branch was defined to include any branch bank, branch office, branch agency, additional office, or any place of business where the regular business of a bank is transacted. No bank was permitted to move a branch without the consent of the Comptroller of the Currency.

8. Any state member bank which had, on February 25, 1927, established and was operating a branch or branches could continue to operate such branches while remaining or becoming a member of the Federal Reserve system. The establishment of branches outside the city of the parent institution was prohibited to all member banks after February 25, 1927.

The enactment of the McFadden-Pepper Bank Act in 1927 had the effect of repealing or modifying certain provisions of the Board's regulations regarding the operation of branches by member banks. The Board in its regulations of 1924 had provided that, under certain conditions, the Board might consent to permit a member bank to establish an out-of-town office or branch. The McFadden-Pepper Act provided that no member bank could establish branches or become a member of the system with branches outside the city of the parent bank which had been established after February 25, 1927. This was a direct attempt to prevent the growth of statewide branch banking in the Federal Reserve system. In an earlier regulation, the Board had sought to make possible the approval of applications to establish branches not only in the city of the parent, but in territory contiguous to the city in which the head office of the bank was located. The new act strictly limited branches to the city of the parent bank.

The passage on June 16, 1933, of the Glass-Steagall Bank Act completes to date the legal steps taken in this country to extend or provide for the establishment and operation of branches by national banks. This act now gives national banks the right, with the approval of the Comptroller, to operate branches on a statewide basis provided state banks and trust companies have that right in the state in which the national bank or banks are located. This change is intended to put national banks on a par with state banks so far as branches are concerned. It falls somewhat short of that, since the capital requirements for national banks operating branches outside the city of the parent is larger than for state banks.

The act does not provide for a direct extension of branches which could not have been made before the passage of the bill, provided, of course, that the bank would have done so under state laws. It makes possible for national banks to do what non-member state banks in this respect could have done before the new legislation was enacted. There are certain provisions in the Glass-Steagall Act which will, it is believed, have a very marked influence on the development of branch banking in this country in the future. These provisions are as follows:

1. Minimum capital for national banks of not less than $50,000, for all new banks organized in the future. This will tend to limit the number of new banks and will make it impossible to charter new banks in many places, hence there will be a demand for branches in such communities to supply the banking facilities needed in that locality.

2. Prohibition of the payment of interest on demand deposits. This provision will tend to reduce the attractiveness of the large correspondent bank to many smaller banks. Smaller balances will be carried in the city banks. Loss of business by the large city banks in this way will make them more anxious or willing to enter the branch-banking business. In the course of time, this factor will be likely to play an active part in creating a more favorable sentiment in favor of branch banking throughout the country.

3. The guaranty of bank deposits. The new act imposing membership in the Federal Reserve system upon banks which may expect to remain permanently in the guaranty fund system will force a number of banks to increase their capital in order to be eligible. This many of them cannot do. Being small banks they will probably find their deposits disappearing and going to larger banks, hence leaving many communities without banking facilities. This will make it more necessary to have branches than at the present time. The effective operation of the guaranty system will tend to encourage the extension of branch privileges throughout the country.

CHAPTER IX

BRANCH BANKING IN CALIFORNIA

The state of California has held a unique position in the development of branch banking in the United States during the past two decades, and especially since the close of the World War in 1918. The influence of the movement in that state cannot be fully measured merely by comparing the growth in the number of branches with similar developments in other states. Such comparisons are interesting and valuable, but fail to indicate the full significance of the changes taking place. California is one of the fifteen or sixteen states which permit the establishment and operation of branches on a state-wide basis. A careful study of the fundamental factors involved in the movement in that state will aid us in estimating the probable development in other states, provided the laws governing banking in this country be broadened to permit branch banking on a wider basis. These principles would apply, in part, if we should adopt either a nationwide system or take a Federal Reserve district, as our geographical unit. What are the conditions in California that make it the most prominent in the development of branch banking? Before summarizing these conditions, let us first review briefly the status of branch banking in the other states which permit state-wide branches.

Delaware and Rhode Island, which permit the operation of branches on a state-wide basis, are small states. The branch-banking situation in each of these states is comparable, fundamentally, to that existing in Maine, where banks are limited to the county or adjoining county in the establishment and operation of branches. In the three southern states of Virginia, North and South Carolina, each larger than either Delaware or Rhode Island, no one bank operates many branches. The banking situation in these states is, therefore, quite similar in many respects to that in the states where only unit banks exist. Arizona and Vermont have few banks of any kind, limited banking resources, and comparatively few banks with branches. Perhaps branch banking in Maryland is most nearly analogous to that of California, but even in Maryland the geographical unit is small and the banks, with one possible exception, have but few branches.

In all other states where branch banking is permitted the branches are restricted to the city, county, or adjoining county of the parent bank. The number of branches and the volume of banking resources owned by the banks operating branches in the state of New York are both far greater than in the state of California. Yet New York State does not represent a branch banking system comparable to that of Canada, or any other national branch system common to all the leading commercial and industrial nations with the single exception of the United States. In some respects the system in New York is little different from unit banking. In fact it is frequently regarded as essentially a unit system, both by many of those who oppose and those who favor an extension of branch banking throughout this country. The branches are located within the corporate limits of the city of the parent institution, and consequently are likely to be called upon to do the same type of financing in general that is carried on at the head office. In these respects New York is similar to several other states, including Louisiana, Massachusetts, Michigan, Ohio, and Pennsylvania.

LEGAL STATUS OF BRANCH BANKING IN CALIFORNIA

Branch banking, as it now exists in the state of California, was legalized by the Bank Act of 1909. Prior to that year, several branches had been established under authority granted by the Civil Code and by regulations of the state banking commissioners. The Civil Code[1] had been interpreted by the attorney-general[2]

[1] Reference has been made to the Civil Code, the banking laws of the state of California and the banking reports of the banking commissioners during the early years of branch banking in the state.

[2] On October 7, 1903, the attorney-general, in a letter addressed to the bank commissioners, held that the "statutes . . . give express authority to banks in this State to open an agency in the same county in which the said bank is incorporated." Moreover he stated in the same letter that "I am therefore of the opinion that an authorized agency of a bank should do business in the name of its principal." *Banking Laws of California*, compiled by Commissioner Nehemiah Blackstock (1907), pp. 171-74. In 1905 the ruling was again referred to and the right to es-

of the state of California to permit state banks and trust companies to open and operate branches in that state. A limited number of banks had actually opened and were operating branches prior to the time when the first ruling of the attorney-general had been announced. It appears certain, therefore, that the earliest branches were secured or established by the banks on the theory that the right to establish and operate branches had not been denied them by the laws of that state.

The Bank Act of 1909 was enacted following a thorough study of banking conditions in California. This act was the first definite statute covering the organization, operation, and supervision of state banks. It provided for a departmental banking system and made provision for the establishment and operation of branches in that state. The act has been amended at different times, but the changes have been of a minor nature and have not altered in any striking way the original sections governing the opening and operation of branches, either within or without the city of the parent institution.

The original act sought to control the creation of branches by providing that all banks must have the written approval of the superintendent of banks before any branch or branches could be opened for business. Moreover the laws provided that the superintendent might grant or withhold the permit in his discretion, but permission should be withheld by the superintendent of banks until he had "ascertained to his satisfaction that the public convenience and advantage will be promoted by the opening of such branch office."[3] Furthermore the act provided that "no bank or any officer or director thereof, shall open or maintain such branch unless the capital of such branch, actually paid in cash, shall exceed the amount required by this act, by the sum of twenty-five

---

tablish agencies outside the county was considered to be within the meaning of the state statutes and laws:

"It is my opinion that the law cited by me in my former communication applies to the establishment, by a banking corporation organized under the laws of this state, of agencies either within or without the county in which it may have been incorporated or in which it may have its principal place of business." *Ibid.*, pp. 185-86.

[3] Sec. 9, California Bank Act of 1909.

thousand dollars for each branch office opened and maintained."[4] The purpose of the restriction just referred to was evidently to prohibit any bank from opening a chain of branches without adequate capital to protect the depositors, the public, and the stockholders.

The Act of 1909, as modified or amended, still contains the same provisions as regards "public convenience and advantage," and the requirements in connection with securing permission from the superintendent of banks to open a branch or branches. The capital requirements have been changed somewhat. The Act of 1929 provides that:

For each branch office located in the place of business of the parent bank, the paid-in capital, in cash, must exceed by $50,000 the capital required for the transaction of business by a bank in that place.[5] . . .

For each branch office of a bank, other than an exclusive trust company, located in any place in the State other than the place of the principal place of the business of the parent bank, the amount of paid-in capital, in cash, must exceed the amount required by law in the sum required for the organization of a bank in that locality, exclusive of the capital required for a trust department.[6] . . .

For each branch of an exclusive trust company opened or maintained in any place in the state other than the place of the principal business of the parent trust company, the paid-in capital, in cash, must exceed by $50,000 the amount required by law for the transaction of a trust company business.[7]

Other requirements were included:

There are also provisions concerning the discontinuance of a branch, increase of capital upon increase in deposits of branches, fee for the opening of a branch, penalty for violation of the law covering the establishment of branches, advertising by branch, and the establishment of branches by banks located in a city or territory which is annexed by or consolidated with a city or territory of a class requiring a larger capitalization.[8]

The provisions in the various sections of the Act of 1929 provide ample authority for governing the establishment, operation,

[4] *Ibid.*
[5] Sec. 9, *California Bank Act of 1929.*
[6] *Ibid.*, Sec. 9, 19, 23, 28, 60, and 82.
[7] *Ibid.*
[8] *Federal Reserve Bulletin*, April, 1930. p. 259.

supervision, and regulation of branches by state banks and trust companies in the state of California.

ECONOMIC CONDITIONS FAVORABLE FOR BRANCH BANKING

California is a large state with a varied climate. It is a state in which is produced a great variety of agriculture and commercial products. The diversified nature of business is such that branch banking is peculiarly adapted to meet the financial needs. The financial requirements of business men in the southern part of the state do not usually come at the same season that aid is required or needed in the northern part. Business in the coast regions does not coincide entirely with that of the interior. Inasmuch as these various demands arise at different times of the year, the large banks with branches can transfer funds from one community to another easily and cheaply, and in that way provide funds to meet the needs of the different sections of the state with a smaller amount of capital funds in the aggregate than could be done by means of unit banks. The branch bank is in a position to make a more economical use of its funds than is the unit bank. The branch bank is in a better position to judge the financial needs of the various communities than the other type of banking system. It is, or should be, in closer touch with a much larger section of the state than could be expected of a unit bank.

A state-wide system of branches facilitates the transfer of funds from one section, where there is a temporary surplus of funds, to another locality, where the demand for loans at a given time is greater than the volume of available funds for lending. The branch system is, in turn, strengthened, for the reason that the branch bank will not be obliged to employ so large a proportion of its funds in the money markets or in the purchase of investment securities. This should give the bank a more desirable portfolio, while at the same time rendering the maximum service in the financing of current business transactions of a short-term nature. Similar conditions do not exist in many small states, or even in some larger states where the diversification in the types of business carried on is limited. Examples of such states are Rhode Island, where the geographical area is small; or North Dakota, where agriculture of a very specialized type exists. Where the conditions are similar to those in Rhode Island and North Dakota, the branch banking unit must be greater than a single state, if the maximum benefit is to be derived from a well-organized and soundly-managed system of branches.

Branch banking had existed prior to 1909 in California on the basis of rulings of the banking commissioner, or without the direct authorization or approval of the banking authorities. Branches increased gradually from the enactment of the 1909 legislation, but the growth did not assume marked proportions until after the close of the World War, and more especially after the year 1922—the year in which Comptroller of the Currency D. R. Crissinger sanctioned the establishment of city offices or teller windows by national banks located in the states which permitted state banks and trust companies to organize and operate branches. Before discussing the development which followed the Act of 1909, it is desirable to sketch the earlier period in which branch banking had its beginning in the state, and which dates back to 1890, or even a bit earlier.

BRANCHES IN CALIFORNIA PRIOR TO 1909

It is difficult to say, definitely, just when the first domestic branch agency came into existence in California. It is clear that one or more agencies of state banks were in operation before 1890. These agencies were nothing more than mere local offices, and have no significance except from a historical point of view. The Citizens Bank, Nevada City, incorporated in 1876, established an agency at Grass Valley, California, which was reported by the banking commissioner as having been opened in 1888.[9] The Rideout Bank, Marysville, California, incorporated in November, 1890,[10] continued an agency which had been established by the firm or partnership of Rideout and Smith. The agency of the Rideout Bank was located at Gridley, California. Foreign banks had opened branches in the state several years before, but these two banks at Nevada City and Marysville may be regarded

[9] *Annual Report of the Bank Commissioner* (Sacramento, 1890), pp. 161, 174, 252.
[10] *Ibid.* (1891), pp. 176, 252.

as among the earliest to open and operate domestic branches.[11]

During the decade 1890-1900, there was no change of any importance as regards branch banking. The two banks, the Citizens Bank of Nevada City and Rideout Bank, still operated the branches which had been established in the late eighties. There was very little interest in the subject. Branch banking, at that time, had not become a banking issue. The decade from 1900 to 1910 saw a small and significant growth in the number of banks operating branches. In 1903 the following banks were reported by the banking commissioner as being interested in agencies:[12]

Bank	*Location*	*Location of Branch*
Nevada County Bank	Grass Valley	Nevada City
Rideout Bank	Marysville	Gridley
Citizens Bank	Nevada City	Grass Valley
Commercial Bank	San Luis Obispo	Arroyo Grande
Bank of Santa Maria	Santa Maria	Guadalupe

These banks were all small and did only a limited volume of banking business. It is doubtful if the Bank of Santa Maria and the Commercial Bank of San Luis Obispo established or opened branches at that time. No further record was found regarding the latter, and the former is not found in the banking reports again until 1906. The commissioner's report for 1905 shows the following five banks with one branch each:

Bank	*Location*	*Location of Branch*
Carlock Banking Co.	Fort Jones	Etna
Nevada County Bank	Grass Valley	Nevada City
Rideout Bank	Marysville	Gridley
Citizens Bank	Nevada City	Grass Valley
United Bank and Trust Company	San Francisco	San Francisco*

* This branch was discontinued in 1906. See *Report of the Banking Commission, 1906*, p. 18.

In relation to earlier years, there was a substantial propor-

[11] It would probably be more accurate to refer to the offices established prior to 1900 or 1905 as agencies rather than as branches. The distinction is not very important in view of the definition of branches included in the McFadden Act of 1927.

[12] *Ibid.* (1905), p. 46.

tionate increase during the years 1906 to 1908 inclusive. The number doubled in 1906 as compared to 1905. The following table, compiled from the reports of the commissioner of banking, shows the changes during the years 1906 to 1908 inclusive. For convenience there is included in the table the data for the period from 1890 to 1908:

Year	*Banks*	*Branches*
1890	2	2
1895	2	2
1900	2	2
1901	2	2
1902	2	2
1903	5	5
1904	5	5
1905	5	5
1906	10	12
1907	20	24*
1908	22	22†

* The California Bank of San Francisco, with four branches, failed Oct. 30, 1907. The French American Bank, San Francisco, was authorized to open a branch in 1907; the branch was retired during the same year, see *Annual Report of the Bank Commissioner* (1907), pp. 16-18. Four other banks had been authorized to open branches, but the branches did not appear to be in operation on June 30, 1907.

† The California Bank, Oakland, with one branch, was closed. *Ibid.* (1908), p. 18. The Farmers Savings Bank, Lakeport, and the Mission Bank, San Francisco, each closed one branch during the year. Five other banks were authorized to open branches, but these were not in operation on July 15, 1908.

The growth in the number of branches in 1906 and immediately thereafter was due in part to the conditions in San Francisco, following the earthquake and fire in that city during 1906. Many bank buildings were destroyed, and the banks established branches to provide banking facilities in different parts of the city. Some of these branches were established to meet an emergency situation and were, therefore, discontinued as soon as the city recovered sufficiently to make them unnecessary.

GROWTH OF BRANCH BANKING FROM 1910 TO 1918, INCLUSIVE

The changes in the number of branches, or of banks operating branches, directly following the passage of the Bank Act of 1909 were not very marked.[13] No bank is cited in the official reports as undertaking to create many branches during the period 1910-18. The largest number for any bank was twenty-three for the Bank of Italy in 1918, which was an increase of twenty-one branches during the period of nine years. The Home Savings Bank of Los Angeles had seven city branches at the end of June, 1918. No other bank in Los Angeles had more than four branches. A large portion of the branches of the Bank of Italy was located outside the corporate limits of San Francisco. The average number of branches per bank operating branches in 1918 was approximately two.

The following table, compiled from the reports of the state superintendent of banks, shows the number of banks operating branches and the number of branches in operation, by years, from 1910 to 1918 inclusive:

YEAR	NUMBER OF BANKS OPERATING BRANCHES	NUMBER OF BRANCHES	TOTAL NUMBER OF BANKS IN THE STATE	TOTAL NUMBER OF BANKING OFFICES
1910	33	36	455	491
1911	43	49	452	501
1912	52	64	455	519
1913	56	80	468	548
1914	55	77	473	550
1915	63	95	468	563
1916	66	105	460	565
1917	69	126	448	574
1918	75	148	429	577

These statistics in comparison with the data for 1908, the year before branch banking was specifically authorized, show that there were more than three times as many banks operating branches in 1918, and that these banks had nearly seven times as many branches.

The period 1910-18 was one in which no large banks were developed with an extensive system of branches. The banks which established branches were feeling their way. Branch banking was new and had to be entered into slowly and with considerable caution. The slow growth of branches should give some indication

[13] See p. 155 for data covering earlier years. Data for 1909 not available.

of the rapidity with which we should expect the development of a sound and conservative system of branches if the laws are changed to permit banks generally to go into the branch banking business. Reports of the superintendent of banks list a number of branches which were authorized and opened, but proved unsuccessful. Some of these branches were closed and some were sold. The unsuccessful branches were fairly well distributed between local or city branches and those located outside the limits of the city of the parent institution. The experience of the California branch bankers shows that it is not always possible to predict or decide in advance whether or not a branch will be profitable. No doubt the discontinuance of some of the branches during this period was due to a duplication of offices by reason of bank mergers. The number falling in this class was undoubtedly small.

THE DE NOVO RULE

About November 1, 1921, Jonathan S. Dodge, superintendent of banks, announced his future policy regarding the authorization or approval of new branches. This declaration has been generally referred to since as the *de novo* rule. It meant that, as a general policy, the superintendent would not approve the establishment of a branch outside the city of the parent institution, unless it could be shown that "public convenience or advantage" would be served thereby. It meant further that the department would not sanction the opening of new branches in communities outside that of the parent, where there were already a bank or banks in operation, unless such branches arose through a merger or consolidation with one of the existing institutions. One purpose of the rule was to restrict the extension of branch banking, while another was to protect unit banks against "unfair competition."

The *de novo* rule as stated by the superintendent is as follows:

> From and after the date no branch shall be created in any locality other than the city or locality in which is located the principal place of business, except by purchase of, or consolidation or merger with, an existing bank in said city or locality unless the superintendent of banks in his discretion shall find that the public convenience and advantage require it.

This rule was intended to direct the normal growth of branch banking through the purchase or absorption of existing banks, rather than through the creation of new branches in localities where unit banks or other branch banks were already in operation. The effect of this rule may be illustrated by reference to the situation in Los Angeles. During the period from the time the rule was promulgated to June, 1925, 103 permits were granted to open *de novo* branches in that city by banks located there, whereas only one was authorized to the Bank of Italy.

This exception was made because plans for opening the branch were well under way when the rule was issued. The Bank of Italy made application for permits to establish two more branches in Los Angeles, but they were denied under the *de novo* rule.[14]

The Bank of Italy regarded this rule as discriminatory, since without the rule it would have been possible for the bank to establish other branches in Los Angeles.

The Bank of Italy undertook to have the act amended to make possible the securing of branches which it had been denied through the rule issued by the superintendent of banks. Failing in this attempt at legislative action, it filed a petition for a writ of mandate which would compel the superintendent to give his written approval, permitting the Bank of Italy to establish in Los Angeles the branches which had been denied the bank as outlined in the preceding paragraph. The points at issue were twofold: the meaning of Section 9 of the Bank Act, and the validity of construction of the act as expressed in the *de novo* rule. The Bank of Italy held that the *de novo* rule was invalid, since (1) it was not in harmony with Section 9 of the Act, (2) the act did not authorize the superintendent to issue such a regulation, and (3), if it had, the law itself would be unconstitutional, because it involved the delegation of legislative powers.

On December 15, 1926, the Supreme Court of California handed down a decision in which it upheld Section 9 of the Bank Act and the superintendent of banks in carrying out the *de novo* rule, through the

[14] Westerfield, Ray B. "The Branch Bank Crisis in California," *The Annalist*, Sept. 25, 1925, p. 374.

. . . lawful exercise of the powers of the superintendent of banks as a policy to be followed by him and as an indication to applicants for branch bank permits of the showing necessary to be made to entitle them to obtain affirmative action on their applications, but in no sense as restricting, modifying, or controlling his statutory discretion.[15]

The action of the court in this case established definitely the power of the superintendent of banks to regulate branch banking. In the exercise of his discretionary powers in interpreting and applying the principle that the "public convenience and advantage" must be served, the superintendent of banks might thereafter decide that it was in the interest of public policy to abolish or suspend the so-called *de novo* rule.

CHANGES IN BRANCH BANKING AFTER 1918

There was no immediate marked change either in the number of banks operating branches or in the number of branches being operated in 1919 as compared with 1918. The data included in the study following 1918 cover national banks as well as state banks and trust companies, whereas the data for the earlier periods do not contain either national banks or their branches. The number of national banks operating branches in California prior to 1919 was so small that the results would not have been materially different had they been included. In 1919 there were only 2 national banks in the state with branches, and they had only 6 branches between them. The total number of banks operating branches in 1919 was 74, including the two national banks, as compared with 75 state banks and trust companies in 1918. The total number of branches in existence in 1919 was 155, including branches of national banks.

The growth in the number of banks operating branches was very slow until 1922. During that year the total number of national banks, state banks, and trust companies operating branches rose from 79 to 87. Then followed a three-year period in which the number of such banks increased to 106. This proved to be the peak year as regards the total number of branch banks. During 1926 there was a substantial decrease in the number of banks

[15] *Pacific Reporter*, CCLI, 798.

TABLE 16

NUMBER OF BANKS OPERATING BRANCHES IN CALIFORNIA, THE NUMBER OF BRANCHES IN OPERATION AND THE TOTAL RESOURCES OF BANKS, CLASSIFIED ACCORDING TO ALL BANKS OPERATING BRANCHES, STATE BANKS AND TRUST COMPANIES, AND NATIONAL BANKS, BY YEARS, 1919–32*

(In millions of dollars)

YEAR	ALL STATE BANKS, TRUST COMPANIES AND NATIONAL BANKS OPERATING BRANCHES					ALL STATE BANKS AND TRUST COMPANIES OPERATING BRANCHES					ALL NATIONAL BANKS OPERATING BRANCHES				
	Number of Banks	Branches			Total Resources	Number of Banks	Branches			Total Resources	Number of Banks	Branches			Total Resources
		Total	*In*	*Out*			*Total*	*In*	*Out*			*Total*	*In*	*Out*	
1919	74	155	49	106	709	72	149	49	100	584	2	6		6	125
1920	78	171	56	115	933	76	165	56	109	808	2	6		6	125
1921	79	196	70	126	1,042	77	190	70	120	948	2	6		6	94
1922	87	285	122	163	1,343	81	275	115	160	1,102	6	10	7	3	241
1923	100	458	208	250	1,771	86	436	189	247	1,459	14	22	19	3	312
1924	99	534	259	275	2,093	84	505	233	272	1,760	15	29	26	3	333
1925	106	606	300	306	2,456	86	551	249	302	2,081	20	55	51	4	376
1926	87	687	343	344	2,753	72	603	270	333	2,277	15	84	73	11	476†
1927	68	793	318	475	2,818	57	342	184	158	1,483	11	451	134	317	1,337
1928	62	799	304	495	3,024	52	351	168	183	1,468	10	448	136	312	1,554
1929	52	894	326	548	3,402	42	378	155	223	1,407	10	496	171	325	1,995
1930	54	830	274	556	3,217	41	290	107	183	1,109	13	540	167	373	2,109
1931	52	806	262	544	2,872	40	286	105	181	1,104	12	520	157	363	1,768
1932	48	804	267	537	‡	35	276	102	174	‡	13	528	165	363	‡

* Source: Compiled from official reports of the department of banking, with the assistance of officials and employees of the office of the superintendent of banks.

† The large increase in the resources of national banks operating in 1927 and the corresponding decline in resources of state banks is explained largely by the conversion of the Bank of Italy into a national bank. For an explanation of this change, see pp. 161–62.

‡ Not available.

operating branches. This condition applied both to state banks and national banks. Table 16 shows the number of banks operating branches year by year from 1919 to 1932 inclusive. The data are segregated according to national banks, state banks and trust companies. Chart IV shows the total number of banks with branches. There were only 52 branch banks in 1931 (and 48 in 1932), including both state and national banks.

There was a slow growth in the total number of branches during the years 1919-21 inclusive. Beginning with 1922 the number rose quite rapidly till it reached a peak in 1929 with 894 branches. It is interesting to observe that the expansion in the number of branches came after the ruling in 1922 of Comptroller of the Currency D. R. Crissinger, permitting national banks to operate teller windows or additional offices. This increase came first of all among state banks and trust companies, and not among the national banks. The changes in the total number of branches, the number of branches operated by state banks and trust companies, and the number of branches owned by national banks are given in Chart IV. The data on which the chart is based will be found in Table 16.

The number of branches operated by national banks was comparatively small until the passage of the McFadden-Pepper Act in 1927. This act authorized national banks, under certain conditions, to establish branches, and in that way encouraged many national banks to consider favorably the possibility of establishing and operating a large number of branches. There was a striking increase in the number of branches belonging to national banks in 1927, as compared with earlier years. This great advance is accounted for very largely, however, by the conversion of the Bank of Italy into a national bank and the absorption of the Pacific Southwest Trust and Savings Bank by the Los Angeles First National Trust and Savings Bank. The Pacific Southwest Trust and Savings Bank had 101 branches at the time of the merger. The Bank of Italy had a much larger number of branches than the Pacific Southwest Trust and Savings Bank. The change of these two banks from one system to another did not increase or diminish the total number of branches for the state as a whole, but it did change materially the situation for each class individually, by decreasing the number in the state system and by increasing the number of branches in the national system. The shift is set forth also in Chart IV.

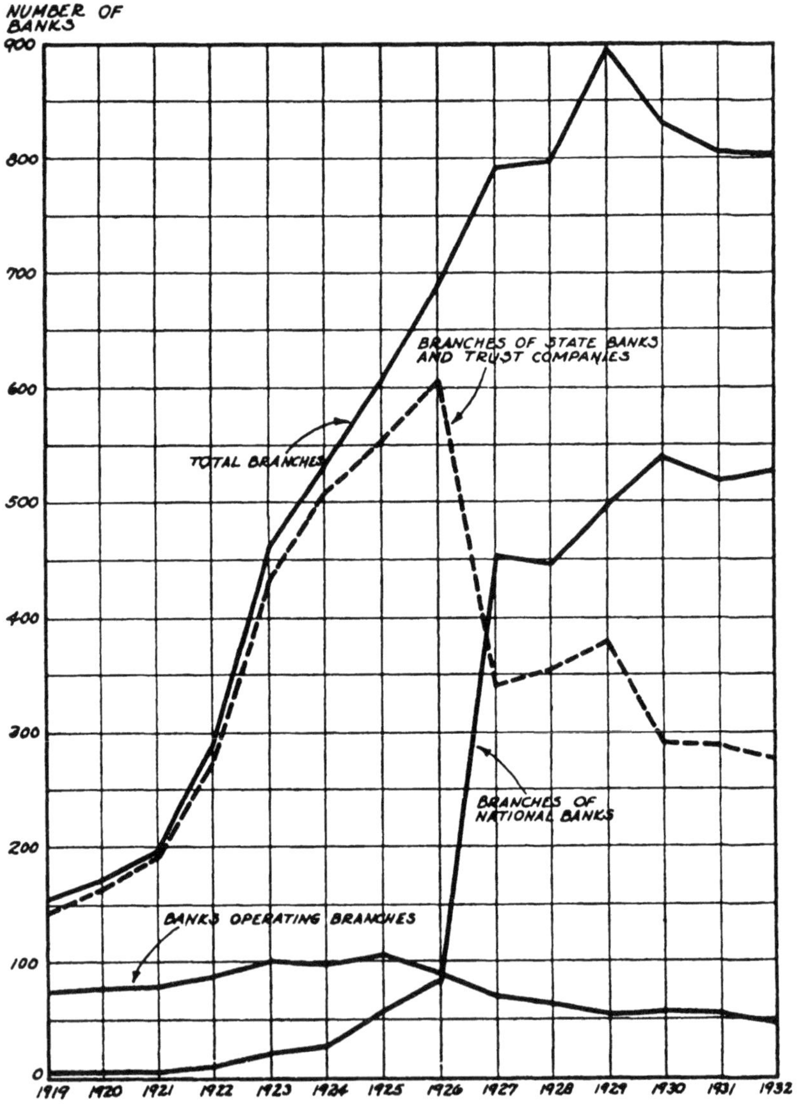

CHART IV. NUMBER OF BRANCH BANKS AND BRANCHES IN CALIFORNIA

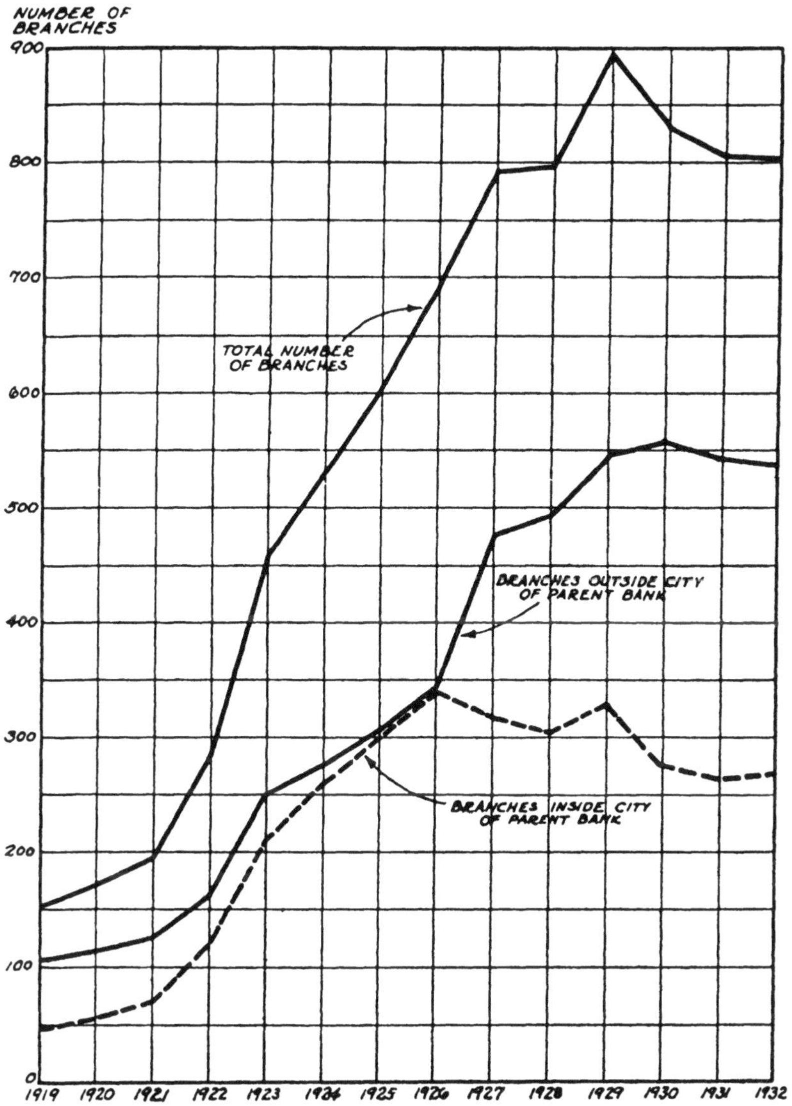

CHART V. DISTRIBUTION OF BRANCHES IN CALIFORNIA, ACCORDING TO LOCATION

A large portion of the total number of branches in existence in the state of California is found outside the city of the parent institution. In this respect the situation differs fundamentally from that in states like Ohio, New York, and Massachusetts, where there is a very extensive system of branches, practically all of which are located inside the city of the parent bank. Prior to 1927 the number of branches operated by national banks for the state as a whole was rather limited. Beginning with and following the year 1927, the total of outside branches for national banks greatly exceeded those located within the city limits of the parent bank. The Bank of Italy has had a powerful influence upon the total number of branches in the state of California. In fact, in later years it has actually owned and operated almost 50 percent of all branches in the state. If its position be measured in terms of total resources, the results are quite different on account of the other large banks operating branches, though they had established only a small number in comparison with the Bank of Italy and its closely allied institutions. Chart V, shows the total number of branches in the state, as well as the number of branches both inside the city of the parent bank and those outside the corporate limits of the city of the parent institution.

The total resources of all branch-banking institutions showed an increase each year from 1919 to 1929. The growth is illustrated by Chart VI. This chart shows a very sharp and decisive upward trend in the total volume of resources of branch banks. The rise was, in fact, almost perpendicular. A comparison of the total resources of national banks with the total resources of state banks and trust companies shows essentially the same relationship between the state and national institutions as regards branch banking as that shown by the comparison of the total number of branches operated by these two classes of institutions.[16] There was a very rapid increase in the resources for state banks and trust companies prior to the year 1927. The three years following 1927 registered large decreases. The total resources for national banks increased slowly from 1921 to 1927, after which there was a striking upward trend during the years 1927 to 1930, inclusive. The difference in the growth or changes in the total resources of state banks and national banks has been explained[17] by the conversion of the Bank of Italy to the national system in the early

[16] For a comparison of the number of branches in this respect see pp. 161-63 above.

[17] See p. 161 above.

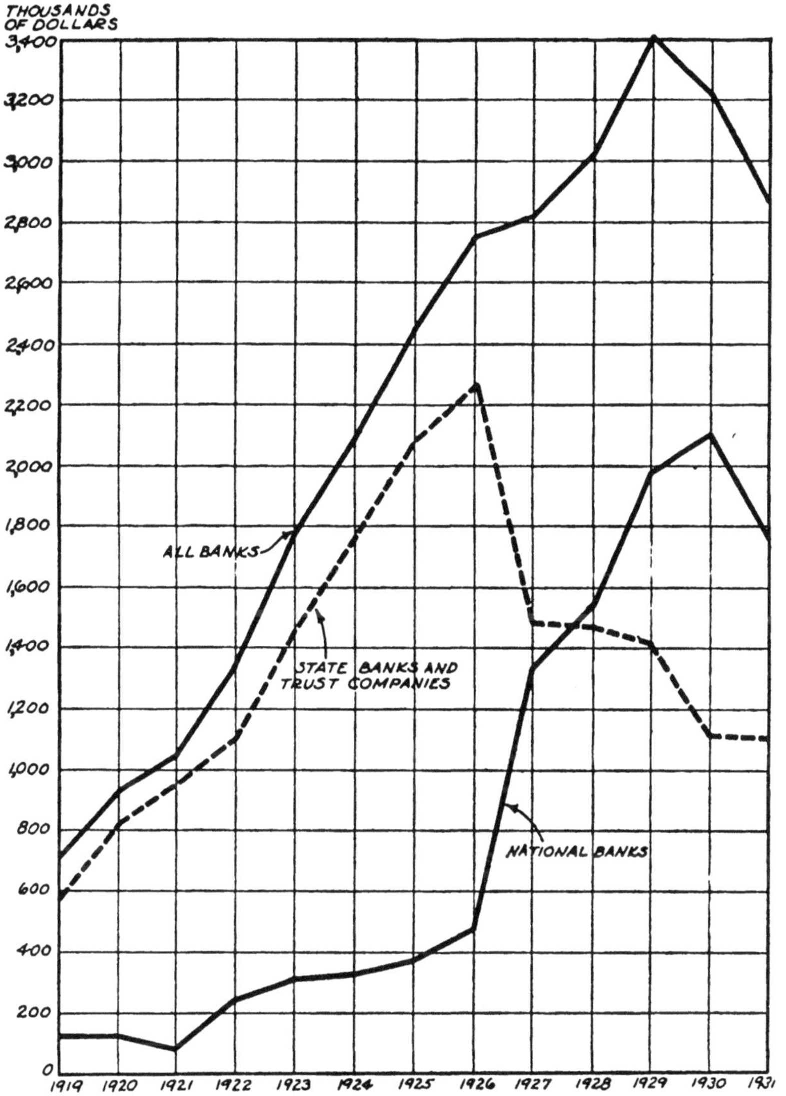

CHART VI. TOTAL RESOURCES OF BANKS OPERATING BRANCHES IN CALIFORNIA

part of 1927, and the absorption of the Pacific Southwest Trust and Savings Bank by the Los Angeles First National Trust and Savings Bank in September, 1927.

TABLE 17

GROWTH OF BRANCH BANKING IN CALIFORNIA, 1919–31*
(In millions of dollars)

YEAR	TOTAL NUMBER OF BANKS	MEMBER FEDERAL RESERVE SYSTEM	BRANCHES			CAPITAL SURPLUS, AND UN-DIVIDED PROFITS	LOANS AND DISCOUNTS	INVEST-MENTS	DEPOSITS			DUE TO BANKS	TOTAL RE-SOURCES
			Total	*In City*	*Outside City*				*De-mand*	*Time*	*Total*		
1919	74	4	155	49	106	68	392	157	184	409	587	10	709
1920	78	17	171	56	115	86	560	199	248	539	786	12	933
1921	79	23	196	70	126	102	633	234	260	626	886	29	1042
1922	87	29	285	122	163	119	727	277	400	733	1133	66	1343
1923	100	34	458	208	250	159	1,112	330	553	932	1484	75	1771
1924	99	33	534	259	275	184	1,290	390	656	1098	1754	113	2093
1925	106	37	606	300	306	203	1,493	519	719	1372	2091	125	2456
1926	87	31	687	343	344	225	1,693	570	762	1559	2319	149	2753
1927	68	22	793	318	475	249	1,926	667	742	1606	2348	143	2818
1928	62	18	799	304	495	297	1,725	822	781	1692	2474	159	3024
1929	52	16	894	326	548	320	1,974	727	828	1920	2748	211	3402
1930	54	17	830	274	556	304	1,778	749	754	1844	2598	212	3217
1931	52	16	806	262	544	302	1,565	811	660	1676	2336	125	2872

* Includes state banks, trust companies, mutual savings banks and national banks. Compiled from official records of the office of the Comptroller of the Currency and of the office of the banking department of California.

TIME VERSUS DEMAND DEPOSITS

A large proportion of the total deposits of banks and trust companies operating branches in the state of California have been, and are, time deposits. In this respect the development of branch banking in that state has been along the lines of savings deposits. Time deposits are much greater relatively for the state of California than for banks operating branches in the country as a whole. The actual figures showing the volume of each class of deposits are shown in Table 17. Chart VII shows the growth of the total volume, as well as for each class of deposits. The relationship between these two classes has remained fairly uniform, though the actual percentage has varied from year to year. Of the total amount for the eleven-year period, slightly less than 70 percent has been time deposits. The volume of total loans and discounts has about kept pace with the increasing volume of demand deposits, while the same ratio obtains as between time deposits and investments. Neither branch banking nor the increase in the number of branches being operated has had any appreciable effect upon the type of portfolio of branch banks in the state. The data show that the time deposits are only partially invested in long-term securities. Time deposits are treated much the same as are demand deposits. It may be true that a large amount of the so-called time deposits are really in the demand class, though included as time deposits for various reasons.

RELATION OF BANK MERGERS TO BRANCH BANKING

The growth of branches in California has been very closely associated with the merger and consolidation movement among banks in that state. In fact, the desire on the part of bankers to secure branches, or locations at which branches could be established, has been the most powerful force at work to bring about bank mergers, which reached their peak in 1927. No other factor has been so effective in bringing to completion a large number of bank mergers and consolidations. The *de novo* rule, adopted and put into effect in the latter part of 1921, has made it necessary for banks wishing to increase or expand their branch-banking activities to absorb or take over existing banks in those localities

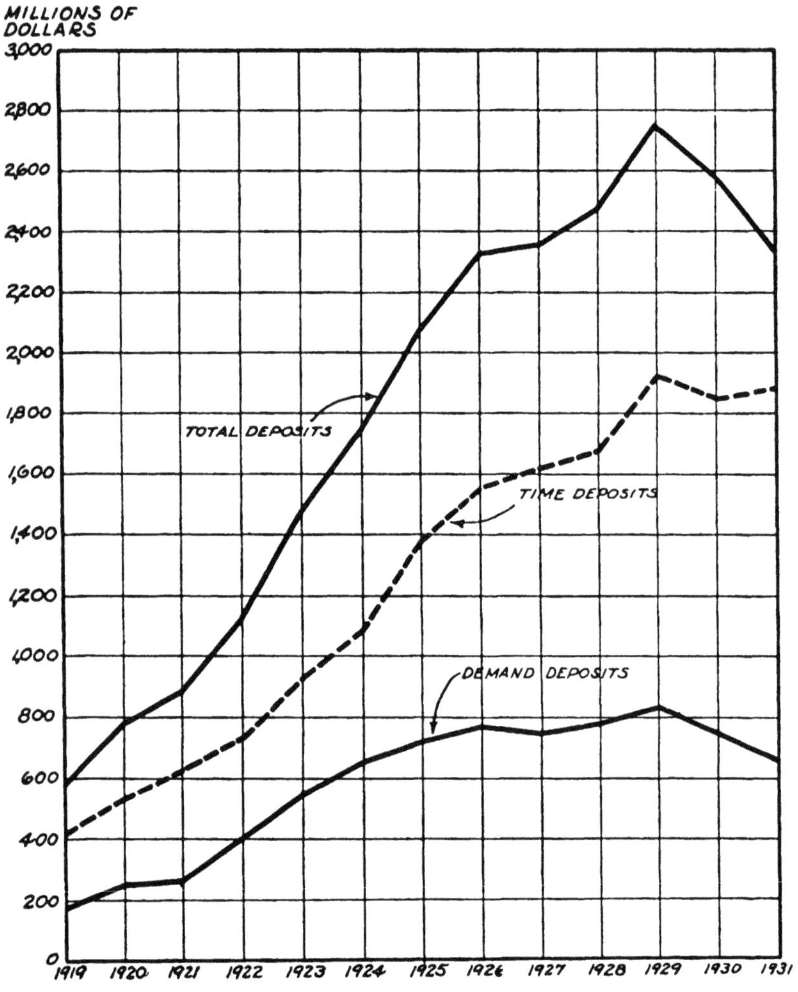

CHART VII. TOTAL DEPOSITS OF BANKS OPERATING BRANCHES IN CALIFORNIA

where the new offices were to be located. The presence of a small bank or banks in most of the communities in the state left little opportunity to find a place where a new branch could be established without conflicting with the *de novo* rule. In this connection the *de novo* rule was most effective.

A large percentage of all branches in operation in the state during the period 1921-32 has been owned and controlled by a small number of large banks. Several banks have been operating branches but, for the most part, such banks have had only two or three branches each, and many have been operating only one branch each. A study of the individual branch banks that operated branches during a part or all of this period shows definitely that the banks with the largest number of branches are the banks that have been most active in absorbing other institutions, either in or outside the limits of the city of the parent bank. A small number of large banks has taken over a comparatively large number of small banks, which have been made branch offices of the larger institutions. The following branch banks stand out prominently as leaders in this phase of the concentration movement:

Bank	*Location of Head Office*
The Bank of Italy (later became a national bank)	San Francisco
The Liberty Bank (later absorbed by the Bank of Italy)	San Francisco
Security Bank and Trust Company	San Francisco*
United Bank and Trust Company	San Francisco
Bank of America of California (later absorbed by the Bank of Italy)	San Francisco
Mercantile Trust Company	San Francisco
Security Trust and Savings Bank (later a national bank)	Los Angeles
Pacific Southwest Trust and Savings Bank	Los Angeles†

* The Security Bank and Trust Company was formerly located at Bakersfield. It later was merged with the United Bank and Trust Company and changed the head office to San Francisco. The latter institution is now a part of the Bank of America National Trust and Savings Association, San Francisco.

† The Pacific Southwest Trust and Savings Bank was merged with the First National Bank and entered the national system.

The eight banks listed above have absorbed a very large percentage of all banks taken over and have been the principal branch banks in the state in so far as numbers are concerned. The first five have been known as members of the Transamerica Corporation group, or the Bank of Italy, and have been dominated by the

Giannini management. The Bank of Italy group has been, by all odds, the most important element in the development of a state-wide system of branches in California. This has been especially noticeable in connection with the extension of so-called "outside branches." The Los Angeles group has been quite active in extending city branches, but less interested in state-wide branches. In brief, the Bank of Italy, or the banks associated or affiliated with the Transamerica Corporation or its predecessors, have been largely responsible for the rapid extension and growth of branches in California and have attained their ends largely by bank mergers and consolidations.

BANK OF ITALY GROUP

During the second half of 1930 the Transamerica Corporation undertook to consolidate its various units. Its work in this connection was described by one public official as follows:

> During the latter part of 1930 the Transamerica Group decided to consolidate or merge all of its various holdings into two banks. An attempt was made to take all of their various nominally independent banks and all branches eligible for conversion to the national system and merge them with the existing Bank of Italy National Trust and Savings Association. The other holdings of the Transamerica Group that were not eligible for conversion to the national system formed the nucleus for a new state bank, the Bank of America, Los Angeles. This latter institution was not a successor to the Bank of America of California, though it acquired a fair portion of the latter's assets. It was simply a new corporation created on November 3, 1930, into which were brought former independent banks and branches of the Bank of America of California which were not eligible for conversion to the national system. Legally, the Bank of America of California was merged into and with the Bank of Italy National Trust and Savings Association and the latter's name was changed to the Bank of America National Trust and Savings Association. This, however, was not a complete merger as explained above, for all of the assets of the Bank of America of California were not taken into the Bank of Italy National Trust and Savings Association.

The most important bank mergers of the banks involving the Bank of Italy and other subsidiary banks of the Transamerica Corporation are shown in Chart VIII. The various holding companies owned and controlled by the Transamerica Corporation are indicated in Chart IX. These two charts, taken together, give us a fairly accurate picture of the extent and scope of this interesting group.

Without bank mergers and consolidations there would naturally have been some extension of state-wide branches, but the devel-

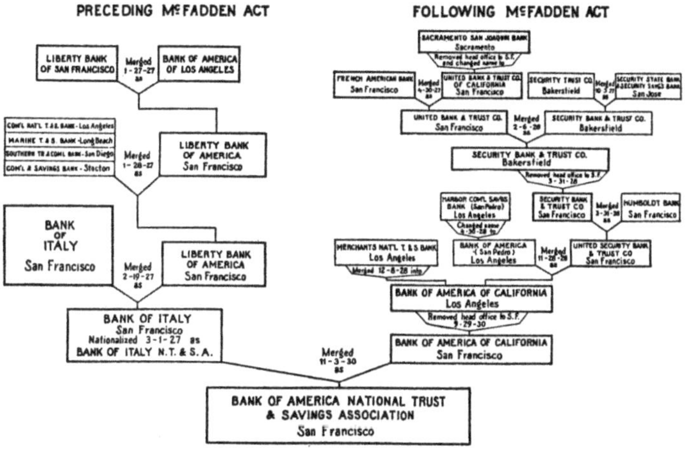

CHART VIII. PRINCIPAL BANKS OPERATING BRANCHES, AND BANKING UNITS MERGED TO FORM BANK OF AMERICA NATIONAL TRUST AND SAVINGS ASSOCIATION, SAN FRANCISCO[a]

[a] Source: Report of the Federal Reserve Committee on Branch, Group, and Chain Banking, 1932, on *Branch Banking in California.*

opment would have been small in comparison with what exists at the present time. Bank mergers and consolidations have been the means not only for expanding branch banking, but also for reducing the number of unit banks throughout the state. In no other state in the Union has the relationship between branch banking and bank mergers been so close as in California. Table 18 summarizes the bank-merger movement in California from 1919 to 1931 inclusive.

CONCLUSIONS

The state of California holds the premier place among states in this country in the development of branch banking, and has had more influence in this direction in recent years than any other state. In this connection, state banks and trust companies held the stage until after the passage of the McFadden Act in 1927, after which, through conversion of state banks into the national

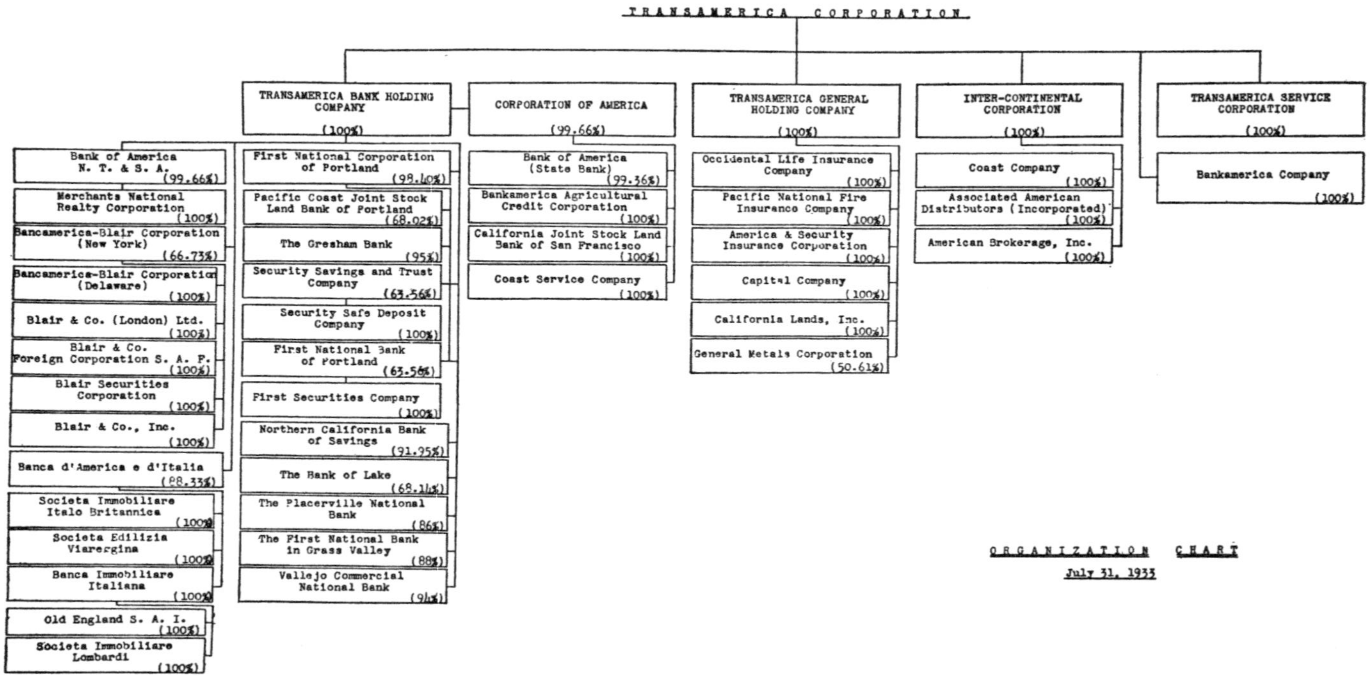

CHART IX. THE ORGANIZATION CHART OF THE TRANSAMERICA CORPORATION AND ITS SUBSIDIARIES

TABLE 18

DATA OF BANK MERGERS AND CONSOLIDATIONS IN CALIFORNIA, 1919–32*

(In millions of dollars)

YEAR	NUMBER OF MERGERS	NUMBER OF BANKS	TOTAL NUMBER OF BANKS ABSORBED	NATIONAL BANKS ABSORBED BY NATIONAL BANKS	STATE BANKS ABSORBED BY NATIONAL BANKS	STATE BANKS ABSORBED BY STATE BANKS	NATIONAL BANKS ABSORBED BY STATE BANKS	DATA OF BANKS PRIOR TO MERGER							DATA OF BANKS AFTER MERGER				
								MEMBER FEDERAL RESERVE SYSTEM	Branches			CAPITAL, SURPLUS AND UNDIVIDED PROFITS	TOTAL ASSETS	MEMBER FEDERAL RESERVE SYSTEM	Branches			CAPITAL, SURPLUS AND UNDIVIDED PROFITS	TOTAL ASSETS
									Total	*In*	*Out*				*Total*	*In*	*Out*		
1919	12	23	12	3		7	2	9				13	138	4				13	167
1920	19	34	19	2	1	10	6	18				36	274	12				42	473
1921	23	51	33	3		13	17	30				47	493	9				51	680
1922	68	88	68	2	1	39	26	43				74	632	12				80	1,066
1923	57	77	57	1		42	14	31				84	943	9				103	1,216
1924	36	48	36		1	19	16	20				82	1,032	7				81	1,127
1925	53	65	57	2	2	36	17	21	194	102	92	65	634	5	234	107	127	55	730
1926	37	50	37	6		23	8	27	309	151	158	80	1,113	10	354	155	199	84	1,199
1927	126	142	126	6	11	70	39	65	322	165	157	169	1,776	12	597	169	428	138	1,693
1928	69	74	69	10	12	33	14	28	449	154	295	119	1,362	3	528	150	378	189	1,461
1929	29	39	29	1	4	13	11	20	337	194	143	216	2,032	4	759	242	517	218	2,446
1930	15	20	15	4	5	4	2	13	439	75	364	150	1,300	4	416	46	307	116	1,223
1931	13	23	13	7	1	0	5	16	417	46	371	125	1,155	4	415	45	370	112	1,119

* Source: *Annual Reports* of the superintendent of banks for the state of California.

system, national banks have been in the lead. The following summary may be made of the California situation:

1. California has a state-wide branch banking system with an extensive system of branches extending over the state.

2. A few large banks own and control a very large percentage of all branches in operation in the state.

3. The number of branches located outside the city of the parent bank is much greater than the number of branches located within the corporate limits of the city of the parent institution. In this respect it differs fundamentally from other large states like New York and Ohio.

4. The volume of time deposits reported for the branch banks in California is approximately double the amount of demand deposits held by the same banks.

5. The so-called *de novo* rule has had a very important bearing upon the method used by banks in establishing branches outside the limits of the city of the parent banks.

6. There has been a very close relationship between the expansion of branches and the number and location of bank mergers throughout the state. In this respect the *de novo* rule has been very influential and has been directly responsible for the extension of branches in this way in many cases.

7. The greatest extension of branches has taken place since the close of the World War. Especially has the growth been marked since 1922, the year in which the Comptroller of the Currency granted the privilege to national banks to establish additional offices under certain circumstances.

8. The commercial, industrial, and agricultural conditions in the state of California are such that the branch system of banking is admirably adapted to meet the needs of the community. Funds can easily be shifted from one part of the state to another. Surplus funds in one part of the state can easily be made available to another part. Banks are placed in a position in which they may more generally use their funds in the state for the purpose of financing industry there than in many other states where such interbank relations do not exist. California branch banks should be, therefore, less dependent upon the money markets in the large centers than are the banks of most states.

CHAPTER X

THE LEGAL STATUS OF BRANCH BANKING

Our multiple system of banking has resulted in a very extensive and cumbersome body of banking legislation. This legislation lacks uniformity in its general provisions regarding the creation of banks and their methods of doing business. A survey of banking legislation in this country, both national and state, shows conclusively that there is absolutely no uniformity in regard to branch banking. The national banking system extends to national banks in the operation of branches the same rights and privileges enjoyed by state institutions of the state in which the national bank is located, not including, of course, foreign branches. National banking laws, as well as the state laws, are more favorable to the extension of foreign than of domestic branches. Some state laws permit the operation of state-wide branches; others prohibit them on any basis. Between these two extremes there are several variations. Local branches are permitted in a few states, while in others there are no references in the statutes to branches. Banking laws in a few states allow banks to operate any branches in existence at the time of the passage of the given law, but prohibit the opening of new branches. In one state, we find that the county is the unit. In Kentucky a limited number of branches are operated as a result of a court decision.

Only a casual or superficial study of the provisions of state banking laws is required to appreciate the complete absence of any definite and permanent national policy toward branch banking. It appears doubtful that many banks in any state have had, from the earliest days, complete freedom in the operation of branches. State banks in Georgia were, for a time, allowed to establish and operate branches on a state-wide basis. Provisions of the laws relative to branches were repealed after the failure in 1926 of several banks which were connected with a large chain of banks some of which had a few branches. Another factor which had considerable influence, perhaps, was the provisions of the McFadden Act prohibiting all member banks from establishing branches outside the city of the parent. By repealing the state law, it put all banks on a more nearly equal basis. In 1929 the laws in Georgia were amended to permit state banks to organize and operate branches either in the city or municipality of the parent bank. In Indiana before the Civil War the State Bank of Indiana successfully operated several branches. The acts of the state legislature in Indiana for 1921 and 1929 denied to state banks the right to establish branches. As a result of the large number of bank failures, the laws were amended in 1930 to permit state banks to operate branches within their respective counties. The laws of the state of West Virginia for a number of years made no specific mention of branches. Legal opinion interpreted the law as being favorable to the extension of branches, but the superintendent of banks ruled against this type of banking. The state legislature in 1929 amended the laws so as to provide definite legislation to prohibit the establishment of branches by state banks and trust companies in that state.[1]

BRANCHES "IN" AND "OUTSIDE" THE CITY

The classification of branches as "city branches" and "outside city branches" has made necessary, in some cases, legal provisions limiting the class of business which may be done by these branches. The designation of the city branches as "additional offices" or "agencies," as distinguished from branches with power to do a full-fledged banking business, has accentuated the tendency to classify branches as "in city" or "outside city." The differences are less marked in this connection than is the case with the capital provisions, but in some instances the administrators regard the difference between an additional office and a branch as fundamental. Some banking officials go so far as to maintain that the latter is branch banking whereas the former is not. To accept the principle that additional offices or the local city offices are not branches,

[1] Despite the laws to the contrary, one or two state banks have operated a branch or branches in that state during the past two or three years.

is to narrow the whole field and, in fact, to relegate it to an unimportant place in our American banking system. There seems to be little justification for this sharp line of demarcation between "city offices" and those "outside" the limits of the parent institution. It is true that until we have had a very considerable development of branches outside the corporate limits of the parent bank, we shall not have the type of branch banking that has won much favor in all other leading industrial and commercial nations. In short we cannot secure the advantages of branch banking generally recognized by branch-banking countries until we have modified our laws so that we may realize the advantages of wide diversification of business, which will reflect itself in the character and quality of the bank portfolios.

THE NATIONAL BANKING SYSTEM

The original National Bank Act,[2] enacted in 1863 during the trying days of the Civil War, contained no provisions specifically for or against the creation and operation of branches by national banks. Branch banking was not an important phase of the banking problem at that time. Two sections included in the act of 1863, however, referring indirectly or by implication to branch banking, were in part as follows:

> The place where its operation of discount and deposit are to be carried on, designating the state, territory, or district, and also the particular county, and city, town or village.[3]
>
> . . . and its usual business shall be transacted in banking offices located at the places specified respectively in its certificate of organization.[4]

In the revision of 1864 of the National Bank Act, the words "offices" and "places" were changed to "office" and "place." The amended sections read as follows:

> . . . its usual business shall be transacted at an office or banking house located in the place specified in its organization certificate.[5]

[2] See Chap. VIII for a discussion of branch banking following the Civil War.

[3] 12 Stat. L., 666; 13 Stat. L., 100, Sec. 6, Senate Document 582 (1910), p. 157. See also Andrew M. Davis' *Origin of the National Banking System*. (Washington: National Monetary Commission Report, 1910).

[4] 12 Stat. L., 668, Sec. 11. See also Sen. Doc. 582, p. 162.

[5] Act of June 3, 1864, 13 Stat. L., 99, Chap. CVI. See also A. T. Huntington and R. J. Mawhinney's *Laws of the United States Concerning Money, Banking and Loans* (1910), p. 334.

The Amendment to the National Bank Act in 1865 provided that a state bank with branches could be converted into a national bank and retain all the branches it had at the time of conversion. Branch banking was discussed from time to time both by bankers and economists, but it was not widely considered again until after the depression of 1893. Discussions of branch banking appeared again in a rather forcible way after the panic of 1907. It seems to have been a practice in this country to discuss this phase of banking after each panic or severe depression. Heavy losses growing out of the panic of 1907, no doubt, had much to do with a revival of interest in this subject which, however, was checked to some extent by the opinion handed down by the Attorney-General, George W. Wickersham, in 1911, to the effect that the National Bank Act did not authorize national banks to operate branches.

Another step in the procession came in 1918 at about the close of the war, which was, in so far as branches were concerned, an amendment or addition to the act of 1865. The act of November, 1918, dealt primarily with the problems involved in the consolidation of banks, whereas the act of 1865, as already pointed out, provided that a state bank could convert into a national bank and retain its branches. The act of 1918 permitted a national bank to take over another national bank and operate any branches which the absorbed bank had at the time such merger took place. This was not an important step in the development of branches, though a few were transferred from one national bank to another under the provisions of this act.

THE MCFADDEN-PEPPER ACT[6]

The McFadden-Pepper Act, approved February 25, 1927, was intended to achieve several results as regards the future of branch banking. The act itself was the result of several years of discussion and reflected the attitude of a group in this country who sought to curb the development of that type of banking. Under the guise of putting the national banks on a competitive basis with state banks and trust companies, it was provided, for the

[6] For a fuller and more complete discussion of the provisions of the McFadden Act relative to branch banking, see Chap. VIII, pp. 144-46.

first time, that national banks could establish branches, with the consent of the Comptroller of the Currency, in states permitting state banks or trust companies to operate branches, provided the branches of such national banks were located within the city of the parent institution. This act, therefore, both recognized the existence of branches and, at the same time, contained provisions designed to restrict a further extension of branches to the city of the parent.

The theory of the McFadden Act is in harmony with the idea back of Comptroller Crissinger's ruling in 1922 in its implication that there is a fundamental difference between the operation of branches within the city of the parent and those operated outside the city. According to this theory, city branches are merely receiving stations for deposits and the cashing of checks. The establishment of such branches is a method of facilitating banking business in a given community or locality. The theory that these "offices" do not make loans and do a general banking business is erroneous. Such branches are under the direction and supervision of the head office just the same as a branch or office is in any other line of business.

More specifically, the act contained the following provisions:

1. The establishment of city branches by national banks was legalized. Any national bank which had been operating an office or branch for twenty-five years without permission was guaranteed the right to continue such office as a legal part of the bank. National banks located in states which permitted state branch banking could, with the approval of the Comptroller of the Currency, establish branches within the city with power to receive deposits and make loans.

2. The act attempted to legalize local branch banking on one hand, and on the other to check a further growth of branches outside the city limits.

3. The act was designed to check the extension of branches by state banks and trust companies, through the control of membership in the Federal Reserve system. The sponsors of this legislation undoubtedly overestimated the hold which the Federal Reserve system had upon a large percentage of the state banks and

trust companies which were interested in the development of an extensive system of branches.

THE BANK ACT OF 1933

An important step was taken in the development of branch banking by national banks by the passage of the Glass-Steagall Bank Act, June 16, 1933. This Act provided that national banks should have the same rights and privileges in establishing branches that had been granted to state banks and trust companies in the state in which the national bank or banks are located. Local branches had been legalized by the McFadden Act in 1927, whereas this new act made it possible for national banks to operate branches on a state-wide basis in all states where state banks were permitted to establish and operate branches. There are about seventeen states and the District of Columbia in which national banks may now operate branches on a state-wide basis, while in a few other states they may operate branches anywhere within the county or adjoining county.[7]

STATE BANKS

From a legal point of view the status of branch banking in the several states may be outlined briefly as follows:

1. *States in which branch banking is prohibited.*—As already indicated, the number of states in this group fluctuates considerably. On September 1, 1933, the following states had legislation prohibiting the establishment of branches by state banks:

Alabama	Minnesota
Arkansas	Missouri
Colorado	Nebraska
Florida	New Mexico
Illinois	Texas
Kansas	West Virginia

The following states included in this group have in operation a few branches even though further extension is prohibited:

Alabama	Minnesota
Arkansas	Nebraska

[7] For a more extensive discussion of the principles and implications of this act, see pp. 146-47.

In the two states of Minnesota and Nebraska only national banks have branches, while in Alabama and Arkansas only state banks have branches. In the case of state banks, the branches were in existence at the time the prohibitory legislation was enacted, but were allowed to continue in operation. There has been a tendency for this type of branch to disappear gradually.

2. *States in which banks are permitted to establish and operate branches on a restricted basis, as distinguished from a state-wide basis.*—The following is a list of the states, together with the territorial unit for branches in each state, in which banks are permitted to establish and operate branches within a very definite and limited geographical area:

State	*Territorial Unit*
Georgia	City or municipality.
Indiana	Same county.
Iowa	Office in contiguous counties if no other bank or office is located in city or town.
Kentucky	By court decisions may establish additional offices or agencies to receive deposits and pay checks.
Louisiana	Municipality or parish.
Maine	County or adjoining county.
Massachusetts	Same town.
Mississippi	Same city.
Montana	In county or adjoining county by continuing offices of bank obtained through merger.
New Jersey	Same city, town, township, borough, or village, or county if branches are secured through merger.
New York	City of parent, or outside New York State.
Ohio	Same city, or city or village contiguous thereto, or county or counties in which municipality containing main office is located.
Pennsylvania	Corporate limits of same place.
Tennessee	County.
Wisconsin	Same city at location of closed bank; and "stations" with limited functions in places denied banking facilities in same county.

The following states are usually listed as having no definite legislation on branch banking:

Kentucky	North Dakota
New Hampshire	Oklahoma
Wyoming	

In this particular group of states, banks operate branches in the following states: Kentucky and New Hampshire.

3. *States in which banks operate branches on a state-wide basis.*—The following are states the laws of which sanction the creation and operation of branches on a state-wide basis:

Arizona	Idaho	North Carolina	South Dakota
California	Maryland	Oregon	Utah
Connecticut	Michigan	Rhode Island	Vermont
Delaware	Nevada	South Carolina	Virginia
District of Columbia		Washington	

In Vermont no provision is made for branches but agencies are permitted on a state-wide basis.

Another fundamental difference between the laws of certain states is found in the provisions setting forth the capital requirements for branches operated by state banks. In a few states the laws provide specifically that the management of each bank must set aside a certain amount of capital funds for the exclusive use of a given branch, while the laws of other states do not require any definite capital fund for use by individual branches. One reason underlying the specific minimum capital requirements is to prevent the bank from expanding unduly the amount of its deposit liabilities without a corresponding increase in capital funds. A more interested, active, and responsible management is usually secured when the stockholders have a substantial investment in relation to risk involved. It has a tendency to prevent the management from spreading its business over too large an area with inadequate capital. Another factor of vital importance is the protection of the depositors and the public. This cannot be accomplished unless the capital funds are increased in proportion to the increase in the line of deposits. In many cases the aim is to require an amount of additional capital equal to the amount necessary to secure a charter for a new bank in the particular community in which the branch is located.

In some states the management may apportion to a given bank any part of its capital that it may deem necessary or desirable. The theory is that the bank and all its branches make up one organization and that the officers and directors are responsible for the acts of each office or branch. If additional funds are needed at any time, they may be quickly supplied by the head office. This method, it is argued, would make possible a more economical use of the resources of the institution. Any losses or profits realized by an individual branch would be immediately reflected in the consolidated statement of the system as a whole. The advocates of this plan maintain that it makes no fundamental difference whether there is a definite segregation of capital funds or not. All that is needed is to have the capital funds in the organization. The objection to this method is that an unscrupulous management would try to operate the head office and the branches on "too thin" a margin of proprietary funds, which would endanger the interests of the depositors and stockholders. If provision is not made for each branch separately, it is desirable to require the head office or the bank to expand its total capital as its deposits and the number of branches increase.

Capital requirements for new banks are generally based upon, or are in proportion to, the population of the city or community in which the bank is to be located. One reason for these restrictions is found in the thought that the amount of business to be done, hence the amount of capital needed, is determined to a large extent by the number of people to be served by the institution. Some other basis might be used if one could be found which would lend itself readily to the purpose. The "population basis" has the distinct advantage of being tangible and easily understood, as well as being readily available. The objection to this method or basis is that the volume of business in a community is not always proportional to the number of people. It is, moreover, an extremely difficult task to ascertain the volume of business to be financed in a given locality. Even though the population is essentially the same in a residential community as compared with an industrial or manufacturing center, the volume of banking business will vary greatly. In other words, the idea that the amount of business depends upon the number of people is in many instances incorrect. To the same degree, the policy of granting charters upon the basis of census reports is subject to criticism.

Adequate capital for banks operating branches is necessary to prevent banks from expanding the volume of business—deposits, loans, discounts, and investments—without a proper increase in capital funds. Banking laws in most states where branches are permitted contain provisions designed to guarantee a proportional increase of capital with the expansion of branches. In many states the laws have been framed with the population basis as the test for additional capital when the number of branches is increased. In other states the laws provide that the bank must have a certain minimum capital, depending upon the size of the city in which it is located, and in addition a certain definite amount for each branch in operation. In Arizona, for example, the bank must start with a paid-up capital of $50,000 and then add $15,000 for each branch. The South Carolina branch-banking law provides that the bank must have additional capital for each branch equal to the amount required for an independent bank in given locality. A bank operating branches in Louisiana is required to have a capital of at least $50,000 for the first branch. For additional offices a graduated scale is specified, so that a bank with a capital of from $250,000 to $300,000 may operate not in excess of seven branches. For each additional unit of $100,000 in capital funds over and above the $300,000, the bank may establish and operate one additional office or branch.

A distinction is made in the requirements of two or three states between commercial banks and trust companies. Usually the requirements are more severe for the trust companies than for commercial banks. This variation in capital requirements is doubtless made for the same reason that impels states to require the trust company to have a larger capital than commercial banks doing business in communities of equal size. The laws of New Jersey illustrate this point.

THE ST. LOUIS CASE

On June 15, 1922, the First National Bank of St. Louis, Missouri, established a branch in that city without obtaining the consent and approval of the Comptroller of the Currency. Plans were announced for the opening of other branches at a later date. This action on the part of the St. Louis bank brought squarely before the public and the courts of that state and the Supreme Court of the United States the question of the right of national banks to establish and operate branches. The Comptroller of the Currency authorized a number of banks during that year to operate "additional offices" or "teller windows" for the purpose of receiving deposits and cashing checks. These were not regarded as branches by the Comptroller of the Currency. Since the St. Louis bank admitted that it had established a branch which was intended to do a complete banking business, the question of the right of national banks to establish "teller windows" did not come before the courts. Moreover the Comptroller of the Currency announced that he would not approve the organization of a teller window unless the state laws of the state in which the bank was located permitted state banks to own and operate branches. Inasmuch as the state banking laws of Missouri denied state banks the right to own and operate branches, the case was new and involved the question of the rights and privileges of national banks to operate branches in states where state banks were denied permission to establish branches.

The state of Missouri brought legal action in June, 1922, to ascertain whether this bank had the authority to establish and operate this branch. It was alleged that, since the National Bank Act had not authorized branch banking, this particular branch was not being operated under Federal laws. Since the National Bank Act did not authorize the branch, the bank was operating the branch contrary to the state laws of Missouri. The Attorney-General, acting for the state of Missouri, took the position that the matter could properly come before the supreme court of Missouri since it was a violation of the laws of Missouri, which prohibited banks from operating branches. The First National Bank, however, held the position that the branch was not a violation of their charter privileges, and furthermore that the bank was a Federal corporation and was not, therefore, subject to the courts of Missouri.

The supreme court of Missouri decided the case against the bank, which immediately carried it to the Supreme Court of the United States for a final verdict. The United States Supreme Court upheld the action of the state of Missouri and confirmed the decision of the supreme court of Missouri.[8] The Supreme Court of the United States held that the bank had not been granted power to operate a branch by its charter and that the action of the First National Bank had violated the laws of the state of Missouri, which did not permit banks to operate branches in that state. This decision left unanswered the question of the right of national banks in Missouri to establish and operate "additional offices" or "teller windows." The decision also left unanswered the question of the right of a national bank to establish and operate branches, either within or outside the city of the parent, in those states where state banking laws permit state banks to operate branches.[9]

Changes in the number of branches in recent years seem to indicate that we have definitely embarked upon a branch-banking era. Sentiment in favor of this type of banking is much stronger than it was a decade ago, yet there is little uniformity in the changes in banking legislation in this respect. In some states there is a tendency toward liberalization of the provisions, in other states increased opposition is noted, while in still others public opinion is indifferent, apparently giving little thought to the matter. The failure in recent years of a large number of banks which were operating branches has created a moderate reaction against the development of branches. In some quarters where branch banking was strongly advocated two or three years ago as a remedy for bank failures, it is not now uncommon to find that a

[8] For a more extended discussion of the legal points involved in this case, see C. W. Collins' *Branch Banking Question* (1926), VI, 59-70.

[9] The McFadden Amendment to the National Bank Act, Feb. 25, 1927, gave national banks the right to own and operate branches within the city of the parent institution in those states where state banks were permitted to own and operate branches by authority of state laws, decisions, or state regulations.

feeling exists to the effect that better bank management is of more vital importance than branches, even though the idea of branch banking is generally regarded with favor. The sentiment has cooled off considerably, so that we may reasonably expect it to have some bearing upon the rate at which the movement is pushed ahead. In the course of time, branch banking will become state-wide in nature and will include a larger and larger number of states. There is little expectation that the laws will be uniform or come with any degree of regularity. It will be a number of years, at least, before we can hope to have anything like a uniform system of state and Federal laws providing for a system of domestic branch banking.

CHAPTER XI

THE EXTENT OF BRANCH BANKING IN THE UNITED STATES

The preceding chapter was devoted to a discussion of the legal status of branch banking in the United States. An attempt was made to set forth as briefly as possible the most essential provisions of the state and Federal laws regarding the rights and privileges of national and state banks, trust companies, and mutual and stock savings banks to own and operate branches, indicating the states in which branch banking may be legally carried on at the present time. The purpose of the present chapter is to show statistically the growth and development of branches in this country. Extensive statistics have been compiled to show not only the increase in the number of banks operating branches and the number of branches in operation, but also to show comparatively the relation of branch banking to the system as a whole. The period which has been covered by these statistics dates back to the year 1918, prior to which the extent of branch banking was quite limited.

The present chapter is more specifically intended to set forth in statistical form certain data regarding the extent and growth of branches over a period of years. The statistical data studied and presented include the following:

1. The number of banks operating branches, including the total number of branches in operation, the total resources of banks operating branches, as well as total loans and discounts, investments, and total deposits, both time and demand. Each of these is considered in relation to similar data for all banks in the United States.

2. The data included in this study have been segregated to show the position of each class of banks—national banks, state banks and trust companies, and mutual savings banks. These data indicate further both the aggregate and the relative growth of each of these groups.

3. The data will be further classified and summarized to indicate the growth and extent of branch banking according to the legal status. Those states in which branch banking is carried on fall into three groups: (1) those permitting branch banking on a state-wide basis; (2) those permitting branches on a more restricted basis; and (3) those in which a few banks operate branches, but in which a further expansion of branches is prohibited by law.

GENERAL BRANCH BANKING DEVELOPMENT

In 1919 there were 476 state and national banking institutions operating 1,082 branches with total resources amounting to more than $7,695,000,000. The number of banks operating branches in 1931 was 737, with 3,375 branches and total resources of over $28,878,000,000.[1] These statistics indicate an increase of more than 54 percent in the number of banks, 212 percent in the number of branches in operation, and 275 percent in the volume of total resources. The marked increase in the volume of branch banking resources means, undoubtedly, that a considerable number of large banks[2] have entered the field of branch banking in those states and cities where branch banking has been permitted. The total number of branches increased more than in proportion to the total number of banks operating branches.

During the period studied, the banking resources for the banking system as a whole made very substantial increases, but the percentage growth was much less than the total for branch banks, or for any particular class, whether it be national banks, state banks and trust companies, or mutual savings banks. The total number of banks in operation decreased from 29,123 in 1919 to 19,163 in 1932.[3] For the same period, the total assets for all banks in the United States increased from $47,615,000,000 in 1919 to $57,245,000,000, in 1932, or, approximately 20 percent.[4]

[1] The largest number of branches reported for any one year was 3,603 in 1929. The number of branches in operation at the close of 1932 was 3,290; see p. 191.

[2] Many banks, it should be noted, increased their resources by absorbing another bank or banks.

[3] See Table 22, p. 208.

[4] Attention is called to the fact that the amount $57,245,000,000 for all banks

Table 19 presents a summary of the number of banks operating branches year by year from 1919 to 1931, inclusive, together with

TABLE 19

SUMMARY OF BANKS OPERATING BRANCHES IN THE UNITED STATES, 1919–31* INCLUSIVE†

YEAR	NUMBER OF BANKS OPERATING BRANCHES			NUMBER OF BRANCHES IN OPERATON			RESOURCES OF ALL BANKS OPERATING BRANCHES (*In millions of dollars*)		
	Total	*State‡*	*National*	*Total*	*State‡*	*National*	*Total*	*State‡*	*National*
1919	476	458	18	1,082	1,030	52	7,695	7,085	610
1920	524	503	21	1,239	1,176	63	9,591	8,491	1,100
1921	535	511	24	1,366	1,292	74	10,266	8,347	1,919
1922	608	552	56	1,715	1,575	140	12,618	9,462	3,156
1923	673	583	90	2,044	1,841	203	14,966	11,129	3,839
1924	716	608	108	2,299	2,050	249	17,878	12,918	4,960
1925	784	640	144	2,586	2,223	363	21,165	14,461	6,704
1926	787	644	143	2,796	2,371	425	22,946	15,963	6,983
1927	833	668	165	3,149	2,227	922	27,152	17,814	9,338
1928	844	682	162	3,307	2,359	948	32,030	20,213	11,817
1929	816	656	160	3,603	2,532	1,071	33,269	21,931	11,338
1930	799	631	168	3,567	2,454	1,113	33,228	21,070	12,158
1931§	737	580	157	3,375	2,101	1,274	28,878	18,192	10,686

* Source: see note to Table 21.

† For more details regarding the number of branches, according to type of bank and legal status, see Table 20.

‡ Including mutual savings banks.

§ For number of banks operating on Dec. 31, 1932, together with the number of branches, see Table 20. Resources and other data for the banks operating branches on Dec. 31, 1932, are not available at this time (Aug., 1933).

the number of branches and the volume of total resources of all banks operating branches.

A satisfactory picture of the branch-banking situation will be obtained from a study of the data including the number of banks operating branches, together with the number of branches in operation classified according to both the type of bank and the legal status of branch banking in the various states. Aggregate totals for the capital, loans, discounts, investments, etc., are pre-

---

in the United States was considerably below 1929, the peak year for number of branches, when total resources for all banks operating branches amounted to $33,269,000,000, or over 58 percent of total assets of all banks in the United States for that year.

TABLE 20

TOTAL NUMBER OF BRANCHES IN OPERATION, CLASSIFIED ACCORDING TO LOCATION AND TYPE OF BANKING INSTITUTION*

YEAR	ALL BANKS OPERATING BRANCHES IN THE UNITED STATES					BANKS OPERATING BRANCHES ON STATE-WIDE BASIS				
	Total	Member, Federal Reserve System	Branches			Total	Member, Federal Reserve System	Branches		
			Total	*In*	*Out*			*Total*	*In*	*Out*
1919	476	134	1,082	631	451	199	18	380	89	291
1920	524	176	1,239	745	494	214	36	433	114	319
1921	535	194	1,366	849	517	213	45	461	132	329
1922	608	246	1,715	1,112	603	250	66	629	224	405
1923	673	275	2,044	1,346	698	281	79	843	335	508
1924	716	296	2,299	1,545	754	285	81	953	405	548
1925	784	335	2,586	1,788	798	277	85	988	436	552
1926	787	334	2,796	1,962	834	260	79	1,070	489	581
1927	833	352	3,149	2,166	983	228	64	1,160	463	697
1928	844	352	3,307	2,271	1,036	222	59	1,177	451	726
1929	816	337	3,603	2,491	1,112	210	57	1,294	490	804
1930	799	330	3,567	2,451	1,116	209	56	1,298	454	844
1931	737	296	3,375	2,293	1,082	191	54	1,214	438	776
1932	747		3,290	2,220	1,070	189		1,194	432	762

* Source: See note, Table 21, p. 199 below.

TABLE 20 *(Continued)*

YEAR	BANKS OPERATING BRANCHES ON A RESTRICTED BASIS					BANKS OPERATING BRANCHES IN PROHIBITED STATES				
	Total	Member, Federal Reserve System	Branches			Total	Member, Federal Reserve System	Branches		
			Total	*In*	*Out*			*Total*	*In*	*Out*
1919	230	95	625	521	104	47	21	77	21	56
1920	264	117	731	611	120	46	23	75	20	55
1921	278	126	833	698	135	44	23	72	19	53
1922	310	153	999	853	146	48	27	87	35	52
1923	348	171	1,115	973	142	44	25	86	38	48
1924	387	190	1,260	1,102	158	44	25	86	38	48
1925	467	227	1,524	1,321	203	40	23	74	31	43
1926	499	239	1,671	1,450	221	28	16	55	23	32
1927	558	266	1,897	1,667	230	47	22	92	36	56
1928	579	272	2,043	1,785	258	43	21	87	35	52
1929	579	265	2,253	1,974	279	27	15	56	27	29
1930	577	266	2,236	1,987	249	13	8	33	10	23
1931	535	236	2,130	1,845	285	11	6	31	10	21
1932	547		2,065	1,778	287	11		31	10	21

TABLE 20 (*Continued*)

YEAR	ALL NATIONAL BANKS OPERATING BRANCHES					STATE BANKS AND TRUST COMPANIES OPERATING BRANCHES					MUTUAL SAVINGS BANKS WITH BRANCHES				
	Total	Member, Federal Reserve System	Branches			Total	Member, Federal Reserve System	Branches			Total	Member, Federal Reserve System	Branches		
			Total	*In*	*Out*			*Total*	*In*	*Out*			*Total*	*In*	*Out*
1919	18	18	52	30	22	446	116	1,005	581	424	12		25	20	5
1920	21	21	63	41	22	488	155	1,148	681	467	15		28	23	5
1921	24	24	74	52	22	495	170	1,263	774	489	16		29	23	6
1922	56	56	140	119	21	532	190	1,538	965	573	20		37	28	9
1923	90	90	203	181	22	553	185	1,792	1,125	667	30		49	40	9
1924	108	108	249	227	22	566	188	1,985	1,266	719	42		65	52	13
1925	144	144	363	343	20	591	191	2,149	1,386	763	49		74	59	15
1926	143	143	425	396	29	590	191	2,291	1,500	791	54		80	66	14
1927	165	165	922	575	347	605	187	2,137	1,516	621	63		90	75	15
1928	162	162	948	607	341	615	190	2,262	1,584	678	67		97	80	17
1929	160	160	1,071	716	355	584	177	2,425	1,684	741	72		107	91	16
1930	168	168	1,113	713	400	557	162	2,346	1,646	700	74		108	92	16
1931	157	157	1,274	886	388	505	139	1,989	1,311	678	75		112	96	16
1932	157	157	1,205	825	380	515		1,961	1,286	675	75		124	109	15

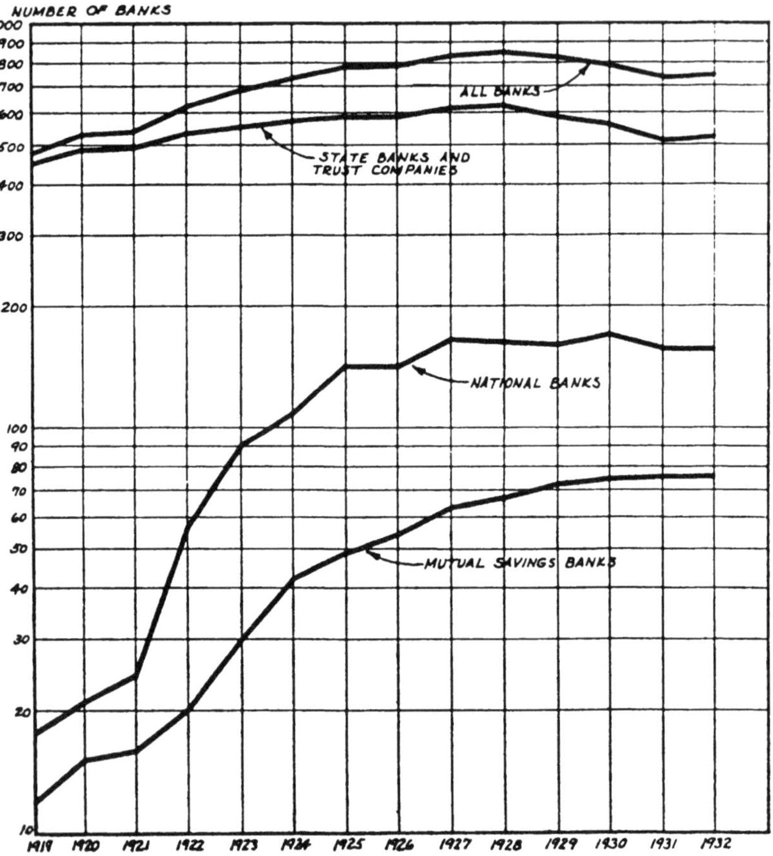

CHART X. TOTAL NUMBER OF BANKS OPERATING BRANCHES IN THE UNITED STATES

sented in tabular form in Table 21. The purpose here is to show the number of banks in the branch-banking business and the number of branches being operated. Table 20 sets forth in considerable detail the extent of branch banking in the United States at the present time and indicates the growth of branches both "in" the city and "outside" the city of the parent bank since 1918.

In 1919 there were 18 national banks operating branches, as compared with 157 in 1931. The number of branches owned and in operation for all national banks increased from 52 in 1919 to 1,205 in 1932. The number of state banks and trust companies was much larger at all times than that of national banks. In 1919 there were 458 state banks and trust companies operating 1,030 branches, including 12 mutual savings banks with 25 branches. The data for state banks and trust companies and mutual savings banks showed that the number of state banks and trust companies had increased in 1932 to 590 with 2,085 branches including 75 mutual savings banks with 124 branches. State banks and trust companies and mutual savings banks had approximately 63 percent of the total of all branches in the United States. The total number of branches operated by national banks showed a relatively greater growth than either state banks and trust companies or mutual savings banks. The branches operated by national banks increased from slightly less than 5 percent of all branches in the United States in 1919, to about 37 percent in 1932. Chart X shows the comparative changes in the number of state banks and trust companies, national banks, and mutual savings banks operating branches.

Branches have been classified according to location, the basis for this classification being the location of the branch, either within or outside the city of the parent. Aggregate figures are given in Table 20. The same data are presented in chart form in Chart XI. It is interesting to observe that the total of each class showed substantial growth, but the branches "in" city increased at a more rapid rate and remained considerably larger during the entire period covered by the statistics. This is only another indication that branches have, to a large extent, been concentrated in the large cities. An extremely important factor in this connection is found in the fact that states like New York, Michigan and Ohio have limited branches to the city of the parent bank. In many cases the great increase in "in" city branches as compared with "outside" branches has been due to the legal status rather than to economic factors.

In Tables 19 and 20 are presented data showing the total number of branches in operation, classified (1) according to the type of bank, and (2) according to the legal status of branches. There has been a marked increase in the total number of branches by state banks and trust companies, national banks, and mutual

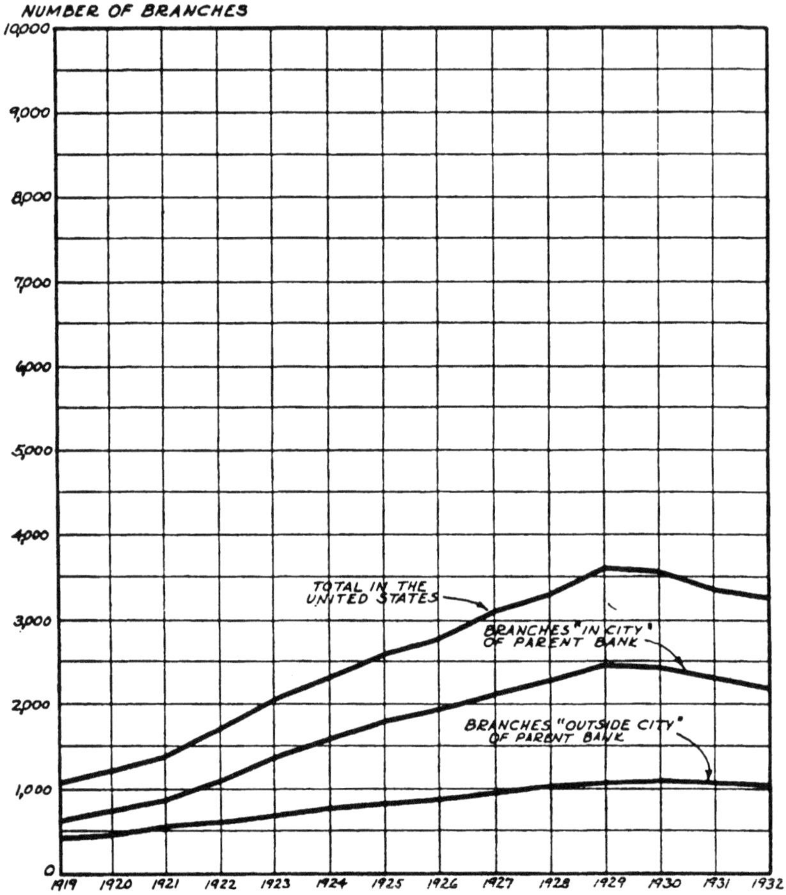

CHART XI. TOTAL NUMBER OF BRANCHES IN THE UNITED STATES, CLASSIFIED ACCORDING TO LOCATION

savings banks. A large percentage of all branches has been owned and operated by state banks and trust companies, as illustrated by Table 20. National banks and mutual savings banks have shown a much more rapid rate of growth in relation to the total number of branches. This favorable showing in the number of branches by mutual savings banks and national banks is due, in part, to the fact that in 1919 there were only a very few banks of either class operating branches. The laws were unfavorable to the creation of branches by national banks. The same applies, in part, to the mutual savings banks. Mutual savings banks are located largely in the states in which there are restrictions on branch banks. A further restriction applied to mutual savings banks—that each mutual savings bank has been generally limited to one or two branches, whereas a national bank may establish several branches.

There has been a very decided increase in the number of branches by banks located in states where branches are limited to "restricted areas," such as the city, county, adjoining county, or contiguous territory. The aggregate totals are not only larger throughout the entire period, but the rate of growth has been more marked in this class than in the state-wide area. In fact the importance of the branches in "prohibited states" declined during the period, as would be expected. The total for each of the other classes showed substantial gains, but, as already noted, the growth in the states permitting state-wide branches has been less marked than in the states permitting branches on a restricted basis.

BRANCHES AND TOTAL BANKING OFFICES

There is no close connection between the total number of banking offices (all banks plus the total number of branches) in operation and the increase in the total number of branches in the United States. It is interesting to make a comparison of the decrease in other countries in the number of unit banks with the extension of branches. In most foreign countries there has been freedom of action in the establishment of branches. There was not present a large number of individual states, such as exist in this country, each with its own body of banking laws. In foreign countries, an extension of branches was generally on a national basis, and it followed as a matter of course that an increase in branches meant a disappearance of a large number of independent banks through bank amalgamations, failures, or liquidations. A comparison of banks with branches in such countries is most informing. To make similar comparisons for the United States as a whole would be useless, for the simple reason that in many states there are no branches and in many others the growth of branches has been so small as to be meaningless.

The most that could be done in this connection would be to

take a few states in which state-wide branch banking is permitted, and even then the conclusions would not be convincing in most of this small group of states. In some cases, however, the number of banking offices has been increased. If the comparison be limited to the eleven leading cities,[5] it is clearly evident that the total number of banking offices has been considerably increased. There has not been a lessening of the number of such banking offices, even if we take into consideration the fact that a number of banks have been absorbed and that several more have failed. This decrease has been more than offset by new banks and new branches.

There are certain states in which the decline in the number of banks has been very striking. This is true in the Northwest, in particular in Montana, North and South Dakota, and in Minnesota. It is likewise true for the state of Florida. The same situation prevails in many other states where branch banking does not exist in any form at the present. The decline in these states has been the result very largely of bank failures, but to a small degree it has been influenced by the merger movement. It is quite evident, therefore, that branch banking to date in this country has not been the major factor in bringing about the rapid decline in the number of independent banking institutions.

If there should be a liberalization of the banking laws in favor of branch banking, as now appears likely to occur in the near future, it may be taken as a certainty that the number of branches will increase rapidly and that this increase will be more rapid, so far as mere numbers are concerned, than the decrease in the number of independent banks. This means that we may look for an increase in the total number of places at which the banking of the country will be done in the future. This means fewer banks, but larger banking institutions with a large number of branches.

BRANCH BANKING IN THE UNITED STATES

Table 21, gives a full summary of the data regarding total capital funds, deposits, loans and discounts, investments, and re-

[5] See Chap. XII, pp. 237-49 ("The Concentration of Branch Banking in Eleven Leading Cities").

TABLE 21

BRANCH BANKING IN THE UNITED STATES: BY TYPES OF BANKS*

(In millions of dollars)

YEAR	ALL BANKS OPERATING BRANCHES IN THE UNITED STATES								
	Number of Banks	Member, Federal Reserve System	Capital†	Loans, Discounts	Investments	Deposits			Resources
						Demand	*Time*	*Total*	
1919	476	134	695	3,967	1,812	4,014	1,653	5,667	7,695
1920	524	176	930	5,123	2,168	4,455	2,434	6,889	9,592
1921	535	194	1,156	5,473	2,431	4,784	2,667	7,451	10,266
1922	608	246	1,376	5,802	3,302	5,973	3,392	9,365	12,619
1923	673	275	1,636	7,740	3,598	6,705	4,445	11,150	14,966
1924	716	296	1,829	9,063	5,009	7,654	5,532	13,186	17,878
1925	784	335	2,164	10,589	5,841	8,620	6,619	15,239	21,165
1926	787	334	2,411	11,569	6,312	9,612	7,616	17,228	22,947
1927	833	352	3,002	14,505	7,979	10,833	9,092	19,925	27,153
1928	844	352	3,549	15,232	8,409	12,418	10,197	22,615	32,030
1929	816	337	4,229	16,501	8,230	12,946	10,366	23,312	33,269
1930	799	330	4,370	14,962	9,376	12,023	11,202	23,225	33,229
1931	737	296	3,941	12,185	10,078	10,425	10,238	20,663	28,877

* Source: The Tables presented in Chaps. XI and XII have been compiled almost entirely from official records. The sources used were the *Annual Reports of the Federal Reserve Board*, *Annual Reports of the Comptroller of the Currency*, annual reports of various state banking departments, special reports, and by direct assistance of many public banking officials and employees. Data for banks operating branches are at or as near the end of each calendar year as it was possible to secure. Where data has been taken from one specific source, it is indicated in a footnote to the table.

† Includes surplus, undivided profit and guaranty fund, and reserves of mutual savings banks.

TABLE 21 *(Continued)*

YEAR	ALL NATIONAL BANKS OPERATING BRANCHES IN THE UNITED STATES								
	Number of Banks	Member, Federal Reserve System	Capital†	Loans, Discounts	Investments	Deposits			Resources
						Demand	*Time*	*Total*	
1919	18	18	56	353	100	302	68	370	610
1920	21	21	100	698	104	529	98	627	1,100
1921	24	24	261	1,186	198	923	133	1,056	1,919
1922	56	56	367	1,775	492	1,595	326	1,921	3,157
1923	90	90	484	2,263	733	1,811	581	2,392	3,839
1924	108	108	533	2,813	944	2,318	747	3,065	4,960
1925	144	144	688	3,569	1,166	2,874	922	3,796	6,705
1926	143	143	743	3,970	1,243	3,195	1,185	4,380	6,984
1927	165	165	1,029	5,474	1,914	3,854	2,020	5,874	9,339
1928	162	162	1,275	6,163	2,155	4,492	2,429	6,921	11,818
1929	160	160	1,430	6,101	1,758	4,428	2,693	7,121	11,338
1930	168	168	1,585	6,362	2,192	4,722	2,994	7,716	12,159
1931	157	157	1,512	5,559	2,417	4,327	2,760	7,087	10,686

TABLE 21 (*Continued*)

YEAR	ALL STATE BANKS AND TRUST COMPANIES WITH BRANCHES								
	Number of Banks	Member, Federal Reserve System	Capital†	Loans, Discounts	Investments	Deposits			Resources
						Demand	*Time*	*Total*	
1919	446	116	628	3,569	1,621	3,712	1,451	5,163	6,939
1920	488	155	797	4,369	1,652	3,926	1,865	5,791	7,985
1921	495	170	860	4,225	1,794	3,861	2,044	5,906	7,822
1922	532	190	964	3,965	2,358	4,378	2,549	6,927	8,899
1923	553	185	1,074	5,404	2,099	4,893	3,030	7,923	10,217
1924	566	188	1,175	6,123	2,952	5,336	3,569	8,905	11,576
1925	591	191	1,297	6,847	3,041	5,747	3,967	9,714	12,547
1926	590	191	1,445	7,379	3,192	6,417	4,384	10,801	13,669
1927	605	187	1,662	8,765	3,648	6,979	4,472	11,451	14,896
1928	615	190	1,940	8,772	3,600	7,926	4,787	12,713	16,890
1929	584	177	2,450	10,019	3,630	8,518	4,497	13,015	18,398
1930	557	162	2,350	8,233	4,103	7,301	4,512	11,813	16,948
1931	505	139	2,031	6,252	4,096	6,097	3,459	9,556	13,772

TABLE 21 *(Continued)*

YEAR	ALL MUTUAL SAVINGS BANKS OPERATING BRANCHES IN THE UNITED STATES								
	Number of Banks	Member, Federal Reserve System	Capital†	Loans, Discounts	Investments	Deposits			Resources
						Demand	*Time*	*Total*	
1919	12		10	45	91		134	134	146
1920	15		32	56	412		471	471	507
1921	16		35	61	438		489	489	525
1922	20		45	62	452		517	517	564
1923	30		78	73	767		834	834	910
1924	42		121	128	1,114		1,217	1,217	1,342
1925	49		178	172	1,635		1,730	1,730	1,913
1926	54		223	221	1,877		2,047	2,047	2,294
1927	63		311	265	2,417		2,601	2,601	2,918
1928	67		334	296	2,653		2,981	2,981	3,323
1929	72		348	380	2,842		3,176	3,176	3,533
1930	74		415	367	3,081		3,697	3,697	4,122
1931	75		397	373	3,565		4,019	4,019	4,419

sources of all banks operating branches in the United States. These data are classified according to (1) the type of banking institution, and (2) the legal status of branch banking.

SIZE OF THE BRANCH SYSTEMS

In 1931 there was a total of 737 commercial banks, trust companies, and savings banks operating 3,375 branches, which was an average of less than 5 branches each. The average number of branches operated per branch bank has gradually increased, but the increase has been so slow as to be comparatively unimportant. In 1919 there were 476 banks operating 1,082 branches. This represented a general average of slightly more than 2 branches per bank. This was not a general increase, but an expansion due very largely to a rapid growth in the number of branches of a few banks. Such banks were located in Detroit, New York City, Buffalo, Cleveland, Los Angeles, and San Francisco. The study prepared by the Federal Reserve Board in 1930 goes into details regarding the number of branches operated by different banks. The report reads in part as follows:

> . . . a large majority of the banks operating branches in the country as a whole were operating only 1 or 2 branches each. Of the 822 banks operating branches, 448, or more than half, were operating only one branch each, 150 were operating 2, and 124 were operating 3 to 5 branches each, the proportion of small systems being not materially different from the proportion shown in February, 1927.[6]

The number of banks with a large number of branches is comparatively small. In this connection the Federal Reserve Board reports as follows:

> At the end of the year (1929), 18 banks were operating each more than 30 branches, including 6 California systems, 1 with 287 branches . . . 3 Detroit banks . . . 7 New York City banks were operating each from 33 to 67 branches; . . . 1 Cleveland bank was operating 57 branches; and 1 Buffalo bank 33 branches.[7]

It is evident that outside of the state of California there are no very extensive branch-banking organizations in the United States. In practically all of the cities referred to, with the ex-

[6] *Federal Reserve Bulletin*, April, 1930, p. 145.
[7] *Ibid.*

ception of Los Angeles and San Francisco, branch banking is limited to the city of the parent institution. No great branch banking organizations are likely to develop in these states until there has been a liberalization in the banking laws permitting state-wide branch banking. Even then, there will be distinct limitations upon the size of the branch organizations. To have branch systems here which will compare favorably with those existing in Canada and England, it will be necessary to enlarge the geographical unit for branches to a nation-wide basis. If this be undesirable, then the next workable unit would, it appears, be the Federal Reserve districts. The conclusion is, therefore, that the size of the individual branch institutions will for some time to come be small and that these areas will be gradually expanded after there have been some fundamental changes in our banking laws, allowing greater freedom in the establishment and operation of branches.

CAPITAL FUNDS OF BANKS OPERATING BRANCHES AND THEIR RELATIONSHIP TO THE CAPITAL FUNDS OF ALL BANKS IN OPERATION IN THE UNITED STATES

The capital funds[8] of banks operating branches in the United States increased from 0.70 billions of dollars to 3.94 billions, or more than 470 percent, during the period 1919-31 inclusive. The capital funds of all banks in operation increased from 5.45 billions of dollars to 9.47 billions of dollars, or approximately 73 percent. This comparison is important in emphasizing and illustrating the rapid growth of the capital funds of banks operating branches in relation to those of the banking system as a whole. The capital funds of banks operating branches were about 13 percent of the capital funds of all banks in 1919, whereas in 1929 the percentage had increased to approximately 42. The relationship between the capital funds of all banks and of all banks operating branches is presented in Chart XII, including a comparison of data of each class of banks operating branches with the totals for all banks operating branches. This chart includes

[8] Capital fund is a term used in this discussion to designate the total capital, surplus, and undivided profits, including guaranty fund, reserve, etc., of mutual savings banks.

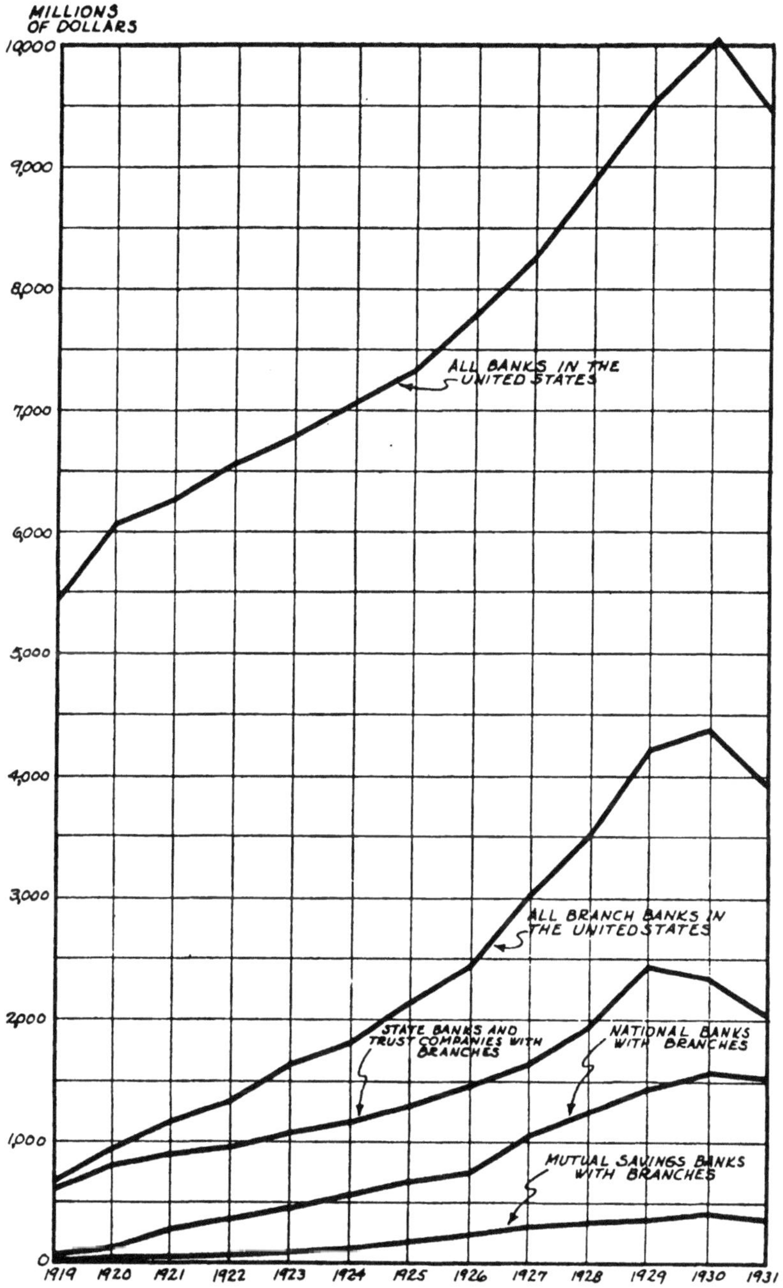

CHART XII. CAPITAL OF ALL BANKS IN THE UNITED STATES AND OF ALL BANKS OPERATING BRANCHES, CLASSIFIED ACCORDING TO TYPE OF BANK

also comparative data for all banks operating branches classified according to type of bank.

If a comparison be made of the amount of capital funds held by banks operating branches on a city or county basis with the total capital funds held by banks in states which permit state-wide branches, it is evident that a large proportion of all capital funds is in the hands of banks which operate branches within the city, county, or adjoining county. The increase in the number of banks with branches limited to the city or county has been somewhat greater than that of banks operating branches in those states which permit state-wide branch banking. The capital funds of those banks operating branches in states permitting state-wide branches declined in proportion to the total for all banks operating branches. This is a rather important result, since it shows that the greatest development of branches has taken place in "city-branch" banking, making due allowance for the situation in the three states of Louisiana, Tennessee, and Maine, which permit the operation of branches on a parish, county, or adjoining-county basis, respectively. The totals for these three states are included in the data classified as city branch banking.

It has been shown that the capital funds of all banks operating branches have increased more rapidly than the total capital funds of all banks in operation. If a more detailed study be made of the data covering the banks operating branches, it is observed that the capital funds of national banks and mutual savings[9] banks have increased faster than the capital funds of state banks and trust companies. Although the total capital funds for state banks and trust companies increased considerably, the increase was not in proportion to that for all banks operating branches. National banks operating branches showed an opposite trend, increasing faster in proportion than the increase for all banks operating branches. State banks and trust companies still held, however, a very commanding lead over national banks in the aggregate in 1931, despite the great increase in both types of banks.

[9] Capital funds, as used here, refers to the total of capital surplus and undivided profits. It is of course understood that mutual savings banks have no capital as distinct from surplus or undivided profits.

DEPOSITS

Total deposits for all banks in the United States increased from 33.78 billions of dollars in 1919 to more than 52.04 billions of dollars in 1931. The data show an increase each year, with the exception of 1921, 1929, 1931, and 1932: The recession of business in 1921 reduced the total deposits from approximately 38.01 billions of dollars in 1920 to 35.85 billions, or a decrease of approximately 5 percent. A comparison of the demand and time deposits for all banks in the United States shows that the increase over the eleven-year period was much greater for time deposits, both as to aggregate increase and the rate of increase. There was an actual increase in the total of time deposits for each year except 1931 and 1932, whereas a decline was registered in the total of demand deposits in the years 1921, 1926, 1928, 1929, 1931 and 1932, as compared with the preceding years in each case. The aggregate figures for all banks in the United States are given in Table 22. Chart XIII presents the relationship between the total deposits for all banks and for banks operating branches, and the various classes of deposits for the same group of banks. Chart XIV shows the comparative rate of growth of the different classes of deposits for banks operating branches and for all banks in the United States.

In 1919 demand deposits of banks operating branches represented more than 16.7 percent[10] of the total deposits for all banks in the United States. In 1931 demand deposits for banks with branches constituted 45.6 percent of demand deposits of all banks. During the same period the percentage of time deposits rose from 17 in 1919 to 35 in 1931. Total deposits of branch banks increased from about 16.8 percent of total deposits of all banks to 39.7 percent in 1931. These figures show conclusively that branch banking, as measured in terms of deposits, was expanding at a much more rapid rate than the banking system as a whole. A rapidly increasing percentage of the total deposits of banks were in the hands of branch bankers. Despite the rapid increase in the totals for time deposits, a larger percentage of all demand de-

[10] See Table 23, p. 211.

TABLE 22

DATA OF ALL STATE BANKS, TRUST COMPANIES, NATIONAL BANKS, MUTUAL SAVINGS BANKS, STOCK SAVINGS BANKS AND PRIVATE BANKS IN THE UNITED STATES BY YEARS, AS OF JUNE 30*

(In millions of dollars)

YEAR	TOTAL BANKS IN THE UNITED STATES	MEMBER, FEDERAL RESERVE SYSTEM	CAPITAL	LOANS, DIS-COUNTS, OVER-DRAFTS	INVEST-MENTS	DEPOSITS			DUE TO BANKS	DUE FROM BANKS	BILLS PAYABLE AND RE-DIS-COUNTS	TOTAL RE-SOURCES
						Demand	*Time*	*Total*				
1919	29,123	8,822	5,445	25,396	12,391	24,030	9,748	33,778	3,890	5,865	2,300	47,615
1920	30,139	9,399	6,089	31,365	11,525	27,794	10,212	38,006	3,708	5,833	3,285	53,079
1921	30,812	9,745	6,357	29,014	11,536	20,638	15,211	35,849	2,809	4,794	2,647	49,671
1922	30,389	9,892	6,575	27,935	12,746	22,262	15,614	37,876	3,244	5,414	1,071	50,425
1923	30,178	9,856	6,806	30,475	13,929	22,612	18,018	40,630	3,610	5,597	1,315	54,035
1924	29,348	9,650	7,053	31,483	14,523	24,681	19,090	43,771	3,928	6,121	798	57,145
1925	28,841	9,538	7,350	33,934	15,736	26,779	20,833	47,612	4,371	6,774	925	62,057
1926	28,146	9,375	7,808	36,283	16,174	25,459	24,267	49,726	4,331	6,769	1,024	64,893
1927	27,061	9,099	8,272	37,314	17,655	26,065	26,382	52,447	4,289	6,900	830	68,133
1928	26,213	8,929	8,897	39,592	19,176	25,794	28,538	54,332	4,081	6,722	1,566	71,574
1929	25,330	8,707	9,506	41,433	17,740	25,494	28,787	54,281	3,629	6,760	1,631	72,173
1930	24,079	8,315	10,013	40,510	18,370	26,045	29,465	55,510	4,337	7,427	666	74,020
1931	22,071	7,782	9,473	35,210	20,507	22,877	29,159	52,036	4,829	7,536	458	70,209
1932	19,163	6,980	8,093	28,090	18,750	17,404	24,774	42,178	3,212	2,920	1,249	57,245

* Source: *Annual Reports of the Comptroller of the Currency.*

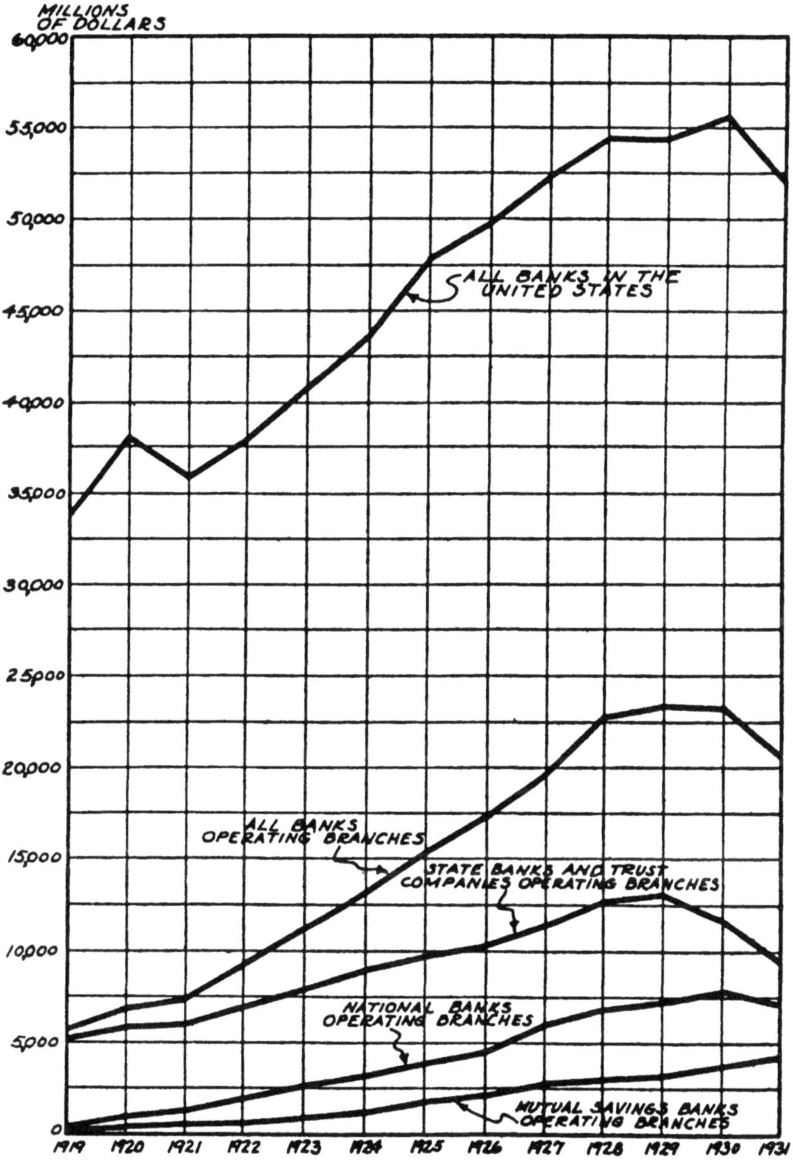

CHART XIII. TOTAL DEPOSITS OF BANKS OPERATING BRANCHES IN THE UNITED STATES, CLASSIFIED ACCORDING TO TYPE OF BANK

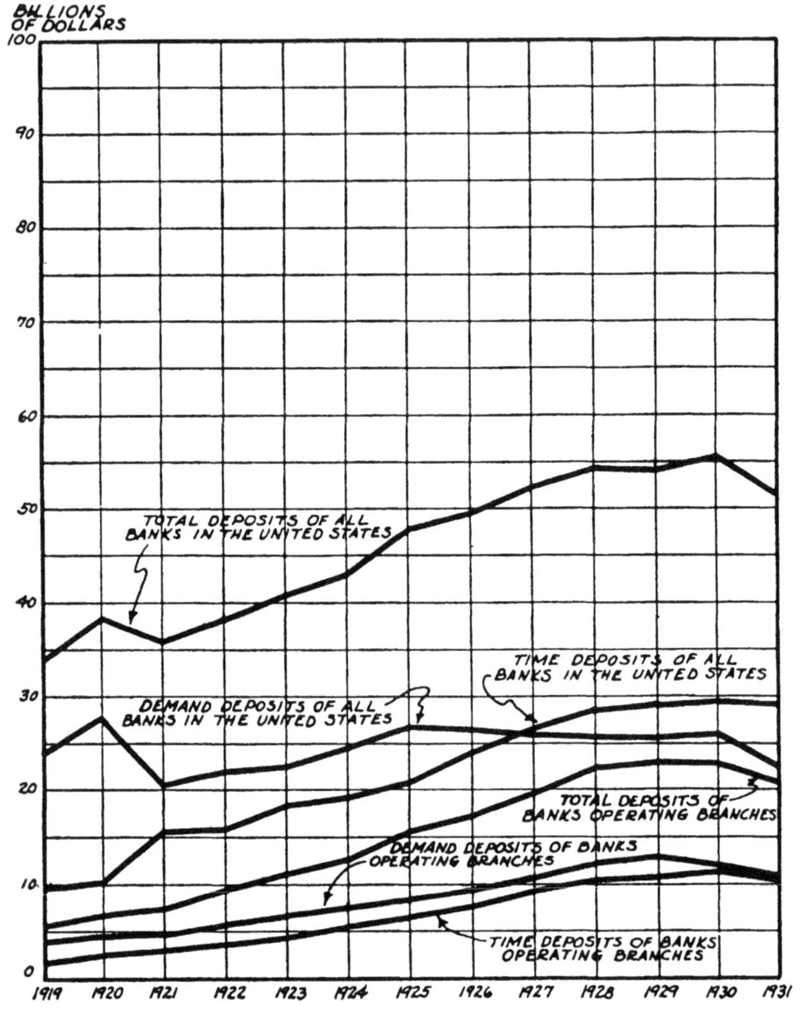

CHART XIV. TOTAL DEPOSITS OF BANKS IN THE UNITED STATES AND ALL BANKS OPERATING BRANCHES IN THE UNITED STATES

posits was owned by banks operating branches than was the case with regard to time deposits. For percentage changes in the demand, time, and total deposits for banks operating branches in comparison with demand, time, and total deposits for all banks in the United States, see Table 23.

TABLE 23

THE PERCENTAGE CERTAIN ITEMS OF BANKS OPERATING BRANCHES ARE OF ALL BANKS IN OPERATION IN THE UNITED STATES*

YEAR	BANKS	MEMBER, FEDERAL RESERVE SYSTEM	CAPITAL†	LOANS, DISCOUNTS, OVERDRAFTS	INVESTMENTS	DEPOSITS			TOTAL RESOURCES
						Demand	*Time*	*Total*	
1919	1.6	1.5	12.8	15.6	14.6	16.7	17.0	16.8	16.2
1920	1.7	1.9	15.3	16.3	18.8	16.0	23.8	18.1	18.1
1921	1.7	2.0	18.2	18.9	21.1	23.2	17.5	20.8	20.7
1922	2.0	2.5	20.9	20.8	25.9	26.8	21.7	24.7	25.0
1923	2.2	2.8	24.0	25.4	25.8	29.7	24.7	27.4	27.7
1924	2.4	3.1	25.9	28.8	34.5	31.0	29.0	30.1	31.3
1925	2.7	3.5	29.4	31.2	37.1	32.2	31.8	32.0	34.1
1926	2.8	3.6	30.9	31.9	39.0	37.8	31.4	34.6	35.4
1927	3.1	3.9	36.3	38.9	45.2	41.6	34.5	38.0	39.9
1928	3.2	3.9	39.9	38.5	43.9	48.1	35.7	41.6	44.8
1929	3.2	3.9	44.5	39.8	46.4	50.8	36.0	42.9	46.1
1930	3.3	4.0	43.6	36.9	53.2	46.2	38.0	41.8	44.9
1931	3.3	3.8	41.6	34.6	51.1	45.6	35.1	39.7	41.1

* Percentages in this table are based upon Tables 21 and 22.
† Capital Funds.

The rapid growth of time deposits of banks operating branches in 1920 over 1919 was due in considerable part to the increase in the number of large mutual savings banks operating branches in New York City. It is perhaps needless to point out that an increase in the deposits of mutual savings banks is registered only in time deposits and does not increase or decrease the aggregate figures for demand deposits. The rate of growth of time deposits of banks operating branches was, until 1926, greater than that of demand deposits. During 1926-27, the changes in the two classes of deposits were about the same, whereas after 1927 the demand deposits showed a tendency to increase at a slightly more rapid rate than time deposits, despite the fact that the data for the period as a whole showed greater increases for time than for demand deposits.

A comparison of the changes of total deposits of banks operating branches, classified according to the class of banks, indicates that the total deposits of national and mutual savings banks, con-

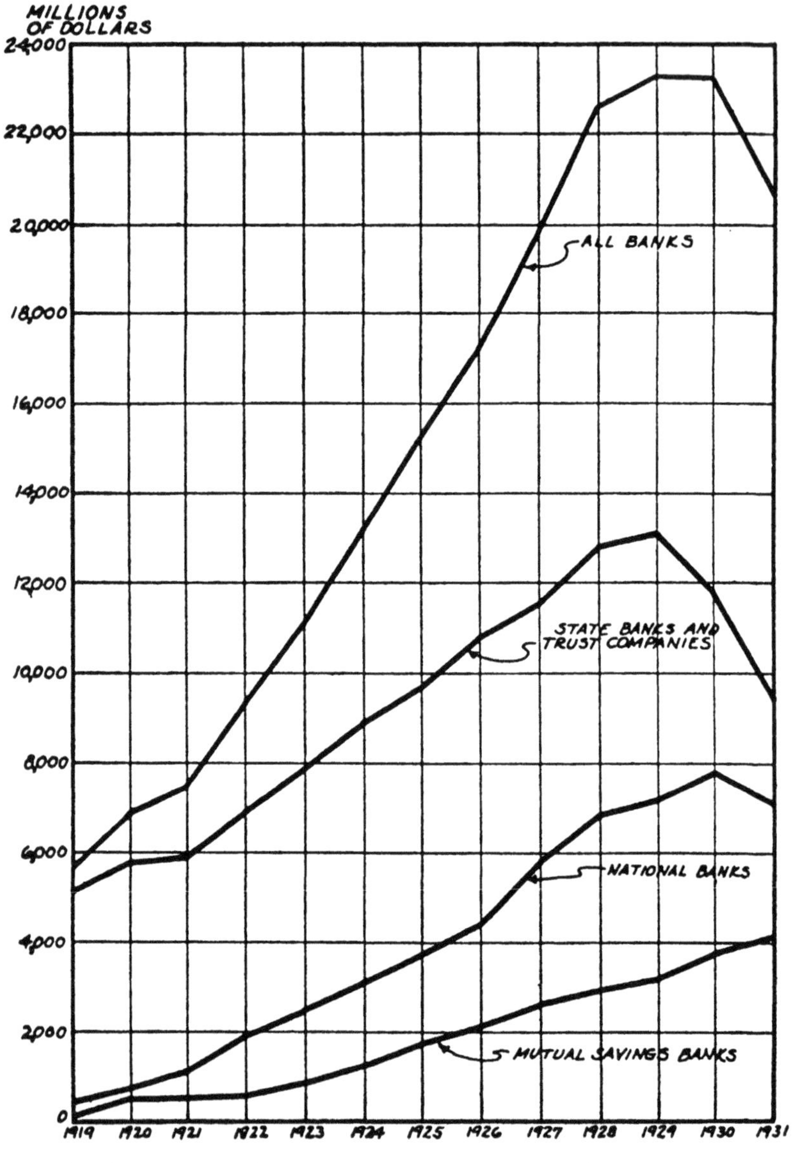

CHART XV. TOTAL DEPOSITS OF BRANCH BANKS IN THE UNITED STATES, CLASSIFIED ACCORDING TO TYPE OF BANK

sidered separately, increased more rapidly than the total deposits of commercial state banks and trust companies. The total deposits of national banks and mutual savings banks, therefore, increased more rapidly than the total deposits of banks operating branches, whereas the total for state banks and trust companies increased more slowly than did the total for all banks. The comparative changes of the deposits for these classes of banks are shown in Chart XV.

When a comparison was made of time deposits of these three classes of banks, it showed results similar to the comparison given in Chart XV for total deposits.

Time deposits of national banks and mutual savings banks, considered separately, increased more rapidly than did the total time deposits of all banks operating branches, while the deposits of state banks and trust companies increased at a slower rate than did the total time deposits of branch banks.

DEPOSITS AND THE LEGAL STATUS

The legal status of the banks offers another basis for the study of the distribution of deposits of banks operating branches, in comparison with all banks. As already pointed out, the states in which branches are in operation may be divided into three classes, as follows: (1) those in which banks operate branches on a statewide basis; (2) those in which banks are restricted in the operation of branches to the city, county, or adjoining county; and (3) those in which the law prohibits a further extension of branches, but which allows a continuation of the branches which were in existence at the time the prohibitory legislation was enacted. The number of states in each of these classes has not remained fixed. In particular there has been a decline in the number of banks operating branches in the third class or division, by reason of the fact that no new banks could establish branches and that occasionally one of the old institutions relinquished in one way or another its right to operate the branches then in existence.

The statistics, when grouped according to this classification, prove that branch banking in this country is restricted to a very considerable extent to city branch banking. The big banks located in the large cities own and control not only a considerable percentage of all branches, but have also a very large portion of all the deposits of branch banks in the United States. In 1919 the total deposits of all banks operating branches were 5.7 billions of dollars, of which more than 4.4 billions (see Table 24) were held by banks located in the states where branches were being operated on a restricted basis. Of the remainder, approximately 980 millions were in the possession of banks located in states permitting state-wide branch banking. In 1931 these two classes held 16.9 billions and 3.5 billions, respectively, or about 99 percent of the total of 20.7 billions for all banks operating branches. Although there was a substantial percentage increase in the deposits of the third class, the aggregate amount of deposits for all banks in this group was so small as to be insignificant from a branch-banking point of view.

The total deposits of all branch banks and of each class are given with other data for the period 1919-31 inclusive, in Table 24.

If the results of Table 24 be reduced to a percentage[11] of all banks operating branches, it will be evident that the relationship of each class to the total fluctuated from year to year. The position of Class 1 remained in the end where it was in the beginning. Banks in states permitting state-wide branches had 17.3 percent of the deposits of banks operating in 1919 and 17.1 percent in 1931. The banks located in the restricted areas held 77.7 percent in 1919 and 81.9 percent in 1931. The net loss came essentially in Class 3, where the percentage was reduced from 5.0 in 1919 to 1.0 in 1931.

The percentage relationship of total resources is most interestingly set forth in Chart XVI.[12]

CAPITAL FUNDS VERSUS DEPOSITS

The question is frequently raised as to whether bank deposits are increasing more rapidly than total capital funds. In considering this question, the inquirer all too frequently refers to the relationship between capital and deposits, disregarding the items

[11] See Table 25, for a more complete picture of these relationships.

[12] Compare with Table 25.

TABLE 24

DATA OF ALL BANKS OPERATING BRANCHES IN THE UNITED STATES, CLASSIFIED ACCORDING TO LEGAL STATUS*

YEAR	ALL BANKS OPERATING BRANCHES IN THE UNITED STATES								
	Number of Banks	Member, Federal Reserve System	Capital	Loans, Discounts	Investments	Deposits			Total Resources
						Demand	*Time*	*Total*	
1919	476	134	695	3,967	1,812	4,014	1,653	5,667	7,695
1920	524	176	930	5,123	2,168	4,455	2,434	6,889	9,592
1921	535	194	1,156	5,473	2,431	4,784	2,667	7,451	10,266
1922	608	246	1,376	5,802	3,302	5,973	3,392	9,365	12,619
1923	673	275	1,636	7,740	3,598	6,705	4,444	11,149	14,966
1924	716	296	1,829	9,063	5,009	7,654	5,532	13,186	17,878
1925	784	335	2,164	10,589	5,841	8,620	6,619	15,239	21,165
1926	787	334	2,411	11,569	6,312	9,612	7,616	17,228	22,947
1927	833	352	3,002	14,505	7,979	10,833	9,092	19,925	27,153
1928	844	352	3,549	15,232	8,409	12,418	10,197	22,615	32,030
1929	816	337	4,229	16,501	8,230	12,946	10,366	23,312	33,269
1930	799	330	4,370	14,962	9,377	12,023	11,202	23,225	33,228
1931	737	296	3,941	12,185	10,078	10,425	10,238	20,663	28,878

* Source: See note Table 21, p. 199, above, regarding source of data for this chap.

TABLE 24 *(Continued)*

YEAR	BANKS OPERATING BRANCHES ON A STATE-WIDE BASIS								
	Number of Banks	Member, Federal Reserve System	Capital	Loans, Discounts	Investments	Deposits			Total Resources
						Demand	*Time*	*Total*	
1919	199	18	126	682	278	408	573	981	1,224
1920	214	36	157	916	325	472	747	1,219	1,527
1921	213	45	174	969	363	464	841	1,305	1,600
1922	250	66	243	1,274	507	771	1,062	1,833	2,301
1923	281	79	289	1,779	585	991	1,327	2,318	2,900
1924	285	81	336	2,011	678	1,142	1,543	2,685	3,348
1925	277	85	365	2,274	832	1,275	1,830	3,105	3,837
1926	260	79	401	2,543	929	1,371	2,069	3,440	4,241
1927	228	64	416	2,730	1,065	1,311	2,128	3,439	4,244
1928	222	59	475	2,572	1,242	1,353	2,302	3,655	4,561
1929	210	57	532	2,903	1,115	1,446	2,544	3,990	5,049
1930	209	56	539	2,693	1,251	1,435	2,518	3,953	4,968
1931	191	54	522	2,324	1,355	1,221	2,302	3,523	4,447

TABLE 24 (*Continued*)

YEAR	BANKS OPERATING BRANCHES ON A RESTRICTED BASIS								
	Number of Banks	Member, Federal Reserve System	Capital	Loans, Discounts	Investments	Deposits			Total Resources
						Demand	*Time*	*Total*	
1919	230	95	538	3,110	1,423	3,452	949	4,401	6,098
1920	264	117	739	4,016	1,738	3,835	1,539	5,374	7,681
1921	278	126	949	4,337	1,957	4,185	1,683	5,868	8,309
1922	310	153	1,071	4,246	2,623	4,959	2,146	7,105	9,726
1923	348	171	1,286	5,664	2,820	5,442	2,906	8,348	11,415
1924	387	190	1,428	6,733	4,109	6,223	3,753	9,976	13,800
1925	467	227	1,733	7,991	4,782	7,059	4,549	11,608	16,612
1926	499	239	1,969	8,801	5,291	8.082	5,423	13,505	18,269
1927	558	266	2,520	11,407	6,775	9,252	6,774	16,026	22,214
1928	579	272	2,996	12,211	7,000	10,755	7,664	18,419	26,639
1929	579	265	3,629	12,234	7,002	11,245	7,649	18,894	27,557
1930	577	266	3,778	12,111	8,041	10,453	8,593	19,046	27,923
1931	535	236	3,387	9,716	8,635	9,086	7,843	16,929	24,122

TABLE 24 (*Continued*)

YEAR	BANKS OPERATING BRANCHES IN STATES PROHIBITING FURTHER EXTENSION								
	Number of Banks	Member, Federal Reserve System	Capital	Loans, Discounts	Investments	Deposits			Total Resources
						Demand	*Time*	*Total*	
1919	47	21	31	174	110	153	131	284	373
1920	46	23	34	191	105	148	148	296	384
1921	44	23	33	166	111	135	142	277	457
1922	48	27	62	282	172	243	184	427	592
1923	44	25	61	297	194	272	211	483	651
1924	44	25	66	319	223	289	236	525	730
1925	40	23	66	324	227	286	240	526	715
1926	28	16	40	226	92	158	124	282	436
1927	47	22	66	367	139	270	190	460	695
1928	43	21	78	449	167	311	231	542	830
1929	27	15	67	364	113	255	172	427	663
1930	13	8	33	157	85	134	91	225	337
1931	11	6	32	145	88	118	92	210	309

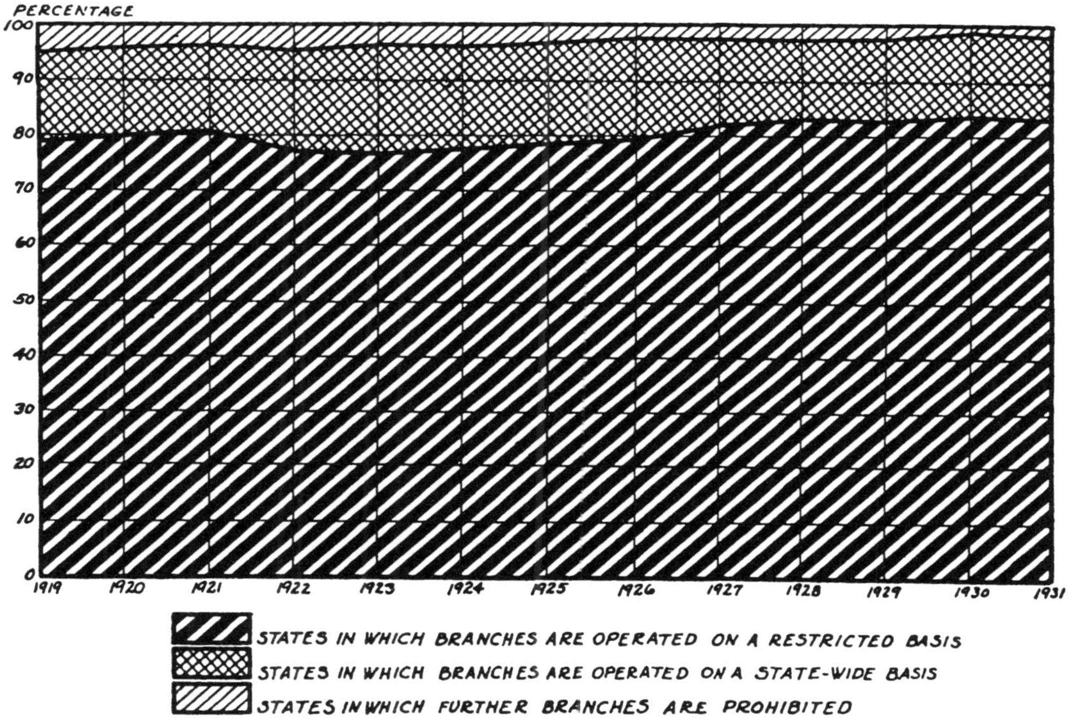

CHART XVI. PERCENTAGE DISTRIBUTION OF TOTAL RESOURCES OF BANKS OPERATING BRANCHES IN THE UNITED STATES, CLASSIFIED ACCORDING TO LEGAL STATUS

TABLE 25

THE PERCENTAGE EACH CLASS OF BANKS (CLASSIFIED ACCORDING TO THE LEGAL STATUS) OPERATING BRANCHES IS OF ALL BANKS OPERATING BRANCHES, INCLUDING SIMILAR PERCENTAGE RELATIONSHIP FOR OTHER ITEMS SHOWN*

YEAR	BANKS OPERATING BRANCHES STATE-WIDE BASIS								
	Number of Banks	Member, Federal Reserve System	Capital†	Loans, Discounts	Investments	Deposits			Resources
						Demand	*Time*	*Total*	
1919	41.8	13.4	18.1	17.1	15.3	10.1	34.6	17.3	15.9
1920	40.8	20.4	16.9	17.9	15.0	10.5	30.6	17.6	15.9
1921	39.8	23.2	15.0	17.7	14.9	9.6	31.5	17.5	15.5
1922	41.1	26.8	17.6	21.9	15.3	12.9	31.2	19.5	18.2
1923	41.7	28.7	17.6	22.9	16.2	14.7	29.9	20.7	19.4
1924	39.8	27.4	18.3	22.1	13.5	14.9	27.8	20.3	18.7
1925	35.3	25.3	16.8	21.4	14.2	14.7	27.6	20.3	18.1
1926	33.0	23.6	16.6	21.9	14.7	14.2	27.1	19.9	18.4
1927	27.4	18.2	13.8	18.8	13.4	12.1	23.4	17.3	15.6
1928	26.3	16.7	13.3	16.8	14.7	10.8	22.5	16.1	14.2
1929	25.7	16.9	12.5	17.5	13.5	11.1	24.5	17.1	15.1
1920	26.2	17.0	12.3	18.0	13.3	11.9	22.5	17.0	15.0
1931	25.9	18.2	13.2	19.1	13.5	11.7	22.5	17.1	15.4

* Percentages presented in this table are based upon data given in Table 24.
† Including capital, surplus and undivided profits.

of surplus and undivided profits. It makes a vast difference in the results of our comparisons whether these two items are included, especially in recent years when the surplus has been increased so greatly. It makes a considerable difference in results, also, whether the total of deposits includes "due to banks." To the writer it appears logical to omit "due to banks" from deposits. In Chapter XII, on "The Concentration of Branch Banking in Leading Cities," the ratios between these two sets of items for different years were worked out, both with and without "due to banks." The reader is referred to that chapter if he is interested in comparing the results in the two cases. For purposes of the present discussion, "due to banks" will be omitted.

Total capital funds of all banks operating branches increased from 695 millions of dollars in 1919 to 3,941 millions in 1931, (see

TABLE 25 (*Continued*)

YEAR	BANKS OPERATING BRANCHES ON RESTRICTED BASIS								
	Number of Banks	Member, Federal Reserve System	Capital†	Loans, Discounts	Investments	Deposits			Resources
						Demand	*Time*	*Total*	
1919	48.3	70.8	77.4	78.4	78.5	86.0	57.4	77.7	79.2
1920	50.3	66.4	79.5	78.4	80.2	86.1	63.2	78.0	80.0
1921	51.9	64.9	82.1	79.3	80.5	87.5	63.1	78.8	80.9
1922	51.0	62.1	77.8	73.2	79.4	83.0	63.3	75.9	77.0
1923	51.7	62.1	78.6	73.2	78.4	81.2	65.4	74.9	76.2
1924	54.0	64.2	78.0	74.3	82.0	81.3	67.8	75.7	77.1
1925	59.5	67.7	80.0	75.5	81.9	81.9	68.7	76.2	78.4
1926	63.4	71.5	81.6	76.1	83.8	84.1	71.2	78.4	79.6
1927	67.0	75.6	84.0	78.6	84.9	85.4	74.5	80.4	81.8
1928	68.6	77.2	84.4	80.2	83.2	86.6	75.2	81.4	83.1
1929	70.9	78.6	85.8	80.2	85.1	86.9	73.8	81.1	82.8
1930	72.2	80.6	86.5	80.9	85.8	86.9	76.7	82.0	84.0
1931	72.6	79.7	85.9	79.7	85.7	87.2	76.6	81.9	83.5

YEAR	BANKS OPERATING BRANCHES IN PROHIBITED STATES								
	Number of Banks	Members, Federal Reserve System	Capital†	Loans, Discounts	Investments	Deposits			Resources
						Demand	*Time*	*Total*	
1929	9.9	15.7	4.4	4.4	6.1	3.8	7.9	5.0	4.8
1910	8.8	13.1	3.7	3.7	4.8	3.3	6.1	4.3	4.0
1921	8.2	11.9	2.9	3.0	4.6	2.8	5.4	3.7	3.5
1922	7.9	11.0	4.5	4.9	5.2	4.1	5.4	4.6	4.7
1923	6.5	9.1	3.7	3.8	5.4	4.1	4.7	4.3	4.3
1924	6.2	8.4	3.6	3.5	4.5	3.8	4.3	4.0	4.1
1925	5.1	6.9	3.1	3.1	3.9	3.3	3.6	3.5	3.4
1926	3.6	4.8	1.7	1.9	1.5	1.6	1.6	1.6	1.9
1927	5.6	6.3	2.2	2.5	1.7	2.5	2.1	2.3	2.6
1928	5.1	6.0	2.2	2.9	2.0	2.5	2.3	2.4	2.6
1929	3.3	4.5	1.6	2.2	1.4	2.0	1.7	1.8	2.0
1930	1.6	2.4	0.8	1.1	0.9	1.1	0.8	1.0	1.0
1931	1.5	2.0	0.8	1.2	0.8	1.1	0.9	1.0	1.1

Table 21), an increase of about 465 percent. During the same period, total deposits of the same group of banks increased from 5,667 millions to 20,663 millions, or an increase of approximately 264 percent. The ratio between capital funds and total deposits for all banks operating branches was 8.16 in 1919, as compared with 5.24 in 1931.[13] This would indicate conclusively that capital funds were increasing more rapidly than total deposits. From that point of view the depositor was receiving greater protection in 1931 than in 1919.

If a comparison be made between these two classes (data for years 1919 and 1931) of items for all banks in the United States, capital funds increased 73 percent, while the total deposits increased only 54 percent. The ratio between total deposits and total capital funds was 6.2 in 1919 and 5.5 in 1931. Here, as in the case of banks operating branches, the developments during the period under study have tended to disprove the contention that the stockholders are now giving the depositor less protection in the form of capital funds than was the case ten years ago. If we go a step further and make a similar comparison, using only the branch banks in the eleven leading cities, the results are substantially the same. From these data, then, the conclusion may be drawn that the depositor was better protected in 1931 than in 1919.[14]

LOANS, DISCOUNTS, AND INVESTMENTS IN RELATION TO DEPOSITS

Total loans and discounts of banks operating branches increased about 207 percent from 1919 to 1931, while investments advanced 456 percent. The combined figures for loans, discounts, and investments showed an increase of about 285 percent. Demand, time, and total deposits increased 160, 519, and 264 percent, respectively. Investments, although increasing more rapidly than loans and discounts, did not increase so rapidly as time de-

[13] See the ratios presented in Table 33, Chap. XII.

[14] Some allowance must be made for the losses sustained by many banks which have not been fully written off. There can be little doubt that as such losses are written off, there will be a considerable reduction in the amount of capital funds reported, which will modify the ratios here arrived at by using bank statistics as stated.

posits. A favorable factor in the situation, however, is the fact that the banks have relatively few bonds and long-term investments and a relatively large proportion of loans and discounts.

For all banks in the United States, time deposits increased 199 percent, while the demand deposits declined approximately 4.8 percent. Loans and discounts for all banks increased 39 percent and investments 65 percent. These figures mean that the huge expansion of time deposits was being used for the purpose of expanding investments, as well as loans and discounts.

TOTAL RESOURCES

In 1919 state banks and trust companies operating branches had more than 90.17 percent of the total resources of all banks operating branches in the United States. National banks and mutual savings banks operating branches had 7.93 and 1.89 percent respectively of the total resources of all banks operating branches. The relative position of each class of banks varied from year to year, but taking the total resources of all branch banks as a whole, the trend of state banks and trust companies was downward, whereas the other two classes were increasing. In 1931 the percentage each class held of the total resources of all banks operating branches was as follows: national banks, 37.0 percent; state banks and trust companies, 47.69 percent; and mutual savings banks, 15.3 percent. The relative position of each of these three classes will be perhaps more easily appreciated by reference to Chart XVII.[16]

From this chart it will be observed that the figures for national banks reached a peak in 1931, when the percentage was 37.0.

If a comparison be made of the volume of total deposits of each class of banks, classified according to the legal status, the results are most convincing with regard to the relative positions of these groups. The banks operating branches on a state-wide basis in 1919 had 15.9 percent of the total resources of all banks operating branches, whereas in 1931 the percentage had declined slightly, being only 15.4 percent (see Table 25). Banks operating branches on a restricted basis, that is, within the city, county,

[16] For a more complete picture of the percentage relationship, see Table 26.

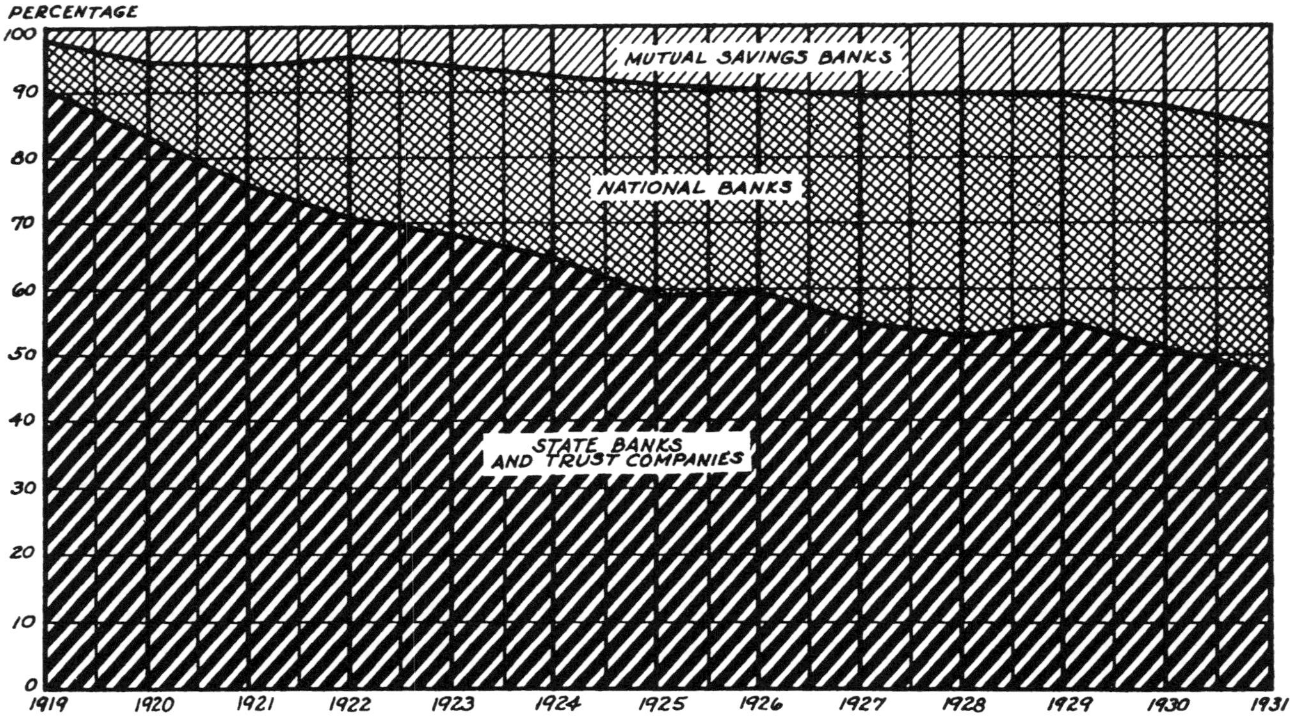

CHART XVII. PERCENTAGE DISTRIBUTION OF RESOURCES OF ALL BANKS OPERATING BRANCHES IN THE UNITED STATES, CLASSIFIED ACCORDING TO TYPE OF BANK

or adjoining county, had 79.2 percent of the resources of all banks operating branches in 1919, a figure which increased to 83.5 percent in 1931. Banks operating branches in those states which prohibited a further extension of branches showed a decline from 4.8 percent in 1919 to 1.1 percent in 1931.

The aggregate total resources of all banks operating branches in the United States are given in Table 21. That table includes detailed data for national banks, state banks and trust companies, and mutual savings banks. Banks operating branches had approximately 41.1 percent of the resources of all banks in the United States in 1931.

The total resources of all banks operating branches increased much more rapidly than did the total resources of all banks in the country. This increase in resources of branch banks was gradual, showing a net gain each year over the preceding year. The greatest expansion came after the ruling of the Comptroller of the Currency in 1922. The total resources of banks with branches increased sharply from 12.6 billions in 1922 to 21.2 billions at the end of 1925. Another period of expansion followed the passage of the McFadden Amendment in 1927. At the end of 1927[16] the total resources of branch banks were 27.2 billions of dollars. The totals for 1929 and 1931 are given above as 33.2 and 28.9 billions respectively. The total resources of all banks increased from 47.6 billions in 1919 to 72.2[17] billions in 1929 and to 70.2 billions in 1931. While this was a very substantial growth, the increase took place more gradually and more uniformly than was the case with branch banks. The importance of each class of branch banks to other classes of banks operating branches and to the banking system as a whole, as measured by total resources, is shown in Chart XVIII.

THE 1922 RULING OF THE COMPTROLLER OF THE CURRENCY

Prior to the ruling of the Comptroller of the Currency in 1922, the number of national banks operating branches was small and limited in certain cities. At the end of 1921 there were in opera-

[16] See Table 21, p. 199.
[17] See Table 22, p. 208.

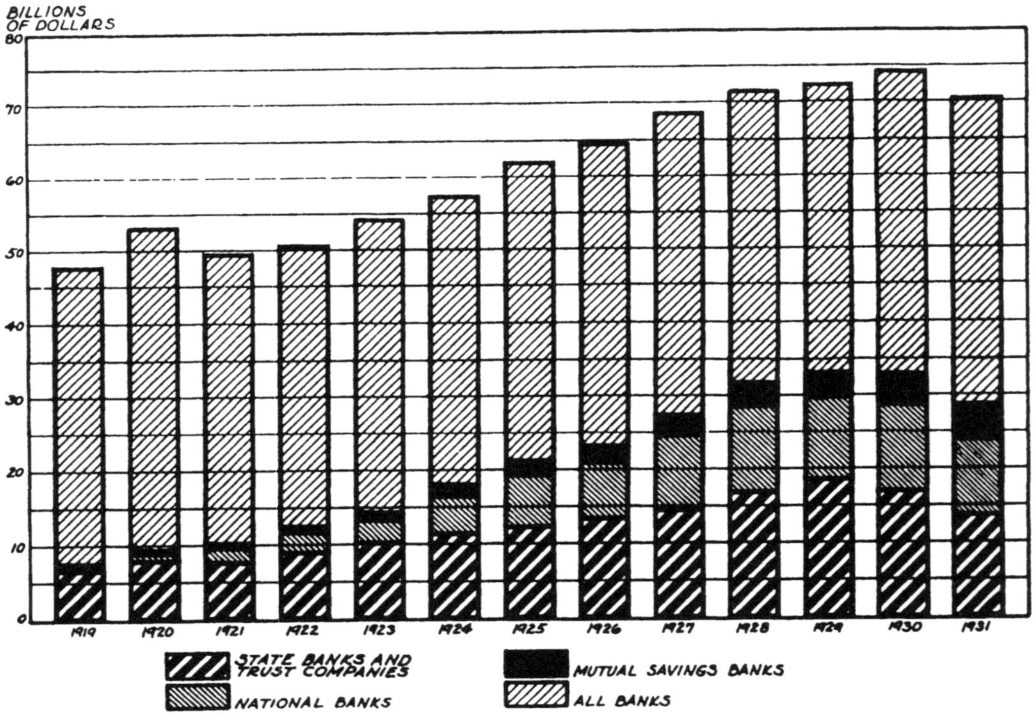

CHART XVIII. RESOURCES OF: (1) ALL BANKS OPERATING BRANCHES; (2) STATE BANKS AND TRUST COMPANIES; (3) NATIONAL BANKS; AND (4) MUTUAL SAVINGS BANKS

tion only 24 national banks with branches. These banks were operating 74 branches, an average of approximately 3 branches per bank. Beginning with 1922 there was a rapid increase in the number of both banks and branches, as compared with earlier years. The total number of national banks operating branches reached a peak in 1927, when 165 banks were operating 922 branches. The number of banks engaged in branch banking declined after 1927, but the actual number of branches continued to increase, reaching the highest point in 1931 with 1,274 branches.

It is quite evident, therefore, that the Comptroller's ruling had a very important influence upon the development of branches among national banks. This influence extended to state banks and trust companies. The number of state banks and trust companies operating branches increased the number of their branches from 1,292 in 1921 to 2,101 in 1931. The action of the Comptroller of the Currency did not change the legal status of branches among state banks and trust companies, but it did have a very considerable influence among state bankers in that they felt that there was to be a greater extension of branches by national banks and that they should, therefore, likewise develop more branches. If the growth of branch banking after 1922 be measured by the total resources of banks operating branches, the results are even more striking. In 1921 all banks and trust companies operating branches had total resources of $10,266,000,000, whereas in 1931 the resources amounted to more than $28,877,000,000. On a percentage basis, the total resources of all banks operating branches was 20.7 percent of the resources of all banks in 1921, as compared with 41.1 percent in 1931. If, on the other hand, it be desired to make a comparison before the passage of the McFadden Act of February, 1927, the results are also marked. The total resources of all banks operating branches were 35.4 percent of the total resources of all banks in the United States at the close of 1926.

THE MCFADDEN ACT OF 1927

The provisions of the McFadden Act were designed to accomplish two objects in regard to the extension of branches: (1) the restrictions of state-wide branch banking by preventing a further extension of "out-of-town" branches by member state banks and trust companies in the Federal Reserve system; and (2) the granting of legal permission to national banks to establish and operate branches in the city of the parent bank in those states which allowed state banks and trust companies to establish branches. The results of this act with regard to the extension of branches within the city limits were rather marked. The number of national banks with branches increased to some extent and the number of branches operated by these showed considerable increase. The total number of branches of national banks increased from 425 in 1926 to 922 in 1927. This rapid growth was largely the result of the conversion of the Bank of Italy in California into the national system in the early part of 1927, shortly after

TABLE 26

THE PERCENTAGE EACH OF THE FOLLOWING ITEMS, OF EACH TYPE OF BANK OPERATING BRANCHES, IS OF THE CORRESPONDING ITEMS OF ALL BANKS OPERATING BRANCHES IN THE UNITED STATES, 1919–29*

YEAR	ALL NATIONAL BANKS OPERATING BRANCHES								
	Number of Banks	Member, Federal Reserve System	Capital†	Loans, Discounts	Investments	Deposits			Resources
						Demand	*Time*	*Total*	
1919	3.78	13.43	8.10	8.89	5.52	7.52	4.11	6.52	7.93
1920	4.00	11.93	10.80	13.62	4.78	11.86	4.03	9.09	11.47
1921	4.48	12.37	22.54	21.67	8.15	19.29	4.98	14.17	18.69
1922	9.21	22.76	26.64	30.58	14.90	26.70	9.59	20.50	25.01
1923	13.37	32.72	29.59	29.23	20.36	27.01	13.07	21.45	25.65
1924	15.08	36.48	29.14	31.03	18.84	30.28	13.49	23.24	27.74
1925	18.36	42.98	31.81	33.70	19.96	33.33	13.92	24.90	31.67
1926	18.17	42.81	30.82	34.31	19.69	33.24	15.56	25.42	30.43
1927	19.78	46.74	34.09	37.37	23.87	35.30	21.94	29.19	34.11
1928	19.19	46.02	35.92	40.46	25.63	36.17	23.82	30.60	36.89
1929	19.60	47.47	33.82	36.97	21.36	34.20	25.97	30.54	34.07
1930	21.03	50.91	36.26	42.52	23.38	39.27	26.72	33.22	36.59
1931	21.30	53.04	38.38	45.62	23.98	41.51	26.96	34.30	37.00

* Percentages presented in this table are based upon data given in Table 21.

† Including capital, surplus and undivided profits of commercial banks and the guaranty fund, reserve fund, etc. of mutual savings banks

TABLE 26 *(Continued)*

YEAR	STATE BANKS AND TRUST COMPANIES WITH BRANCHES IN THE UNITED STATES								
	Number of Banks	Member, Federal Reserve System	Capital†	Loans, Discounts	Investments	Deposits			Resources
						Demand	*Time*	*Total*	
1919	93.69	86.56	90.40	89.96	89.45	92.47	87.78	91.10	90.17
1920	93.12	88.06	85.74	85.28	76.19	88.13	76.62	84.06	83.24
1921	92.52	87.62	74.38	77.20	73.80	80.70	76.65	79.25	76.18
1922	87.50	77.23	70.05	68.33	71.41	73.29	75.16	73.97	70.51
1923	82.16	67.27	65.62	69.82	58.32	72.98	68.16	71.06	68.26
1924	79.05	63.51	64.24	67.55	58.92	69.71	64.51	67.53	64.75
1925	75.38	57.01	59.94	64.66	52.05	66.66	59.93	63.74	59.28
1926	74.96	57.18	59.92	63.78	50.56	66.75	57.56	62.69	59.56
1927	72.66	53.25	55.58	60.81	45.96	64.69	49.79	57.88	55.23
1928	72.86	53.97	54.65	57.59	42.80	63.82	46.93	56.22	52.73
1929	71.56	52.52	57.93	60.71	44.10	65.79	43.38	55.82	55.30
1930	69.71	49.09	53.77	55.02	43.76	60.73	40.28	50.86	51.00
1931	68.52	46.96	51.54	51.31	40.64	58.49	33.78	46.25	47.69

YEAR	MUTUAL SAVINGS BANKS WITH BRANCHES IN THE UNITED STATES								
	Number of Banks	Member, Federal Reserve System	Capital†	Loans, Discounts	Investments	Deposits			Resources
						Demand	*Time*	*Total*	
1919	2.52		1.49	1.13	5.02		8.10	2.36	1.89
1920	2.86		3.44	1.08	19.01		19.34	6.83	5.28
1921	2.99		3.06	1.12	18.04		18.35	6.56	5.11
1922	3.28		3.29	1.07	13.67		15.23	5.51	4.46
1923	4.45		4.77	0.94	21.30		18.76	7.48	6.08
1924	5.86		6.60	1.40	22.23		21.99	9.22	7.50
1925	6.25		8.24	1.62	27.98		26.13	11.35	9.04
1926	6.86		9.24	1.90	29.73		26.87	11.88	10.00
1927	7.55		10.32	1.81	30.15		28.25	12.92	10.65
1928	7.93		9.42	1.94	31.55		29.23	13.18	10.37
1929	8.82		8.23	2.30	34.53		30.63	13.62	10.61
1930	9.26		9.50	2.45	32.86		33.00	15.92	12.40
1931	10.18		10.08	3.07	35.38		39.26	19.45	15.30

the enactment of the McFadden Act. Aside from the Bank of Italy, there have been several branches established by national banks within the city limits. The effects of this act have been to increase very greatly the number of city branches in the national system as well as to check the growth of the other type of branch.

The total number of all member banks and trust companies, including national banks, operating branches showed very little change after the passage of this legislation. The total number of such member banks was 334 in 1926 and 296 in 1931, whereas the member state banks and trust companies were 191 in 1926 in comparison with 139 in 1931. The number of branches established by state banks and trust companies outside the city of the parent declined sharply in 1927, owing to the conversion of the Bank of Italy to the national system. After that year the number of outside branches increased, but at a less rapid rate than before the enactment of the McFadden Amendment.

The McFadden Amendment did not, in last analysis, bring about any very fundamental change in the branch-banking situation. What it did do was to check for a time the growth of branches outside the city of the parent. This decline in the number of new branches would probably have come without the law, for the simple reason that the greatest growth had been in the state of California and the situation had reached a point in that state where it was likely to slow down. The movement has never attained such proportions in other states, and the law could therefore do no more than prevent a growth in the other states where state-wide branch banking is permitted. It accomplished positive results in the expansion of national branch banking and marked an important stage in its growth largely for the reason that it legalized the practice which had been carried on in the system for some time, giving an approval to it which had not previously been extended in this country. Aside from this feature, the McFadden Act can not be regarded as favorable to branch banking.

The (Glass-Steagall) Banking Act of 1933 extended the privileges of establishing and operating branches on a state-wide basis to national banks in those states which permit the state banks and trust companies to operate branches on that basis. The new act attempted to equalize the conditions between state and national banks. This was not fully accomplished for the reason that the capital requirements of national banks operating branches outside the city of the parent are somewhat higher than those for state banks and trust companies. It appears likely that the enactment of this act means a considerable extension of branches in the future.[18]

BRANCH BANK FAILURES

During recent years much discussion has centered around the question of bank failures. The query has frequently been raised as to whether unit banks have been more likely to fail than banks operating branches. The only available statistics covering this phase of the banking situation over a period of years are those prepared under the general direction of the Federal Reserve Committee on Branch, Group and Chain Banking. From 1921 to 1931 inclusive, 179 banks and trust companies operating branches failed. These banks had, at the time of their respective closing, in the aggregate 474 branches, and loans and investments amounting to $1,056,007,000. Of the 179 banks which failed, 134

TABLE 27

SUSPENSIONS OF BANKS WITH BRANCHES, 1921–31

YEAR	NUMBER OF SUSPENSIONS	PERCENT OF TOTAL	NUMBER OF BRANCHES				LOANS AND INVESTMENTS (000 OMITTED)	PERCENT OF TOTAL
			In Head-Office City	*Outside Head-Office City*	*Total*	*Percent of Total*		
1921	6	3.4	3	3	6	1.3	$33,911	3.2
1922	2	1.1		2	2	0.4	1,921	0.2
1923	4	2.2		6	6	1.3	2,629	0.2
1924	4	2.2		5	5	1.0	1,867	0.2
1925	2	1.1	1	1	2	0.4	2,652	0.3
1926	11	6.1		33	33	7.0	11,724	1.1
1927	3	1.7		7	7	1.5	2,226	0.2
1928	3	1.7		7	7	1.5	2,843	0.3
1929	10	5.6	7	11	18	3.8	23,213	2.2
1930	40	22.4	109	38	147	31.0	434,074	41.1
1931	94	52.5	166	75	241	50.8	538,947	51.0
TOTAL	179	100.0	286	188	474	100.0	$1,056,007	100.0

[18] For a more general discussion of the possible effect of this act, see pp. 146-47.

TABLE 28

SUSPENSIONS OF STATE AND NATIONAL BANKS WITH BRANCHES, 1921–31

YEAR	STATE BANKS					NATIONAL BANKS				
	Number of Suspensions	Number of Branches			Loans and Investments (000 omitted)	Number of Suspensions	Number of Branches			Loans and Investments (000 omitted)
		In Head-Office City	*Outside Head-Office City*	*Total*			*In Head-Office City*	*Outside Head-Office City*	*Total*	
1921	6	3	3	6	$33,911					
1922	2		2	2	1,921					
1923	4		6	6	2,629					
1924	4		5	5	1,867					
1925	2	1	1	2	2,652					
1926	11		33	33	11,724					
1927	3		7	7	2,226					
1928	3		7	7	2,843					
1929	10	7	11	18	23,213					
1930	38	107	38	145	383,407	2	2		2	$50,667
1931	85	144	74	218	483,564	9	22	1	23	55,383
TOTAL	168	262	187	449	$949,957	11	24	1	25	$106,050

were closed during the years 1930-31. Table 27 is reproduced here to show more fully the extent of branch-bank failures during the years 1921-31.[19]

The relationship of national branch-bank failures to that of failures among state branch banks and trust companies is shown in Table 28. Only 11 national banks failed, all of them closing their doors in 1930-31.[20]

The data in Table 29 indicate the relationship of the number of failed branch banks to all banks operating branches in certain branch-bank states.[21] This comparison shows a relatively high number of failures of branch banks, but the banks which failed operated few branches, less than two on an average.

TABLE 29

SUSPENSIONS OF BANKS WITH BRANCHES, 1921–31, AND ACTIVE BANKS WITH BRANCHES, DECEMBER 31, 1931, IN IMPORTANT BRANCH-BANKING STATES

STATE*	ACTIVE BANKS WITH BRANCHES DECEMBER 31, 1931		SUSPENSIONS OF BANKS WITH BRANCHES 1921–1931	
	Number of Banks	*Number of Branches*	*Number of Banks*	*Number of Branches*
California	50	801	5	15
Maryland	27	108	4	17
Louisiana	39	98	12	18
North Carolina	23	84	24	40
South Carolina	11	77	9	24
Maine	19	73	3	5
Virginia	30	57	6	7
Tennessee	25	58	4	5
TOTAL	224	1,356	67	131

* Only those states are given in which a substantial number of branches have been in operation outside the city of the head office for several years, although the number of branches shown includes both those inside and outside the city of the head office of the bank.

During the year 1932 the number of bank failures declined considerably as compared with 1931. While there are no sum-

[19] Report of the Federal Reserve Committee on Branch, Group, and Chain Banking (1932), on *Branch Banking in the United States*, p. 231.

[20] Report of the Federal Reserve Committee on Branch, Group, and Chain Banking (1932), on *Branch Banking in the United States*, p. 232.

[21] *Ibid.*, p. 235.

mary data available to show the scope and extent of these failures, it is known that several branch banks operating branches failed. These were mostly small banks with few branches. Many banks operating branches found themselves in serious difficulties following the bank holiday in March, 1933. The failure of two large branch banks in Detroit, together with certain banks in Ohio, Maryland and elsewhere, has led many to believe that branch banks are just as likely to fail as unit banks. It is a fact, of course, that the type of branch banking we have had in this country did not fare very well in recent months. The causes for the failure of the large branch banks in Detroit were probably the same as those for other banks in Michigan and adjoining states, frozen loans and unsound management.

Until we have adopted and tried a branch-banking system on a much wider scale, we shall be unable to determine whether such a system will work satisfactorily in this country. It is clear, I take it, that the unit bank has failed to meet the needs of the country. Branch banking has succeeded fairly well in many countries. We have yet to adopt and establish a branch system comparable to those of foreign countries.

SUMMARY

1. The total number of banks operating branches increased from 476 in 1919 to 737 in 1931. Total resources of all banks with branches during the same period advanced from $7,695,000,000 to $28,878,000,000, an increase of approximately 275 percent. Total deposits expanded 264 percent, while the total number of branches rose from 1,082 to 3,375.

2. Total resources of all banks operating branches in 1919 amounted to 16.2 percent of the total resources for all banks in the United States, but in 1931 the branch banks had 41.1 percent of the total for all banks.

3. The number of branches increased rapidly, following the ruling of the Comptroller of the Currency in 1922 and the passage of the McFadden Act in 1927. Total resources and total deposits of all banks with branches showed similar gains following these changes.

4. If branch banks be classified according to the legal status

of the branches, the largest gains were made by banks located in those states which restricted branches to city, county, or adjoining county of the parent bank. Substantial gains were made by banks operating branches in those states permitting state-wide branches. If the total resources of banks operating branches in states permitting state-wide branches be expressed as a percentage of the total resources of all banks operating branches, this class showed a slight decline.

5. Branches located in the city of the parent institution registered much greater gains than did the number of branches located outside the city of the parent.

6. Time deposits of banks operating branches have shown a greater increase in relation to the total deposits of all banks operating branches than have time deposits of all banks in relation to total deposits of all banks in operation in the United States.

7. The net increase in the total resources of state banks and trust companies operating branches between 1919 and 1931 was 6,833 millions of dollars, whereas national banks and mutual savings banks showed net increases of 10,076 and 4,273 millions of dollars respectively. If the changes be measured in terms of percentages of all banks operating branches during this period, the results show that the total resources of all state banks and trust companies operating branches declined from 90.17 to 47.69 percent of the total resources of all banks operating branches. Similar percentages for national banks and mutual savings banks increased from 7.93 and 1.89 percent to 37.00 and 15.30 percent respectively of the total resources of branch banks. Despite the aggregate increase in the resources of state banks and trust companies, there was a marked change in the relative position of this group of branch institutions. National banks and mutual savings banks made greater percentage gains than state banks and trust companies. The total resources of state banks and trust companies with branches still remain considerably larger than the combined resources of national banks and mutual savings banks with branches.

8. With the exception of a few banks which operate a substantial number of branches, the average size of the branch systems

or the number of branches operated by any one bank is small. Although there has been a tendency to increase this average, the growth has been quite slow. Our system remains, therefore, essentially a unit system with a few large banks operating a considerable number of city branches. This excludes the Bank of America, National Trust and Savings Association and a few other systems in California, and perhaps The Citizens and Southern National Bank of Savannah, Georgia.

9. Total capital funds of banks operating branches have increased approximately 467 percent, whereas total deposits of the same banks have increased only about 264 percent. This would seem to indicate greater protection to depositors by reason of the greater amount of capital funds in relation to the deposit liabilities of the branch-banking institutions.

10. Loans, discounts, and investments of banks operating branches showed a greater percentage increase than did total deposits. Time deposits increased more than 519 percent from 1919 to 1931, whereas total investments increased only about 456 percent.

11. Investments of branch banks increased about 456 percent, while total loans and discounts expanded approximately 315 percent, during the period under discussion.

CHAPTER XII

THE CONCENTRATION OF BRANCH BANKING IN LEADING CITIES

As has already been pointed out, the growth in the number of banks operating branches has been very largely concentrated within a few states. Branches of these banks have been highly concentrated within certain cities or are owned by branch banks whose head offices are located in these leading cities. States in which the greatest concentration has occurred are New York, California, Michigan, Ohio, Pennsylvania, Louisiana, Massachusetts, and Maryland. If one were to include in the list only the first five states listed, a large percentage of all branches in the country would be included. The two outstanding states are, perhaps, New York and California. New York City and Buffalo have a large number of banks operating branches, all of which are located within these two cities and are classed as "city" branches. California, on the other hand, has state-wide branches with two large branch cities—Los Angeles and San Francisco. More "outside" branches are located in the state of California than in any other state in the Union.

A comparison of the resources of all banks in the United States,[1] the resources of all banks operating branches,[2] and the resources of all banks operating branches in the eleven leading cities,[3] shows that the growth in either or both classes of banks operating branches was much more rapid than that for all banks in this country. The percentage changes occurring in total resources of all banks operating branches were almost identical with the percentage changes taking place in the resources of banks operating branches in the eleven leading cities.

It is of interest to study banking concentration on the basis

[1] See Table 22.
[2] See Table 21.
[3] See Table 31.

of the expansion in these eleven cities which have taken a leading position in the development of branch banking. With this idea in mind, separate statistics have been compiled for the banks operating branches in the eleven leading branch-banking cities. These data include a large percentage of all the deposits and resources of all banks operating branches within the United States.

CONCENTRATION OF BRANCH BANKING IN LEADING CITIES

Branch banks located in the eleven leading cities[4] have developed branches in such numbers that they have a large proportion[5] of all the branches in operation in the United States. The number of branches operated by the banks in these cities[6] has varied from year to year, showing a rapid increase during the period from 1919 to 1931 inclusive. In 1919 there were 486 branches owned by banks located within these centers, or 44.9 percent of all branches being operated in the United States at the end of that year. In 1932 the total number of branches for all banks operating branches in the United States was 3,290, as compared with 2,032[7] branches for the eleven leading cities, which was 61.7 percent of the total. Even though the concentration was noticeable in 1919, so far as the number of branches was concerned, the number increased very rapidly in these centers as well as in other parts of the country. It is probably true that, had the state laws permitted banks to operate branches in certain other states, the number of city branches would have been considerably larger than they are, both in the aggregate and in the total percentage of all banks operating branches in the United States. This is, of

[4] The eleven cities included are Baltimore, Boston, Buffalo, Cincinnati, Cleveland, Detroit, Los Angeles, New Orleans, New York, Philadelphia, and San Francisco.

[5] The cities of Chicago, St. Louis, Minneapolis, Kansas City, Dallas, Seattle, and Denver are other centers where branches would probably have been established, had the state banking laws not prohibited that form of banking.

[6] It should be noted that some of the branches operated by banks located in these eleven cities are situated outside the corporate limits of the parent institution, and are frequently referred to as "outside" branches.

[7] The peak in the number of branches was reached in 1929, both for all banks operating branches in the United States and in the eleven leading cities. The numbers for the two classes were 3,603 and 2,286, respectively.

TABLE 30

NUMBER OF BRANCHES IN EACH OF ELEVEN LEADING CITIES*

CITY	1919	1920	1921	1922	1923	1924	1925	1926	1927	1928	1929	1930	1931	1932
Baltimore	27	28	28	35	43	52	54	58	62	65	76	71	70	71
Boston	22	20	21	25	32	34	40	51	53	59	66	72	64	56
Buffalo	20	26	29	39	47	50	53	62	68	72	65	79	79	69
Cincinnati	12	16	22	24	29	35	41	46	49	52	46	56	61	58
Cleveland	31	46	67	76	76	77	79	86	90	99	102	104	105	108
Detroit	111	124	147	191	201	236	285	291	318	298	314	294	275	233
Los Angeles	23	31	43	94	171	231	273	334	378	252	389	294	217	218
New Orleans	23	32	32	39	39	41	42	44	46	47	44	46	45	44
New York	161	191	205	227	272	308	371	403	479	540	630	574	569	552
Philadelphia	14	18	27	31	39	50	77	90	104	119	143	126	92	89
San Francisco	42	42	48	76	144	170	201	243	423	463	411	468	523	529
TOTAL IN ELEVEN CITIES	486	574	669	857	1,093	1,284	1,516	1,708	2,070	2,066	2,286	2,184	2,100	2,032

* Source: See note, Table 21, p. 199.

course, merely conjecture, since we can do no more than estimate what the results might have been under different conditions.

While there has been a general upward trend in the number of branches operated by the banks located in the eleven leading cities, the expansion has been especially rapid among banks located in Detroit, Los Angeles, New York, Philadelphia, and San Francisco. Banks located in these five cities had 1,676 branches in operation in 1931, which was about 50 percent of all branches in the United States. The number of branches being operated by the banks of these leading cities is shown for each city, year by year, for the period from 1919 to 1932 inclusive, in Table 30.

The total resources, in 1931, of those branch banks located in the "big five" cities[8] which operate branches amounted to more than $18,560,000,000, or slightly over 64 percent of the total resources of all banks operating branches in the United States. Banks operating branches in New York City alone had more than $15,600,000,000[9] in total resources in 1930, which was over 46 percent of the total resources of all banks operating branches in the United States. At that time the New York City banks were operating 574 branches, or 16 percent of all branches in operation in this country.

The importance of the eleven cities in the development of branch banking in this country will be more fully and clearly appreciated by a study of statistics showing the volume of resources and other items indicating the size of the institutions involved. In 1919 the total resources of banks operating branches in the eleven cities amounted to more than $5,926,000,000, as compared with $7,695,000,000 for all banks operating branches in the United States. In 1931 the total for the eleven cities was $21,957,000,000 as compared with $28,878,000,000 for all banks operating branches throughout the country. The eleven cities held 77 and 76 percent, respectively, of the total resources of all banks operating branches in the United States in these two years. These percentages fluctuated from year to year during the period from 1919

[8] New York, San Francisco, Detroit, Los Angeles, and Philadelphia.

[9] The number of branches was 569 in 1931, while the total resources had declined to $13,245,000,000 for the same year.

to 1931 inclusive, but never varied greatly above or below these two percentages. In fact, the lowest percentage for these cities was 76.0 in 1931, while the highest for any year was 79.7 percent in 1921.

A comparison of the items of total capital and surplus and undivided profits, loans and discounts, investments and total deposits of the two classes of banks, shows about the same percentages as those given in the preceding paragraph for total resources. These data show the banks operating branches in the eleven cities have on an average slightly more than 75 percent of all the business and assets of all banks operating branches in the United States.

It is interesting to note that although the volume of total deposits held by the banks operating branches in the leading cities remained close to 75 percent throughout the period studied,[10] an analysis of the time and demand deposits shows that there was considerable variation in these two when considered separately. The demand deposits in these centers decreased from 84.2 percent of the demand deposits of all banks operating branches in the country in 1919, to 79 percent in 1931, with a strong tendency during the later years to be approximately 79 or 80 percent. The time deposits, on the other hand, showed an increase. In 1919 time deposits amounted to 58.6 percent, and in 1931 to 70.6 percent, of the deposits of all banks operating branches in the United States. This development followed the general trend of time deposits as compared with demand deposits for all banks in the United States, though the increase of time deposits was less marked in the leading cities than for the country as a whole.

Changes in the concentration and development of branch banking in the eleven cities are shown in Table 31, which includes the aggregate changes for all banks operating branches in these centers in comparison with the percentage changes (see Table 32) of the data for the banks operating branches in these cities, together with similar data for all banks operating branches in the United States.

[10] See Table 32.

TABLE 31

DATA OF ALL BANKS OPERATING BRANCHES IN ELEVEN LEADING CITIES*

(In millions of dollars)

YEAR	NUMBER OF BANKS	MEMBER, FEDERAL RESERVE SYSTEM	BRANCHES			CAP-ITAL	LOANS, DIS-COUNTS	INVEST-MENTS	DEPOSITS			DUE TO BANKS	DUE FROM BANKS	BILLS PAY-ABLE, REDIS-COUNTS	TOTAL RE-SOURCES
			Total	*In City*	*Out-side City*				*De-mand*	*Time*	*Total*				
1919	121	54	486	447	39	525	3,129	1,328	3,381	969	4,350	380	645	357	5,926
1920	128	71	574	530	44	720	3,921	1,651	3,660	1,578	5,238	429	811	427	7,502
1921	130	77	669	614	55	929	4,269	1,897	4,026	1,757	5,783	814	809	180	8,178
1922	149	90	857	766	91	1,060	4,819	2,523	4,838	2,248	7,086	1,050	979	63	9,704
1923	180	97	1,093	932	161	1,231	5,774	2,971	5,341	3,058	8,399	1,138	1,015	91	11,442
1924	197	109	1,284	1,088	196	1,406	6,899	3,876	6,184	3,861	10,045	1,641	1,279	29	13,823
1925	228	120	1,516	1,287	229	1,684	8,139	4,574	6,892	4,795	11,687	825	1,833	112	16,604
1926	239	122	1,708	1,418	290	1,874	8,801	4,915	7,760	5,479	13,239	1,029	1,732	121	18,145
1927	239	120	1,969	1,542	427	2,305	11,017	5,984	8,539	6,348	14,887	1,248	2,149	109	20,797
1928	231	113	2,066	1,608	458	2,763	11,540	6,283	10,037	7,154	17,191	1,266	2,721	232	25,027
1929	216	104	2,286	1,766	520	3,334	12,411	6,313	10,361	7,347	17,708	2,393	2,641	311	25,935
1930	199	100	2,184	1,663	521	3,403	11,224	7,436	9,509	7,932	17,441	2,730	1,305	59	25,743
1931	168	84	2,100	1,590	510	3,055	8,960	7,867	8,232	7,233	15,465	1,864	1,108	235	21,957
1932	163		2,032	1,608	424			.							

* Source: Compiled from *Annual Reports of the Comptroller of the Currency*, Annual reports of various banking officials, and from other official reports.

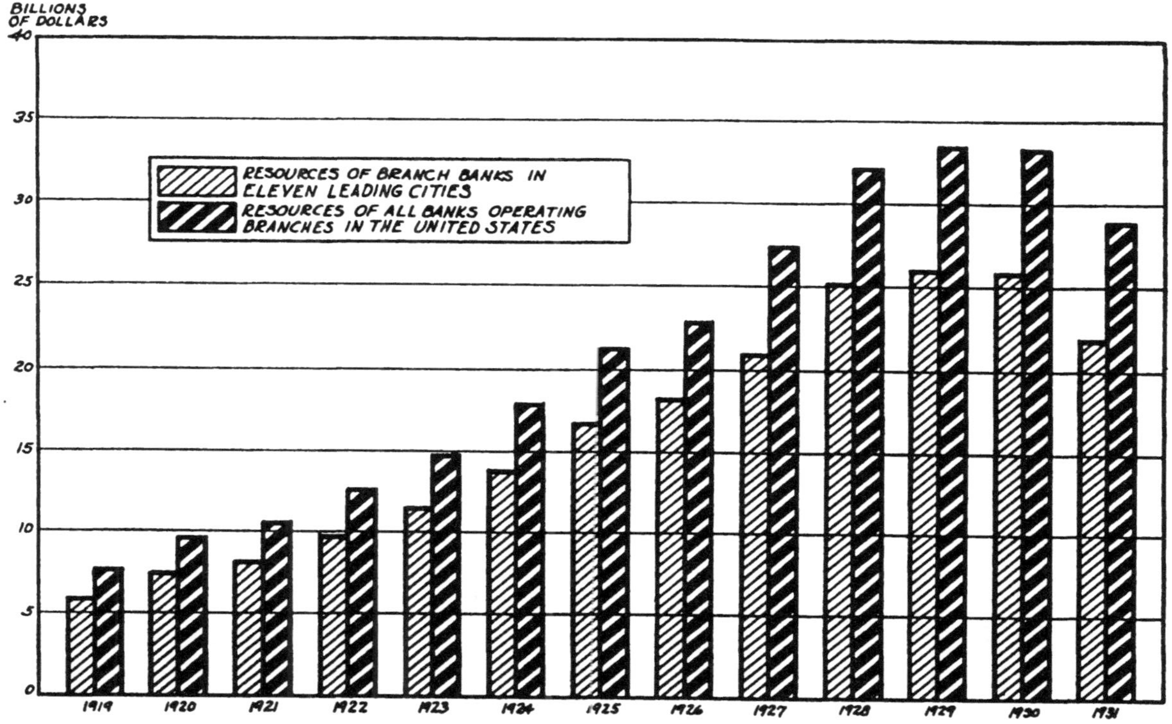

CHART XIX. RESOURCES OF ALL BANKS OPERATING BRANCHES IN THE UNITED STATES, AND RESOURCES OF ALL BANKS OPERATING BRANCHES IN ELEVEN LEADING CITIES

TABLE 32

THE PERCENTAGE BRANCH BANKS LOCATED IN ELEVEN LEADING CITIES AND OPERATING BRANCHES, ARE OF ALL BANKS IN THE UNITED STATES WHICH OPERATE BRANCHES*

YEAR	NUMBER OF BANKS	MEMBER, FEDERAL RESERVE SYSTEM	CAPITAL	LOANS, DIS-COUNT	INVEST-MENTS	DEPOSITS *De-mand*	DEPOSITS *Time*	DEPOSITS *Total*	RE-SOURCES
1919	25.4	40.3	75.7	78.9	73.3	84.2	58.6	76.8	77.0
1920	24.4	40.3	77.5	76.5	76.2	82.2	64.8	76.0	78.2
1921	24.3	39.7	80.3	78.0	78.1	84.2	65.9	77.6	79.7
1922	24.5	36.6	77.0	83.1	76.4	81.0	66.3	75.7	76.9
1923	26.7	35.3	75.2	74.6	82.6	79.7	68.8	75.3	76.5
1924	27.5	36.8	76.9	76.1	77.4	80.8	69.8	76.2	77.3
1925	29.1	35.8	77.8	76.9	78.3	80.0	72.4	76.7	78.5
1926	30.4	36.5	77.7	76.1	77.9	80.7	71.9	76.8	79.1
1927	28.7	34.1	76.8	76.0	75.0	78.8	69.8	74.7	76.6
1928	27.4	32.1	77.8	75.8	74.7	80.8	70.2	76.0	78.1
1929	26.5	30.9	78.8	75.2	76.7	80.0	70.9	76.0	78.0
1930	24.9	30.3	77.9	75.0	76.1	79.1	70.8	75.1	77.5
1931	22.8	28.4	77.5	73.5	75.1	79.0	70.6	74.8	76.0

* Source: The percentages presented in this table are based upon data given in Tables 21 and 31.

A comparison of the total resources of all banks operating branches in the eleven leading cities with the same data for all banks operating branches in the United States, for the period from 1919 to 1931 inclusive, is made in Chart XIX.

The total volume of business carried on by banks may be determined by a study of the total deposits, loans, discounts and investments, and resources. A comparison of each of these items with the total amount of capital funds employed or contributed by the stockholders should give an indication of the profitableness of a given institution or group of institutions. These comparisons are best expressed in the form of ratios. A comparison of such ratios of banks operating branches with similar ratios for all banks in the United States will show which of these two classes of banks is doing the larger volume of business on a given amount of capital funds. A similar comparison of the ratios of all banks operating branches with the ratios for banks located in the eleven leading cities and operating branches, will indicate which of these two

TABLE 33

RATIO OF CAPITAL FUNDS TO: (1) TOTAL LOANS AND INVESTMENTS; AND (2) TOTAL DEPOSITS*

YEAR	ALL BANKS IN THE UNITED STATES			ALL BANKS OPERATING BRANCHES			ALL BANKS OPERATING BRANCHES IN ELEVEN LEADING CITIES			ALL BANKS IN UNITED STATES NOT INCLUDING MUTUAL SAVINGS BANKS		ALL BANKS OPERATING BRANCHES NOT INCLUDING MUTUAL SAVINGS BANKS	
	Loans and Investments	Deposits		Loans and Investments	Deposits		Loans and Investments	Deposits		Loans and Investments	eposits Not Including Due to Banks	Loans and Investments	Deposits Including Due to Banks
		Not Including Due to Banks	*Including Due to Banks*		*Not Including Due to Banks*	*Including Due to Banks*		*Not Including Due to Banks*	*Including Due to Banks*				
1919	6.94	6.20	6.92	8.32	8.16	8.79	8.48	8.27	9.00	6.53	5.75	8.25	8.09
1920	7.04	6.24	6.85	7.84	7.41	7.93	7.74	7.28	7.87	6.63	5.79	7.60	7.15
1921	6.38	5.64	6.08	6.84	6.45	7.20	6.64	6.23	7.10	5.90	5.12	6.61	6.21
1922	6.19	5.76	6.25	6.62	6.81	7.70	6.93	6.68	7.67	5.76	5.33	6.46	6.65
1923	6.52	5.97	6.50	6.93	6.82	7.64	7.11	6.82	7.75	6.10	5.54	6.74	6.62
1924	6.52	6.21	6.76	7.69	7.21	8.27	7.66	7.14	8.31	6.10	5.80	7.51	7.01
1925	6.76	6.48	7.07	7.59	7.04	7.91	7.55	6.94	7.43	6.38	6.13	7.36	6.80
1926	6.72	6.37	6.92	7.42	7.15	8.01	7.32	7.06	7.61	6.37	6.04	7.21	6.94
1927	6.64	6.34	6.86	7.49	6.64	7.54	7.37	6.46	7.00	6.31	6.04	7.36	6.44
1928	6.61	6.11	6.57	6.66	6.37	7.28	6.45	6.22	6.68	6.27	5.78	6.44	6.11
1929	6.22	5.71	6.09	5.85	5.31	6.19	5.62	5.31	6.03	5.81	5.31	5.54	5.19
1930	5.88	5.54	5.98	5.66	5.31	6.02	5.48	5.13	5.93	5.48	5.17	5.28	4.94
1931	5.88	5.49	6.00	5.80	5.24	5.80	5.51	5.06	5.67	5.41	5.04	5.17	4.70

* The ratios contained in this table have been derived by comparing data found elsewhere in this study, or are derived from material presented in this volume.

classes grants the largest amount of loans and carries the greatest volume of deposits, or does the largest volume of business upon a given capitalization.

The volume of business, determined by a comparison of total loans, discounts and investments, and total deposits, to the capital funds, is much greater for the banks operating branches than for all banks in the United States. This is true not only for all banks operating branches in the United States, but also for those banks operating branches which are located in the eleven leading cities. The ratios of loans, discounts and investments to capital funds, for all banks in the United States, for all banks operating branches in the United States, and for all banks located in the eleven leading cities and operating branches, were 6.94, 8.32, and 8.48, respectively, for the year 1919.[11] The same ratios for 1931 were respectively 5.88, 5.80, and 5.51.[12] These ratios show that the banks operating branches do the larger volume of business and, other things being equal, should yield a larger return in the form of dividends to their stockholders. It might be argued that since the amount advanced by all banks is smaller, the banks not operating branches are safer. The statistics for bank failures, however, do not indicate that banks operating branches are more apt to fail than non-branch banks.

The ratios in Table 33 show a marked drop for the year 1929 as compared with 1928. The sudden decline at that time is due, in part at least, to the rapid increase in capital funds during that year, in comparison with the growth in total loans, discounts and investments, as well as the increase in total deposits. Despite the falling off in the ratio of total deposits to capital funds for all banks in the United States, the decline was somewhat sharper for banks operating branches. Growth in capital funds was greater for banks operating branches. The increase in the capital funds among the banks operating branches was due in part to the greater efforts made to sell new stock as compared to banks in the smaller places. Loss of capital funds was probably much less through bank failures

[11] See Table 33, p. 245.
[12] *Ibid.*

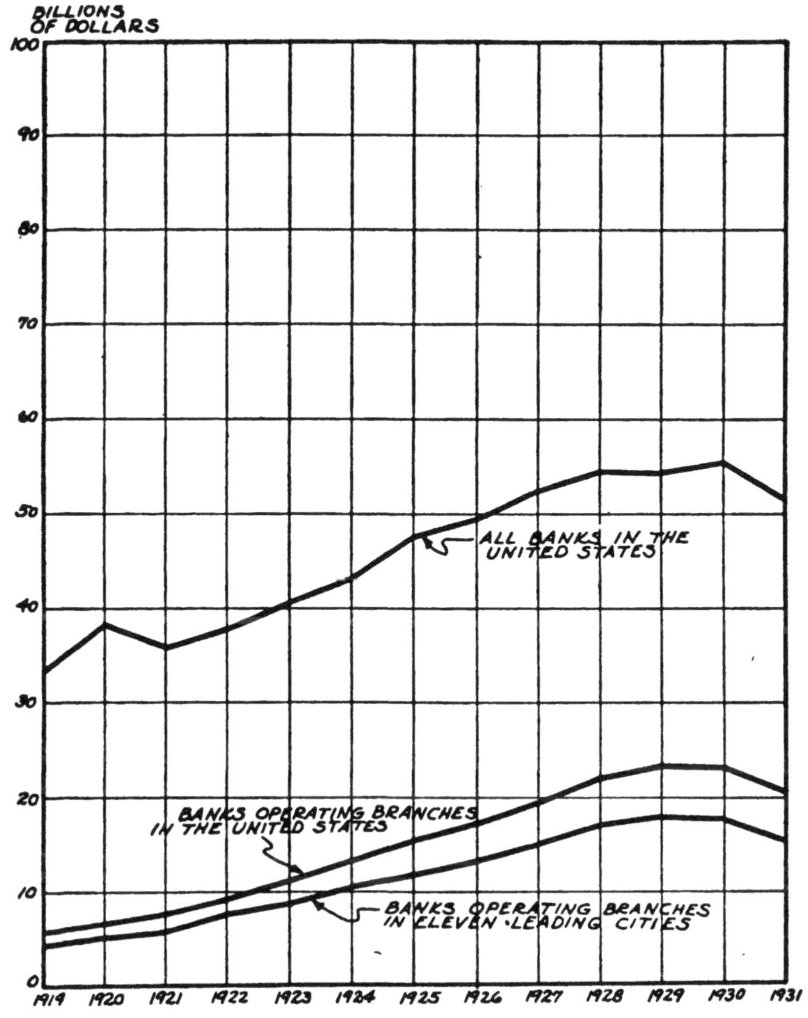

CHART XX. TOTAL DEPOSITS OF: (1) BANKS IN THE UNITED STATES; (2) BANKS OPERATING BRANCHES IN THE UNITED STATES; AND (3) BANKS OPERATING BRANCHES IN ELEVEN LEADING CITIES

in the large cities, and among banks operating branches in the less densely populated localities.

A study of Table 33 shows a general decline in the ratios, which would seem to indicate that depositors have greater protection now than a few years ago. Such a conclusion is not warranted for the reason that capital funds are and have been carried at book value and are undoubtedly too high in many cases, owing to the failure of directors to write off losses and to mark down the stock to represent its actual value especially in recent years.

The relative changes in the total deposits of all banks in the United States, total deposits for all banks operating branches, and the total deposits of banks operating branches in the eleven leading cities, is shown in Chart XX.

The changes in the two classes of banks operating branches have been uniform and have, for the most part, moved together. Total deposits of all banks have increased greatly, but have not expanded so rapidly as have the total deposits for the banks operating branches.

Time deposits have increased faster than demand deposits, in banks operating branches. This is true of all banks operating branches, as well as of banks operating branches in the eleven leading cities. Demand deposits of all banks operating branches and of those operating branches in the eleven leading cities have moved together.

SUMMARY

Despite all the claims to the contrary, the development of branches by banks in the United States has been highly concentrated or restricted geographically. There has been a marked concentration of branches among a limited number of banks located in eleven leading branch banking cities. More specifically, the following summary may be drawn from our study of branch banking in these leading cities:

1. About 25 percent of all banks operating branches in this country in 1919 were located in these eleven leading cities. During the period covered, this percentage varied somewhat. The lowest figure for any year was 22.6 percent in 1931, while the highest was 30.4 percent in 1926. These same banks held approximately 78 percent, on the average, of all resources of branch banks throughout this period.

2. The branch banks located in the eleven leading cities held

more than 75 percent of all deposits of all banks operating branches in the United States during the period under study.

3. Time deposits of banks operating branches in the leading cities increased from 58.6 percent in 1919 to 70.9 percent in 1929, and then declined in 1931 to 70.6 percent of the time deposits of all banks operating branches in this country. Demand deposits of branch banks in the leading cities declined from 84.2 percent of the demand deposits of all branch banks in 1919 to 79.0 percent in 1931.

4. The branch banks located in the leading cities had 486 branches in 1919 as compared with 1,082 for all branch banks in the country. In 1931 these same banks owned 2,100 branches out of a grand total for all branch banks in the United States of 3,375.

5. This study shows conclusively that the branch-banking resources of this country are largely concentrated in these eleven leading cities. This is true even though we consider only the states in which branch banking is permitted, leaving out of consideration those states in which there are no branches.

CHAPTER XIII

BRANCH BANKING AND MUTUAL SAVINGS BANKS

Mutual savings banks as a general rule have few, if any, branches. The mutual savings banks operating branches are located primarily in the four states of Maryland, Massachusetts, New York, and Pennsylvania. Even in these states the branch movement has not assumed the importance that it has attained among the commercial state banks and trust companies. Legal restrictions in different states differ as regards the location and number of branches by mutual savings banks. They also differ frequently, even in any one state, when compared with the privileges extended to commercial state banks and trust companies with regard to the establishment and operation of branches. In New York State, for example, a mutual savings bank may establish only one branch which must be located in the same city or borough as the head office, whereas the state banks and trust companies may establish a number of branches within the city of the parent institution.

Mutual savings banks in New York may, however, have more than one branch if the additional branches have been obtained by a merger or consolidation with another mutual savings bank. In Maryland, the privileges of the two classes of banks are quite similar. The laws of Massachusetts are more favorable toward mutual savings banks. Trust companies there may establish one branch in the city of the parent institution. This provision does not apply, however, to the branches established prior to April 29, 1902, or to "offices" taken over by a merger with a trust company or a national bank located in the same town, provided the Commissioner of Banking approves, on the ground that the public convenience would be served thereby. On the other hand, the laws governing mutual savings banks provide that a mutual savings bank may operate one or more branches in the city or town

TABLE 34

DATA OF ALL MUTUAL SAVINGS BANKS IN THE UNITED STATES*

LOCATION	1919			1931			1932		
	Number of States	*Number of Banks*	*Resources (millions of dollars)*	*Number of States*	*Number of Banks*	*Resources (millions of dollars)*	*Number of States*	*Number of Banks*	*Resources (millions of dollars)*
New England States	6	400	$2,011	6	381	$3,804	6	379	3,711
Eastern States	5	197	3,009	5	197	6,998	5	195	7,047
Middle West States	4	24	141	4	17	235	4	16	221
Pacific States	1	1	10	2	5	154	2	4	155
TOTAL	16	622	$5,171	17	600	$11,191	17	594	$11,134

* Source: *Reports of the Comptroller of the Currency.*

or within a radius of 15 miles, where no savings banks are in operation. The reasons, therefore, for the few branches opened by mutual savings banks cannot be explained wholly by legal restrictions.

Mutual savings banks are located for the most part in the eastern and New England states. It is a well-known fact that mutual savings banks have not been established to any marked extent in the southern and western states. According to statistics compiled by the Comptroller of the Currency there were 622 mutual savings banks on June 30, 1919, and 594 on June 30, 1932.

Table 34 shows the geographical distribution of these banks. The bulk of the business performed by mutual savings banks during the period from 1919 to 1932 was done by the banks in the six New England and five eastern states. There has been no marked change in the relative position in the three periods selected even though the total volume of business carried on has increased very materially. The eastern states included in 1931 are: New York (147), New Jersey (25), Maryland (14), Pennsylvania (9), and Delaware (2). New York, the leading state involved, as measured in terms of total resources, had more than $5,811,846,000 of assets in 1931, while Massachusetts ranks second with total assets of more than $2,377,795,000. These two states alone had about two-thirds of all the banking resources of all mutual savings banks in the United States. It is not surprising to find that these two states also possess a very large percentage of the total resources of all mutual savings banks operating branches, as well as of the number of branches actually operated.

The scope and extent of the development of branches by mutual savings banks, together with the number of such banks, are more clearly shown in Table 35, in which the total number of savings banks is given in comparison with the total number operating branches. It will be seen from this table that only a small percentage of all mutual savings banks are operating branches in this country. A similar comparison of the total number of mutual savings banks, in the particular states in which there are branches in operation, shows that there is likewise a proportionately small number of branches.

TABLE 35

COMPARISON OF TOTAL MUTUAL SAVINGS BANKS OPERATING BRANCHES, WITH TOTAL MUTUAL SAVINGS BANKS IN THE UNITED STATES, AND TOTAL MUTUAL SAVINGS BANKS IN STATES PERMITTING BRANCHES*

YEAR	ALL MUTUAL SAVINGS BANKS IN UNITED STATES		ALL MUTUAL SAVINGS BANKS IN BRANCH STATES		ALL MUTUAL SAVINGS BANKS OPERATING BRANCHES			NUMBER OF BRANCHES IN OPERATION		
	Number of States	*Number of Banks*	*Number of States*	*Number of Banks*	*Number of Banks*	*Percent of the United States Total*	*Percent of Total in Branch States*	*Total*	*In*	*Out*
1919	16	622	5	282	12	1.9	4.3	25	20	5
1920	16	620	6	422	15	2.4	3.6	28	23	5
1921	17	623	6	424	16	2.6	3.8	29	23	6
1922	17	619	6	422	20	3.2	4.7	37	28	9
1923	17	618	6	421	30	4.9	7.1	49	40	9
1924	17	613	6	421	42	6.9	10.0	65	52	13
1925	17	611	6	383	49	8.0	12.8	74	59	15
1926	17	620	6	408	54	8.7	14.1	80	66	14
1927	17	618	7	408	63	10.2	15.4	90	75	15
1928	17	616	7	408	67	10.8	16.4	97	80	17
1929	17	611	8	408	72	11.8	17.6	107	91	16
1930	17	606	8	407	74	12.2	18.2	108	92	16
1931	17	600	8	403	75	12.5	18.6	112	96	16
1932	17	594	8	399	75	12.6	18.8	124	109	15

* Source: Official reports and records of state banking departments, and *Annual Reports of the Comptroller of the Currency.*

The extent of the movement cannot be adequately presented merely by comparing the total number of banks operating branches with the non-branch banks. The comparative size of each class, as well as the total volume of business done, throws most interesting and valuable light upon the subject. Table 36 shows a comparison, expressed as percentages of the total number of banks, guaranty fund, etc., loans and discounts, investments, deposits and resources, of all mutual savings banks operating branches in the United States, with the same data for all mutual savings banks in the United States and with all mutual savings banks in those states where mutual savings banks operated branches for the period from 1919 to 1931 inclusive:

TABLE 36

DATA OF ALL MUTUAL SAVINGS BANKS OPERATING BRANCHES IN THE UNITED STATES, EXPRESSED AS PERCENTAGES OF: (1) ALL MUTUAL SAVINGS BANKS IN THE UNITED STATES; (2) ALL MUTUAL SAVINGS BANKS IN THOSE STATES WHERE MUTUAL SAVINGS BANKS OPERATE BRANCHES*

YEAR	BANKS OPERATING BRANCHES		GUARANTY FUND, SURPLUS, ETC.		LOANS AND DISCOUNTS		INVESTMENTS		DEPOSITS		RESOURCES	
	Percent of the United States	*Percent of the Branch States*	*Percent of the United States*	*Percent of the Branch States*	*Percent of the United States*	*Percent of the Branch States*	*Percent of the United States*	*Percent of the Branch States*	*Percent of the United States*	*Percent of the Branch States*	*Percent of the United States*	*Percent of the Branch States*
1919	1.9	4.3	2.6	7.1	1.9	5.7	3.7	9.6	2.8	7.8	2.8	7.9
1920	2.4	3.6	7.6	9.3	2.1	2.5	15.2	19.4	9.1	11.2	9.0	11.1
1921	2.6	3.8	7.9	9.6	2.7	2.6	15.2	19.0	8.8	10.8	8.7	10.7
1922	3.2	4.7	8.1	9.7	2.1	2.5	15.0	18.5	8.9	10.9	8.9	10.8
1923	4.9	7.1	12.9	15.5	2.2	2.6	24.1	29.6	13.3	16.2	13.2	16.0
1924	6.9	10.0	18.4	21.9	3.4	4.0	34.6	43.0	18.2	22.1	18.2	19.2
1925	8.0	12.8	23.8	28.9	4.1	4.9	48.8	61.5	24.2	29.5	24.2	29.4
1926	8.7	14.1	26.8	32.1	4.8	5.7	55.1	70.2	27.0	33.0	27.2	33.2
1927	10.2	15.4	33.8	39.0	5.2	6.0	68.6	83.8	32.2	37.9	32.4	38.1
1928	10.8	16.4	33.4	38.8	5.4	6.1	70.7	86.6	34.4	40.4	34.3	40.3
1929	11.8	17.6	35.9	44.6	6.6	7.5	75.3	91.7	35.3	41.3	35.3	41.4
1930	12.2	18.2	39.4	51.9	6.2	7.1	88.9	95.3	40.1	46.9	40.0	46.8
1931	12.5	18.6	35.0	45.8	6.2	7.1	87.3	93.2	40.1	46.4	39.5	47.2

* The basic aggregate amounts from which the percentages in this table have been computed are given in full in Tables 21 and 22, Chap. XI, pp. 199–202, 208 above.

The importance of the growth of this form of branch banking becomes more apparent when a study is made of Table 36. The total resources of mutual savings banks operating branches were small in 1919, amounting to 2.8 and 7.9 percent of the resources of all mutual savings in the United States and of the total mutual savings banks in states permitting branches, respectively. These percentages increased gradually year by year until they had reached 39.5 and 47.2 percent, respectively, in 1931. Similar percentage changes are to be noted in a comparison of total deposits and total investments for the three groups of banks. The average size of the banks and the volume of business done by banks operating branches increased at a more rapid rate than did the number of savings banks operating branches. This is, of course, what we should expect, since branches are operated largely by the largest mutual savings banks. Moreover the largest number of savings banks which have branches, as already pointed out, are located in New York and Massachusetts, where the largest individual mutual savings banks are located.

It is quite evident, therefore, that an increasing percentage of the volume of business is being done by those mutual savings banks which are operating branches. It is probably not too much to expect a liberalization in the near future of the law governing mutual savings banks as regards the operation of branches. This has been realized to a small degree recently in New York State. It was during the year 1930 that mutual savings banks there were permitted for the first time to have more than one branch each. They may now (1933) have a larger number, if the additional branches are secured through a merger or a consolidation. The attitude of the state banking department is favorable toward broader powers for mutual savings banks.

RELATION TO THE CONSOLIDATION MOVEMENT

The changes taking place among mutual savings banks have had very little, if any, connection with the large number of bank mergers and consolidations going on in those states where mutual savings banks are in operation. It is, of course, true that a few such savings banks have been involved in mergers or consolidations in some of the eastern or New England states, but the number has been so small, and in some cases with no branches involved, that we are justified in drawing the conclusion that the relationship is not important so far as this part of our study is concerned at this time. A few mergers have taken place between mutual savings banks themselves, but the number is too small to be of any significance. Moreover, in most cases there have been no branches transferred or established as a result of the consolidation.

It seems possible that in the future the consolidation movement may have a more direct influence on mutual savings banks. In New York, for example, the situation appears to be slowly changing. Mutual savings banks may now secure branches as a result of mergers. There is also a desire on the part of the banking authorities to broaden the powers of mutual savings banks in order that more than one branch may be established by each mutual savings bank if it is deemed desirable. There is also the feeling that mutual savings banks may operate branches quite satisfactorily in certain communities denied such facilities under existing conditions. The Sargent bill, introduced into the New York State Assembly in 1930, was designed to bring about such changes. No such legislation has been passed. The need for such a modification is no doubt keenly felt by a few of those operating mutual savings banks, as is evidenced by the recent changes in location of branches. A number of old branches have been discontinued and new ones opened, this being necessary since the law limited each bank to one branch.

LIMITED DEMAND FOR BRANCHES

The demand for an extension of branches by mutual savings banks is limited. The chief single reason for this at the present time is the absence of the motive for making large profits, though other factors play a part.

Mutual savings banks, as has already been pointed out, have developed mostly in the eastern and New England states. Public sentiment in these states has been, for the most part, rather opposed to a broad extension of branch banking in any form.

In three states, Massachusetts, New York, and Pennsylvania, where a large percentage of the resources of mutual savings banks are found, branches for both commercial and savings banks are restricted to limited geographical units. Naturally the sentiment and restrictions tend to apply to mutual savings banks with even greater force than to commercial banks and trust companies.

The original and underlying motive in the organization and promotion of mutual savings banks was more philanthropic than in the case of big commercial institutions. They came into existence to encourage the small wage earner and salaried individual to put away a certain amount each week or month. These institutions were intended to provide a means for taking care of the "small man." In fact, they may well be regarded as the small man's bank. The sentiment attached to the building up and operation of these institutions precluded, more or less, the question of extending the field of activity to other communities. It was felt that an extension might be looked upon with disfavor. At any rate there was little, if any, desire on the part of the management to establish branches.

The profit motive was largely absent. The trustees or directors of these institutions cannot, of course, own stock, for there is none. All of the net income realized by the management is supposed to be turned over to the depositors with the exception of the amount set aside as a surplus or guaranty fund to take care of any losses which may be incurred by the officers through the making of loans or investments. The directors or trustees benefit only in proportion to the amount of funds they have on deposit in the bank itself. Moreover, they are not salaried individuals, so that they can, at most, get very little directly in the way of financial returns for serving on the Board of Trustees. This situation makes it unlikely that they will be over-anxious to establish branches in other communities.

Another factor of considerable importance in the establishment of branches by commercial banks and trust companies is that of stockjobbing or the selling of stock. This takes the form sometimes of marking up the market price of the stock with a view to unloading it on the public. This has proved to be quite profitable for the promoters in some cases. In some instances security affiliates are involved. Holding companies are sometimes organized to buy control of a bank, with the idea of selling out later for a substantial profit. The commercial bank is always after new business, and branches offer, or are thought to offer, a new mechanism for securing business which would otherwise go to some other financial institution. If the branches are successful the result is an increase in the profits, yielding larger dividends and increasing the net worth or value of the assets back of the outstanding stock. No such opportunities are offered in the operation of mutual savings banks.

ADVANTAGES OF MUTUAL SAVINGS BANKS

In many respects mutual savings banks may operate branches quite successfully, both for the good of the community and for the benefit of depositors. It is not desirable to have too many savings banks, especially in the smaller communities. A larger population is required to support a mutual savings bank than is the case with a commercial bank or trust company. The average size of the balance carried by the depositor is much smaller so that the bank requires a large potential body of depositors in order to realize a body of deposits sufficient to support such an institution. It is not financially possible to organize an independent mutual savings bank in many smaller communities which would nevertheless contribute substantially to the fund if the opportunity existed. The most economical way to provide such facilities is through the extension of branch banking.

From the point of view of the depositor, one of the fundamental questions in any banking system is that of safety. Depositors need this protection more than any other one group. Where this is admittedly absent, chaos is likely to be followed by heavy losses for both depositors and stockholders. During recent years the number of failures of commercial banks and trust companies has been large. In this connection it is interesting and important to compare the record of the mutual savings banks with that of other types of banking institutions. The results are unmistakably in favor of the mutual savings banks, very few of them having failed, as compared with national banks or commercial state banks and trust companies. The losses have been proportionately lower in the savings institutions. These conditions prevail in states which permit mutual savings banks to operate branches, as well as in other states where mutual savings banks are not operating branches.

The average depositor of a savings bank is a man with limited financial means. His deposits are small, as are also his loans, if any. He desires safety of principal above all else. Many such individuals have found a great deal of comfort in having their funds on deposit with this sound class of institutions during financial depressions. Other individuals might have been in a better position if they, too, could have had the advantages of such facilities. Some states do not provide for mutual savings banks. In other states the laws governing the operation of savings banks are not as sound as those now in existence in New York and Massachusetts. The nature of the business of a savings bank makes it practically impossible to establish mutual savings banks in places where there is not a substantial population from which to draw deposits. Since there are many places in which it is impossible, or at least undesirable, to establish mutual savings banks, the only alternatives are to extend to other communities and localities the advantages and services of mutual savings banks now in operation, or to increase the protection of savings depositors in other types of banking institutions by the segregation of assets back of savings or thrift deposits to such an extent that such assets will be available, first of all, to meet the claims of the savings depositors. In fact there is much to be said in favor of promoting both plans at the same time. Certainly there does not appear to be any basic reason why strong and ably managed mutual savings banks should not, if they desire, extend their services to other communities.

Another argument in favor of extending branch privileges to this class of financial institutions is that of convenience of access. Strong branches will not only encourage the opening of savings accounts and thereby increase the savings of many small wage earners, but they will be a distinct asset to the community. They will also increase the volume of capital which may be used for the purpose of further production.

The type of business carried on by a mutual savings bank is largely that of receiving deposits and investing the funds thereby secured. The same will be true to a greater extent in the case of branches of such institutions. Mutual savings banks make only a limited number of direct loans, other than mortgage loans, to individuals. Generally speaking, the borrowers from a savings bank are entirely different from the depositors.

One argument so frequently advanced against an extension of branches by commercial banks and trust companies is to the effect that the services rendered by the branch managers would tend to be less desirable than those now rendered by the officers and directors of the unit banks. The anti-branch bankers usually contend that the branch managers would be slow to lend funds to the business men of the community and that they would actually prefer to send the funds to the central money markets and keep them employed in collateral loans, rather than to lend for commercial purposes in the local community. The very nature of handling savings funds make it necessary that they be invested in first-class investments, which usually requires that the bonds or stocks, as well as the mortgages, be such as to reduce to a minimum the risk involved. The branch of a mutual savings bank would therefore be largely a receiving station for savings funds, rather than a place at which the business men of the community would go for bank loans to finance their current business operations. On the other hand, there should be nothing to prevent the mutual savings banks from buying, through their branches, any first mortgages arising in the local sections, if such mortgages met with the primary tests of first-class mortgages.

Certain economies of operation may be easily realized by an extension of branches. Branches may be operated with lower overhead costs. Rent will be less, owing to the fact that smaller and less expensive quarters will meet the needs of local offices. The amount tied up in fixed capital, or buildings, furniture and fixtures, will be less. Light and heat bills will be smaller, as will the annual outlay for the upkeep of the property in connection with a branch, as compared to that where an independent bank is established. The personnel will be smaller, since fewer people will be needed to carry on the work. The expenses in connection with the investing of funds and investigating mortgages and real estate will, to a marked extent, be consolidated in one general office. This will reduce the percentage cost of the work for the branches, as well as direct costs of operation of the head office.

The reserves and reserve balances carried in commercial banks will be reduced through the pooling of the reserves for several branches. This will in no way injure or lessen the safety of the branches or of the bank as a whole. The branches will be in a position to rely safely upon the head office should they need additional cash to meet withdrawals.

Despite the criticisms that have been made against the operation of branches, there are several very powerful arguments in favor of a further extension of branches by mutual savings banks, regardless of our attitude toward branch banking in general. More liberal provision for this type of banking would undoubtedly increase the safety of our banking system, at the same time adding to the facilities by providing adequate offices for the convenience of the small wage earners and others who are not in a position to avail themselves of the opportunities offered at the larger commercial banks and trust companies.

CHAPTER XIV

BRANCHES AND THE CORRESPONDENT SYSTEM

The very nature of modern business enterprise makes it necessary that some means be available for transferring funds from one place to another and from one person to another to settle or adjust the claims arising out of business transactions. Banks provide these services. They also act as intermediaries between those who have funds to lend and those who wish to borrow. To render such services, banking institutions establish connections or relations with other banking institutions, both in their own community and elsewhere. In some cases these connections become international in scope, while in other cases they are less extensive and to some extent indirect. Regardless of the fact that we are accustomed to think of the deposit and discount functions as the most important functions performed by a commercial bank, it is, nevertheless, true that banks perform a useful service also in handling collection items and in transferring funds from one part of the country to another.

In most of the leading industrial and commercial countries, these interbank services are provided for by an extensive system of branches, supplemented by a limited number of correspondents or agents. Prior to the growth and development of branches in these countries, such business was transacted largely by bankers and other financial houses through direct contacts and agreements. This method has been, in part, replaced, in many countries by the development of a large number of branches. In the United States the work has been performed very largely by unit banks through correspondent bank accounts.

The branch systems which had been developed to a considerable extent in the United States, especially in the South and the West, prior to the Civil War, were local in nature and did not provide the proper facilities for settling balances and transferring funds, either short or long-term or both, on a national or international scale. In order to take care of this type of business, which was increasing in volume and scope with the rapid growth of the country, bankers therefore recognized the need for and participated in an extensive development of the correspondent relationships among banks throughout the country. As this class of business proved to be quite lucrative with its increasing volume, many large city banks made strenuous efforts, through personal representatives and otherwise, to secure as much of it as possible. In the absence of a national branch system, the correspondent method of transacting both national and international banking business secured a firm hold on the business and economic life of the country.

The rapidity with which the correspondent system developed soon made it an essential part of our banking mechanism. The need on the part of banks for branches was thus lessened, since this business at a distance could be handled through correspondents. Local interbank business was easily taken care of by local arrangements. Scarcity of capital in the early days made it possible for the banks to use all the funds they could obtain very profitably in their own communities. The local demand was so great that most bankers had no desire to extend their business outside their communities, except in so far as they were acting as agents for their customers. Such business as their depositors had could be handled easily through correspondent banks. The success of this system made it unnecessary to establish additional offices. These conditions explain in part why there was no strong sentiment favoring branch banking in the period following the Civil War.

Once we had a system for interbank business well established it was natural for bankers to use it and, at the same time, to resist or discourage changes relative thereto. Especially was this true when it meant that local banks might be forced out of business in many instances. The small bankers were therefore opposed to any encroachment upon their domain by branches of other banks. Large city bankers, on the other hand, took only a passing interest in the subject of branches, regardless of their personal opinions, for the reason that, if they advocated branches, they were in danger of losing the business of bankers who were opposed to an extension of branches. Hence the long period in our banking history in which there was little, if any, discussion of branch banking. The organization of a small bank required much less capital and was regarded as a desirable field of endeavor. During this period the correspondent system continued to increase, both in the total volume of business transacted and in the importance which it assumed in our banking system as a whole.

THE CLEARING AND COLLECTION OF CHECKS

In those countries which have an extensive system of branches, it is customary for banks to make collections through them whereever possible, rather than through correspondents, as is largely the case in this country. A branch system simplifies the process of handling checks and other items for collection. In the United States the existing practice was changed to some extent by the adoption of the Federal Reserve system. It would not be possible in many countries, for example, England or Germany, for a controversy to develop concerning par clearance of checks, such as has arisen in the United States since the inauguration of the Federal Reserve system. The question of collection charges with another bank would not be likely to arise for the reason that the checks would be handled almost entirely by the branches.

INTERBANK LOANS

Small banks frequently borrow or rediscount their paper during certain seasons of the year. If these banks are not members of the Federal Reserve system, they have logically only one place to go for these funds—to the correspondent or large city bank. Under a branch system the local branch would, of course, secure the funds through the head office. Such a system, it is contended, leans toward monopoly, while under our unit system the bank is independent. In reality, it should be pointed out, the unit bank is only partly independent of the large city correspondent. If the country bank wishes to borrow from its city correspondent, there are certain rather rigid conditions which must be complied with. It is here that the influence of the large city banks upon their country correspondents becomes important. Before such advances are made, the country banks are usually investigated. They must frequently secure these advances by pledging certain types of collateral or by providing satisfactory endorsements. They are constantly under the observation of the city bankers.

By reason of the fact that the country banks must hold certain acceptable classes of collateral, they are practically compelled to purchase securities representing business enterprises outside the community. In fact the whole argument that a bank should keep all of its funds invested or loaned out in the same community in which it gets the bulk of its deposits is a weak one, unless the business of that particular community is well diversified, which is not generally true except in the so-called money-market centers.[1] It is to the best interests of the depositors, as well as of the community as a whole, for the funds to be properly diversified in order to secure the desired safety. By reason of the large area covered by branch banks operating many branches outside the locality of the head office, we normally find greater diversification in the branch system than in the unit banks.

Country banks may change their correspondents if the requirements become too rigid, whereas the branch has no alternative in the matter. Even though the country banks change correspondents, the new correspondent will require essentially the same protection as the old. Competition has forced or will force all the large city banks to offer about the same type of service to smaller banks. This being the case, there is not a very fundamental difference in their requirements over a period of time. Thus in the end, so far as influence or control of large banks or financial centers is concerned, the results are quite similar in the correspondent and branch systems. Critics of both unit and branch banking have generally failed to emphasize this point properly.

RELATION TO THE BANKING SYSTEM

The effect of the correspondent relationship becomes vastly more important and pronounced when studied from the point of view of the banking system as a whole. Where such connections

[1] Certain economies are realized by having the reserves for a given bank and all its branches handled by the head office. For a discussion of this phase of the problem, see Chap. XV, pp. 279-80.

exist between many out-of-town country or small city banks on the one hand, and the large metropolitan banks in the financial centers on the other, it means that the shifting of funds, the granting of advances to a certain community or group of banks, rests very largely in the hands of the so-called "big banks" in New York, Chicago, St. Louis, Los Angeles, San Francisco, and a few other leading financial centers. This condition places the large city banks in a position where they may and do exert a powerful influence regarding the transfer and use of banking funds.

Prior to the passage of the Federal Reserve Act we had a highly developed system of interbank balances and reserves carried by the country banks with their city correspondents. The reserve funds of national banks were concentrated to a marked degree in central Reserve and Reserve cities. This resulted in greater concentration in New York and Chicago, perhaps, than in any other cities. The passage of the Federal Reserve Act changed materially the location of the actual legal reserve funds of the national and state banks and trust companies which became members of the Federal Reserve system, even though the old conditions which had reached a peak prior to the passage of the Federal Reserve Act continue to an appreciable extent even today. If we assume that the large metropolitan banks are carrying accounts for two, three, or four thousand country and small city banks, it must be evident to all thoughtful students and bankers that the influence of the large city bankers in such a system is enormous.

The results are clearly demonstrated in the case of the small banker who, in substantially the same position as the branch manager of a large bank would be, finds himself in the possession of a considerable volume of funds which are not needed, at least temporarily, by the local community. He will strive, as all good bankers do, to keep his funds busy rather than idle. When this situation arises it is a very common practice for the small banker to call upon the metropolitan bank, his correspondent, for advice, on the basis that the city bank is in closer touch with the market and will be better able to select the best securities or commercial paper. In many cases the local or country banker will rely directly and almost entirely upon the advice of the city correspondent. Not infrequently the funds are sent to the correspondent with instructions to invest the amounts in bonds or commercial paper at his discretion. The branch of a large branch bank could do no more under similar circumstances.

In other cases the funds are simply transferred to New York with the request that they be employed in the New York money market. Or again, the funds are sometimes placed on deposit in the large bank in return for a specified rate of interest on the average balance maintained. The influence of the city correspondent in such cases is very great, even though it is presumably acting as the agent for the out-of-town correspondent bank.

The agreement entered into at the time the correspondent relationship is established provides that a certain stipulated average balance must be maintained by the smaller bank with the larger one. As the holder of reserves and free balances, the large city correspondent is in a dominant position and exercises a profound influence on the shifting of funds, though this is often emphasized as one of the disadvantages of branch banking. In either case, it is not so much a question of transferring funds, for that will be necessary under a system either of independent banks or of branches. The fundamental question is, of course, which plan best serves the needs of the country as a whole. In the correspondent system the country and smaller city banks are somewhat less under the dominance of the metropolitan banks than branches would be, but the branch bank is in a position generally to transfer funds more directly from one part of its territory to another. Thus when funds are not needed for commercial purposes in a given locality, the bank with branches may have a demand for such funds in another part of its district. It is in reality less likely that funds will flow into the central money or stock market under the branch system than under an independent system. The branch bank, if honestly and efficiently operated, will be in a position to handle such funds more economically. It should reduce the amount of funds which is kept on deposit in the form of bankers' balances. This is important from the standpoint of profits for banks as a whole throughout the country.

One of the principal reasons, perhaps the predominating one in most cases, in extending branches through the absorption of banks already in operation, is to secure the most favorable location in the community and to obtain a substantial volume of business while at the same time eliminating a strong competitor. Banks generally find it more profitable in the long run to pay more for a successful bank than to take over the ones which are more easily and cheaply obtained. There is an interesting connection between the methods of conducting interbank business on the one hand and the bank-failure epidemic and the growth and development of group banking on the other. During recent years the continued failure of banks has cut into the correspondent business enjoyed by the metropolitan banks. The absence of branch banks and the growth of group banking have induced some large city banks to undertake, through their affiliates, to buy up the stock of weak banks which they hope to restore to a sound basis.

Control and ownership of interior banks by this method offers some very attractive commercial possibilities. The fact that the small interior or country bank is not in a prosperous condition makes it possible to secure control at very small outlay frequently far below the real value. Such banks may be easily converted into profitable offices or additions by reducing overhead expenses and improving the management. (If this is not possible, of course the little bank may prove to be a very costly investment at any price.) In many cases the management of a small bank fears a failure and is therefore willing to take a low price and sometimes even to sell at a loss. The bank's affiliate may realize a substantional profit in the purchase of such properties. A second inducement is found in the fact that the city bank will retain or receive a larger part of the correspondent business of the purchased bank or banks. If the bank is allowed to fail or to fall into the hands of another group, the metropolitan bank will lose business, a thing which all bankers will avoid if possible. A third reason is sometimes found in the fact that the city banks anticipate a greater extension of branch banking and want to be in a position to have branches located at very strategic points when such a development takes place.

FINANCING FOREIGN BUSINESS

Under any system of banking, it is not feasible for the smaller banks to establish direct connections with banks in foreign countries. The potential volume of business to be transacted by these institutions precludes such an arrangement. Yet most of the small banks do occasionally experience demands for that type of service. Such services will be needed to finance imports and exports, to meet the needs of tourists and travelers, and to transfer funds from one country to another. In such cases the small bank must rely upon connections made and maintained by the large metropolitan banks. Such large institutions can perform these services both for themselves and for their correspondents. If the local business man wants a letter of credit, it will be provided generally by the local bank acting through its city correspondent in New York or Chicago. In other words, the practices followed are determined by the large banks. The influence exercised by the large banks is therefore even more powerful in connection with the foreign business than in domestic trade and commerce.

LOCAL VERSUS STATE OR NATION-WIDE BRANCHES

There is a very interesting relationship between the attitude of large city bankers toward branches and the business which has been and is enjoyed by these bankers from their country correspondents. There can be no doubt that some of the large banks in this country have failed to take an active part in the discussions regarding the merits and demerits of branch banking. When a large city bank has an enormous business with country or small city banks located in sections or states in which banks are not permitted to operate branches, it is only fair to expect such bankers to take an attitude in harmony with the interests of those who provide them with business. This does not necessarily indicate a weakness on the part of the large city bankers, for, after all, they are in business to make profits for their stockholders. They merely refrain from pressing the matter, preferring to let the development take its own course even though they are confident that the banking system is undergoing a change.

In the case of city branches, in New York or Cleveland, the

bankers are likely to take a more aggressive position. These city branches are frequently regarded as merely an extension of the activities of the head office and not as full-fledged branches, such as the large banks in England operate in various parts of that country. This type of branch does not compete to any marked extent with the banks which the large city banks hope to place on their correspondent list, except, perhaps, in a few instances where the smaller bank is located in the same city. With this in mind, the large city bankers can, and frequently do, go on record as favoring an extension of city branches, but at the same time either oppose the development of branches on a state-wide basis or evade the subject as far as possible. With the prohibition of interest on demand deposits by the (Glass-Steagall) Banking Act of June, 1933, this factor will be of less importance in the future than it has been in the past.

The purpose of this chapter is to indicate, to some extent at least, how influential the correspondent system of banking has been in this country. We do not contend that the influence of the large city banks, operating a number of branches, will be identical with the influence exerted by large city banks with an extensive list of correspondents throughout the country. Of course the bank with branches has a more direct influence and perhaps it occupies a more powerful position, but we must realize that, through the development of the correspondent system, the large city banks have had a very profound influence upon the thought of small bankers as well as upon the policies and practices followed by them. It is further believed that the influence of the correspondent banks is largely ignored by those who are strong advocates of the unit system. The introduction of a system of branch banking in this country would not alter the source of banking power and influence to any marked extent, considering the system as a whole. It might change the amount, the direction, or the distribution of certain loans or certain funds, but it would not have the extraordinary effect of suddenly transferring control over all these funds to the large cities. Since a considerable measure of that control has already passed to them, it is not likely that the situation would be profoundly altered. In fact, it is believed that a sound branch-banking system would take funds away from New York, Chicago and other metropolitan centers, even though the power was centered there. Bankers usually lend their funds where it is most profitable and desirable, all things considered. By properly distributing their funds in their own district, many banks would have less funds to send to the financial centers. There would be a corresponding decline in the demand by interested banks for loans in the money market centers. This would tend to reduce the cost to the banking system in handling surplus funds.

Moreover, the assumption that an extension of branches in this country would mean the disappearance of all the small banks seems to the writer to be fallacious. We shall always have a large number of banks in this country, as compared with the total number in England or Canada. Certainly this will continue to be the case for many, many years to come. This being true, the correspondent system will continue to operate. The greater the extension of branches, the less will be the importance of the old correspondent system. There are, and have been, too many small banks in this country, so there need not be any fear of losing a sizable number of them. A stronger banking system will result, even though we have only a limited development of branches. Such a change would not deprive the local bankers of all their power and influence, though it would probably reduce them.

CHAPTER XV

BRANCH BANK MANAGEMENT

The policies formed and the methods used in the establishment and operation of a system of branches by any bank or banks are most vital and important. The success of the system, measured in terms either of the services rendered or the net earnings or profits to the stockholders, will depend, to a great extent, upon the character and type of management employed. If the management is narrow-minded, selfish, unmindful of the interests of the community served, there will be a tendency for the business of the branch to decrease. Such management will, moreover, invite competition either in the form of new unit banks or new branches of other banks, or both. If a branch-banking system is to be permanent and successful, it must demonstrate that it will, all things considered, provide a safer, more economical, and more serviceable system than the unit banks have afforded in the past.

From a broad economic point of view, the ultimate test of success must be whether the system provides proper and adequate banking facilities at a reasonable cost and in a way that meets the financial needs of the business community. Banking success depends upon the business of the country and any system not adapted to that business will not endure. It is true, of course, that business enterprise in turn depends upon some type of banking. That does not, however, imply that banks and bankers are not dependent upon other types of business. The banker is a middleman and must, in the end, adapt his methods to those which prevail under a given economic system. If the banker fails, he should expect criticisms and proposals for changing or modifying the methods followed. This is just as inevitable in the field of banking as it is in any other line of business, as for example the railroad business, or the methods used in marketing and distributing various commodities. The management of a branch must, to be successful, seek first of all to provide the services needed. With these general statements in mind, let us consider certain practical questions, as well as other factors, which are considered by the management of a branch-banking system in the establishment and operation of a system of branches.

The owners or stockholders of a bank judge the success or failure of the enterprise very largely by its profitableness—the same basis used by the stockholders of an enterprise in any field of business. The branch office must make good on this basis if it is to continue. There is abundant evidence to prove that a branch will not be continued indefinitely unless it is a profit-making undertaking. Branches have been moved from one point to another, have been merged with other branches, and have often been closed for no other reason than that they did not yield a satisfactory net profit. If a unit bank is unprofitable, it is not always easy to liquidate it voluntarily; but instead it is too often allowed to continue in operation, getting into worse and worse condition until finally it must be closed. Some of the more important phases of branch-bank management have to do with the proper location of branches, local control, allocation of a certain amount of capital to each branch, methods of establishing branches, the securing and training of managers and employees, the restrictions placed on managers regarding the amount and character of the loans to be made, the policy of transferring funds from place to place, the method followed in conserving the bank reserves, and the investment policy between the head office and each of its branches.

BANK POLICY TOWARD BRANCHES

The expansion of branch banking in this country has been due to a variety of factors. The reasons vary with different bankers and in different parts of the country. Assuming that the laws are favorable toward an extension of branches, some bankers are constantly making inquiries and investigations to determine the places where the potential volume of business is sufficiently large to warrant opening a branch. Estimates are frequently made regarding the amount of business which may be secured in a given community. If a community has inadequate banking facilities, it may offer an immediate field. If the population and business of a community is small but rapidly increasing, it may be desirable to establish a small branch and let it expand with the business of the community. When the location is selected wisely, the future will provide business to make the branch profitable for the stockholders, while suitable banking services are provided for the community at a time when there would perhaps be no possibility of establishing a unit bank.

The advantage of an early start is frequently a strong argument for the creation of a branch in a small but growing community. The first bank on the ground generally has a decided advantage, other things being equal, over its competitors. Customers are not likely to leave the branch once they have established relations, provided the branch renders the services required. This is one of the reasons why Canadian banks have often gone into small localities and established branches, some of which were kept open only two or three days per week. Later, when the volume of business had increased, the work of the branch was enlarged. Branches were made to serve the needs of business. Banks have, for the most part, found this method quite satisfactory.

Competition may be the controlling factor leading some bankers to embark upon a branch-banking policy. In the large cities there is a tendency, as the city grows, for the business man to become further and further removed from the head office of a bank. This makes it necessary for the bank to consider, sooner or later, the question, "How may the services of the bank be carried to the old customer?" If this cannot be done, some other unit bank or branch is likely to get a large share of the business of such customers. This will be due not to any dissatisfaction on the part of the depositor, but rather to his preference for having his banking connection near his place of business, simply for the sake of convenience. Under conditions like these, the head office of a bank may become very much interested in the question of establishing new offices in order to retain business. There can be little doubt that many offices or branches have been established in certain localities for this reason.

The same policy followed with regard to city branches applies to the practice of establishing new branches outside the city of the parent bank. Banks may be, and in many cases are, fully justified in seeking to establish a branch or branches in order to retain the business of their old customers who have found it necessary to transfer their place or places of business. It is a doubtful policy for a bank to establish a branch because a competitor has done so. The pursuit of such a policy is likely to lead to questionable banking methods which will in most cases prove costly. Wholesome competition between large banks is desirable. Within bounds it will reduce the overhead costs and make for a sounder banking system. It becomes dangerous when the methods lead to the establishment of too many offices or to the assumption of too heavy expenses not justified by the volume of available banking business.

The location of a branch will depend upon a number of factors. In many instances it will depend upon the banking facilities already available. In casting about for a location, it is only natural that the management should select a place where the opportunities are greatest. These advantages are generally found in a community or section where the banking facilities are limited in proportion to the volume of banking business. It would be pure folly to locate a branch in a town or city, or in a particular part of a city, where the number of banking offices is already adequate to take care of all the business in that section. Yet that frequently takes place. It seems that the large banks in certain cities feel that they must have an office in the center of the city, in some cases for the very reason that other banks have opened branches there. Such a policy will, in the end, do more harm than good, not only to the banks but to the business community as well. Branches should be established because there is business to be done, because there exists a real need for a branch.

If the business is too small or limited at a given time, it may be in the process of being developed, or the business of the community may normally be expected to increase so that within a short time it will be quite sufficient. Under such conditions, a bank may be justified in establishing a small office which will involve a limited outlay and which will not require a large personnel or a heavy overhead. As the volume of business increases[1] the branch can expand its facilities. In such a case the bank, though making little if any profits in the beginning, may be performing a valuable service and laying the foundation for a very profitable and prosperous branch in the future. Where there is business to be developed, the bank may consider the future as well as immediate returns.

The legal status of branch banking in the several states has much to do with the policy adopted by the banks in establishing branches. In those states where branch banking is limited to the city, the problem is much easier than in states like North Carolina or California where the problem of out-of-town branches must be considered. In Maine, Louisiana, and Tennessee, where banks may have branches in the county, adjoining county, or parish, the question of a location is only slightly different from that of the banks in those states where branches are limited to the city of the head office or contiguous territory. In all states there is a very definite boundary line beyond which it is, in most cases, impossible to pass.

There are two well-known methods of securing or establishing branches. The first is that of establishing the branches outright. A location is secured, permission of the banking authorities is obtained, and the branch is opened for business. This method is frequently referred to in California and other places as the *de novo* method. The second way is for the branch bank to select a town or city in which one or more banks are being operated, provided of course that the branch is to be outside the corporate limits of the city of the parent bank. A merger is arranged on some basis with one or more of the banks in that town or city. The bank absorbed is operated as a branch of the continuing bank. Despite

[1] The minimum amount or volume of deposits necessary to place a branch upon a satisfactory basis from the point of view of the management varies somewhat. In 1924 the president of one New York City branch bank estimated that a branch should have at least $1,000,000 in deposits. "A bank that is once established and that is operating branch banks and tellers' windows can cover its expense in one of these offices with deposits of about $1,000,000. That will cover our expense." *Hearings before the Committee on Banking and Currency*, House of Representatives, 68 Congress, 1 Session, H.R. 6855 (April, 1924), p. 97. This would be too small for many branches in New York City. This amount should be regarded more as a minimum for the offices having low overhead costs.

the fact that the second method has been subject to some criticism on the ground that small banks are sometimes forced to sell out through pressure of the larger banks, it is generally the more satisfactory. It is less likely to result in an over-banked community. There is less effort to get business away from other institutions.

Some banks have adopted a very definite policy of buying out the controlling interest of old, well-established institutions and continuing them as branches of the other bank. This practice has been followed rather extensively by some of the large banks in the state of California in building up a large number of out-of-town branches. The method to be followed will depend to a considerable degree upon the problems involved in a particular community at the time the branch is to be established. To refuse to allow a new branch in a community that has a branch or a unit bank, might result in preventing the community from securing the proper banking facilities, for the reason that undesirable people might get hold of the best locations and then refuse to merge with another group and at the same time fail or refuse to provide the full banking services required by that locality. Under such conditions the banking officials should not hesitate to authorize the establishment of other institutions.

The branch bank should select its branch managers with the greatest care. Capable managers are not enough. They must be that as a matter of course, but they either must have or must develop a genuine interest in the community in which they are located. The complaint is frequently made that the managers are shipped into the community and have no genuine interest in developing the community or remaining there. They are ready to leave as soon as a promotion is offered which will place them in a larger office or city. It is a general criticism, just or unjust, that the managers who are brought in from outside do not try to give the community the best service or the services that are required. They are accused of being "yes" and "no" men, who are interested in avoiding any risks even if, as a result, they are compelled to transfer the funds to other centers for investment or for lending. The unit banker, it is maintained by the critics, takes a more personal interest in the community and hence cannot be replaced by branch managers without a loss to the community. The branch banks must overcome this objection, in so far as it is genuine.

Branch managers should be selected who will take an interest in the community. The branch cannot grow unless the community is prosperous. The success of one means greater success to the other. This question of personal contact, however, while important, is frequently overemphasized. There is no doubt that the depositor or borrower of a branch is further removed from the management of the head office than is the case in a unit bank. There appears to be little doubt that there is somewhat less of a personal relationship existing in the branch than in the unit bank. While there are advantages in a branch system, it must be realized that there is a loss, to a certain degree, of what may be termed the personal touch. Managers refer frequently to the head office for advice or instructions. This practice may result in delay in granting loans or giving advice to depositors.

Many bankers undertake to meet the above criticism by securing new branches through the buying up or merging of a unit bank already in existence in the community. When the merger has been completed, the officers of the unit bank become officers of the continuing bank and are placed in charge of the branch. Of course they are under the supervision and regulation of the head office, but they should certainly be as alive to the best interests of the community as before the merger. In fact, they are under such circumstances a part of the community. They know the business men of the community and are therefore in a position to render most capable service, both to the branch bank and to the community or business interests of the locality in which the branch is situated.

In other cases the branch banker with the utmost care trains future managers in the methods followed at the head office. These men are then sent out as assistant managers to the branches, with the thought that they will ultimately be made managers. Under this plan they have an opportunity to study the business interests of the community before being placed in charge of a branch. If this policy is followed, the branch should have managers that are fully acquainted with the needs of their particular customers. It is true that the managers are changed from time to time, but so is the management of unit banks. The turnover is, perhaps, more marked in the case of branches than in the other type of bank. It is unfortunate that we have no definite and reliable information regarding the length of tenure of branch managers, as well as that for officers of unit banks. We must rely upon opinions and these are not always very definite, convincing or reliable.

BANK RESERVES

Branch banking has certain advantages in connection with the bank reserves. The problems growing out of the handling of reserves are among the most important which the individual banker has to solve. Safety and liquidity of bank assets make it imperative that the banker keep sufficient reserve (including legal reserves and cash in vault) to meet the demands of his depositors. In order to do this, the bank usually keeps a secondary reserve which may be easily converted into cash if the occasion arises. One important purpose of the reserve is to restrain the banker from extending his lines of credit too far. The character of the earning assets should have considerable influence upon the amount of reserves required, as well as upon the volume of funds kept in the form of a secondary reserve. A well-diversified portfolio growing out of different lines of business is the one most likely to be convertible into cash or available funds with which to meet the demands of depositors.

A branch-banking system established on a national basis or on some other wide geographical basis would normally have a more diversified portfolio than a unit system, even though we concede that the management is of the same quality. Unit banks, except the large ones, are not generally in a position to secure this diversification of loans, discounts, and investments. The head office of a branch system is in a position to take care of such situations more economically than is a unit bank. Branch banks may by careful coördination secure a better use of their funds, by reason of the diversified character of the business being financed. The ability to shift funds easily from one branch to another makes it possible for the bank to reduce the amount of available cash in the system, and thus to curtail overhead costs, without lessening the security or assurance that depositors will be protected in the event of heavy withdrawals from the banks, since the withdrawals are not apt to take place in the different branches at the same time. Some branches are normally reducing their loans while others are expanding. Some sections are increasing their deposits while in others there is a decline due to increased demand for funds.

It is customary for the branch system to keep its reserves largely in the head office. Each branch is required to carry only till money to meet the local needs and even this may be somewhat less than for a corresponding unit bank of similar size, for the reason that cash can easily be obtained from the head office. One branch banker[2] has stated that it is the policy of his bank to keep all the legal reserve at the head office, as well as the secondary reserve. The branches "carry till money; that is all." When the demand for funds in one community is slack, the banker will generally have calls from other branches for help. If not, the main office is in a position to invest the surplus funds in commercial paper or other desirable short-term paper or high-grade bonds. Of course it must be remembered that the transfer of funds in this way will take place only in case the branches are being operated on a wide geographical basis, and not within a single city. This tendency to reduce both the legal reserves and the vault money brings a corresponding increase of income to the bank. It is unlikely that any considerable number of branches will ask for assistance at a given time. Ways and means can easily be devised for keeping a close check on the reserve balances in order to keep funds available for transfer whenever they are needed by any branch. By these methods the branch should realize a higher and more satisfactory return from the use of its funds.

The administration and supervision of banks operating branches on a state-wide basis varies considerably. In some cases a large

[2] *Hearing before the Banking and Currency Committee,* House of Representatives, 68 Congress, 1 Session, H.R. 6855 (April, 1924), p. 74.

stockholder, if there be one or more in the community, is elected as a director of the bank. Such a director forms a connecting link between the head office and the branch. When the branch is obtained through the absorption of a bank already in existence, it is a common practice to retain one or more of the officers or directors as officers or members of a local committee for the branch. One purpose of this policy is to have the depositors feel that the branch is a part of the community as well as a branch of a large bank located elsewhere. The board of directors frequently appoints an advisory board which endeavors to keep in touch with the work of the branch. A common practice is to have the local directors act as an *ex-officio* discount committee for the branch. This type of branch management and control serves to attract and hold deposits at the branch, as well as to lessen the opposition to outside ownership and control.

In Canada, where branch banking is highly developed, the territory is divided into districts and a superintendent appointed to supervise all branches in his section. Under this system, the branch managers have been allowed a great deal of freedom in handling the affairs of the branch. The extent of such powers depends upon the ability and experience of the managers. The lending power varies from $1,000 for a new manager to $5,000[3] for the more experienced men. Requests for loans in excess of these amounts are referred to the superintendent for his approval. With the approval of the superintendent, the managers may lend up to $25,000. Applications for loans in excess of $25,000 are generally referred to the head office for review and final approval.[4] The branch managers have almost, if not completely, unlimited power in rejecting a loan. It would not ordinarily be considered good banking practice to overrule the managers in this respect.

The powers and duties of branch managers in the United States vary considerably. The extent of their lending power depends to a large degree upon the type of managers that a given bank em-

[3] Some writers give the loan limits as ranging from $2,500 to $10,000. See Bernard Ostrolenk's *Economics of Branch Banking* (New York: Harper and Brothers, 1930), p. 168.

[4] McGibbon, D. A., Commissioner, *Report on Banking and Credit with Respect to the Industry of Agriculture in the Province of Alberta* (1922), pp. 44-47.

ploys. In some banks the branch managers are scarcely more than clerks and have little power. Other banks have adopted the policy of placing vice presidents in charge of the branches. Under the latter policy the managers may have very broad powers and privileges in making loans and taking care of the needs of their depositors. Nearness of the branch to the head office determines to a certain degree what powers are granted to the managers. In general, however, the managers of branch banks in this country and in Canada have a definite policy mapped out for them and are expected to refer all matters to the head office if the questions fall outside the powers conferred.

As stated above, branch managers are frequently given power to make loans and advances up to a certain maximum, depending upon the borrower or his collateral. The manager reports such loans or advances as a matter of routine to the head office. In some cases a manager may be allowed to exceed his maximum, after which the loan is reviewed by the head office. This privilege will be withdrawn if the judgment of the manager proves to be unreliable. Beyond this special privilege, the manager is required to submit applications to the head office for approval before advancing the funds. Delays in making loans may be partly overcome by applying in advance to the head office for the approval of a line of credit to be given a customer. If this policy is followed, the manager is in a position to advance the funds to his borrower as soon as the request is made. In any event the time required will not be much, if any, greater than that required by the president of a unit bank who refers his large loans to the executive committee for its approval.

Some banks have adopted the policy of permitting the managers of branches created through the absorption of an old bank to lend an amount as large as would have been possible when the bank was a unit bank.[6] There will naturally be some variation in this respect as between the policies of different institutions. In some

[6] Elliott, Edward, vice president of the Security Trust and Savings Bank, Los Angeles, California: "In any place where we have taken over a bank, the manager of that branch now lends to his customers without consultation in advance with the head office just as much as could have been loaned when he was a unit bank, to the individual." *Hearings before the Committee on Banking and Currency*, House of Representatives, 68 Congress, 1 Session, H.R. 6855 (April, 1924), p. 73.

cases the limitations are stated specifically. The by-laws of one branch bank in the South provide that:

Loans not exceeding two thousand dollars ($2,000) may be made by an assistant cashier at a branch bank in a town having no local directors, but where there is a local director or vice president, the consent of one or the other shall be had before making a loan of over one thousand dollars ($1,000). No loan in excess of two thousand ($2,000) shall be made without the consent of the president or cashier, or, in their absence, by three members of the discount committee.

The president of the First National Bank, Detroit, Michigan, placed the limit at a smaller figure.[6] He stated that

The branch, as a rule, makes no loans. The branch manager, of course, has authority to make loans up to a certain limit (say $500 to $1,000) to his customers, but all applications for loans above this limit go before the officers and directors of the bank.

There are certain advantages in branch banking, as compared with unit banks, in the carrying out of an investment policy. It is a common practice in this country for banks to invest a portion of their funds in bonds, and in the case of some state banks, in stocks of other corporations. If these funds are to be invested on a sound and conservative basis, the investing banks must make a careful study or analysis of the securities before they are purchased. Many banks for one reason or another do not do this. Too many banks buy what security salesmen recommend. The time and expense involved in a careful investigation of a security are often too great to be undertaken by the smaller institutions. In a large branch system the volume of funds to be invested in this way is large enough to justify the organization and maintenance of a department to analyze and check securities both before and after purchase. As a consequence of the lack of careful analysis, such heavy losses have been sustained by many banks that they have been virtually forced into liquidation through an unsound investment policy. The same principle holds true as regards the credit work of many small banks throughout the country. In these respects the branch-banking system organized on a broad basis has distinct advantages.

The branch-banking system has certain advantages over unit

[6] Clark, Emory W., article, *Bankers Monthly*, Oct., 1922, p. 36.

banks in the use of capital funds. All banks in this country are required to provide a specified minimum capital before the bank may open for business. These capital requirements are generally based upon the population of the various communities in which banks are located. The theory is that the stockholders should invest sufficient capital to furnish adequate protection to the depositors. In some communities the volume of business is so small that it will not provide sufficient income to show a reasonable profit, even on the small capital invested. The branch bank with a large capital can usually allot only the amount needed in a given community and thus use its funds more economically. In most cases there is a minimum amount required for a branch, but the amount specified is usually in proportion to the size of the community. In some states, however, no allocation of capital to the various branches is required. This is true of California. In fact it makes little, if any, difference whether a given amount of capital is or is not assigned or allocated to a given branch or branches. The all-important thing is that the individual bank and its branches should jointly have sufficient capital to protect the depositors.

CHAPTER XVI

RELATION OF BANK MERGERS TO BRANCH BANKING

To what extent has the bank consolidation movement contributed to the growth of branch banking in the United States? The bank-failure epidemic covering the last decade has led many bankers and economists to seek a remedy. Branch banking has been regarded by many as the most desirable method of relief that can be adopted. The growth in the number of branch banks in the past few years has given rise to various studies to ascertain just what part several factors have played in stimulating this development. Among the various reasons assigned, bank mergers and consolidations have held a very prominent place. Great as may be our interest in this development, it must be kept in mind that branch banking is not permitted in many states where there have been large numbers of bank mergers. This phase of our study is at this time, therefore, limited to certain states where branch banking is permitted. The relationship between branch banking and bank mergers is important in the following states: California, New York, North Carolina, Maryland, South Carolina, and New Jersey. The development is of great interest in certain of the larger cities in the states of Louisiana, Massachusetts, Michigan, Ohio, and Pennsylvania.

There is certainly a close connection between the development of branch banking in the United States and the growth in the number of bank mergers and consolidations in those states where branch banking is permitted. In many cases, of course, the merger had its origin in the desire of a group to extend its branches into other localities or parts of the same city, and the feeling that the best way to accomplish this was to take over a bank with or without branches in order to obtain a branch or branches. A limited number of banks have absorbed a number of other banks without branches and continued the head office of the merged institution as a branch. There are other cases where the continuing bank absorbed institutions which were themselves operating branches. Where consolidations were completed in such cases, additional offices were not created, but there was a change in the management. The consolidation did not necessarily mean that additional capital was provided. In fact, in many instances it meant just the opposite, for the capital of the continuing bank was often less than the combined capital of the banks before the merger had been effected.

Notwithstanding the fact that an individual bank may participate in a number of mergers and consolidations, thus securing branches, the same bank may be, at the same time, engaged in the creation of new branches in which no other bank is directly involved. Under such circumstances, it is difficult to determine accurately the percentage of growth in the number of branches which have been the result of bank mergers. Our data in Table 11, pages 56-58, dealing with the number of branches both before and after the merger should therefore be considered only as indicative of the changes going on, and in no instance does an increase of branches mean that this was due entirely to mergers which had been completed. In not a few consolidations the increase in the number of branches is entirely a direct result of the merger. The securing of branches in this way has been more common in the state of California than in any other part of the country. The practice has also been quite common in the states of New York, Ohio, and Michigan. To a smaller extent we find the same tendency in recent years, in some of the southern states, notably South Carolina. On the other hand, it is interesting to observe that a large number of mergers took place in those states where there were either no branches, or where further extension is absolutely prohibited. This situation is found throughout the Middle West, where branch banking has, until recently, been largely illegal.[1]

As stated above, banks have obtained branches through bank

[1] The state legislatures of Indiana and Iowa have recently enacted laws which permit banks to establish and operate branches on a very restricted territorial or geographical basis. Mergers and branch banking in these states will no doubt be closely related in the future, if there is any substantial growth in the number of branches.

consolidations more commonly in California than in any other state. The *de novo* rule[2] has been an important factor in this development. Whenever a bank can take ove rand convert another bank into a branch, the absorbing bank secures a substantial volume of new business, and at the same time eliminates a certain amount of what would otherwise be competition for a new branch. In California the banking department certainly has refused in a considerable number of cases to permit the establishment of a new branch without the elimination of the already-existing unit bank. This policy avoided a part of the criticism which would have arisen on the ground that the larger institution was using unfair methods to force the small unit bank out of business. The Bank of America National Trust and Savings Association, San Francisco, has without doubt obtained more "outside" branches through absorptions than any other bank, not only in California, but in the country as a whole. The passage of the McFadden Amendment in 1927 had a restraining effect on members banks, with the result that the development in this connection has since slowed down to a certain extent—especially as regards mergers and consolidations between banks not located within the corporate limits of the same city.

What would be the result if the branch area were extended geographically in the states which now permit city branch banking, or even in those states which do not permit it at this time? There appears to be little, if any, doubt that the extension of branch banking would involve bank consolidations to a very great extent. Perhaps the connection would be much closer for the reason that the small-bank problem is better understood now than formerly. Many small bankers realize more fully than ever before the futility of trying to operate a small institution under unfavorable circumstances. The larger banks realize that it is frequently more economical to buy out the small bank than to start a new bank and compete with the already-existing institution. The branch will find itself on a profit-making basis much sooner, and the feeling toward the branch is likely to be much better—a thing which large banks fully appreciate. There seems, therefore, good reason

[2] For a fuller statement concerning the *de novo* rule, see Chap. X, pp. 157-59.

to believe that with an extension of branch-banking territory, many mergers and consolidations will take place, leading to the growth of branches in this way.

In referring to the relationship between the growth of branch banking and bank amalgamations in England, Sykes, an able writer on this subject, stated:

> The progress of the system of branches, widespread over the United Kingdom, has in large measure accrued from the amalgamation policy pursued over a period of one hundred years. Up to a point, the results of this have been economically and socially beneficial, not the least important of these being the growth of effective, keen, and incessant competition. Of late years both the opening of branches and competition have been carried beyond desirable limits, and this has been produced by amalgamation moves the justification for which was questionable.[3]

It seems fair to assume that our experience in the future will follow closely that described by Sykes regarding the development of English branch banking during the past hundred years. In some states at the present time serious objections are raised against branch banking, but, even so, in many states an extension of branch banking is preferred to bank failures. The same or similar conditions prevail in other states where branch banking is now prohibited. An extension of the branch privileges would give rise to mergers not only for the purpose of preventing failures, but also to secure new business through branches. In this connection one state superintendent made the following comment:

> As a general proposition, I do not regard branch banking as being as satisfactory as unit banking. If, however, I can prevent a weak bank from failing by merging it with a stronger bank which will continue the office as a branch of the larger bank, I shall not hesitate to do so. In short, while I do not favor an extension of branch banking, I prefer it to bank failures.

One well-known and widely-used method of avoiding bank failures is to effect mergers between weak and strong banks. There are two or three reasons why a strong institution may be willing or can be induced to assist the weak institution: (1) to avoid a bank failure in its own community; (2) to lessen competition; and

[3] Sykes, Joseph, *The Amalgamation Movement in English Banking, 1825-1924* p. 187.

(3) to secure new business. If the banks are not located within the same city, the difficulty of carrying out the details of a merger is greatly increased.

One banking superintendent gave his reasons for encouraging mergers as follows:

> When two small banks in a town are struggling for existence and neither making more than operating expenses, and in many cases not able to care for the needs of their customers, it has been the policy of the department, if possible, to bring about a merger or consolidation of them, thereby making one good strong bank, able to take care of the commercial needs of the community, and at the same time earn a fair return to the stockholders upon their stock investment.

The absorbing bank may not be able to retain the business of the absorbed institution, either for the reason that it is not convenient to the depositors or because the depositors are dissatisfied with the new management, feeling that the bank was absorbed for the direct benefit of the newcomers. Frequently, the problem is greatly simplified by operating a branch at the place of the absorbed bank. Since state-wide branch banking is prohibited in all except a few states, and county branch banking (or other modifications of this plan) is restricted to a still smaller number of states, it becomes quite evident that under present conditions there is a definite limit to the extent to which branches will come into existence through the medium of bank mergers or consolidations, except within the corporate limits of the city of the parent institutions. And it is difficult at times to see how the management of one bank can justify its action to its stockholders in taking over an institution in another community. The use of the merger as a means of preventing or postponing bank failures has its limitations. The right to operate branches of the stronger or absorbing bank would, in many cases, greatly simplify the problem.

Under chain and group banking a form of combination is secured that is different from that in which actual mergers and consolidations take place. In building up a group of banks, a number of banking institutions and resources are brought under the control of a central management, just as in the case of a consolidation; but in the case of a chain or group the separate legal entities or corporations still remain. In theory there is supposed to be a great deal of freedom for the local organization. In fact the management exercises extensive supervision over the units.

In chain or group banking, the purpose is to bring together a large number of institutions without interfering with their charters. To "merge" in the common meaning of the term would be undesirable in many states for the reason that the various offices could not be kept open. In some instances the holding company buys up more than one bank in a given community and then merges the banks in order to cut down the overhead. A number of mergers have been effected in this way. In the main, however, we must look for the most important effects in this direction from the bringing together of large resources under one management, rather than from the reduction of the actual number of banking institutions through mergers and consolidations. It may be stated in general, however, that an increase in group and chain banking does not necessarily mean any corresponding increase in bank consolidations. In fact it may mean just the opposite.

The economic results of this development are just as important and far-reaching as in the cases where the mergers are completed in the ordinary way. In the future, as branch banking increases and its advantages are more clearly seen and understood, there is likely to be an increase of this type of mergers.

A very interesting case developed in Massachusetts following the passage of the Consolidation Act of 1918 and the McFadden Act of 1927. The McFadden Act provided, among other things, that a bank which had been operating a branch for twenty-five years prior to that time could continue to operate it. The Consolidation Act of November, 1918, provided that national banks could consolidate within county limits. The national bank referred to took over a bank at Fitchburg and continued in operation the branch of the Fitchburg bank. This office was moved to the location formerly occupied by the head office of the Fitchburg bank. It then merged several other banks in the same county and consolidated the capital and surplus with that of its own institution. Under the restrictions regarding national banks' establishing new branches outside the city of the parent institution, these offices could not be continued as branches. A holding company was organized. The stock of this corporation was trusteed with the stock of the national bank, in order to keep complete control in the hands of the management of the national bank. This holding company then established small banks in each of the communities where the national bank had absorbed the other institution. What really took place, then, was a merger between the national and other county banks, with the substitution of a smaller bank in each locality. These small institutions were under the control and direction of the holding company, which was in turn controlled by the national bank. This is very close to being branch banking though it is not so termed. At any rate, it shows how closely bank mergers, branch banking, and group banking are connected. There appears to be little doubt that these banks would be operated as branches if the national act permitted it. In the last analysis it may almost be said that this is a modified form of branch banking.

RECENT DEVELOPMENTS

An important tendency in recent branch-banking legislation, both state and Federal, is to tie up an extension of branches on a state-wide or county basis directly with bank mergers and consolidations. This is being done by prohibiting a bank from establishing a branch in a town or city in which a bank is already in operation, unless the branch bank absorbs a bank already in existence in that community. The aim is to prevent the development of too many banking offices in a given locality. It is not intended to encourage mergers as such, but rather to avoid a competitive struggle among banks to establish branches which would be located in communities already being served by unit or other banks.

The process of securing branches in some states is dependent almost entirely on this type of banking concentration, as for example Wisconsin and Montana. In other cases branches may not be established in a community where a bank is already in operation except through the absorption of a bank already in existence. This is well illustrated by the recent banking laws in the states of Connecticut, Oregon, Utah, and Washington. The recent Bank Act of 1933 provides for extension of branches on a state-wide basis by national banks.

It is evident that the relationship between bank mergers and consolidations and an extension of branch banking will be much closer in the future than in the past. In the future we may expect that any extension of branches will be accompanied by a substantial increase in the number of bank mergers. There will be, no doubt, many small branch systems built up and later absorbed by a larger branch bank. In this way the growth and extension of branches in various sections of the country will be accompanied by an increase in the number of mergers and a decrease in the total number of individual banks. The number of mergers will tend to be large for a few years. With a decline in the total number of banks, the number of mergers will decline, but the mergers will be likely to involve larger banking resources on the average, and hence to continue to be an important factor in the concentration movement of banking in the United States for several years.

In conclusion, it can be said that there is without doubt a vital connection between the growth of bank mergers and consolidations and the extension of branch banking. The modifications which are being made in the laws regarding bank mergers and branch banking in the United States have done much to promote the acquisition of branches through mergers. Development along these lines is limited to those states which have laws favorable to a development of branch banking, either on a state-wide basis or on a liberal restricted basis. Since there is a marked tendency to liberalize the laws relative to the extension of branches in several states, it is only logical to conclude, in view of what has taken place in certain states in the past, that efforts will be made to restrict the creation of new branches except through the purchase of banks already in operation in the locality where a branch is desired. Such a restriction would undoubtedly serve a most useful purpose in preventing the creation of additional banking offices in localities where the business is too small to support them. The development of branches should therefore be closely associated with consolidations in the future, just as it has been in England in the past. Such development would no doubt tend to strengthen our banking system immensely and at the same time avoid a great deal of harmful competition and bad banking, which is usually paid for in the long run by the depositors of the banks involved.

CHAPTER XVII

SOME ECONOMIC ASPECTS OF BRANCH BANKING

Many phases of the branch-banking question have now been discussed. Statistics have been compiled to show the scope and extent of branch banking in this country, both in the aggregate and in comparison with all the banking resources of this country. The relationship of branch banking to the correspondent system has been considered, as well as the branch-bank management problem. The historical development of branch banking has been briefly traced from the early days of the American Republic. The special development in the state of California and the legal status of branch banking, both state and national, have been outlined. These are all very interesting aspects of the subject of branch banking. As students of banking, we are, however, in the last analysis interested most deeply in the economic effects which would be produced if we adopted a branch-banking system either on a nation-wide or a Federal-Reserve-district basis. What effect will branch banking have upon the services to be rendered by the banking system? Will branch banking strengthen our system so as to increase the services rendered to business and the community and, at the same time, reduce the extremely heavy losses which depositors and stockholders have suffered in this country for the past hundred years through bank failures, especially the heavy and most burdensome losses of the last decade? More specifically, let us consider a system of branch banking in relation to the following:

Convenience of access, to both borrowers and depositors
Safety of funds
Mobility of bank funds
Diversification of loans and investments
Concentration of banking capital
Availability of bank credits

Interest rates and cost of accommodation
Arguments against branch banking

CONVENIENCE OF ACCESS

The question of service to the individual and to the community at large is one of the most important problems to be considered in making a comparison of branch banking with a unit system. The convenience of a bank or a branch involves two questions. (1) the physical location of the banking office at which the business is to be transacted, and (2) the difficulty or red tape which must be encountered by the individual customer in coming in contact with the officers of the bank or the branch, as the case may be. It is frequently claimed (see page 277) by the opponents of branch banking that the management of the branch is such that the manager is only a figurehead and that all the more important business must be referred to the officers at the head office of the bank, who may be many miles away. For that reason, it is argued, the officers of the bank never fully understand either the wants or needs of their branch depositors. These critics maintain that under the unit system they can come in direct contact with the officers of the bank and thus secure greater and more prompt service from the bank. The question is one of great importance in our banking system. Are the officers of a branch system more hard-boiled and slower to negotiate loans than in the unit system? Is it true that the officers of a branch system do not understand the needs of their distant branch depositors? Are these officers any less sympathetic than in the unit system?

The first of these two questions is anwered primarily by the number of banking offices established and maintained. In this connection the advantage is in favor of the branch system. The free development of such a system would reduce the number of independent banks considerably, but the actual number of offices or banking places should be, on the whole, increased. Branches can be established with a smaller amount of capital, a smaller operating force, and with less expensive banking quarters. There are many places in which a bank with the minimum capital required for a national bank could not succeed for the simple reason that the volume of business is too small to support such a capital investment. Many small localities could support a small branch which may or may not be open every day. The total number of banking offices could be greatly increased with profit to the stockholders and with additional banking facilities for the community at large.

With regard to the ease with which the officers of the two systems may be reached, there are two problems to be considered: (1) is the relationship less personal, and (2) will the branch system be more rigid and thus tend to restrict credit more than is the case in the unit system? The second question will be discussed in another section (see page 300), under the "Availability of Credits." There seems to be no doubt that the relationship between the bank and its depositors will be less personal and that there will be some loss of sympathy between the officers of the bank and the customers of the distant branches. This cannot be avoided. This is, I believe, fully realized by branch bankers in other countries where branch banking has been in general operation for many decades. Many depositors of the branches will never come in contact with the senior officers and directors who determine the policy of the branch at which they do business. This is unavoidable in a branch-banking system which is wide in its scope. There seems to be no adequate way of completely overcoming this weakness in a branch system, though it may be, and is, obviated to a certain extent by securing able and sympathetic branch managers who understand the needs of their particular community and who strive to represent their interests with the officers of the head office. In this way much can be done, but it is not possible to bring the officers and all their customers together as is common in a unit system.

The final decision regarding branches must rest upon other comparisons between the two systems. Branch banking must be justified on other grounds if it is to be accepted.

SAFETY OF FUNDS

One of the primary considerations in any banking system is the question of safety both for the stockholders and the depositors.

The nature of a branch-banking system is such as to insure greater protection to the depositors than is the case in the unit system. In the United States there has been a very large number of bank failures in comparison with the number of failures in countries where branch banking has been highly developed. A large number of banks with branches in this country have failed, but the aggregate is small when compared to the total number of banks which have failed here. In most cases only small banks have failed. Exceptions are found in the failure of the Bank of United States and the Chelsea Exchange Bank and Trust Company in New York City, the Bankers Trust Company in Philadelphia, the National Bank of Kentucky and the Peoples State Bank of Charleston, South Carolina, with forty-eight branches. It is very doubtful whether the experience which we have had in the United States in regard to failures of banks operating branches can be taken as any criterion of what should be expected under a strong, capable management. Any banking system with inferior management is likely to suffer heavy losses. Branch banking is no guarantee except in so far as it may be successful in the development of better managers of banks. To the extent that this is accomplished, the funds of depositors will be safer.

It may be argued that the past decade is unusual and that we cannot predict what will happen to the unit banks that survive the present depression. Records show that a wave of bank failures has followed practically all major depressions in this country during the past hundred years. When diversification of loans and investments is considered in connection with the safety of funds, it becomes more evident that the advantage lies with the branch system. Better and more complete credit information may be had, for reasons that have already been pointed out.

Bank failures in Canada have resulted largely from the mismanagement and dishonesty of officers located in the head office, such dishonesty being concealed from the auditors.[1] A study of the systems of Australia and England seems to lead to the conclusion that either of these two systems, measured in terms of bank failures, is superior to that of Canada, while the Canadian

[1] Willis and Beckhart, *Foreign Banking Systems* (New York: Henry Holt & Co., 1929), p. 479.

system, in turn, has suffered fewer losses than have occurred in the United States.[2]

MOBILITY OF BANK FUNDS

A branch-banking system established on a nation-wide basis, or on a basis covering a wide geographical or territorial area, possesses a distinct advantage over a unit system in the ease with which it can transfer funds from one part of its territory to another. The unit bank must rely upon its correspondent, whereas the branch system, through its head office and various branches, has little difficulty in moving funds from a branch where they are not needed to another branch where they may be used in commercial or industrial loans with a short-term maturity. This process is accomplished with less cost and time, and hence results in a more economical use of the funds of the bank and its branches.

The mobility of funds is especially important where banks are called upon to finance one-crop regions. Under such circumstances, the unit bank will find itself in the position of needing more funds than it has at one season, and having more than it needs at another. At one time the unit bank must borrow from its correspondent and at the other period it must seek an outlet for its funds, which is usually done through the large city correspondent. The head office of a large branch system will know the requirements of the various localities in which it operates branches, and can adjust its financing to supply the various sections without calling on outside banking institutions. The funds of the branch may be more economically used and a larger return realized than where the unit bank acts through another bank. The branch banks in California have maintained that this is one of the principal advantages of the branch system in that state. The same benefits have been attained by the Canadian banking system in the transfer of funds from the eastern to the western provinces, or vice versa, as the needs of these different sections vary from time to time.

DIVERSIFICATION OF LOANS AND INVESTMENTS

One of the advantages of a branch-banking system is realized in connection with the diversification of the portfolio of the bank. This is made possible for two or three reasons. Many small banks

[2] *Ibid.*, p. 484.

have only a limited volume of funds to employ and frequently find it very difficult to diversify properly without overextending their credit resources, or without reducing the average size of the loan to a point where it is expensive to handle in relation to the income derived. It is necessary to have a fairly large fund before it can be well diversified, especially when the bank undertakes to meet the needs of the community in which it is located. The branch systems secure a sufficiently large volume of deposits so that their funds can be more scientifically invested, even if we assume the same degree of ability in the management of the unit and the branch bank. Of course there are large banks which may accomplish this end either through the large volume of their funds or by reason of their desirable location. Reference is here made to the conditions that surround unit banks in general in this country. Moreover, it is the banking system as a whole, and not the individual banks in certain favorite locations, that must be considered.

A large and well-managed branch-banking system will have its branches widely distributed geographically. Various kinds of business will naturally be carried on in the different sections covered by a branch system. Under such conditions, the head office will be in a position to secure easily a well-diversified portfolio. If too many funds are invested in a particular one-crop region, the branch bank may offset this condition by loans to other lines of business through branches located in other industrial or commercial centers. The bank, with all its branches, will thus secure the needed diversification. If one industry undergoes a setback, it is not likely that the same condition will exist in all other industries. The bank can normally expect some sections to be in a position to meet their obligations, even though extensions may have to be made to borrowers in the depressed communities. The branch bank is especially well situated to diversify its loans, discounts, and investments, and to transfer the funds from place to place as required.

The branch bank, with its larger resources and greater volume of business, is in a position to secure the services of well-organized credit and research agencies and thus to keep itself better informed about business conditions in the different parts of its territory, as well as in other parts of the world. This enables the bank to spread its activities with safety. The bank management knows more accurately the various classes of business which it will be called upon to finance, as well as the individual borrowers. The problem of the use of surplus funds is to a considerable extent solved, since the bank and its branches find a more regular use of the funds in their own territory by transfers from one community to another as needed. The policy of the bank in connection with investments is thus improved. The bank is in a position to investigate the securities to be purchased and does not run the risk of purchasing high-interest-yielding but speculative bonds in order to earn a high return. The bank with branches can organize a large investment department in the head office to serve all the branches. The cost of such an organization spread over a large number of branches is small proportionately, though large in the aggregate.

The opponents of branch banking contend that a large branch bank is interested in securing the deposits of the various small agricultural or industrial communities for the purpose of transferring such funds to the large financial centers for use there, neglecting the needs of these smaller localities. The very reverse should be the object of the branch system. Under our correspondent system, with a large number of small banks, each with one or more correspondents in the large cities, it is the usual thing for the small banks, when they have funds not needed in their own communities, to transfer them to the large cities where they are used all too frequently in the stock market or for other speculative purposes. In other words, the correspondent system brings about the very evil which the critics of branch banking say would appear under a branch system. As a matter of fact, it would be easy, under a system as already pointed out, to transfer funds from one section to another, and thus use them for commercial, industrial, or agricultural purposes, rather than in the large financial centers. Branch banking should, therefore, reduce rather than increase the amount of funds going to the large financial centers.

CONCENTRATION OF BANKING CAPITAL

Under a branch-banking system the control of banking will be placed in fewer hands than is the case in the unit system. This concentration of management or control is inevitable in any line of business when large-scale production develops. Concentration of power does not necessarily lessen the public interest in buying and holding bank stocks as an investment. In fact, it should, if properly handled, tend in general to increase the desirability of bank stocks as a type of investment. Better management should and will, in time, bring more uniform earnings and fewer losses, and thus increase the dividends on bank stocks. There will be fewer banks, but these will have a larger average capital and the shares will be more widely distributed.

The total amount of capital invested in the banking business will, no doubt, be less proportionately than it is today under the unit system. The larger individual banks will require larger capital, but the increase will not be in proportion to the increased volume of business. That will lessen the amount of capital stock outstanding and increase the net earnings which may be distributed among the many shareholders. The losses should be less by reason of improved management and credit analysis. In brief, there will be a smaller proportional amount of capital invested, and it will be more widely distributed. This concentration of control will develop, as time goes on, in either the unit or the branch system of banking.

AVAILABILITY OF BANK CREDITS

The anti-branch bankers maintain as one of their primary arguments the claim that customers of the various branches will in general have less access to bank funds than they now enjoy under the unit system. The contention is made that since the branch managers will not be in as close touch with the community as are the officers of the unit banks, and since funds will be siphoned off from the many local sections and transferred to the head office to be used in the metropolitan centers or in stock-market financing, difficulties will be encountered by the depositors of the branches in borrowing. The branch managers will be instructed to require more and specific kinds of collateral against loans and discounts. Specific stock-exchange or listed securities will be demanded, which in many cases will not be held by the borrowers. This course, if pursued by the branch-banking authorities, will make it difficult for the borrowers to meet the requirements of the banks. These criticisms resolve themselves into the question of the services offered by the branch system as compared with those of the unit system.

It is difficult to understand why a bank should go to the expense of developing branches and nursing them along until they yield net profits unless it intends to do a regular banking business in the various localities in which branches have been established. The primary purpose in securing accounts is to do a banking business with such customers. A bank cannot hope to secure deposits from a business community unless it, in turn, grants such accommodation as is needed in the community. The banking business is two-sided, the securing of deposits and the making of loans. It is from the latter, together with investments, that banks as a whole receive the greater part of their income. The interest rate paid by small borrowers or borrowers from commercial banks is generally higher than that received by banks in the large financial centers for the funds loaned in the call-loan market or in the money markets, where commercial paper or bankers' acceptances are the principal types of paper to be had.[3] It appears logical to conclude, therefore, that the management of a branch system would advance funds to the business interests of a given community in accordance with the needs of that community for carrying on its commercial, industrial, and agricultural operations.

The contention that fewer loans and discounts would be made under a branch system than are made under the unit system is mere conjecture so far as this country is concerned. Without in any way condemning the unit banks for their past actions, it is no doubt true that many unit banks would be in operation today instead of in the hands of receivers if they had not concentrated so largely on local business. In other words, the unit bankers would themselves, in many cases, be far better off had they invested more of

[3] In Canada, funds are shifted from the maritime provinces to the western provinces to secure a higher interest return. Willis and Beckhart, *Foreign Banking Systems*, pp. 465-66.

their funds in other than local paper. The branch bank which has taken care to have its branches widely separated should be in a position to lend larger amounts safely in a given community by reason of its diversified portfolio, which is made up of the total loans, discounts, and investments of several branches, representing many different industries and sections of the country. Instead of the branches being unable to give the services needed, they should be peculiarly fitted to give better service than the unit system can. At certain seasons of the year the head office should be able to transfer large amounts of funds to the branches where they are needed, these in turn to be transferred to another center at another season, as demand dictates. Of course these advantages may be of no avail if there is dishonest or selfish management, seeking to use the funds for personal ends. In such hands any system will fail to give the banking services needed in a business community.

The experience of other countries cannot be taken as the ultimate test of what would occur in this country, were we to adopt a national branch-banking system. It should throw some light upon the problem, however, as such systems illustrate the advantages as well as the disadvantages of branch banking. The experience of other countries in this respect is decidedly in favor of branch banking. The Canadian branch banks have not siphoned off funds from the western provinces to be used in the larger cities in the eastern districts. The large chartered banks located in Toronto and Montreal have given special attention to the needs of the western or agricultural provinces, and have loaned out in that part of the country as much as they have received in deposits from that section. In fact, in not a few instances, the loans and discounts made by these banks in the western provinces have been greater than the deposits held by these branches. The experience in other countries is much the same, and there does not appear to be any logical reason why the same results should not be attained in the United States under a well-organized and regulated branch-banking system. Surplus funds tend to accumulate in populous centers, but under a well-managed branch-banking system these funds will be available and will be generally loaned out in those communities where the funds yield the largest returns consistent with sound and conservative banking policies.

The opponents of branch banking maintain that there are necessarily great delays in making loans and that the borrowers will not be able to secure loans so quickly, even though these may be granted in the end. These delays, it is claimed, are due to the fact that the branch managers are not given full lending powers and requests for loans must be referred to the head office. The approval of the head office may be necessary in some cases but, even so, it should not ordinarily cause a long delay. The borrower should apply for his funds sufficiently in advance of his needs to give the bank time to make an adequate credit investigation, whether he is dealing with a branch or a unit bank. Where the borrower is in actual need of funds and can show good reason for his request, he is not apt to be denied or held up for long.

Branches usually have the power to make loans up to a certain amount on an unsecured basis. There is generally more freedom in the making of secured loans, providing the classes of security are of a standard or listed variety. The same principle applies to the making of loans at the head office by the officers of the bank. Here the officers are given a certain amount of freedom, but if the loans exceed a certain amount, they must be approved by another officer or two, or by the loan and discount committee, and in some cases they are referred to the board of directors before the loans are finally approved. The essential difference is one of degree. A little more time may be required at certain branches, but these delays, if they come, should not greatly handicap the borrower, since he may make his arrangements in advance, as he must or should under either a branch or unit system. Under a well-managed system of branch-banking there need not, therefore, be any cause for complaint on this ground.

INTEREST RATES

An extension of branch banking in this country on a wide scale would tend to bring about lower and more uniform interest rates. A bank operating branches would tend to make its rate of interest uniform in all its branches. There would be a difference in the rates charged to different classes of borrowers, which is true in the large city banks at the present time and is likely to continue in the future. The management of a branch system would tend to charge the same rate at the different offices on loans and discounts of a similar nature, however. There would not be the wide spread now existing between the rate paid by a farmer in one section of the country and that of a farmer in another section, unless there was a material difference in the risk and the liquidity of the loans advanced. Any banking system with branches organized on a national basis would be likely to apply a more nearly uniform rate for funds than is charged by a large number of independent banks widely separated. The same would be true even though the branch system were limited to a smaller area, provided the territorial unit was not too small.

The experience of this country is quite limited as to the actual interest rates charged under a branch-banking system. The results in the state of California[4] seem to indicate that the extension of branch banking has been accompanied by a decline in the average interest rates, in certain parts of the state at least. One banker testified in this connection as follows:

> Our uniform practice has been to adopt a maximum rate of 7 percent. For instance, when we entered the San Joaquin Valley, where we found on entry that the prevailing rate of interest on loans was 8, 9, and in some instances 10 percent, we immediately brought every one of the loans then in the pouch down to a maximum of 7 percent, and enunciated a rule that interest on such loans should thereafter be at the rate of 7 percent.[5]

In England, where there is a far greater concentration of banking control than exists here, the same results have been secured that are claimed for the state of California. The effects of the concentration movement on interest rates in England are described by Sykes as follows:

> With the increase of the number of branches belonging to one bank . . ., and the growth of associations of bankers, rates and charges have

[4] Hearings, on H. Res. 141, Vol. I, Part 4 (1930), p. 505. (See also *Report of the Joint Commission of Agricultural Inquiry*. House of Representatives, 67th Congress, 1st Session. Report 408).

[5] *Ibid.*, Vol. II, Part 11, p. 1525.

tended to become more uniform and to be reduced. This tendency has now been crystallized into effective practice by the development of competition. . . . it is improbable that loaning and interest rates ever varied so widely in the more compact banking area of England as in the heterogeneous divisions of America . . ., undoubtedly the differences were sufficient to be economically undesirable.[6]

He further states that

. . . in the days of the private bankers, who were generally located in their own single districts, there was little uniformity of rates.[7]

In discussing the relation of the Canadian branch-banking system to interest rates, Professor Beckhart states:

While the quantity of data available is not as complete as would be desirable, all evidence seems to bear out the view that interest rates are lower in western Canada than in similar sections of the United States and that the borrower secures his accommodation at a reasonable cost.[8]

The opinion of one able Canadian banker was that, if single-province banks were operated in the West, they would not be as able to supply the needed funds to the various western provinces as are the banks which have branch offices in the East from which they may shift deposits.[9] Beckhart adds that

. . . without exception the bankers who testified lay great emphasis on the higher costs in the West as justification for the higher rates of interest.[10]

It seems clear from the experience of both Canada and England that the rates of interest have been made both more uniform and lower under a branch system than under the unit system. The same results appear to be indicated by American experience which, however, in recent years at least, has been quite meager. It seems reasonable to expect that a well-organized branch-banking system in the United States would bring about the same results. The greater economies of operation, the ease of transferring funds, and the greater diversification of risks would all tend to reduce the actual costs of providing banking services. These advantages

[6] Sykes, Joseph, *The Amalgamation Movement in English Banking, 1825-1924*, p. 149.

[7] *Ibid.*, p. 148.

[8] Willis and Beckhart, *Foreign Banking Systems*, p. 453.

[9] Testimony of H. C. McLeod, *Minutes of Proceedings, Evidence*, Committee on Banking and Commerce, Appendix, No. 2 Ottawa: C. H. Parmelee, Printer, p. 119.

[10] Willis and Beckhart, *op. cit.*, p. 461.

could, in part at least, be passed on to the borrowers by means of a lower interest charge.

ARGUMENTS AGAINST BRANCH BANKING

1. *Branch banking is un-American.*—The supporters of unit banking frequently put forth the argument that branch banking is not "natural" to this country. It has been adopted by foreign countries but never by the United States. To initiate or inaugurate a system of branch banking now would be to renounce a long, historic policy of unit banking. This country has been financed largely by a system of unit banks and to change that now would be to reject a time-honored institution which has been one of the primary elements in the growth of this country. The reply that is frequently made to this argument is that this country started out with a branch system and used it quite extensively until about the close of the Civil War. Since then there has been a limited number of branch banks at all times, though the number during much of the period was so small as to make branch banking unimportant. Interest sprang up from time to time, but it was not until after the close of the World War that the growth of branches really assumed importance. Moreover, it is claimed by branch-bank advocates that there is nothing sacrosanct about unit banking and that what we desire is the best possible type of banking system. It is, therefore, the American method to change our methods when better results may be obtained. The question is not, "Is branch banking un-American?" but rather, "Would our banking system be improved? Would we have safer banking institutions with a smaller number of bank failures?" There is nothing in a system of branch banking that could be regarded as un-American. It is customary for other corporations to establish distant offices wherever they may prove profitable. Well-known examples of this type of organization are found in the development of chain stores.

2. *Tendency toward monopoly.*—Branch banking tends to drive out of existence small or unit banks. The management of branch banks is continually looking for locations for branches. If the system is a growing one, new branches will be established until the available territory is thoroughly covered by branches. These

branches will be established through the taking over of other banks or by the *de novo* method. The argument is generally made that the large branch bank will, in many cases, when it is unable to buy or merge the smaller unit banks, enter into vigorous competition and continue this until it has driven the smaller unit bank out of existence. This competition may, it is contended, take the form of lower interest rates which will be maintained until the small bank is forced to close, after which the rates may be increased to the point where they will become burdensome to the community.

Monopoly would appear in connection with the extension of credit. This might result in a system in which the management would restrict the flow of credit in certain directions. Those who were not in the good graces of the management would not be granted the amount of credit needed. Again, funds could easily be transferred to another community or class where they would be loaned to those closely associated with the management of the branch system. In the opinion of the writer this argument is not very convincing. Such a development has not occurred in those countries where branch banking has attained its greatest development. It is possible under a dishonest or selfish management, but it would not be in the best interests of the bank in the long run. It does not seem likely, therefore, that an intelligent management would attempt any such a policy. There is no doubt, however, that the branch bank would try to extend its services through the extension of new branches. Some banks might try unfair methods, but this would probably not be true of the banking system as a whole.

3. *Examinations and supervision.*—There is greater difficulty in making the proper examinations of a bank with a large number of branches. If the present policy of examining banks and branches were followed it would require a large number of bank examiners. If all branches were examined simultaneously, a very large staff would be required, larger in fact than the state could afford to employ at all times. The reply to this argument is usually found in the contention that it is not necessary to examine all the branches at one time. It is maintained that better results would be obtained if the examination were begun with the head office as of a given date, and then worked out to each branch as of that date. In this

way a satisfactory examination could be made with a much smaller examining staff. There is much to commend this policy.

Public supervision would be at a further disadvantage owing to the fact that we have an extensive development of both state and national banks in this country. Moreover, each state has its own laws and would not consent readily to have banks from other states operate branches within its borders. If this barrier were broken down, supervision would be complicated by the fact that two or more states would have to examine certain branches. A bank located in Ohio and operating branches in Kentucky would, if the bank were a state bank, be subject in part to both jurisdictions. The state officials of the state in which the head office was located would encounter serious obstacles if they undertook to examine a branch in another state. If both state and national banks were operating branches, there would be difficulties in keeping the two systems up to the same degree of efficiency.

4. *Drainage of funds into the money-market centers.*—Many of the critics of branch banks see in an extension of the branch system, as has already been indicated, a means for draining the funds out of many small communities into the large centers. It is the contention that the managers would not feel it worth while to lend out funds in the local communities, since the risk involved in relation to costs and profits would be too great. Rather than spend the time and energy to ascertain the position of the local borrowers (so runs the argument), the managers would largely ignore the needs of the various communities and transfer the funds to a place where they could be advanced against listed securities or used to buy bills in the money market.

The methods of financing through the correspondent banks in this country, as was indicated above (see page 266), has tended strongly to bring about just this result. It is doubtful if a greater concentration of funds in the financial centers could be attained under branch banking than has already been realized under the unit system which has been in operation in this country for many years. The tendency for funds to concentrate in New York is one of the fundamental criticisms leveled against the unit system during these many years. Branch banking should, under good management, produce just the reverse tendency, since the network of branches would facilitate the transfer of funds from one local community to another. In this way the funds could be used to a greater extent in the financing of commercial and industrial types of business, and less for more speculative purposes.

5. *Lack of interest in the welfare of the community.*[11]—Some people foresee a grave danger that the methods adopted by the management of a branch bank would not be in harmony with the best interests of the community. This would arise, it is claimed, from the fact that the manager would regard his connection with a branch as only temporary and that he would expect to move in due time to a larger or more remunerative branch. He would not therefore be interested in developing the business of the community, but rather in transferring funds to the head office. In this way the business interests of the local community would suffer, and its development would be less rapid than would have been the case under the unit system. The branch would never become an integral part of the community in the sense that unit banks do.

The depositors at the branches would never come into contact with the officers of the bank, who really determine its policy and who in the last analysis actually approve the loans made through the various branches. The business men doing business with a branch would always be at a great disadvantage, because the head office would not understand the needs of their locality. The branch managers would be less sympathetic and would make more onerous the terms on which funds would be lent. The managers would be instructed to secure a type of collateral which would in many cases be scarce and hard for the local business man to provide.

There is little doubt in the mind of the author that this criticism is well founded in some respects. The larger the institution and the further removed the real management, the slighter the contact between the depositors and the officers of the bank. This has its bad features. On the other hand, the results must be measured in their entirety. The question of most importance is, "Would the branch system be stronger than a unit system?" This should be the deciding factor. If the banking system is safer and stronger,

[11] See above, p. 277-78.

the loss of personal contact between the officers and depositors may be more than offset by these advantages. The depositors are more interested in a safe banking system than in anything else. It can be said truthfully, no doubt, that many unit banks have been too easy in their credit policy and that a certain amount of tightening up is necessary. In any case, this possible disadvantage of branch banking seems to the writer to be far outweighed by the advantages. That there are some disadvantages in branch as compared to unit banking is not disputed.

6. *Loss in local taxes.*—Some of the strong advocates of unit banking hold the position that a development of branch banking in this country would result in a very considerable loss in local taxes for many communities. It is held that the unit banks contribute substantially toward the expenses of local government. A considerable part of this would be lost, since the most that could be expected under a branch-banking system would be to tax the property owned for the purpose of the operation of the branch. This investment would be small as compared with the amount now held by the unit banks. This would cut down the amount of taxes paid by the banks for a given community. In short, an extension of branches would, it is claimed, mean a loss in local revenue which would increase the burden upon other business interests and would, in not a few cases, work a hardship upon certain local communities. This does not appear to be a very convincing argument, for the reason that a banking institution, be it a branch, a unit bank, or a large bank with many branches, cannot maintain a large establishment in a community unless the volume of business is sufficient to pay the expenses involved and yields in addition a fair return upon the investment. The loss would not be serious in the way of local taxes, it is believed, even though such a loss would perhaps arise in some instances.

CHAPTER XVIII

BRANCH BANKING AND THE FEDERAL RESERVE SYSTEM

One of the arguments advanced against an extension of branch banking is that it would have an unfavorable effect upon the Federal Reserve system. Many advocates of the unit system maintain that if we were to adopt a branch banking system it would materially alter the Federal Reserve system. This is an interesting as well as an important question. In order to answer the query, it is necessary to consider many phases of the system and the probable effect upon the system as a whole. The answer will no doubt vary considerably, depending upon the interest of the person who is considering the problem. It appears to the present writer that undue importance has been attached to this phase of the discussion.

The principal question involved in a discussion of branch banking is, "What would be the primary advantage to our banking system as a whole if we were to adopt branch banking?" Or, to put it in a negative form, "What is the primary objection to a development of branch banking in this country?" The purpose of banking reform of any kind should be to improve the banking system. The aim should be first of all to increase the safety of the system in relation to the services which are being performed. If this premise be accepted, it is proper to consider just what the results would be, were a branch banking system adopted and put into operation on a wide scale. A broad extension of branch banking would tend to modify or change certain relationships between the commercial banks and the Federal Reserve banks. the most important of which are the following:

Interbank relationship
Membership
Number of Federal Reserve banks
Volume of rediscounting at the Federal Reserve banks

Relation to credit control
Relation to the commercial-paper market

INTERBANK RELATIONSHIP

Under the unit banking system it is necessary to develop interbank connections between the various banking institutions. These interbank relations take different forms and grow out of the business needs of the community. The most important relations developed among banking institutions involve the following:

1. Clearing and collecting checks
2. Bank balances
3. Bank loans and advances
4. Credit information
5. Foreign banking services and connections
6. The placing of short-term funds in the money and call-loan markets

1. *Clearing and collecting checks.*—Under the unit system the banks must exchange checks and other credit instruments which are received by one bank drawn upon another. Banks are under the necessity also of collecting notes, drafts, and bills of exchange for their customers. These must be handled by other banks or agencies in the process of actually presenting them to the drawee for payment. The handling of such items has become recognized as one of the functions of a commercial bank. The safest and most satisfactory method for doing this type of work is by forwarding such credit instruments to another bank or banks for collection. This practice has been highly developed in our system of banking. A certain amount of this business will always be present in any modern commercial banking system where there is more than one bank in a country. In the carrying on of foreign banking business, it is difficult to imagine an international banking institution which would not be forced to use a correspondent bank for some part of its foreign business.

The methods of handling these various credit instruments would be greatly modified if branch banking were substituted for the unit system. Some of this interbank business would remain, but each bank or branch would send all this business through its branches wherever possible. The collection of such checks, notes, and other credit instruments would be carried out through the branches wherever this was possible. Since the Federal Reserve system has been and is being used extensively for the handling of this business between banks located in different communities, there would be considerable change in this respect. The volume of such business would in all probability be reduced very greatly.

2. *Bank balances.*—The adoption of the Federal Reserve system brought about a great change in the carrying of interbank balances by unit banks. The provision requiring all legal reserves to be carried either in the Federal Reserve banks or in the vaults of the bank itself was instrumental in concentrating the bank balances to a great extent. When the Federal Reserve Act was amended in 1917, requiring all legal reserves to be kept in the vaults of the Reserve banks, the concentration was carried as far as it could be. This did not eliminate all bank balances by any manner of means. The banks found it necessary to carry large balances, in many cases, in cities outside the Federal Reserve district in which the member bank was located. In addition, there were state banks and trust companies which never became members of the Federal Reserve system. These banks continued to need the correspondent relationship for reserve purposes as they had done before the Federal Reserve system had been established. These balances are maintained partly for reserve purposes, partly for meeting the requirements in connection with national or international banking business in the financing of customers of the bank, partly to meet the requirements in connection with interbank loans, and partly to provide balances against which drafts may be drawn.

If there were established a branch-banking system on a wide basis, a considerable change would be involved, both among the banks which are now members of the system and among those banks which are outside the Federal Reserve system. The member banks would still be required to carry their legal reserve, but other balances would be largely eliminated, for the reason that the head office would be relied upon to handle the surplus funds, if any. There would be a more important shift in sections of the country now being served by non-member banks. The head office in this connection would act as the central agent for all the branches and would reduce the desire or need for such banking connections.

3. *Bank loans and advances.*—Individual banks operating as a part of a large branch banking system would not generally be obliged to rely upon a correspondent for large loans. The head office would act as an intermediary for the purpose of transferring funds from one community to another. This would lessen the amount of bank borrowing. The small banks, now in the habit of borrowing from the large city banks or the Federal Reserve, would be branches and hence would rely upon the head office for such assistance as was needed. The total amount of funds actually borrowed should be considerably reduced, even though the actual amount of funds transferred from one section or community to another might be very greatly increased, as compared with the present volume of banking business. The head office might find it necessary from time to time to call upon the Federal Reserve system for help, but the total should be much less than the total for all the banks under a unit system. If the large branch banks failed to become members, which does not appear likely, the volume of rediscount or direct borrowings at the Federal Reserve would be very greatly reduced. It is likely, therefore, that the total amount of interbank borrowing would be reduced considerably, and that the Federal Reserve system would get a larger percentage of this business for the banking system as a whole than it at present enjoys. The large branch banks would probably be less dependent upon the Federal Reserve system, which might have its advantages in that the Federal Reserve might find it necessary to extend its services to member banks in order to hold them in the system. Under such a system it is quite conceivable that the Federal Reserve banks could do much to strengthen the system and at the same time attract a large number of the large, strong banks into the system. Moreover, at the present time the Federal Reserve must provide a different type of service for the country bank as compared with the needs of the larger banks. This service would be more uniform under branch banking.

4. *Credit information.*—An extension of branch banking on a

wide area would lessen the volume of interbank credit work being done at the present time. Some of this work is done by or through the Federal Reserve banks. Under a branch system the head office would act as a clearing house for all the branches. The effect of an extension of branches would be greater in this regard among the commercial banks themselves than between the commercial banks and the Federal Reserve system. The amount of credit information sent to the Federal Reserve banks would be less if there were a smaller amount of borrowing from the Reserve banks, or if the rediscounts were less.

5. *Foreign banking services and connections.*—The growth of branch banking would curtail the number of interbank connections growing out of the financing of foreign trade and other international financial transactions. Since very little service of this nature is rendered by the Federal Reserve system, there would not be any marked changes in this regard in so far as it is concerned. The large branch banks would be likely to have foreign connections to a much greater extent than is now the case. Since the number of banks would be much smaller, the head office of the branch systems would take care of such business itself, thus making unnecessary the formation of interbank connections for the purpose of handling international financial transactions. Branch banks would find it necessary, in many cases, to rely upon such connections until sufficient time had elapsed to build up the foreign branches required to finance their foreign business.

6. *The placing of short-term funds in the money and call-loan markets.*—Under the present system of unit banks, there is an actual need for these interbank accounts for the purpose of handling the surplus funds of the various small or interior banks which wish to diversify their portfolios by placing a part of their funds in short-term obligations based upon business transactions independent of the locality in which the bank is being operated. This desire on the part of bankers has done much to bring about a growth of the business between the correspondents. If we were to adopt a branch system, a considerable change would be brought about for the reason that the head office of the branch system would handle these funds and would probably send a smaller pro-

portion of them to the financial centers. They would be transferred instead to another part of the bank's branch territory where they were more urgently needed and from which a larger interest rate might, in many cases, be received.

This method of handling funds should enable the Federal Reserve system to control or influence more easily the volume of funds going into the call-loan market. Here again the influence on the Federal Reserve would be indirect, rather than direct. The greater change would come about among the commercial banks as the number of branches increased over a wider and wider area.

MEMBERSHIP

Any extensive development of branch banking will necessarily result in a marked change in the number of state banks and trust company members, as well as in the total number of national banks. The number of commercial banks in the country will be materially reduced, which will in turn be followed by a reduction in the number of banks in the Federal Reserve system. There are a large number of small unit banks with a capital of less than $25,000 which may not become members of the Reserve system. Under a branch system, these small banks would be branches of larger banks which could, in turn, be members of the Reserve system, thus extending the Reserve advantages to a considerable part of the banking community not now receiving them. If results be measured in total number of members, there will be a substantial decline. There are other tests by which the importance of membership in the system may be determined, however. The number of member banks would be altered so that the percentage of the commercial banks in the Reserve system, measured in terms of total resources, would be very considerably increased. On the other hand there is good reason to believe that as the banks became larger and larger, and the number of branches increased, there would be a tendency for banks to enter the system, so that in the end a larger percentage of the total banking resources of all commercial banks would be included in the system than is now the case.

Another phase of the membership question arises in connection with the control of the Reserve system. If this country were to adopt a branch system based upon the Federal Reserve district as a territorial unit, the total number of banks in the district would in time become quite small, so that the control of the Reserve banks, at least in some districts, would be concentrated in a few hands. This would become more and more marked as the number of small banks declined and the number of large banks decreased with the increasing number of branches throughout the district. This would place the small bank in an increasingly unfavorable position in meeting the competition of the large banks and in its representation on the board of the Federal Reserve bank.

NUMBER OF FEDERAL RESERVE BANKS

The total number of banks needed and likely to continue in operation under a branch system will depend to a great extent upon the geographical unit adopted for branch banking. If we were to adopt the Federal Reserve district as the unit for the extension of branches, then the total number of Federal Reserve banks is likely to remain constant, at least for a considerable number of years. If, on the other hand, a nation-wide system of branches were permitted, the number of Federal Reserve banks should be decreased within a few years. The number of large banks would be gradually reduced under such conditions until there would be no good reason for the existence of all of the Reserve banks.

What we can say at the present time is that with any substantial development of branch banking there will be fewer commercial banks in the United States. There will, therefore, be fewer banks in the Federal Reserve system, but the banks that are included will be very much larger on the average than are the member banks at the present time. This will probably alter to some extent the method of electing directors of the Reserve system. The present method of dividing the member banks into three groups for the purpose of electing Class A and Class B directors may need revision to meet new conditions.

VOLUME OF REDISCOUNTING AT THE FEDERAL RESERVE BANKS

What changes, if any, would take place in the method, time, or extent of member-bank rediscounting under a branch system, as compared with the unit system? Would the branch banks be able to get along with less frequent appeals to the Federal Reserve banks than are the unit banks? The answer would seem to be that the branch banks should be able to operate with less rediscounting than is now necessary. Under our present system there are two fundamental reasons for shifting funds by commercial banks. One is diversification of the portfolio and the second, the surplus of funds existing at certain seasons of the year. It is frequently necessary to send funds to a distant money market in order to keep such funds busy and to secure the desired diversification. This practice is now carried out by some banks at the same time that other banks near by are in need of additional funds and are obliged to go to the Federal Reserve bank or to some correspondent to borrow or to rediscount paper. The branch bank, with its large capital and connections through its branches, is in a position to transfer these funds from one point, where they are not needed, to another where they may be loaned out to business concerns that are in need of assistance.

The branch bank in thus transferring its funds accomplishes two things: (1) it secures greater diversification in many cases, and (2) at the same time avoids the necessity of sending these funds temporarily to the money market. The commercial bank may then more easily restrict itself to the financing of commercial, short-term business needs than at the present time, when it must invest some of its funds in bonds, and place a part in the money market, to find its way in part at least into the call-loan market to finance speculation in securities. The Federal Reserve banks under a branch system would then be called upon less frequently to rediscount for their members, for the very good reason that the member banks would keep themselves in a more liquid condition and would therefore need less assistance from the central bank. This should mean that the proportion of funds kept in the money market would decrease. It would not necessarily mean that the Federal Reserve system would be reduced to a place of less importance.

RELATION TO CREDIT CONTROL

There are several aspects of this relationship. The change brought about by branch banking will depend upon the extent to which it is developed and the area over which individual banks may establish branches. If branches should be limited to the state of the parent institution, it is unlikely that there will be any very substantial modifications in the existing conditions, except that the banks are likely to be on the average somewhat fewer and larger. This would not materially, it is believed, alter the power of the Federal Reserve system to control credits. On the other hand, if the member banks were allowed to extend branches throughout the Federal Reserve district, the banks would be much fewer in number and likely to be stronger financially, in the long run, with less dependence upon the Reserve system for rediscounts. This would tend to change the position of the Federal Reserve system, in that the Reserve banks would have less direct contact with their members from the point of view of borrowers. However, the branch banks would tend to send less funds to the large financial centers, so that the Federal Reserve banks would be in a position to make their rate changes more effective, since the volume of market funds would be smaller and hence more sensitive to Federal Reserve policy.

If we assume a further extension of branch banking to include all of the United States, with each branch bank free to establish and operate branches in any part of the country, there would be a very substantial change or modification in the position of the Reserve system. There would be fewer member banks—in fact few banks of any kind. The banks would be much larger and stronger financially. This would, or at least should, place the banks operating branches in a more independent position, where they would be less likely to borrow from the Reserve banks. There would be a tendency to develop a small number of banks with branches in a given Reserve district, which would control a very large percentage of all the banking resources in that district. This would, in turn, permit such banks to elect whomsoever they wished as directors of the Reserve bank. In fact, the movement would almost certainly go further and reduce the number of Reserve banks. This would give us a system in which each Federal Reserve bank would cover a larger territory and deal with much larger and more independent institutions. It would tend to change the activities of the Reserve banks to some extent, but it would not eliminate the need or necessity for the Reserve system. The money markets would probably get smaller amounts of funds, thus leaving the Reserve banks in a stronger position so far as controlling the money market is concerned.

In conclusion, there is no reason for thinking that the development of branch banking in this country would eliminate the need for a Reserve system, though the system would probably be changed to some extent. Branch banking will not result in a monopoly to such an extent as to make the Reserve system ineffective. The system will not lose its power and influence if it is operated along proper lines. It will find new or somewhat different functions to perform, as conditions change from time to time.

RELATION TO THE COMMERCIAL-PAPER MARKET

A type of commercial paper known as open-market commercial paper, which is bought and sold by commercial-paper houses, has played a very important rôle in banking and finance in this country for a great many years. Its importance has steadily decreased in recent years, but it is still regarded as one of the most important phases of the American method of financing. This type of financing is not found in those countries which have had a very extensive development of branch banking. The reasons for its large place in American finance are many. From the point of view of the local bank, it was desired because it offered an outlet for funds at a certain season of the year, thus affording a very substantial income for the banks. In other cases this type of paper was wanted for the purpose of properly diversifying the portfolio. Both these conditions are more fully met by a branch bank in the countries where branch banking is permitted on a large scale. The bank secures diversification by reason of the fact that the combined portfolio of the bank and all its branches represent a large number of borrowers widely separated both geographically and in the type of business being conducted by the borrowers. The bank and its branches thus secure diversification and at the same time are in a position to keep their funds more fully employed through the bank's own direct customers.

From the standpoint of the borrower, the branch bank is generally able to supply all the funds the borrower needs, which is not always true in the case of the unit bank, especially if the bank is small. This condition makes it necessary for the business man to do business with two or more banks in order to secure all the funds that are needed at certain seasons of the year. In many cases, the business man turns to a commercial-paper house to secure the funds needed rather than go to two or more commercial banks, securing at each only a part of the funds required. The borrower does this for two or three reasons. The borrower at times feels that selling his commercial paper in the market gives him some very desirable advertising. In other cases, he finds that his bank balances may be reduced through the use of commercial-paper houses. In still other instances, the deciding factor is the prevailing interest rate. The borrower realizes that it is frequently less expensive to borrow his funds in the open market, since the interest rate there is lower than it is at his own bank on customers' paper.

Under a branch-banking system, these conditions do not exist generally. The interest rate is more uniform throughout the country under a branch-banking system than under the unit system. This largely does away with the element of cost so far as the borrower is directly concerned. The commercial branch banks are not in the market for this type of paper, so that there is no market for such paper; or at most it is a narrow one which tends to increase the cost to the borrower rather than to lower it. In short, the conditions are so fundamentally different that commercial-paper houses and branch banking do not thrive side by side. It is fair, therefore, to assume that with a development of branch banking in this country, we shall witness a further decline and perhaps a disappearance of the commercial-paper business of the character we have been discussing.

CHAPTER XIX

CHAIN BANKING

A type of banking concentration which has received much attention during the past two decades in the United States is chain banking. Closely related to the discussion of chain banking is another different type of banking commonly referred to as group banking. There is considerable difference of opinion among bankers, economists, and business men in regard to the distinctions, if any, which should be drawn between these two phases of the American banking system. The present writer, in discussing the subject of chain banking in 1925, did not undertake to differentiate between it and group banking.[1] The developments which have taken place since then make it desirable now to treat the two separately. The term group banking was used in only a very restricted way as far back as 1925. It was used in the state of Texas to a very limited extent. During the past three to five years, the subject of group banking has received the greater amount of attention. What, then, is the essential difference between these two forms of banking control and ownership?

In this discussion the term chain banking will be used to refer to that form of concentration of ownership and control in which an individual or group of individuals own and control two or more independent unit banks, whereas group banking will be applied to that type of ownership in which the stock is held by a holding company. In either case, the banks owned have separate charters and each retains its own identity as regards the management and personnel. Another characteristic generally common to group banking is that the member banks in a group are centered or clustered around a large metropolitan bank. Supervision by the holding company is apt to be more thorough and complete, for the reason that the holding company and its officers assume a greater

[1] Willis, H. P., "Banking Inquiry," 1925, Vol. VI by John M. Chapman. Typescript in the Library, School of Business, Columbia University, New York City.

responsibility than is usual in the chain systems. The chain systems were frequently built up secretly, whereas the holding companies are more open in their efforts to obtain and manage or supervise the banks. While it is not always true, the individual banks owned by the holding companies are generally larger than the individual banks found in the chain systems. With these distinctions in mind, this chapter will be devoted to a discussion of the problems arising in connection with chain banking, while the next chapter will deal with the question of group banking.

ORIGIN OF CHAIN BANKING

It is not possible to state definitely when inter-bank control of this form first appeared in this country. Doubtless it has existed in one form or another for many years. Control of two or more banks first originated through the ability of one man or a small group of men to buy up or establish a number of banks for the purpose of securing either a larger profit or a greater volume of funds with which to finance more adequately some particular business in which these individuals were interested.

The first chains or banking affiliations, according to one able student of chain banking, were probably formed in the eastern states, the idea gradually finding its way to the West and the South. In the Northwest chains were formed as early as the eighties.[2] The scarcity of capital at that time was no doubt fundamental in bringing about this type of concentration. The development has been much greater since 1900 than before. The growth has been marked in certain parts of the country, especially in some of the southern states, where perhaps the largest chain in the entire country had its headquarters, size in this case being measured by the number of banks involved.

[2] Mildred L. Hartsough has presented a very interesting and detailed account of the early chains in the Northwest in *The Twin Cities as a Metropolitan Market* (Minneapolis: University of Minnesota Press, 1925). She cites many illustrations of the growth of small chains in and around Minneapolis. The early development in the South is briefly treated in an article, "Group or Chain Banking Grows," *Wall Street Journal*, Oct. 18, 1929, p. 16. This article points out that Wm. S. Witham started, in Georgia in 1889, a chain that bore his name for many decades.

Chain banking is not limited to any particular geographical section of the country.[3] On the contrary, it is widely scattered through different states. There are not more than one or two Federal Reserve districts in which chain banking does not exist,[4] or has not heretofore existed, in some form. The extent of chain banking varies widely in different states, as well as from time to time in the same state. Some state banking authorities and officials of the Federal Reserve banks have maintained in times past that there were no such organizations within certain areas or states. Even in some states in which it is freely admitted that chain banking exists, banking officials maintain that the relation of the chain banks to the system as a whole is insignificant. As early as 1909 the commissioner of banking of Wisconsin observed:

> A new feature in banking has manifested itself of late which, if permitted to go unhindered, will eventually result in a monopoly control of banking business. I refer to the so-called holding companies which are increasing with alarming rapidity in various parts of the country. One of these companies, with headquarters in Minneapolis, Minn., owns a controlling interest in more than fifty banks in Minnesota, Iowa, Wisconsin and the Dakotas. In Wisconsin, eight or ten banks are now controlled by this one company; two other companies have recently been organized at Minneapolis, Minn., for the purpose of getting control of banks either by buying up a majority interest in banks now in existence, or by organizing new banks. The same objection that has repeatedly been advanced against branch banking or chain banking applies with equal force to this new method of manipulating the banking business. The representatives of the holding company are usually elected to the offices of president and cashier of the bank, and while they generally have some local directors, the management is dominated by the holding company influence, and the loans are in the majority of cases made to parties residing outside of this state. Legislation should be had to discourage this evil in every possible manner.

Despite the fact that the holding company is referred to in this quotation, the methods of operation and control of such organizations were like the old chain system rather than the present-day

[3] Chain Banking had been carried on in New York City for at least half a dozen years by 1907. Noyes, Alexander, *Forty Years of American Finance* (New York: G. P. Putnam's Sons, 1909), p. 365.

[4] It is likely, if the whole truth be known, that small combinations or chains exist in some form, though the number of banks has been so small as to escape observation in the past.

group organizations. The situation in the Northwest has been admirably described as follows:

There are companies now located in the Twin Cities which make it a part of their business to act as agents in the purchase or sale of country bank stocks, and advertisements sometimes appear in trade journals of companies who are in the market for these stocks on their own account or for their clients. The Ross-Davidson interests, which in 1904 controlled 13 banks, had increased this number by 1910 to 22, and other companies experienced a similar growth. By 1916 it was the claim that over 300 banks were included in chains which were operated with Minneapolis as headquarters.

It was noted earlier that the first chains were mainly restricted to North Dakota, but that is no longer the case. Banks in Minnesota, in South Dakota, in Montana, and even in Wisconsin, Iowa, and Michigan, are included in lines which are controlled from Twin Cities. In fact, by far the largest number of banks included in the northwestern chains is now in Minnesota, with North Dakota and Montana following in importance. Not all of the interests which control these banks operate from the Twin Cities. Most of the chains even at the present time, have been built up through the purchase, by country bankers, of stock in banks in their locality.

There were in 1920 ten or twelve major lines of banks in the Northwest, each controlling from ten to thirty-five banks, and at least thirty or forty smaller ones, controlling from two to ten banks each. A majority of the banks controlled are state institutions, but many national banks are included. Most of the chains are confined to one or two states, but some concerns have banks in three or even four.[5]

In discussing the problem from a slightly different point of view, the same author commented as follows:

It was the estimate of a banker in the head office of one line company that not more than 50 percent of the banks in the Northwest are now entirely independent institutions. Though this is almost certainly an overstatement of the fact, it indicates that, aside from the purely academic interest in the subject, the problem of investigaion is one of a wide and practical interest to everyone concerned with banking principles and practice.[6]

In Texas the movement made considerable progress, being termed, by some, "group banking." It is doubtful if the methods of operation and control were essentially different from the so-

[5] Hartsough, op. cit., p. 147.

[6] *Ibid.*, p. 145.

called chain systems of other states. Another section of the country which has been a very fertile field is that of the Middle West in the states of Illinois and Iowa. The growth in Iowa has not been as marked probably as it was in the Northwest, or in Georgia or Florida. Indications point to a very high degree of this form of concentration in the territory surrounding Chicago.

Chain banking has never been limited to the non-branch banking states. Several small chains have been organized and operated in California as well as other far-western states. Chains have existed (as already indicated) in Georgia, a state in which the branch banking privileges have varied from state-wide organization on the one hand to complete prohibition on the other. Branch banking does not, therefore, prevent or crowd out chain banking altogether, though it has had the effect of keeping the size of the chains somewhat smaller and also that of limiting their influence, with the exception, perhaps, of Georgia. The stronger bankers do not look with favor upon what has been defined as chain banking. They prefer branch or group banking. There are no political or state boundary lines so far as chain banking organizations are concerned. They often extend into several states as well as into different Federal Reserve districts, involving both state and national banks.

Mr. Cousins, Commissioner of Banking for Wisconsin, in 1922 described or outlined as follows the extent as well as the method of building up chain systems:

> Corporations exist in several neighboring states engaged in the business of purchasing stock in banks. Ordinarily they try to purchase a sufficient amount of stock to give them control. They sometimes purchase all the stock. One Minnesota corporation is the owner of stock in twenty-three Minnesota banks, several Wisconsin banks, two North Dakota banks, and one Michigan bank, making a total of thirty-three banks. There are other corporations engaged in this same business and indications are that additional holding companies will be formed. This chain system might not be objectionable if the management of the controlling corporation was always conservative and their total investment in paper limited to a very small amount. This policy is not always followed by the controlling corporation. It was in January, 1919, I believe, that one chain system met with disaster in Minnesota resulting in the banking department of that state closing fourteen banks of the chain in one day.

It was found that all of the banks were loaded to the limit with the same class of paper. Officers of the corporation and several officers of banks were sent to the penitentiary as the result of this crash.

The Wisconsin banking department has had experience with efforts of promoters to gain control of Wisconsin banks. Within the past two years a North Dakota citizen who owned several banks in that state, in Minnesota, Illinois, and Indiana, sought to purchase control of several Wisconsin banks. His method was to pay for the stock out of the assets of the bank, substituting North Dakota paper for the good Wisconsin paper, which he turned over to the shareholders in payment for their shares. Fortunately, the department learned of his efforts and prevented the carrying out of his plans. He is now under indictment in other states, and four of his banks have been closed.[7]

A very extensive search was made in 1925 to ascertain the extent of chain banking in the United States. Printed reports were examined, state and Federal officials were consulted both by personal interviews and correspondence, and the offices of some of the chains were visited, in an effort to secure as large a volume of data as possible regarding the scope and extent of the movement. The collection of that material was the work of several individuals, all of whom were associated with the work in connection with the banking inquiry of 1925.[8] There can be little doubt that the data secured were incomplete. The very nature of chain banking made it practically impossible to secure complete data. The writer learned later of chains that were in existence in 1925 of which the state banking officials had no knowledge. The data are, however, such that they give a fair picture of the extent of the movement at that time. A summary of them is presented in Table 37.

In some states even the banking departments take little or no notice of the situation. Some of the combinations listed or included in the table were holding companies, but at that time there was no general distinction between the individual and the holding-company methods of control. Some banking officials stated that there were no chains within their own state, or that there was no chain-banking problem. In other states, it was maintained that the banking system was no better or no worse by reason of chain

[7] *Twenty-eighth Annual Report of the Commissioner of Banking of Wisconsin* (Madison: Homestead Printing Co., 1923), p. xvii.

[8] *Ibid.*, "Banking Inquiry" (1925).

TABLE 37

SUMMARY OF BANKING CHAINS AND AFFILIATIONS REPORTED IN THE UNITED STATES IN 1925*

STATE	NUMBER OF CHAINS	NUMBER OF BANKS		
		National	*State*	*Total*
Arizona	4	1	14	15
Arkansas	2	7	17	24
California	20	43	23	66
Colorado		Two or three reported; banks failed.		
Florida	1	5	49	54
Georgia	2		163†	163
Idaho	18	36	37	73
Illinois	3		18	18
Iowa	8	21	24	45
Massachusetts	1	Reported for an earlier date in Boston.		
Minnesota	5		103†	103
Mississippi	2	1	16	17
Missouri	1	3	3	6
Montana		Some reported, the number not given.		
Nebraska	2	2	9	11
Nevada	1	2	7	9
New Jersey	6	11	15	26
New Mexico	2	2	6	8
New York	10	23	12	35
North Dakota		Some reported, the number not given.		
Oklahoma	6	22	23	45
Oregon	6	7	15	22
Pennsylvania	2	3	13	16
South Dakota	1		6	6
Texas	2	5	23	28
Utah	9	21	31	52
Washington	16	32	37	69
Wisconsin	2		14	14
Wyoming	1	5	3	8
TOTAL	133	252	681	933

* No chains were reported for the other states. The table gives a representative picture of this type of interbank control, it is believed.

† Data not available to make a separation. Some were doubtless national banks.

banking. In still other states it was claimed that the chain banks were the strongest banks in the state, or that there were no reasons for dissatisfaction with that type of control. In some states the results have been very bad, as for example, Montana, Colorado, Iowa, and Georgia. In some instances all the banks involved in certain individual chains failed with very heavy losses to the depositors. More recent states afflicted in this way are Arkansas, Tennessee, and Kentucky. Yet in all these states, branch banking has not been generally acceptable.

The lack of interest in or attention to the problem is chiefly due to the lack of knowledge regarding the purpose and methods of operation. Another factor which explains in part the lack of concern about the spread of chain banking is the fact that most of the banks involved are small and not very strong financially. Larger banks located in the centers where chain banking has had its greatest development are not generally included in chains. Yet it is these larger banks that are frequently most feared by the country, or smaller bankers. Again,the public is often misled by the fact that each bank has a separate charter, and generally has local representation on the board of directors of the bank, even though the bank may be owned and controlled very largely by the individual or individuals who have built up the chain.

During the year 1926 the Witham chain failed, including a large number of banks located in the states of Georgia and Florida. This was followed by the failure of one or two smaller chains in Iowa and some in other states during the next two or three years. One large chain, the A. B. Banks chain of banks, in Arkansas, failed in 1930. These failures increased the criticisms against chain banking and emphasized in a forceful way certain weaknesses of this type of banking control. It is doubtful if these failures had any substantial effect upon the general attitude toward chain banking. Certainly they did not result in any attempts to regulate these systems. There was no striking change in the number of banks engaged in what we have here defined as chain banking.

One of the defects of the data that have been compiled in practically every investigation of the subject is that no effort has been made to segregate the data to show a difference between group and chain banks. The data compiled by the Banking Inquiry in 1925, by the Economic Policy Committee of the American Bankers' Association, and that by the Federal Reserve Board, were tabulated to show only totals for both group and chain banking jointly. In fact, in all these discussions the two types were treated as a single phase of the American banking problem. It would be most helpful if the data were arranged so as to show whether the more recent type of organization (here called group banking) has been more successful than the earlier type. If it could be shown that group banking is more desirable from actual experience in operation than chains have been in the past, it would be most valuable information.

Statistics (see Chapter XX) will be presented later to show the scope and extent of group and chain banking, though it is impossible to present data for the two separately. The statistics will, however, show the extent of the two types jointly in comparison with all banks in the United States. These data indicate the changes taking place in these two types of banking control.[9]

METHODS OF BUILDING CHAINS

There are several well-recognized methods by which control of a chain of banks may be secured. One method which has been employed to some extent has been to use the stock of one bank as collateral to secure bank loans and thus obtain funds for buying up the stock of other banks. A well-known writer in discussing the panic of 1907 described this method as follows:

> One of the characteristic incidents of the era of speculation, watched by conservative financiers with much uneasiness, had been what was called "chain banking." In New York City, half a dozen banking institutions of the second rank had been bought up by a speculating financier. He had used his stock in one institution as collateral on which to borrow money; the proceeds he had used to buy stock in another bank; repeating the process with each new acquisition. Controlling his "chain of banks" on such a tenure, he had utilized the whole of them to promote his personal speculations. This had been going on during half a dozen years. On Wednesday, October 16, 1907, one of these institutions, the Mercantile National of New York City, a bank with $11,500,000 deposits, applied to the other banks of the Clearing House for help.[10]

The stockholders of the banks secured by the method described may then become the officers or directors, and thus be in a position to dictate the policy of each of the banks. This method has been effectually used in various cases in controlling a number of

[9] The data showing the extent of chain and group banking are presented in Chap. XX, because they were collected and compiled by the Federal Reserve Board more especially as a result of what has been termed group banking in this study.

[10] Noyes, Alexander, *Forty Years of American Finance*, p. 365.

banks. The plan followed to some extent in Texas has been described by one writer as follows:

> The operation of group banking is the controlling interest of a number of banks, located in towns close to one another, held or owned by one or two or more individuals, who usually are directors or officers in each of the banks they control, and through these individuals the policy of the banks is formed, and the group brought to a head.

A chain was organized in Nevada,[11] consisting of nine banks, controlled largely by two men who became respectively president and vice president of each of these banks. In Wyoming a chain was formerly in operation which centered around a bank in Omaha. All the members of the Wyoming chain were reported to have failed. This chain was likewise reported to be controlled by two men who held positions as directors in each of the several banks. In Arkansas one chain, which failed in 1930, was reported, in which one man held the position of president and director in at least nineteen different banks. The Arkansas chain was tied up with an insurance company, which acted in the capacity of a bankers' bank for this group of banks. If they needed bank loans, they applied to the insurance company for help, rather than to another bank. Two chains existed in Mississippi in which one man was officially connected with nine different banks in connection with control of one chain, while in the other a single individual was associated with at least eight banks.

A second method for building up a chain is to organize new banks at various locations where the situation is such as to give promise of success to the enterprise. Under this method it is, of course, necessary to give the bank being organized the semblance at least of being a local institution and largely under the control of local interests. While it is no doubt true that this system has been used effectively in some instances, it is not believed that it has been used so extensively or so effectively as that of quietly buying up banks already in existence.[12] More opposition is likely

[11] This chain encountered serious difficulties in the autumn of 1932 and was taken over by the state banking department in Dec., 1932.

[12] In one or two cases it is reported that one or more persons made large profits through the organization of small banks in railroad towns in the Northwest. These banks were later sold to citizens of the community at a substantial profit to the promoters.

to be encountered from state banking authorities in building up chains by establishing new banks than in the use of the other methods.

A third method is followed in some states where the group or head of the chain gets substantial control through acting as a fiscal agent for a number of so-called independent banks. Under this plan the controlling interests in some cases own a majority interest in the stock, in others, a minority interest, and in others, none. In the latter case the influence is exerted through the fiscal relationship established between the bank and the company acting as fiscal agent. This, as pointed out in another paragraph of this chapter, is on a flat minimum basis. The banks establishing such connections sometimes enter into a contract, the term of which varies considerably, with the controlling company or group in which the company is to act as fiscal agent. Under this contract, the fiscal agent performs some or all of the following services for each of the banks: the investment of surplus funds with other needy banks, outside borrowing, the arrangement of excess loans to one person for other banks, meetings with local boards of directors if necessary, the examination and passing on credits if needed.

Still another method used to a limited extent in bringing about chains or interbank control has been the development of interlocking directorates. The dangers of this method have been discussed at different times, and the abuses growing out of certain cases have brought about the enactment of legislation against it, especially with reference to national bank directors. This took special form in Section 8 of the Clayton Act of 1914, which reads as follows:

8. That from and after two years from the date of the approval of this Act no person shall at the same time be a director or other officer or employee of more than one bank, banking association, or trust company organized or operating under the laws of the United States, either of which has deposits, capital, surplus, and undivided profits aggregating more than $5,000,000; and no private banker or person who is a director in any bank or trust company organized and operating under the laws of a State, having deposits, capital, surplus, and undivided profits aggregating more than $5,000,000, shall be eligible to be a director in any bank or banking association organized or operating under the laws of the United States. The eligibility of a director, officer, or employee under the

foregoing provisions shall be determined by the average amount of deposits, capital, surplus, and undivided profits as shown in the official statements of such bank, banking association, or trust company filed as provided by law during the fiscal year next preceding the date set for the annual election of directors, and when a director, officer, or employee has been elected or selected in accordance with the provisions of this Act it shall be lawful for him to continue as such for one year thereafter under said election or employment.

No bank, banking association, or trust company organized or operating under the laws of the United States, in any city or incorporated town or village of more than two hundred thousand inhabitants, as shown by the last preceding decennial census of the United States, shall have as a director or other officer or employee any private banker or any director or other officer or employee of any other bank, banking associatoin, or trust company located in the same place: *Provided,* That nothing in this section shall apply to mutual savings banks not having a capital stock represented by shares: *Provided further,* That a director or other officer or employee of such bank, banking association, or trust company may be a director or other officer or employee of not more than one other bank or trust company organized under the laws of the United States or any State where the entire capital stock of one is owned by stockholders in the other: *And provided further,* That nothing contained in this section shall forbid a director of class A of a Federal reserve bank, as defined in the Federal Reserve Act, from being an officer or director, or both an officer and director, in one member bank: *And provided further,* That nothing in this Act shall prohibit any private banker or any officer, director, or employee of any member bank or class A director of a Federal reserve bank, who shall first procure the consent of the Federal Reserve Board, which board is hereby authorized, at its discretion, to grant, withhold, or revoke such consent, from being an officer, director, or employee of not more than two other banks, banking associations, or trust companies, whether organized under the laws of the United States or any State, if such other bank, banking association, or trust company is not in substantial compentition with such banker or member bank.

The consent of the Federal Reserve Board may be procured before the person applying therefor has been elected as a class A director of a Federal reserve bank or as a director of any member bank.

When any person elected or chosen as a director or officer or selected as an employee of any bank or other corporation subject to the provisions of this Act is eligible at the time of his election or selection to act for such bank or other corporation in such capacity his eligibility to act in such capacity shall not be affected and he shall not become or be deemed amenable to any of the provisions hereof by reason of any change in the affairs of such bank or other corporation from whatsoever cause, whether specifically excepted by any of the provisions hereof or not, until the expiration of one year from the date of his election or employment.

This legislation has not been effective in curbing chain banking because it applies to the larger institutions which have not been, as a general rule, interested in building up chains of banks. In fact, the sentiment among the large banks as a whole is evidently opposed to chain banking, even though many of them favor branch banking. Also, the effectiveness of the legislation has been greatly lessened by the further fact that it does not apply to most of the small state banks. It is the latter class of banks which have fallen a prey to the chain system in certain parts of the country.

The state of Wisconsin has recognized the problem at different times and, in its effort to prevent chains, it has placed a resident requirement on all bank directors. This has not been very successful for the reason that the law can be circumvented fairly easily by the appointment of dummy directors. A better law would perhaps require that a certain percentage of all the stock of a bank be owned and controlled by residents of the state in which the bank is located. Such a law would, however, not prevent state-wide chains, unless the requirements provided for a smaller geographical unit than the state. Neither would it prevent working agreements between banks in different states.

The efforts of the state department in Wisconsin were described by the commissioner in his 1922 report as follows:

In an attempt to prevent control of banks in this manner the legislature several years ago incorporated into the law a provision providing that directors must be residents of Wisconsin. This provision has been ineffective. The controlling corporation will assign a few shares, possibly one share apiece, to residents of Wisconsin, and ask them to permit the use of their names as directors. The management is under the controlling corporation. The directors have little or no financial interest in the banks. The officers do not look to the directors for their instructions and the directors do not feel that they should perform the duties expected of them under the law. They are directors in name only. The orders come from the controlling corporation.

The remedy is hard to find. Possibly a law requiring that at least a majority of the shares should be owned by residents of Wisconsin and by individuals rather than by corporations might be a safeguard. The matter is one for the careful consideration of the people and their representatives in the legislature.

If branch banking is undesirable and is a danger, the chain banking system is tenfold more so.[13]

SIZE OF INDIVIDUAL CHAINS

It was definitely ascertained by those making the inquiry in 1925 that there were no "average-sized" chains. The number of banks owned or controlled by a single chain varied considerably, ranging from 5 or less to 175 or more. One estimate of the Witham chain of Atlanta, Georgia, in 1925, placed the number of banks involved at 200 or more. In this connection, the Federal Reserve Board stated that:

> In the absence of laws permitting branch banking there has been, in certain sections, a considerable development of so-called chain banks—banks owned or controlled in groups by individuals or by holding companies. The largest of these systems includes some 175 small banks.[14]

It appears certain that the large chain referred to by the Board was the Witham chain with headquarters in Atlanta, Georgia. That was probably the largest chain in existence in 1925. A large number of banks owned and controlled by that chain failed in 1926. In some states the number of banks within a given chain is small, in others much larger. The growth of group banking and the large number of bank failures had a very marked effect upon the extent and size of banking chains in certain parts of the country. The A. B. Banks chain of banks, with headquarters in Little Rock, Arkansas, was an example of a chain in which there was a large number of small banks tied up together. This chain failed in 1930,[15] along with the failure of several other banks in the states of Arkansas, Kentucky and Tennessee.

CHAIN VERSUS BRANCH BANKING

Chain banking is frequently confused with branch banking. The two are essentially different and should be so classified. In branch banking there is only one legal entity—each branch being a part

[13] *Twenty-eighth Annual Report of State Banking Commissioner* (1923), p. xvii.
[14] *Annual Report of the Federal Reserve Board* (1922), p. 6.
[15] See below, p. 329.

of the head office, or parent institution. The parent and all its branches form one unit. A chain of banks, on the other hand, is made up of a number of banks each having a separate charter and forming legally a separate corporation. Each bank has its own location, capital, and organization, and makes its own reports. Theoretically each bank acts on its own initiative, but practically there is a central controlling body which frequently determines the common policy of all the members.

With respect to the supervision and control, chain banking differs widely from branch banking. The ownership of a bank which is operating a system of branches is common knowledge. Such is frequently not the case with a chain of banks. The public is often not aware of the relationship existing among several supposedly independent banks. This makes the problem of government supervision more difficult, because there are certain phases of the relationship which cannot be so easily ascertained or supervised as they could be in the case of branches.

Branch banks have, in most cases, been established under state laws or regulations which set forth the conditions under which such business may be carried on. Chain banking is often possible by reason of the very fact that there are no laws governing such relationships. In most cases the state laws contain no provision whatever regarding the ownership of the stock of a bank, except to provide that one state bank may not own the stock of another state bank or corporation—or at most not more than a certain amount, usually 10 percent. No provision is made concerning the amount of stock a single person may own in separate banks or corporations. As a result, the same ends may be secured that the former provisions have attempted to prevent, namely, a majority control of a number of so-called independent banks. The state laws are generally weak in this respect. If the provisions prohibiting one bank from owning a majority of the stock of another bank are correct in principle, then the controlling of the majority of the stock of a number of banks by one individual, a group of individuals, or even a holding company, should likewise be prohibited.

The state commissioner of banking in the state of Wisconsin in 1922 advocated that a law be passed requiring all banks in that state operating branches "to close or incorporate such branches within a certain period of years." Laws had already been enacted prohibiting the establishment of any new branches. It was regarded as an improper form of banking, and the commissioner wished to emphasize the potential danger by reason of the then recent action of Comptroller Crissinger regarding the operating of branches by national banks. At the same time, the Wisconsin commissioner took a very decided stand against chain banking. In this connection he stated his position as follows:

> There is a much more serious situation existing and no law on the statute book controls it. Everything that has been said or can be said against branch banking applies to this condition to a much greater degree. I refer to the chain banking system which exists to some extent in Wisconsin. It is an increasing evil.[16]

OPERATION AND CONTROL

There is no uniform policy as regards the method followed by the controlling interests in managing and supervising the various members of a particular chain. It has already been shown that the control is exercised in some cases through certain officers and directors who take an active part in the affairs of each member of the chain. They often go from one bank to another to supervise the business and to attend the directors' meetings. In many cases the banks have a local board of directors who are presumably determining the policy, whereas as a matter of fact the control really rests in the hands of the absentee members of the board. In other cases, the local directors are in last analysis merely dummies.

The extent to which the bank is supervised likewise varies considerably. The purpose may be to secure funds for financing a given business. In that case the primary purpose would be to so shape the lending policy as to secure all the funds possible. Management of the local business is usually placed in the hands of the local officers and directors, so long as it does not interfere with the larger policy, that of serving the controlling interests. Some chains have a central organization for lending their surplus funds or for

[16] *Twenty-eighth Annual Report of the Commissioner of Banking of Wisconsin* (1923), p. xvii.

borrowing from outside sources when such funds are needed. This organization frequently has charge of the investments for all of the banks in the chain. At other times it takes an active part in the supervision of the credit work of the bank. The problem of checking and passing on collateral for loans is often considered a function of the head office.

The controlling organization frequently takes a very active part in the reserve policy adopted and carried out by the chain members. In such cases the volume of reserves carried by the system as a whole is greatly reduced, since funds may easily be transferred from one bank to another in case the reserves of any one bank or banks become too low. This practice, if properly carried on, could be made very profitable to all the members, since they could do a large volume of business on a given reserve. If, on the other hand, the policy is not well formulated and wisely carried out, it will tend to weaken the members of the chain.

In most cases, the work of opening and maintaining correspondent relationships in the larger financial centers is done by the controlling interests for all the members. One chain is reported to have secured members in one eastern state because the eastern banks thus obtained were often in the position of having surplus funds which could be made available to other members. This method of securing interbank accounts is not a "pure" correspondent relationship, but it takes the place of that relationship in some cases, because the controlling group might, without this connection, find it necessary to establish borrowing accounts with other banks in order to secure the needed funds.

Another way in which supervision and oversight is maintained is through the method of reporting. The members are usually required to submit regular reports of their operations to the head office. These are gone over with care. The frequency with which these reports are filed varies with different chains and under different circumstances. Some reports are made daily, others weekly, and some monthly. It is not unusual for the head office to maintain or organize an auditing division which inspects the accounts of each bank very carefully at least once each year, and oftener if necessary. Such reports, when submitted to the head office, give the managing officials a very satisfactory check upon the activities and standing of the various members.

DIFFICULTY OF EXAMINATION

At the present time the difficulty of properly examining a large chain of banks is in many instances practically unsurmountable. This situation is inherent in the organization of large chains as at present constituted. If the chain is a small one and all members are located within the boundaries of a single state, the banking department finds it comparatively easy to make a simultaneous examination of all the members at one time, provided it is fully known just what banks are contained within a single system. This is often difficult, for banking departments do not have complete data as to members. Such a condition renders the problem very complex and trying, even for those examiners who are fully alive to the situation.

The most extensive and powerful chains often extend through two, three, or even four or more states. Where one has developed in this way, it is practically out of the question to get an adequate examination of an entire system as of a given date. If one state is more rigid in its requirements than the other states in which a given chain is operating, the management of the system might transfer questionable assets from one bank to another, if by so doing it could avoid the criticism of the superintendents or examiners. When such conditions prevail, even if all the examiners are alert, it is not possible in most cases to get coöperation of state authorities in other states to examine all the members of a single chain on the same dates or in the same way.

The difficulties involved in the examining and supervising of these chains is fully appreciated by many banking departments, yet they find it impossible to guard the public to the extent which they desire, and to which the public is justly entitled. Many examiners would welcome an opportunity to apply more rigid tests if they had the power to include all the members within their examination. This is not possible, especially where a chain extends through states from New York to Florida or from Nebraska to Idaho. It is interesting to note that this situation has been realized for more than a decade, even though we must admit that little of a concrete nature has been accomplished to remedy it. Referring to the conditions in North Dakota in 1913, the state examiner said:

> Examinations of closely affiliated institutions, where the same people jointly owned or were interested in banks in that state as well as in North Dakota, have been conducted on the same date with the Minnesota examiners. The information exchanged subsequently between departments has been of mutual benefit in determining the condition of the banks.[17]

The situation might in part be remedied if all the banks were located in a given Federal Reserve district, and were also members of the system. In such cases it would be possible for the Federal Reserve bank examiners to make proper examinations as of a given date. This check, however, is of interest only in theory, because of the great difficulties involved in putting it into practice. In the first place, a large percentage of the state banks involved in chains are not members, and hence would not be subject to the examination of Federal Reserve banks. In the second place, these chains often extend into two or three different Federal Reserve districts, which would lessen the effectiveness of Federal Reserve bank supervision on exactly the same grounds as state supervision is partly defective at the present time. The difficulties encountered in properly examining and supervising the operation of a chain are illustrated in the case of a chain which is reported to own stock in banks located in Iowa, Minnesota, and the Dakotas. Such a chain covers at least two Federal Reserve districts—Chicago and Minneapolis. In the same way, the banks fall under four or five different state banking jurisdictions.

CONCLUSIONS

From the foregoing discussion, it is now possible to arrive at certain conclusions regarding the control, operation, and effects of chain banking as it has been conducted in certain sections of this country during the past few decades.

1. Chain banking in one form or another has existed in the

[17] *Report of the State Examiner to the State Banking Board and Report to the Governor* (Public Document 11), (Devils Lake, N.D.: Journal Publishing Co., June 30, 1914), p. 6.

United States for more than four decades, appearing perhaps first in the eastern states and later in the West and the South. Its growth has been more marked since 1900 and it is now to be found in a large number of states from New York to California.

2. Owing to the lack of statistics and complete information, it has not received the attention which the movement warrants. More recently, with the rapid growth of group banking since 1926, more attention has been devoted to it, but in many cases no distinction is drawn between group and chain banking. In the more recent discussions, the major attention is given to group banking.

3. The manner in which the chains are built up, and the extent of the territory frequently covered by a single chain, make it an extremely difficult problem for Federal and state examiners to control such a system of banks. In fact no method has yet been devised which enables the examiners satisfactorily to examine chains extending through two or more states. This aspect of chain banking is very dangerous because of the possibility that a system which is not properly operated may bring ruin to a large number of depositors, as well as to the stockholders.

4. If a chain of banks were properly organized, capably and honestly operated, it could bring about very desirable results by assisting in the transfer of funds, in the handling of large loans, in the diversifying of loans and investments, and in the financing of local industry. The dangers in the system are also very considerable for the reason that such extensive powers may not be honestly or efficiently exercised. Some have been successful while many have failed. Others have neither materially improved nor weakened the situation. On the whole the dangers outweigh the possibilities for good.

5. Chains possess all the disadvantages frequently ascribed to branch banking, without most of the virtues of branch banking. Branch banks are usually operated under adequate laws and proper supervision, but chain banks often have neither. Banks may be held responsible for their branches, but the same can not be said of the chain systems, since each bank is a separate corporation. The ownership and control of branches are well known, but that is not always the case with chain organizations.

6. The state banking laws are wholly inadequate to deal with the problems growing out of chain banking. State banking officials are generally powerless to prevent the formation of a chain by a small group of individuals, regardless of the fact that it is likely to result in bad banking or heavy losses to the community and the depositors. Furthermore, the organization is often formed and in operation for a considerable period of time before the situation is fully appreciated by the state banking department.

7. It would seem desirable for Congress to pass a law that would place all chains which extend beyond state boundary lines under the supervision of the Federal Reserve Board or the Federal Trade Commission, with full power to compel such groups to carry on a sound and conservative banking business or be forced into liquidation. The list of banks included in the various chains should be published as frequently as possible. If this type of supervision and regulation is not possible, then something should be done to prevent this kind of banking concentration.

8. Chain banking is found most extensively developed and is having its greatest growth in those states which do not permit branch banking. Some of the small chains in California have been absorbed by banks operating branches.

9. As a rule chains are built up by bringing a group of small banks under a single or unified control. Large banks are seldom included. The amount of capital required to control the larger institutions is a bar to the extensive development of chains among the larger banks. That being the case, the system is apt to include several weaker banks.

10. Chain banking in this country has not on the whole been successful. One cannot regard chain banking favorably as a means of overcoming the many failures and weak spots found in our unit banking system.

CHAPTER XX

GROUP BANKING

In the chapter on "Chain Banking," a general distinction was made between group and chain banking. Control by a holding company is the fundamental characteristic of group banking, while one or more individuals exercise control in the chain system. The origin of the term group banking is of comparatively recent date, especially as it is used in banking terminology at the present time. The first time the writer came in contact with the term as applied to a type of banking control[1] was in 1925, when it was being used in the state of Texas by one organization to refer to the kind of concentration existing in connection with a few banks in that state. It is doubtless true that there was no essential difference between that organization and other combinations in other states commonly referred to at that time as chains of banks. The term was not generally used until 1927.

Holding companies as a form of banking control began many years ago, even during the early days of chain banking. Such control was then generally classed as chain banking. The earliest holding companies were probably formed in the Northwest, in or around Minneapolis. This was one of the two principal sections of the country[2] in which there was a marked development of chain banking before 1910. The Adam Hannah Company, organized in 1900 in Minnesota, was one of the earliest companies organized for the purpose of gaining control of small banks. From that date there was a limited number of these small holding companies being organized in certain parts of the country, though the total was never large.[3] The following is a partial list[4] of the earlier holding com-

[1] One writer, in describing the practice in Texas, said in part: "The operation of group banking is the controlling interest of a number of banks, located in towns close to one another, held or owned by one or two or more individuals, who usually are directors or officers in each of the banks they control, and through these individuals the policy of the banks is formed and the group is brought to a head.

[2] The other section was in and around Atlanta, Georgia.

[3] No attempt is made to give a complete list of these companies organized in any

panies which the writer has considered in studying this movement:

	Year Organized
Adam Hannah Company	1900
Farm Mortgage Loan and Trust Company, Carrington Montana	1902 or earlier
John F. Sinclair Company	
The Union Investment Company	1903
Union Securities Company, Spokane, Washington	1909
Continental Securities Company	1910
Grandin Investment Company	1914
Bankers Holding and Investment Company	1917
Ulland-Mealy-Carey Company	1919
John W. Black and Company	1919
Mortgage Securities Company	

This list is by no means complete, but it indicates in a general way the tendency in the Northwest to resort to the use of the holding company in building up a chain of banks alongside of the individual type of concentration of management.

There are certain differences between the early type of holding company and that now typical in group banking. In the first place the latter type is much larger and more pwerful financially. Earlier types had smaller amounts of capital funds and could not secure control of the larger banks as is being done by many holding companies of the present day. Other factors of considerable importance are the method of distributing the securities and the methods of raising funds. In the formation of chain systems in the beginning, the public was not invited to participate, as it has been in the case of the later holding companies. The capital stock was usually owned by a few persons, whereas today it is not unusual for the

part of the country at any time. It is the intention of the writer to outline what he regards as the important principles involved and the results of this type of banking, using such historical data as are needed to indicate the appearance and growth of group banking.

[4] This list was taken almost entirely from Hartsough's *The Twin Cities as a Metropolitan Market*, pp. 144-154.

holding company to have a large issue of stock underwritten[5] and sold to the public by investment bankers.[6] In this way a much larger volume of funds is secured than is usually obtained through a direct appeal to the public. The influence and extent of the control is, therefore, much more extensive than was possible under the older type.

DEVELOPMENT OF GROUP BANKING

In the preceding section, dealing with the early history of group banking, mention was made of the rapid expansion of group banking beginning with and following 1927. Since that date the development has been marked. The status of chain banking in this country in 1925 has already been indicated (see Chapter XX, p. 343). In 1929 Andrew Price, President of the Marine Bancorporation, Seattle, made a study of group and chain banking. This study, while interesting and important, was not as extensive as the more recent studies of the Federal Reserve Board, the Economic Policy Commission of the American Bankers Association, and the Federal Reserve Committee on Branch, Group, and Chain Banking. The data compiled by the latter organizations are much more complete, up-to-date, and informative than any other data published. Of the three, the reports of the Federal Reserve committee are the more thorough and up-to-date. Unfortunately this Report has not been published, but it has been submitted to the Banking and Currency Committee of the United States Senate. We shall first consider briefly the report of the Economic Policy Commission[7] and later review the work of the Board.

[5] In Sept., 1929, Stone, Webster and Blodget and other investment houses offered 1,000,000 shares of Marine Midland Corporation, a bank-holding organization, to the public at $60 per share. During the same month, Otis and Co., and The First Citizens Corporation offered 120,000 shares of Bank Ohio Corporation at $43 per share.

[6] At the present time a number of such holding companies have their stock listed on the stock exchanges. The Transamerican Corporation and Marine Midland Corporation in New York, the Marine Bancorporation in Seattle and Northwest Bancorporation in Chicago and Minneapolis are some of the holding companies which have listed their stock on security exchanges.

[7] The data compiled by this commission include both groups and chains of banks. There was no attempt to separate the data along the lines of distinction followed in the present study. There are no representative data available to show the growth and extent of group banking alone.

REPORT ON GROUP AND CHAIN BANKING AMERICAN BANKERS ASSOCIATION[8]

The growth of group banking and the widespread interest developed therein during the year 1929 were instrumental in inducing the Economic Policy Commission of the American Bankers Association to make a rather extensive study on the scope and development of both group and chain banking. A report was published in October, 1929, and preceded the reports of the Federal Reserve Board, although in many respects not so complete and satisfactory. In the study made by this commission, group and chain banking were treated as one, although there were recognized certain differences as regards the methods of control. Upon the basis of the type of ownership, these groups were classified as follows:

1. Groups or organizations in which a particular bank is the controlling element. In this class there were reported to be 78 chains or groups, involving 407 banks with total resources of approximately $6,473,000,000.

2. Groups or chains in which a non-banking holding company, not subsidiary to any particular bank, was the dominant element in the control of the institutions. There were reported 28 chains in this group, involving 380 banks with total resources of about $5,335,000,000.

3. Groups and chains in which the dominant control was exercised by an individual or group of individuals acting for themselves. In this class there were reported 167 chains, involving 1,071 banks with total resources of approximately $1,468,000,000.

The conclusions of this interesting and timely report of the Economic Policy Commission are succinctly stated in two paragraphs of the report:

> These three classes represent a total of 273 chains involving 1,858 banks and over $13,275,000,000 in aggregate resources. Some of these chain systems comprise 50 to 100 banks each. If there are now approximately 25,000 banks in the country with resources of $72,000,000,000,

[8] This section is a summary of the *Study of Group and Chain Banking*, by The Economic Policy Commission of the American Bankers Association (New York, Oct. 14, 1929), of which commission R. S. Hecht was chairman.

these figures indicate that almost 7½ percent of our banks and over 18 percent of our banking resources are enmeshed in the great web of chain banking that now covers almost every part of the country.

Of one class or another chain head offices appear in our figures in all but nine of the forty-eight states and the District of Columbia; and as to these our information is chiefly negative, and we cannot say positively whether there is chain banking going on there or not.[9]

The movement included all but nine states. The largest number of chains or groups reported by any state was 34 for Minnesota. These 34 organizations had 435 banks (also the largest number of banks controlled by groups in one state) with total resources of about $995,350,000. New York State had 17 chains or groups, involving 117 banks with total resources of $4,206,790,000, or approximately 31 percent of the total resources of all banks in the country owned or controlled by group or chain organizations.

Results shown by the study of the Economic Policy Commission are, moreover, similar to those of the Federal Reserve Board covering group and chain banking for the same period, although the Board's study did not appear until some time later. The Economic Policy Commission reported that 7½ percent of all banks, as compared with 7.7 percent reported by the Board, were involved. The Board took as a measure of growth the total loans and investments, while the Commission used total resources. In 1929 the Board reported that chains and groups controlled 19.5 percent of the total loans and investments of all banks, whereas the Economic Policy Commission's report indicated that these organizations had about 18 percent of the total resources of all banks in operation at that time.

The Economic Policy Commission performed a great service in showing the extent of the movement at a time when our information was far from complete, but it rendered a greater service in calling attention again to fundamental changes which had been going on in our banking system during recent years. The work of the Federal Reserve Board in compiling data on these types of banking rendered it unnecessary for the commission to continue collecting these data.

[9] *Ibid.*, pp. 7-8.

THE FEDERAL RESERVE BOARD

Like the other studies which have been made, that of the Federal Reserve Board did not segregate the data referring to group and chain banks, but represented both in combined tables and charts. The investigation of the Board covers only a short period of time, but it is adequate to show the extent of the movement in 1927 and the changes which have since taken place. The Federal Reserve Board, in compiling its data on chain and group organizations, recognized three types, as follows:[10]

1. Instances where control is exercised by a holding corporation, which has usually been formed by interests connected with one or more of the principal banks belonging to the system.

2. Instances where control is exercised by the principal bank of the system, either through direct ownership of stock by the bank, or through ownership of directors of the bank.

3. Instances of ownership of controlling or substantial interest in a number of banks by an individual, family, or group of individuals.

The scope and extent of chain and group banking in the United States will be more clearly appreciated by a study of the data showing the number of such organizations, together with their total loans and investments. These facts[11] are presented, for the years from 1929 to 1931 inclusive, in Table 38.

A study of Table 38 reveals very interesting facts. The actual number of chains and groups reported decreased from 321 on June 30, 1929, to 273 as of the end of 1931, or approximately 14.9 percent. The total number of banks owned on December 31, 1931, was 1,886 as compared with 1,921 on June 30, 1929. These figures indicate also that chain and group banking have fluctuated considerably as regards total loans and investments.

The important position held by chains and groups in the banking system as a whole makes this subject a vital one at the present time. It justifies careful analysis. It must be considered in any dis-

[10] *Federal Reserve Bulletin*, April, 1930, pp. 149-50. The description of these three types has been quoted verbatim. It is essentially the same as that used by the Economic Policy Association (see above, p. 346).

[11] This table was compiled by combining certain data given in the Report of the Federal Reserve Committee on Branch, Group and Chain Banking (1932), on *Banking Group and Chains*, Table 7, p. 35 and Table V, Appendix p. xx.

TABLE 38

NUMBER OF BANKS AND THE LOANS AND INVESTMENTS IN CHAINS AND GROUPS, JUNE 30, 1929–DECEMBER 31, 1931

DATE	NUMBER OF CHAINS AND GROUPS	NATIONAL BANKS		STATE MEMBER BANKS		NON-MEMBER BANKS		ALL BANKS	
		Number of Banks	*Loans and Investments (Millions of dollars)*	*Number of Banks*	*Loans and Investments (Millions of dollars)*	*Number of Banks*	*Loans and Investments (Millions of dollars)*	*Number of Banks*	*Loans and Investments (Millions of dollars)*
June 30, 1929	321	715	5,012	106	3,008	1,100	1,748	1,921	9,768
Dec. 31, 1929	332	854	6,336	124	3,786	1,187	1,971	2,165	12,093
June 30, 1930	325	886	6,765	126	3,876	1,217	2,125	2,229	12,766
Dec. 31, 1930	316	872	6,649	121	3,390	1,161	1,817	2,154	11,856
June 30, 1931	305	863	8,099	116	3,543	1,092	1,713	2,071	13,355
Dec. 31, 1931	273	805	5,818	98	2,398	983	1,426	1,886	9,642

cussion of the extension of branch banking or banking control, or even of banking supervision and regulation. The old type of chain system could never have attracted such large volumes of capital. It could not, for that reason alone, have attained such a growth as has been made possible through the introduction of the holding company on a wide scale. The number of chains is probably as great as, perhaps much greater than, the number of groups, but the banks involved are much smaller and are more likely to be institutions located in the less populated areas.

SIZE OF GROUPS AND CHAINS

While a few of the chain and group organizations have become very large, with tremendous financial resources, the greater number of such combinations owned or controlled comparatively few banks. Table 39 gives the number of banks owned by various chain or group systems:[12]

TABLE 39

SIZE OF GROUPS AND CHAINS

Number of Banks	*Number of Systems*
3 banks	64
4 banks	56
5 banks	39
6 to 9 banks	86
10 to 19 banks	32
20 or more	10
Total	287

Of the total number of systems, 159 groups or chains had not more than five banks each. The predominance of small groups or chains is further emphasized by the fact that 245 of these systems had less than 10 banks each. In this respect the size of the groups resembles that of the branch banks. In either case, only a few organizations embraced a large number of institutions.

BRANCH BANKING IN CONNECTION WITH GROUP BANKING

On December 31, 1929, there were 119 banks owned by members of groups and chains which were operating branches. These

[12] *Federal Reserve Bulletin*, April, 1930, p. 148.

banks operated 1,415 branches, or approximately 40 percent of all branches reported by the Federal Reserve Board at that time. Group and chain banks on that date had $11,177,000,000 in loans and investments, of which banks with branches held approximately $6,264,000,000, or more than 50 percent of the total for all banks which were members of groups or chains. The number of branches owned by chain and group banks had increased to 1,627, representing 48 percent of the total number of branches in operation on June 30, 1931.

From these data it is evident that a number of banks and organizations were involved in both chain and group banking, while at the same time certain of the banks were deeply interested in the development of branches. The number of branches owned by banks controlled by or belonging to groups and chains showed a marked increase within the short period of one and one-half years. Group and chain owners and managers increased the percentage of the loans and investments which they held of all banks operating branches. These types of management had very greatly extended their control through the ownership of individual banks. The Transamerica Corporation of California and the Marine Midland Corporation of New York are two nationally known financial institutions which have expanded through the absorption of individual banks and through the creation of new branches.

REASON FOR THE GROWTH OF GROUP BANKING

A number of reasons may be advanced for the development of group banking in this country. This expansion has been accompanied by a declining interest in what we have referred to as chain banking. Group banking is not merely a development of chain banking under a new name. It is believed that there is sufficient difference between the two to explain very largely the decline of one and the expansion of the other. The difficulty of measuring the importance of the two is aggravated by the fact that the data compiled to date regarding them have not been segregated. Another difficulty lies in the fact that many writers refuse to recognize any fundamental differences between the two. Let us now consider the various factors which have helped to bring about the development of group banking during and following 1927:

1. *Desire for profits.*—A desire for profits on the part of the organizers and managers of the holding company has been the deciding factor in many cases. It is hoped, by bringing together a group of banks and improving the management, to increase the earning power of the banks and thus to secure a substantial income for the stockholders of the holding company as well as larger personal incomes for the officers and managers of the banks and the holding company.

2. *Opportunities for stockjobbing.*—During the heyday of the big bull market, there were many opportunities for the sale of securities of practically all kinds. These stocks and bonds could frequently be sold at prices which made possible large profits for the promoters. Efforts of the stockjobber were greatly facilitated by the organization of the holding company. There were two opportunities for securing a profit from the building up of a chain of banks. The first was through the organization of a holding company and the sale of its securities to the public for a substantial sum, the proceeds thus obtained being used to buy up the controlling interest in a few banks, which, in turn, might be sold to another group or company for a large profit. In the second case the presence of the holding company, with a desire to obtain a list of banks, created a situation in which certain individuals would go out and buy up or secure an option on the stock of one or more banks, which they sold to the holding company. In this way the promoters often realized a huge profit by marking up the price of the stock of the banks involved in the transaction. It is believed that the opportunities thus created had much to do with the rapid development of the holding company type of management, once it had started.

3. *Laws prohibiting branch banking.*—Several cases have existed where the organizers of group systems preferred to establish branches, but the banking laws did not permit them to do so. Under such conditions, the holding company was adopted as a means of accomplishing an end not otherwise possible. The branch plan has frequently been employed as far as it was feasible to extend the activities of the bank, while the holding company was then used to extend the work of the bank where branches were either pro-

hibited or limited for one reason or another. This latter method of building up control was used extensively by the Transamerica Company in connection with its operations in the state of California. Outside the state and sometimes within the state, the Transamerica Company was the holding company by means of which the organization secured control of other banking resources. This method enabled the company and its subsidiary organizations to extend its operations to a nation-wide basis, and even to become international in scope. The former case is represented by such organizations as the Marine Bancorporation of Seattle, Washington, which has publicly announced its policy of converting independent group institutions into branches when, as, and if the laws were so modified as to permit them to do so.

4. *The bad reputation of chain banking.*—During the history of chain banking in this country, there have developed several very unpleasant situations with regard to the manner in which control has been obtained and the way in which that control has been exercised. One of the most famous cases of this kind developed in connection with the Witham chain, which failed disgracefully in 1926, carrying with it untold losses for the depositors, the public and the stockholders, in the two states of Georgia and Florida, to say nothing of the indirect losses to organizations outside of these states which had been doing business there. Several cases of failure had occurred at earlier dates in and around Minneapolis. The failures of other chains in the South, and failures in Iowa and Colorado, have all contributed to a general distrust of chain banks. A more recent debacle in Kentucky, Tennessee and Arkansas, which among other things brought down the A. B. Banks chain of banks, has served to emphasize still further the bad elements of chain banking.

5. *Fear of losing correspondent business.*—The development of group, chain or branch banking will have a very important effect upon the correspondent method of doing interbank business. An attitude of indifference on the part of some very large and powerful banking organizations toward branch banking has been due in part to the fact that it was realized that to encourage and extend branch banking would alter many correspondent accounts. Large banks

have feared at times that if they advocated an extension of branches, that by itself would bring about a loss of correspondent accounts. So long as the laws prohibited branch banking, things were allowed to drift. However, when the movement toward group banking began, the laws were not a protection against the extension of this type of banking, which was also bound to affect very materially the correspondent business. At first there was no particular interest manifested by the large banks, but more recently this inactivity has disappeared and a limited number of large banks have taken steps to obtain control of certain banks in order to hold the business which they now have in a particular community or section of the country.

ADVANTAGES OF GROUP BANKING

There are certain advantages in group banking not found in a unit system. Some of these advantages are common to branch banking; in fact, some could be more successfully secured under a branch system than by group banking. The most important of these advantages may be summarized as follows:

1. *Larger lines of credit may be granted.*—Under a unit system where the banks are small, or even in larger institutions, it is not possible for one bank to provide the amount of credit needed in many cases by large business organizations. Group systems can secure better, more complete and up-to-date information concerning their credit risks, and for that reason alone are in a more desirable position to pass upon loans and discounts. The fact that there may be a considerable number of banks in a system enables it to grant loans which often would be too heavy for any single institution in the group. Large loans may be apportioned among the various members so that no one has an excessive amount and at the same time the funds may be made available to the borrower through one bank. This gives the group a decided advantage over unit banks. Under a unit system the logical thing might be for the large borrower to apply to a city bank, and thus take away from the smaller institution a desirable type of business. Since the small banks could not supply all that was needed, they would not be permitted under such circumstances to share any part of it. The group

plan overcomes this in part. These results may be, and are, secured through branch banking in many countries.

2. *Greater diversification in loans and investments.*—A small local institution with limited funds is at a great disadvantage for the reason that it frequently cannot afford to make the same investigation or credit analysis that a large institution can, in order to secure a proper diversification of its portfolio. Unit banks are restricted to a considerable extent to their own community. They cannot afford so elaborate a type of credit department or investment advice as can the group management. This narrows their field of activity greatly. A group organized on a wider geographical basis is in a position to transfer funds from one locality to another, or to shift borrowers' paper from one section to another, so that a given bank has greater diversification, not only as regards the maturity, but, which is more important, as regards the type of business represented by loans and discounts. The per-unit cost should be less for the group than for the independent unit bank with a limited territory and a smaller volume of funds.

3. *Reserve policy.*—A well-organized system of branches or group of banks can utilize the most profitable methods of handling reserves, including secondary reserves. A smaller amount of cash may be held than is safe for a unit bank, since balances may be easily and quickly shifted from one member to another. The volume of loans and investments may be proportionately increased. The amount of legal reserve would not be changed unless by reason of a group taking its members either into or out of the Federal Reserve system. There could and should be a great improvement made in handling the secondary reserve problem. A group should in the first place have a more widely diversified portfolio and would therefore actually need less in the form of the so-called commercial paper or prime bankers' acceptances. More of its own loans would be composed of short-term commercial paper, secured directly through the discount of good customers' paper. Inasmuch as the group as a whole would have a large amount of this class of paper, it would regard the customers' paper itself as desirable first-class secondary reserves.

4. *Trust functions.*—A large financial institution is desirable if

adequate trust services are to be provided. Liability and responsibility of trustees and trust companies are such that stockholders should be required to make a considerable capital investment, in order to give the necessary financial protection to those being served by the trust organization. Such an investment is impossible in many communities, where the quantity of available capital funds is distinctly limited. It can, however, be raised and the necessary protection given by means of the group system. Under group management, it is not necessary to provide the trust services at each individual office or bank. In fact the head office of the holding company or group could provide at one office the necessary talent to operate the trust department, and this division could then supervise smaller sections of the various member banks so as to provide a requisite volume of business to justify the maintenance of a separate department. In this way the group secures a certain volume of business which might otherwise go undeveloped, and at the same time affords an outlet for investment funds.

5. *More specialized personnel.*—Bringing together a group of small or medium-sized banks under one central management makes possible a better type of management for the banks. Individual units will receive the advice and assistance of the officers of the holding company as well as the officers and directors of the larger banks within the group system. The holding company will have a large number of employees, and will, under these conditions, be in a position to do a great deal of work of an educational nature which will tend to raise the standard of efficiency of all employees. There are many ways in which this type of employee may demonstrate his superiority over the type which has prevailed in far too many localities in this country in the past. The personnel should also get a greater satisfaction out of their work, aside from any financial returns either to themselves or to their employers.

6. *Larger volume of capital funds for certain localities.*—In many communities there are insufficient funds available to permit the operation of a bank on a sound and successful basis. The group organization would be of service in these communities if it established and operated smaller but sound banks. Branch banking has

a decided advantage over the group system in meeting the needs of the small communities.

7. *Advice on investments.*—A holding company could build up a securities department, not with the idea of selling stocks or bonds to the various banks in the system, but to render at cost or a reasonable price, the best advice possible to its member banks, to the end that these smaller institutions will have advice comparable to that now secured by the larger banks which maintain investment departments. This advice would be helpful and profitable to the banks, and for this service the members of the group should pay enough to give the securities department a fair profit. It would, or at least should, eliminate a large proportion of losses now sustained by banks which buy speculative securities because they are offered to them by some forceful, high-priced salesman.

8. *Advantages to the community.*—A large financial organization should be of considerable value to a community. It ties up the smaller localities with the larger financial centers. It makes possible the securing of the needed funds for developing the community. It gives a certain recognition to the community which is otherwise lacking.

9. *Central control.*—A group system offers a centralized control not found in unit banks. The holding company brings unity into the system and gives the smaller banks the benefit of better accounting methods, methods of securing and training the personnel and in general added strength in the various communities in which the group operates.

10. *Economics of operation.*—The group system should reduce the costs of bank operation. Credit work and the work involved in the analysis of securities will be performed at lower per-unit costs. There will be a reduction in the personnel, or, what amounts to the same thing, a more economical use of the force employed. Lower prices would be possible on all purchases of supplies and equipment. One central organization could do all the buying and thus secure prices which in the course of time would amount to large savings for the corporation. Better accounting methods would be easily attainable at a less cost in the aggregate than that now paid by the various organizations or banks acting separately.

DISADVANTAGES OF GROUP BANKING

Group banking may be good or bad, depending upon the way in which the holding company has been organized, together with the amount of capital provided and the character of the management in charge of operating the organization once it has become a going concern. Bank management may be "bad" whether the type of organization is that of group, chain, branch or unit banking. No type of organization will prevent dishonest or inefficient management. The nature of group banking makes it somewhat more liable to certain undesirable practices than either unit banking or branch banking. The advantages of group banking have been outlined above. The disadvantages may now be considered under the following heads:

1. *Stockjobbing.*—One of the reasons for the growth and extension of group banking has been the opportunity for stockjobbing. In some cases this has been carried to an extreme. Stocks have been bid up far above their value based upon potential earning power.[18] Bank stocks have been purchased at high prices and then unloaded on a holding company at a still higher price. In other cases the stock of the holding company has been sold to the public with the thought of buying up bank stocks. There are some instances where the holding company was organized with the idea of building up a group which could be sold later to another group at a price to yield a fancy profit. Bank stocks were often marked up with the expectation of resale to a new group. Such practices might have been highly profitable to the promoters, but the results were not in the best interests of the depositors or the community, which had, in the end, to pay the costs.

2. *Dishonest management.*—There are several cases on record where the officers or managers of chain banking have proved unworthy of the confidence, power, and trust confided in them. The Witham Chain in Georgia failed in 1926, the McCauley chain in Oklahoma suspended in 1929, and the A. B. Banks chain in Arkansas went down in 1930. Smaller chains had failed earlier in Minnesota and Iowa. The history of group banking is shorter and the number of cases of dishonest management that have come to light

[18] *Hearings*, 1930, p. 1431.

is smaller. There are instances, however, if not of dishonest management, at least of unethical and dangerous practices. The way in which the Banckentucky was handled is a case in point. The managements in a few other holding companies certainly do not have very satisfactory records. There is little doubt, in fact, that a limited number of groups is in anything but a sound or liquid position. It should be added, again, that this criticism does not apply to all groups by any manner of means. There is no doubt that the management of many groups is both capable and honest. The possibilities for harm, however, are multiplied in a group or chain system, as compared with the unit bank when the management, regardless of the outcome to depositors and stockholders, seeks to operate the various units of the group for its own personal gains.

3. *Double liability of stockholders.*—The question has been properly raised regarding the ability of holding companies to make good their double liability in case of bank failure. This question has been raised on the theory that the holding company will have very little in the way of assets aside from the stock it holds in the various member banks of the group. Although some holding companies have made an effort to provide against this potential liability, there is no doubt that many of them have practically no assets except the bank shares which have been purchased. This question regarding the ability of the holding company to meet its double liability implies that there is grave danger that if one member of the group fails, others, perhaps all, will fail. Further, the liabilities thus created through the actual failure of these banks will be so large as to consume all of the assets of the corporation leaving an insufficient amount to meet the double liability requirements. In fact, under such circumstances the question may be raised: "Will the failure of the banks wipe out the equity of the holding company by reducing to zero the value of the bank shares held by the holding company—the bank shares constituting the main bulk of the holding company's assets?" There is no use denying the fact that the double liability feature is circumvented in many cases when the ownership passes into the hands of the holding company. This feature is fully recognized by some banking officials throughout the country.

Of course this disadvantage in many cases is more theoretical than real. The past record of recoveries by assessment of bank stockholders shows that a considerable portion of the amount legally due under the double liability feature is never actually collected. The loss sustained by the depositors as a result of this shift in ownership is not as fundamental as some would have us believe. However, the depositors are justly entitled to all the protection possible and the protection of double liability should not be taken away unless something else is given instead.

There is a possibility that laws might be enacted to enforce double liability upon the shareholders of the holding company, so that each individual shareholder would be liable for bank stocks held by the holding company to the extent of the individual stockholder's proportionate share of the bank stock held by the holding company to that of the entire stock of the holding company. This does not hold out a very promising method of protecting the depositors of banks.

4. *Difficulties of examination and supervision.*—Difficulties of examining a group of banks are similar in many respects to those of chain systems outlined in the chapter on "Chain Banking" (see Chapter XIX, page 339). Groups generally include larger banks, and in some instances banks in different states, so that it is practically impossible at the present time to get a thorough examination of the banks in a group at one time. Such conditions provide opportunities for fraudulent or unethical practices. There is not only the difficulty of maintaining a sufficiently large staff for the purpose, but examiners in one state have no authority in another state. Likewise the national examiners are not in a position to examine state banks or vice versa. Members of some groups are as widely separated from other members of the same group as New York is from California.

ATTEMPTS AT PREVENTION

There exists in many states,[14] among certain classes in the banking community, a very strong feeling not only against chain and

[14] No attempt is made here to give an exhaustive list of the states in which there are restrictions against this type of control. The reader, if interested in the particular states in which these supposed limitations exist, is referred to the study of the Eco-

group banking, but against any type of multiple banking which will lessen the importance of the unit bank. This opposition has been especially directed toward branch banking. In recent years there has been a feeling in some localities that both chain and group banking should be restricted definitely by law or regulation. In the days before group banking was differentiated, the state of Wisconsin made vigorous efforts at times to prevent the formation of chains in that state (see Chapter XIX, page 334). More recently, laws have been enacted which were designed to limit the amount of bank stock which may be owned by one holding company. Similar efforts have been made in the states of West Virginia[16] and New Jersey to try to make illegal the extensive development of the holding company as a means for owning and controlling a group of banks.

Studies by the Federal Reserve Board clearly show that these efforts have been for the most part ineffective. It is likely that groups own or control one or more banks in each of the three states mentioned above, to say nothing of the greater extension in other states. If the laws prohibit the holding-company method of control, some of the state banking officials are either out of harmony with existing legislation or very lax in their enforcement of banking laws. This form of concentration has become a part of our banking system and has extended its control over a substantial volume of banking resources. The writer has very grave doubts that the attempts at prohibition will prove a real hindrance to the further extension of this type of control, so long as the holding companies themselves deem it a profitable or desirable field in which to expand. In the state of West Virginia it seems evident that the laws prohibit a corporation or holding company organized under the laws of that state from building up such a system, but it is extremely doubtful whether the state laws can prevent a corporation organized under the laws of Delaware or any other state from buying up control of banks in West Virginia.

---

nomic Policy Association, the Summary or Digest by the Federal Reserve Board, published in the *Hearing on Branch, Chain and Group Banking before the Committee on Banking and Currency, House of Representatives, 1930;* and Gaines T. Cartinhour's *Branch, Group, and Chain Banking* (New York: The Macmillan Co., 1931).

[16] The West Virginia law was passed in 1929.

The same thing holds true in most of the other states, especially New Jersey and Wisconsin. Most states do not have any laws bearing specifically upon the situation. At any rate the efforts to date have not been effective and are not likely to be so with the existing body of legislation. If a branch-banking law were enacted within the near future, the problem would in large measure be solved. Many groups would be converted into branch systems. This way of escape would not take care of the cases in which a holding company is operating in a number of states. Unless the problem is solved in this way, the next few years are likely to see a further increase in the importance of group banking.

CONCLUSIONS

1. Group banking, when honestly and efficiently organized and operated, has certain advantages over a unit system of banking. These advantages in part take the following forms:

(1) Greater diversification of portfolios
(2) A larger and more skilled personnel
(3) A larger and better-manned credit department
(4) Ability or power to extend larger lines of credit
(5) Lower overhead expenses in the operation of small banks

2. A great saving may be realized through a more skillful handling of the reserves of the small banks. The reserves may be kept in somewhat different form and the amount of actual cash reduced for the group as a whole, which would not be possible for banks acting independently of each other.

3. The management may organize a trust unit for the group system as a whole, in cases where the individual banks are unable to operate a trust department by reason of the small volume of business in a given community. A central organization can have a very small trust section in the small banks. In fact, in some cases it may be expedient for the trust business in some localities to be transferred at once to the head office, or to one of the larger banks. Under such circumstances it could be cared for, in part, by the management of the local bank in the community where the customer lives.

4. The group system simplifies the raising of capital funds in

certain localities. In many cases a group bank can be operated in a community with a smaller capital than would be safe for a unit bank, by reason of the strong support of the holding company for the local bank.

5. At times the holding company will be in a position to give helpful and constructive investment advice, not only to its own members but to the business community in which certain of its member banks are located.

6. A member of a group system has the advantages growing out of a centralized management and control such as can be offered only by a large organization.

7. It is difficult to examine and supervise large chains or groups of banks. This is especially true when such groups include state and national banks, which are located in different states and subject to different jurisdictions.

8. Groups have been organized in many cases for the purpose of making a profit out of selling the stock of the corporation or in the marking up of the market price of the bank stock itself. This is familiarly known as stockjobbing.

9. Depositors lose in part at least the double-liability feature attached to bank stocks when such stocks are held or owned by corporations whose principal business is that of buying and owning bank stock, but which are not in turn subject to double liability.

10. If the management of the group is either inefficient or dishonest, there is serious danger of failure. Since the group includes many institutions, the potential loss is very great. There is always danger that if one of the members fail, it will affect all other members, and in this way cause widespread loss to several communities.

11. There are no fundamental advantages ascribed to group banking that can not be secured by a well-organized and operated branch-banking system. This is certainly true as regards commercial banking business. The branch system will in all probability establish branches in many small communities in which the group organization would not find a unit bank profitable, considering the amount of capital needed, together with certain other overhead expenses, for these will generally prove greater for group organi-

zations than in the case of branch banks. The central organization of a group system may in considerable degree provide the same oversight and managerial ability supplied by the head office of a branch bank to its individual branches, but the responsibility is not as firmly placed in the group as in the branch system. Legal responsibility must be assumed at the head office for each of its branches. This is in itself a very important advantage of the branch system over the other type. In the matter of providing capital for small communities, the branch system is infinitely better situated, since it would simply allot whatever capital was needed for each branch, regardless of the capital requirements for the organization of a new bank in that particular community.

Branch systems should be more easily supervised by banking officials than group or chain systems. There are likely to be fewer jurisdictions involved. Moreover the bank would be required to secure permission from the banking authorities before establishing a branch, and would consequently be obliged to submit to whatever supervision and regulation was necessary from the point of view of the Comptroller of the Currency and the various state banking officials. In this respect, the public welfare would be much better served by branch banking.

CHAPTER XXI

CONCLUSIONS

The relationship between branch banking and bank mergers has been outlined at some length in the preceding chapters. The growth and the scope of each of these major phases of the banking concentration movement have been analyzed statistically and certain of the data presented in chart form to indicate developments more clearly. Both bank mergers and branch banking have been considered, in turn, in relation to bank failures, chain and group banking, and the changing size of the unit bank. Effort has been made to consider both the legal and the economic background for the more important and fundamental changes. The history of branch banking in this country as a whole has been briefly traced. In like manner we have reviewed the branch-banking developments in the state of California where the most extensive and interesting branch-banking situation in this country is found. All these have been considered in relation to the banking system as a whole, in order to draw certain conclusions as to the validity of the arguments offered by both those who favor and those who oppose branch banking, as well as other phases of the concentration movement.

Our study has led us to certain conclusions regarding the probable future tendencies in the field of commercial banking. In the United States branch banking has made substantial progress in some sections of the country in comparison with unit banking. Legal restrictions have served to limit the area of branch banking to particular states, and many of these states further limit the operations of branches to the county or city of the parent institution. Despite these restrictions, running over a long period of years, there were during the first half of 1933 marked changes in the legal status of branch banking. National banks were given the right, under certain conditions, to establish branches on a state-wide basis in states permitting state-wide branch banking.

In addition several states enacted laws during 1933 permitting the operation of branches on a state-wide basis. Regardless of the decline in the number of branches during the years 1930-32 inclusive, there is substantial and convincing evidence to indicate that there will be more, rather than less, branch banking in this country in the future.

Public sentiment has changed considerably in the United States during recent years by reason of the large number of bank failures and the realization of the fact that the unit bank has, in far too many cases, proved unsuccessful. As a result of the heavy losses through failures, a better understanding has been developed both of the advantages and the disadvantages of branch banking. The large number of smaller cities and towns having lost all local banking facilities, has brought home to many that what is needed is a sound banking system, be it based on the branch or on the unit principle. The trying difficulties of the small bank have fairly definitely shown that some form of multiple banking is needed unless the community is prepared to get along with fewer places at which banking business may be conducted. Many bankers in the smaller localities have been converted to the principle of branch banking, or at least have ceased to oppose it, by reason of the trouble they have encountered in keeping open their own banks or in merging them with other stronger institutions.

Threatened bank failures and the difficulties of salvaging property through mergers have shown in many states the urgent need for some form of branch banking. Many banks might have been saved had stronger banks been permitted to absorb and convert them into branches before they reached the last stages of decadence through the decline of security prices and through bad management. The experiences growing out of such efforts to save the banks have been powerful influences in breaking down some of the opposition to multiple banking. Branch banking has gained many supporters as a result.

Experience, to date, with chain and group banking has been of such a nature as to create serious doubts regarding the advisability of relying upon these systems as a means for improving our banking facilities. The record of chain banking is certainly anything but gratifying. Methods employed in building up chains and the lack, oftentimes, of responsible management and control have caused many to look upon branch banking as a more promising way out of the difficulty. Many of those in control of the most successful group systems have already signified their willingness and intention of converting the banks of their group systems into branches as soon as the banking laws will permit. There are few, if any, real advantages in group banking that could not be enjoyed under a branch system if the laws permitted the operation of branches on the same geographical basis as that enjoyed by the groups.

It must not be assumed that the branch system has always proved successful. Several individual banks operating branches have failed, just as there have been unit-bank failures. Resultant losses have often been extremely heavy, as for example in the case of the failure of the Bank of United States, New York City, in 1930. Branch banking must have capable and honest management to succeed; otherwise it will encounter difficulties. There has been a considerable number of branch-bank failures in this country since 1929. In addition, there are a substantial number of banks which have been unable to survive the bank holiday and have been forced to operate on a partial basis or to close entirely. In fairness, however, we should not compare the results of branch-bank failures in this country with the unit system unless we concede that the type of branch banking which has been most successful in other countries has been largely lacking in the American banking system. Experience abroad has been far more satisfactory in this connection than our own.

It should be pointed out that there is not often a meeting of the minds of those who advocate branch banking and those who oppose it. The former praise the results attained by branch banking in foreign countries, while opponents emphasize the bad showing of many of the banks which operate branches in this country. It should be carefully noted that the situation in the United States where branch banks are in operation is not at all similar to that existing in the countries where branch banking prevails in its most successful form. Before we can draw conclusions regarding the results of branch banking, we must give it a trial in this country on a wider basis. If we are not willing to do so, we should condemn only the form of branch banking common in the United States. This, in the last analysis, is not a genuine system of branch banking.

Perhaps the most convincing argument against branch banking is found in connection with the relationship between the bank and its own customers. There is no denying the fact that the real management is further removed from depositors and borrowers in those countries where branch banking prevails than is true under the unit system. In the latter, it is often more inconvenient to reach the authoritative man, but even so the disadvantages of branch banking are often overstated. Yet it is undoubtedly true that such aloofness exists in some localities. With these general observations, certain more specific results of the study should be presented.

1. The larger number of bank failures in this country provides ample proof that there have been and still are serious defects in our banking system. Statistics show that on the average the small banks in this country have been less profitable and more susceptible to failure than the larger institutions. The situation has given rise to considerable dissatisfaction with the small unit banks not because they are small but because they have been so costly to the community through failures and the consequent tying up of depositors' funds for long periods of time, aside from the actual loss realized by stockholders and depositors through liquidation. The failure situation has emphasized the need for some type of banking reform to increase the soundness and stability of our banking system.

2. Another phase which has assumed a position of importance in recent years, and has been closely related to the bank-failure situation in certain parts of the country, is the merger and consolidation movement. This movement has been related to several phases of the banking system and should not be thought of too narrowly. The following are its more important relationships:

(1) *Bank failures.*—In many places owners, managers and banking officials have coöperated to effect one or more mergers

among banks to ward off, if possible, a pending bank failure. In many cases these efforts have been rewarded by the prevention of bank failures, or, what amounts to the same thing, saving the community from heavy losses. On the other hand, in many instances these efforts have been unsuccessful; while in still others the absorbing bank failed later, thus reflecting still heavier losses in the end than would have been the case had a merger never been effected.

(2) *Branch banking.*—The desire to secure branches has been one of the principal causes of bank mergers and consolidations in those states which permit banks to operate branches. The relationship has been marked in states like California, New York, Ohio and Michigan. With an extension of the branch-banking laws the real relationship will become even closer for some time to come.

(3) *Trust business.*—In many places the entry of commercial banks into the fiduciary field has been accompanied or preceded by a merger in which a trust company was involved, the commercial bank realizing the advantages of securing a certain line of commercial business as well as a substantial volume of trust business, the latter being the more fundamental in mergers effected in order to control fiduciary business.

3. The most important phase of the present study is seen in connection with the history and development of branch banking in the United States. Branch banking has existed in some form or other from the earliest days of this country to the present time. It is true that both the extent of, and current interest in, branch banking has varied considerably from time to time, yet, there has remained an underlying feeling among certain students and bankers that ultimately our unit-banking system would give way in this country to branch banking, as has so largely happened in other commercial and industrial countries. The following stand out as interesting and important phases of this part of our study:

(1) The principles of branch banking were widely accepted before the Civil War. That conflict and the enactment of the National Bank Act, as later revised and amended, influenced also by the amendments to the Revenue Act of 1865 placing a tax

upon the note issue of state banks, had the effect of eliminating practically all branch banking in this country. Following the war era there gradually developed a body of opinion in favor of unit banking which eliminated any broad and thoughtful consideration of the branch-banking problem. It has been only during the past two decades that branch banking has made any substantial progress.

(2) The enactment of the state-wide branch-banking law in California in 1909 gave new life to the movement. Since then there has been a slow but gradual growth in favor of this type of banking. That law was followed, several years later, by a ruling of the Comptroller of the Currency (1922) permitting national banks to operate "teller windows" in the city of the parent bank, provided state laws gave state banks the right to establish and operate branches in the state. This ruling was followed by the McFadden Act of 1927, legalizing city branches for national banks while at the same time attempting to curtail state-wide branches through the power to regulate and supervise member state banks and trust companies. The Banking Act approved June 16, 1933, extended to national banks the right to establish, under certain conditions, branches on a state-wide basis in those states where state banks had such privileges. During the first six months of 1933 some six or seven states enacted laws permitting state banks and trust companies under certain restrictions to operate branches on a state-wide basis.

(3) At the present time, (August, 1933), there are about 16 states in which state banks, trust companies and national banks may operate branches on a state-wide basis, and 15 other states in which banks may operate them in the city, county or adjoining county. There are indications in a few other states pointing to a liberalization of the banking laws in this respect. So noticeable have these signs become that we may feel justified in predicting a more extensive development of branches in the future than we have seen in the past.

(4) The attitude of both the office of the Comptroller of the Currency and the Federal Reserve Board has changed from time to time, depending upon the persons in charge. The change of

policy of the Board in 1933 was intended to curb the growth of branch banking on a state-wide basis by prohibiting a further extension of branches on that basis by member banks of the Federal Reserve system. The ruling of the Comptroller of the Currency in 1922 has had a tremendous influence on the trend of branch banking in this country during the past decade. Past experience in this country has definitely shown that we cannot expect a definite course of action until there has been enacted specific legislation permitting or prohibiting branch banking. Such legislation will be considerably delayed by reason of the number of the state banking systems and the lack of uniformity among them.

(5) There has been an interesting development of branches by mutual savings banks in New York, Massachusetts and Pennsylvania. The number is not large in any state, but it has shown some growth and meets a specialized need. This field of branch banking has distinct limitations for two reasons: mutual savings banks are limited to comparatively few states, and large numbers of potential depositors are needed in order to assure a sufficient volume of business to make such branches profitable.

4. Chain banking has been in existence for a number of years. It has not been confined to any particular section of the country, but its growth has been greatest in those states which prohibited branch banking. Certain states in the Northwest and the Southeast have had the largest chain systems; hence our conclusions are based largely upon the developments in these regions. This type of banking has met with tremendous losses through bank failures, the greatest being the collapse of the Witham Chain in Georgia in 1926. During later years the movement has been subjected to very severe criticism. As a movement it has not been generally acceptable to the banking community, and has probably passed its zenith. With a further development of branch banking, there will be less and less effort on the part of bankers and others to establish and operate chain systems.

5. Group banking, as distinguished from chain banking, is closely associated with the holding-company type of management and control whereas the individual type of ownership and control

prevails in chain banking. The management of certain group systems through public sale of stock has been able to raise large amounts of capital funds, and hence has been able to control much larger banks. It has certain advantages that are not possessed by chains. Thus it can raise larger amounts of capital, secure better management and coördination of its several members through the holding company. The management assumes greater responsibility than has been the case generally with chain systems and has consequently been more successful than chain banking. Yet it has been in many cases merely a substitute for branch banking where the latter was prohibited by law. Many group bankers contemplate the conversion of their group systems into branch systems as soon as the laws are changed to permit them to do so.

Group banking as we know it today has developed in this country very largely since 1927. The data showing the extent of this movement are usually associated with chain banking. A statistical presentation was not possible of this system alone. During the years 1931-32, it has probably just about held its own numerically. With the growth of branch banking and a liberalization of the branch-banking laws, it seems likely that the extent of group banking will rapidly decline, since it is, or has been, so largely a substitute for branch banking.

Group banking, if properly managed, should strengthen the banking system in the states where branches are not permitted. It has no outstanding advantages not provided by branch banking, and lacks the centralized management and responsibility common to the branch system. It seemingly represents only a temporary phase in the development of the American banking system and will largely pass with the growth of branch banking.

In conclusion, it should be stated that there are many phases of the concentration movement, especially when viewed in its broader aspects. It is world-wide in its scope and includes many branches of our business and economic life. If the subject were covered fully, such a study would include a consideration of the changes taking place in fields like marketing, transportation, manufacturing and commerce. These changes are not limited, in other words, to any particular branch of our economic life. Our particular and immediate interest has been and still is in the general field of banking and the changes and developments going on there.

The concentration movement when limited to the field of banking includes practically all the leading industrial and commercial countries of the world. The development in the United States have followed similar changes in England, Germany, France, and Canada, as well as some other countries. In England and Canada, for example, the number of banks remaining is small, while the number of branches operated is large. More specifically, the amalgamation movement in England has reduced the number of independent banks to a very small fraction of what it was fifty or one hundred years ago. The tendencies in this country are the same as those in England, but far less advanced.

Study of the concentration movement of banking in this country thus leads to the general conclusion that the banking system is and has been for a number of years undergoing a gradual change which will, in the end, give us comparatively few banks with a large number of branches. The decline in the total number of banks will no doubt, in the long run, make necessary certain changes in the central banking system. This change will probably result in less, not more, concentration of funds in the large financial centers. That should give the central banking system greater power and influence in controlling the volume of credit, and should enable it, through this control to exercise a very wholesome influence on the growth and expansion of business generally. These changes taken as a whole should, if properly directed, strengthen the banking system, rendering it safer and more efficient.

BIBLIOGRAPHY

Books

Baldwin, W. E., *New York Banking Law*. Annotated. The Banks Law Publishing Co., New York, 1926.

Barnett, George E., *State Banks and Trust Companies*. Vol. VII, "National Monetary Commission Report," Washington, Government Printing Office, 1910.

Beckhart, B. Haggott, The Banking System of Canada. Reprinted from *Foreign Banking Systems,* Henry Holt and Co., New York, 1929.

Blackstock, Nehemiah, *Banking Laws of California*. 1907.

Cable, John Ray, *The Bank of the State of Missouri*. Columbia University Press, New York, 1923.

Cartinhour, Gaines T., *Branch, Group and Chain Banking*. Macmillan Company, New York, 1931.

Catterall, R. C. H., *The Second Bank of the United States*. University of Chicago Press, Chicago, 1903.

Collins, C. W., *The Branch Banking Question*. Macmillan Company, New York, 1926.

Davis, Andrew M., *The Origin of the National Banking System*. "National Monetary Commission Report," Sen. Doc. 582, Washington, 1910.

Dewey, D. R., *State Banking before the Civil War*. Vol. IV, "National Monetary Commission Report," 1910, Washington.

——— *The Second Bank of the United States,* Vol. IV, "National Monetary Commission Report," Washington, 1910.

Dowrie, G. W., *The Development of Banking in Illinois, 1817-1863*. University of Illinois, "Studies in Social Sciences," Vol. II, No. 4, Urbana, 1913.

Esarey, Logan, State Banking in Indiana, 1814-1873. *Indiana University Bulletin,* Vol. X, No. 2, Bloomington, 1912.

Haggerty, John S. and Sidney A. Schulte, *Laws relating to Banking*. Revised ed. Franklin Dekeleine Co., Lansing, 1929.

Hamilton, Alexander, Report on a National Bank, Dec. 1790. *Report of the Secretary of the Treasury, 1837,* Vol. I.

Harr, Luther A., *Branch Banking in England*. University of Pennsylvania Press, Philadelphia, 1929.

Hartsough, Mildred L., *The Twin Cities as a Metropolitan Market: A Regional Study of the Economic Development of Minneapolis and St. Paul*. University of Minnesota Press, Minneapolis, 1925.

Hepburn, A. Barton, Branch Banks and the Currency Problem. *Sound Currency*, Vol. IX, No. 1, March, 1902.

Huntington, A. T. and Robert J. Mawhinney, *Financial Laws of the United States concerning Money, Banking, and Loans, 1778-1909*. Sen. Doc. 580, "National Monetary Commission Report," Washington, 1910.

Knox, John J., *A History of Banking in the United States*. Bradford Rhodes and Co., New York, 1903.

McGibbon, D. A., *Report of the Commission on Banking and Credit with respect to the Industry of Agriculture in the Province of Alberta*. Mimeographed Copy, 1922.

McLeod, H. C., Testimony of, *Banks and Banking; Minutes of Proceedings, Evidence, etc.*, Appendix 2, Committee on Banking and Commerce, C. H. Parmelee, Ottawa, 1913.

Noyes, Alexander, *Forty Years of American Finance, 1865-1907*. G. P. Putnam's Sons, New York, 1909.

Ostrolenk, Bernard, *Economics of Branch Banking*. Harper and Brothers, New York, 1930.

Preston, H. H., *History of Banking in Iowa*. State Historical Society of Iowa, Iowa City, 1922.

Richardson, James D., *A Compilation of the Messages and Papers of the Presidents, 1789-1908*. Vol. IX, Bureau of National Literature and Art, New York, 1909.

Root, L. Carroll, States as Bankers, *Sound Currency*, Vol. II, No. 10, 1895.

Report of the Indianapolis Monetary Commission. University of Chicago Press, Chicago, 1898.

Schulte, Sydney A., co-author, *see* Haggerty, John S.

Semingson, Gilbert, *Laws relating to State Banks, Savings Banks and Trust Companies in the State of North Dakota*. Bismarck, 1929.

Southworth, Shirley D., *Branch Banking in the United States*. McGraw-Hill Book Company, Inc., New York, 1928.

Starnes, George T., *Sixty Years of Branch Banking in Virginia*. Macmillan Company, New York, 1931.

Sumner, Wm. G., History of Banking in All Leading Nations. *Journal of Commerce and Commercial Bulletin*, Vol. I, 1896.

Sykes, Joseph, *The Amalgamation Movement in English Banking, 1825-1924*. P. J. King and Son, Ltd., London, 1926.

Tippetts, Charles S., *State Banks and the Federal Reserve System*. D. Van Nostrand Company, Inc., New York, 1929.

White, Horace, National and State Banks, *Sound Currency*, Vol. II, No. I, Sound Currency Committee of the Reform Club, New York, 1894.

Willis, H. Parker, *The Federal Reserve System*. Ronald Press, New York, 1923.

——— *Banking Inquiry of 1925*. Typewritten Manuscript, School of Business Library, Columbia University, New York.

——— and B. H. Beckhart, *Foreign Banking Systems*. Henry Holt and Co., New York, 1929.

Wright, Benjamin C., *Banking in California, 1849-1910*. H. S. Crocker Company, San Francisco, 1910.

Periodicals

Bankers Magazine, New York, Vol. II, Feb. and March, 1848; Vol. XI, May, 1857; Vol. XV, June, 1861; Vol. XXXII, Aug., 1877; Vol. XLVI, Jan., 1892; Vol. LII, Jan., 1896; Vol. LXIV, April, 1902; Vol. LXV, April, 1902.

Clark, Emory W., Branch Banking in Detroit. *Bankers Magazine*, CV, No. 4, Nov., 1922. The Bankers Publishing Co., New York.

Cooke, Thornton, Branch Banking for the West and South. *Quarterly Journal of Economics*, XVIII, 97-113, Nov., 1903.

Dana, Wm. B., Company, Publishers, *The Commercial and Financial Chronicle Resolutions of Federal Reserve Board Restricting Branches of State Banks Seeking Membership—Minority Report—Opinion of Counsel*, Nov. 10, 1923, New York.

Eckardt, H. M. P., Branch Banking among the State Banks. *Annals of the American Academy of the Political and Social Science*, XXXVI, 148-61, Nov., 1910.

Federal Reserve Bulletin, Dec., 1924; April, 1930; July, 1932; March, 1933.

Group or Chain Banking Grows. *Wall Street Journal*, Oct. 18, 1929, New York.

Platt, Edmund, Branch Banking before the Civil War. *Proceedings* of the New York State Bankers' Association, 1925.

——— Branch Banking for Country Banks. Address before Alabama Bankers' Association, Birmingham, May 20, 1927 (Mimeographed Copy), Washington, 1927.

Sprague, O. M. W., Branch Banking in the United States. *Quarterly Journal of Economics*, XVII, 242-60, Feb., 1903.

Westerfield, Ray B., The Branch Bank Crisis in California. *The Annalist*, Sept. 25, 1925, New York, pp. 373-75.

Public Documents and Reports

Annual Reports of the Comptroller of the Currency, 1876-1932.

Annual Reports of the Federal Reserve Board, 1915-31.

Annual Reports of the Secretary of the Treasury, 1855-61, 1890-97, and 1918-30.

Annual Reports of the Bank Commissioners, Sacramento, California, 1890-98.

Annual Report of the State Examiner to the State Banking Board and Report to the Governor. Public Document II, Journal Publishing Co., Devils Lake, N.D., 1914.

Annual Report of the Commissioner of Banking of Wisconsin, 1922, Homestead Printing Company, Madison.

Hearings before the Committee on Banking and Currency, House of Representatives, 68th Congress, 1st Session, on H.R. 6855, April, 1924.

Hearings before the Senate Committee on Banking and Currency on S. 3316 and H.R. 8887. Consolidation of National Banking Associations, 68th Congress, 2d Session, 1925.

Hearings before the Subcommittee of the Committee on Banking and Currency, United States Senate on S. 1782 and H.R. 2, Consolidation of National Banking Associations, 69th Congress, 1st Session, 1926.

Hearings before the Committee on Banking and Currency, H.R. 71st Congress, 2d Session, under H.Res. 141, Government Printing Office, Washington, 1930.

Hearings on Branch, Chain, and Group Banking before the Committee on Banking and Currency, H.R. 71st Congress, 2d Session, H.Res. 141, Government Printing Office, Washington, 1930.

Proceedings of the Forty-fourth Annual Convention of the Iowa Bankers' Association, 1930.

Reports of Federal Reserve Banks:

Operating Costs and Profits in 1926. Federal Reserve Bank of Boston.

Comparison of the Operating Ratios of the Representative Member Banks in the Second Federal Reserve District for the Year 1929. Federal Reserve Bank of New York, New York, April 29, 1930.

Analysis of Operating Costs and Profits of Member Banks in the Philadelphia Federal Reserve District. Federal Reserve Bank, Philadelphia, 1928, 1930.

Analysis of Member Bank Earnings and Expenses in 1926 and 1928. Chicago Federal Reserve District, Federal Reserve Bank, Chicago, May, 1928, and Oct. 1929.

Monthly Review of Business Conditions. Federal Reserve Bank of San Francisco, Dec. 20, 1928.

Report of the Federal Reserve Committee on Branch, Group, and Chain Banking, 1932, on *Bank Suspensions in the United States, 1892-1931*. Mimeographed Copy.

Report of the Federal Reserve Committee on Branch, Group, and Chain Banking, 1932, on *Banking Profits, 1890-1931*. Mimeographed Copy.

Report of the Federal Reserve Committee on Branch, Group, and Chain

Banking, 1932, on *Branch Banking in California*. Mimeographed Copy.

Report of the Federal Reserve Committee on Branch, Group, and Chain Banking, 1932, on *Branch Banking in the United States*. Mimeographed Copy.

Report of the Federal Reserve Committee on Branch, Group, and Chain Banking, 1932, on *Banking Groups and Chains*. Mimeographed Copy.

Report of the Joint Commission of Agricultural Inquiry, Report 408, H.R. 67th Congress, 1st Session, Part II, Government Printing Office, Washington, 1921.

Report of the Treasury Committee on Bank Amalgamations, His Majesty's Stationery Office, London, 1918.

Report of the Economic Policy Commission of the American Bankers' Association, R. S. Hecht, Chairman, New York, Oct. 14, 1929.

INDEX

COLUMBIA UNIVERSITY PRESS
COLUMBIA UNIVERSITY
NEW YORK

FOREIGN AGENT
OXFORD UNIVERSITY PRESS
HUMPHREY MILFORD
AMEN HOUSE, LONDON, E.C. 4

Bei Fragen zur Produktsicherheit wenden Sie sich bitte an:
If you have any questions regarding product safety,
please contact:

Walter de Gruyter GmbH
Genthiner Straße 13
10785 Berlin
productsafety@degruyterbrill.com